The Masculinities Reader

The Masculinities Reader

Edited by

STEPHEN M. WHITEHEAD
and FRANK J. BARRETT

Polity

First published in 2001 by Polity Press in association with Blackwell Publishers Ltd

Editorial Office:
Polity Press
65 Bridge Street
Cambridge CB2 1UR, UK

Marketing and production:
Blackwell Publishers Ltd
108 Cowley Road
Oxford OX4 1JF, UK

Published in the USA by
Blackwell Publishers Inc.
350 Main Street
Malden, MA 02148, USA

ISBN 0–7456–2688–2
ISBN 0–7456–2689–0 (pbk)

A catalogue record for this book is available from the British Library and has been applied for from the Library of Congress.

Typeset in 10/12pt Sabon
by Kolam Information Services Pvt. Ltd, Pondicherry, India
Printed in Great Britain by MPG Books Ltd, Bodmin, Cornwall

This book is printed on acid-free paper.

Contents

Part III   Masculinities in the Public Domain

Part IV   The Private Lives of Men

Part V   Endings and Beginnings: The Practices and Politics of Changing Men

Acknowledgements

My part in the writing and editing of this book is dedicated to my sons
Gavin, Jay and Robert.

Stephen Whitehead

I would like to dedicate my effort on this book to my father, my grand-
fathers, my uncles and all the Irish, working-class men who have pre-
ceded me and make me proud of my heritage.

Frank Barrett

We both would like to thank Sophie Ahmad of Polity Press for her
invaluable advice and guidance throughout the process of compiling
the material for this reader. Thanks also to Deborah Kerfoot for her
continued support and for bringing us together for this project.

The editors and publishers wish to thank the following for permission to
use copyright material:

Beacon Press for material from Michael Messner, *Power at Play* (1992)
pp. 91–102. Copyright © 1992 by Michael A. Messner;

Blackwell Publishers for material from Arthur Brittan, *Masculinity and
Power* (1989) pp. 1–6; Scott Fabius Kiesling, 'Power and the Language of
Men' in S. Johnson and U. L. Meinhof, eds, *Language and Masculinity*
(1997) pp. 65–85; David Collinson and Jeff Hearn, 'Naming Men as
Men: Implications for Work, Organization and Management', *Gender,
Work and Organization*, 1:1 (1994) pp. 2–22; and Frank Barrett, 'The
Organizational Construction of Hegemonic Masculinity: The Case of the
US Navy', *Gender, Work and Organization*, 3:3 (1996) pp. 129–42;

Human Kinetics Publishers, Inc. for material from Richard Majors, 'Cool Pose: Black Masculinity and Sports' in M. A. Messner and D. F. Sabo, eds, *Men and the Gender Order* (1990) pp. 109–14;

Institute for Social Research, Oslo, for material from David H. J. Morgan, 'Family, Gender and Masculinities' in A. Leira, ed., *Family Sociology and Social Change*, nr. 18 (1994) pp. 55–66; Men's Studies Press for material from A. Segal, 'Masculinity, School, and Self in Sweden and the Netherlands', *The Journal of Men's Studies*, 8:2 (2000) pp. 171–94;

Open University Press for material from John MacInnes, *The End of Masculinity* (1998) pp. 45–60;

Oxfam Publishing for material from Katherine Wood and Rachel Jewkes, 'Violence, Rape and Sexual Coercion: Everyday Love in a South African Township', pp. 41–6, and Niels Sampath, 'Crabs in a Bucket: Reforming Male Identities in Trinidad', pp. 47–54, in C. Sweetman, ed., *Men and Masculinity* (1997);

Polity Press for material from Robert W. Connell, *Masculinities* (1995) pp. 67–86;

Sage Publications, Inc. for material from Michael S. Kimmell, 'Masculinity as Homophobia: Fear, Shame and Silence in the Construction of Gender Identity', pp. 45–60, and David Gutterman, 'Postmodernism and the Interrogation of Masculinity', pp. 219–34, in H. Brod and M. Kauffman, eds, *Theorizing Masculinities* (1994); Ralph R. Donald, 'Masculinity and Machismo in Holywood War Films' in S. Craig, ed., *Men, Masculinites and the Media* (1992) pp. 124–36; and R. W. Connell, 'Masculinity Politics on a World Scale' from 'Men and Masculinities', *Men and Masculinities*, 1:1 (1998) pp. 3–23;

Taylor and Francis Books Ltd for material from Deborah Kerfoot, 'The Organization of Intimacy' from S. Whitehead and R. Moodley, eds, *Transforming Managers: Gendering Change in the Public Sector,* UCL Press (1999) pp. 184–98; and Stephen Whitehead, 'The Invisible Gendered Subject?', *Journal of Gender Studies*, 10:1 (2001);

The University of Chicago Press for material from Peter M. Nardi, *Gay Men's Friendships: Invincible Communities* (1999) pp. 189–206;

Virago Press for material from Lynne Segal, *Slow Motion* (1997) pp. 205–17;

Westview Press, a member of Perseus Books LLC, for material from Alfredo Mirande, *Hombres y Machos: Masculinity and Latino Culture* (1997) pp. 118–22, 132, 136–8. Copyright © 1997 by Westview Press;

Every effort has been made to trace the copyright holders but if any have been inadvertently overlooked the publishers will be pleased to make the necessary arrangement at the first opportunity.

Publisher's Note

An ellipsis [...] has been used whenever material from the original has been omitted. Where a paragraph or more has been excluded, a line space appears above and below [...].

Apart from the omission of material discussed above, each chapter has been presented as it was originally published. The decision to do this has necessarily entailed inconsistencies of style and spelling between the chapters.

The Sociology of Masculinity

*Stephen M. Whitehead and
Frank J. Barrett*

During the last two decades research into men and masculinities has emerged as one of the growth areas of sociological enquiry. The past decade alone has seen over 500 books published, the introduction of two specialist journals, and a proliferation of websites all providing a particular slant on the condition of men at the turn of the millennium. In the USA there are now some fifty universities offering specialist programmes in this subject. Beyond the USA, and across Australasia and Europe in particular, a similar surge in feminist-inspired writings on men and masculinities has occurred. Whereas only two decades ago critical insights into masculinities were relatively few, today there are no areas of men's activities that have not been subject to some research and debate by both women and men. Whether they study sport, families, organizations, management, media, violence, power, identities, crime, education, ethnicity or sexualities, the social science student and researcher is now required to have some critical knowledge or appreciation of gender, and increasingly men's sense of gender as constructed through dominant representations of masculinity.

The aim of this book is, then, to provide students and researchers with an accessible and comprehensive overview of the key debates in the sociology of masculinity. In so doing, the volume will introduce not only the most influential concepts, but also emergent themes in this field. However, given the depth and breadth of research now available on men and masculinities, the writings chosen for this reader should be considered neither definitive nor exhaustive of the genre. Rather, the chapters in this volume are illustrative of an often complex and still developing area of study. Just as feminist theory has moved through first, second and now third waves of critical enquiry (Farganis, 1994), so has the sociology of masculinity. It is an area of sociology that has, since the mid-1950s, drawn on many theories, including structural functionalism, Marxism, psychoanalysis, critical structuralism, and, more recently, post-structuralism and theories of the post-modern (see Whitehead, forthcoming, for discussion). It can be seen then, that unlike feminist theories, which can be traced back at least to the eighteenth-century writings of Mary Wollstonecraft (Tong, 1993; see also Rendall, 1985), the sociology of masculinity is relatively recent, only coming into being in the latter half of the twentieth century. Since the 1950s, the USA has proved to be an especially fertile ground for research into men, with the studies undertaken by Pleck (1976), Hacker (1957), Hartley (1959), and David and Brannon (1976) being particularly influential in the early stages of the genre's development. In recognizing the importance of US scholarship in this field, it is entirely appropriate, then, that over half of the twenty-one chapters in this volume originate from North America.

Despite the exponential increase in research into men and masculinities, there has, to date, been no reader published which draws on key writings from all parts of the globe. In this respect at least, this volume is unique. This is an important point, for it should be recognized that the critical study of men and masculinities is not confined to any particular national border, ethnic group, or identity politics. The sociology of masculinity now draws on a highly pluralistic scholarship, and as a consequence enjoys a vast and diverse audience. A further key characteristic of this volume is the fact that most of the twenty-one chapters remain in their original state. As a consequence, the book provides the student or researcher with the fullest introduction to the debates as is possible, while offering indications of the periodic shifts in this field of sociology.

Given the amount, richness and variety of the writings in this area, it is inevitable that good and influential works have, unfortunately, had to be omitted. While the writings chosen are all excellent examples of the field, several key authors who have made important contributions to the sociology of masculinity have, by virtue of space and design, not been included, though in some instances their publications do provide the vehicle for chapters in this volume. Recognizing this, we would like to acknowledge a number of writers not directly included in this book, but who have made important contributions to the sociology of masculinity. In particular, we would mention Harry Brod and Michael Kaufman (1994), Mike Donaldson (1993), Tony Jefferson (1998), Ian Craib (1987), Jonathon Rutherford (1992), Andrea Cornwall and Nancy Lindisfarne (1994), John Stoltenberg (2000), Victor Seidler (1994), Martin Mac an Ghaill (1994), Donald Sabo (1985), Peter Middleton (1992),

Alan Petersen (1998), Joseph Pleck (1995), Michael Roper (1994), David Jackson (1990), and Andrew Tolson (1977).

Feminist parentage

It is increasingly recognized that feminist theories have not only constituted a most influential scholarship within academia, they have also had a profound impact on the subjectivities of countless numbers of women worldwide. This has led to immense personal and political transformations, the consequences and direction of which are still unfolding. Recognizing such, we would go so far as to suggest that feminism was the single most powerful political discourse of the twentieth century, shaping up to have an even greater impact in the twenty-first. For while the dynamic of feminism continues to change across European, American and Australasian countries, its form and impact in Asia, Africa, the Middle East and the Far East is increasingly powerful, exciting, and certainly should not be underestimated. Indeed, so subversive and political is feminist thinking within and beyond the West, that many commentators consider the rise in religious fundamentalism to be a direct response by men to the changing position and expectations of women. Anthony Giddens describes it as an 'attempt by men to stall the (global) gender revolution' (Giddens and Hutton, 2000: 27).

Such a threatening reaction from men to women's new-found sense of power and self should not be too surprising, for one of the direct consequences of feminist thinking and action has been to expose and highlight the power, position and practices of men. In so doing, feminism has explicated the continuing inequalities between women and men as they exist across ethnic groups and cultural and social borders. Feminism is political inasmuch as it is about seeking change towards what Bob Connell describes as 'gender justice'. In pursuit of this aim, feminism puts men and masculinities in a critical spotlight, in the process centring on the practices of men in ways many men would prefer it not to, not least because there may well be costs to them as a result. Certainly in terms of sustaining unequal material advantage, opportunity, status and privilege, men have much to lose with the rise of feminist thinking. Conversely, we would also argue that men have much to gain, not least in achieving emotional well-being, empathy with others, quality of relationships, reflexivity, and balance in their lives. For the sake of this and future generations it can only be good that men recognize they have a gender, rather than perceive gender to be about women and, thus, peripheral to how they experience the world. In this respect, men are central to the gender transformations that characterized the late twentieth century and continue into the twenty-first. However, as feminists have long argued, the historical centrality of malestream writing, philosophy and political practice has served to make men invisible, particularly to themselves. As Whitehead in chapter 20 illustrates, it is a condition that continues for many males.

Yet despite many men's propensity for self-denial in the face of direct and obvious shifts in women's subjectivities, large numbers have responded to the challenges posited by women's movements since the 1960s. The contrasting responses of men to feminism have been well charted by Clatterbaugh (1990) and Messner (1997). Briefly, these responses range from the avidly anti-feminist men's movements, increasingly flexing their political muscles in the West via groups such as the Christian Promise Keepers, through to a possibly more accommodating mythopoetic movement (see Kimmel, 1995, for discussion), and on to the pro-feminist response typified by the writings in this book (Gutterman in ch. 3; Connell in ch. 21). Across this gendered political terrain lie the increasingly important gay men's movements (see Nardi, ch. 16), and the black (see Majors, ch. 11) and Chicano/Latino (see Mirandé ch. 19) men's movements.

The point to stress, then, is that writings in this volume originate from both women (feminists) and men (pro-feminists) and, as such, declare their feminist parentage and affiliation quite openly. In this respect, the volume has a clear political dimension in that each contributor has a personal/political alignment with women and 'Other' men in their fight for gender, racial, and sexual justice.

The state of men

The notion that women still have equality battles to fight at the start of the twenty-first century would strike some as quite odd. For is it not the case that women now 'have it all'? Do we not live in a 'post-feminist era'? Are not men the ones now 'in crisis'?

In order to have an understanding and appreciation of the state of men at this point in history it is important to first address the above assumptions. The idea that women 'have it all' is beguiling, but before assuming it to be the case one must put it in context of both social movements and cultural differentiations. Taking the latter point first, it is obvious to any observer that acute structural gender inequalities exist across the globe.

For those of us who live in the West, it may be less apparent that women in other countries suffer physical and mental hardship, violence, abuse, political disenfranchisement, inequality in law and material disadvantage, are frequently denied educational opportunity, and are in many cases treated in every respect like an underclass. But such is the daily reality of life for millions of women, and not only in openly misogynistic countries such as Saudi Arabia and Afghanistan. However, Western societies themselves are in no position to pontificate on gender inequalities in Asia, Africa, and the East. Men's abuse and violence towards girls and women is endemic across the West, with male aggression remaining the 'dark side' of masculine role performance in all 'modern' societies (Bowker, 1998; see also Wood and Jewkes, ch. 7). In terms of employment, Western women have made significant progress yet still receive lower wages for the same job as men and can expect to pay a substantial 'gender forfeit' in terms of loss of salary over a working lifetime in comparison to men (Creighton, 1999; Office of National Statistics, 2000). Similarly, over the past decades women in countries such as the United Kingdom have made great strides in educational achievement, yet leave education for work only to suffer discrimination in respect of both comparative incomes with men and opportunities to progress to the highest levels of organizational life (Collinson and Hearn, 1996; see also ch. 8). While wider economic and social changes have combined to provide women with work and lifestyle choices unimagined by their mothers and grandmothers, women still carry the burden of multiple roles, a situation that has become more acute as work intensification pressures combine with the continued stereotypes many men hold about housework, childcare, caring roles, and emotional labour (Hochschild, 1989; Franks, 1999).

We would argue that so long as the above situations exist in any part of the globe there can never be a 'post-feminist era'. Furthermore, it is salutary to look more closely at those changes that have benefited Western women over the past five decades or so, and to place them in wider contexts. For example, many of the freedoms and opportunities now available to women have come through science and technology (i.e. the Pill); economic transformations (i.e. the rise in service industries); educational opportunity (i.e. the emergence of the knowledge economy); and greater political pressures towards equality in law (i.e. the European Court). None of these changes is a direct result of men changing. The social, economic and political transformations outlined above have come about in spite of, not because of, men. Such changes as we have seen have been driven by financial imperatives, not so much a desire for equal opportunities. Increased opportunity for women has, in some areas, been a consequence, but not the original intention. In that respect, any notions of a so-called 'post-feminist era' are dangerously premature. For if the financial imperative ever changes, and there are always pressures for it to do so, then women could well find themselves having to re-fight battles many had thought long won.

This brings us to the third assumption – that men are in crisis.

Of all the current discourses surrounding transformations in gender relations, that of a male crisis is particularly potent and apparent. The male crisis, or 'crisis of masculinity' thesis, has assumed, for many, almost the status of a defining characteristic of Western societies at the turn of the millennium (see, for example, Faludi, 1999; Clare, 2000; Horrocks, 1994; Bly, 1990; also MacInnes, ch. 17). The common theme within this debate is that the displays of manhood considered appropriate prior to, say, the 1950s, are socially stigmatized and debased fifty years on. Many men still yearn to perform and validate their masculinity through 'conquering the universe', but the aggressive, dominant, emotionally repressed behaviour that such yearnings engender are increasingly seen as (self)-destructive, if not derisible. Various views are put forward as to why such a comprehensive shift in gender perspectives has come about, but most writers in this area draw on three key social markers for evidence. They assume that men are being reduced to this confused, dysfunctional and insecure state through a combination of, firstly, rampant, soulless consumerism; secondly, women's (feminism's) successful assault on male bastions of privilege; and thirdly, more widespread social and cultural disapproval of traditional displays of masculinity.

Such ideas have a popular appeal in that they appear to provide an 'answer' to the complex changes that have occurred between women and men and to many men's apparent inability to accommodate women's new-found confidence. However, like the idea of a 'post-feminist era', the male crisis discourse requires putting in context in order to achieve a better purchase on its veracity. Each of the main three social conditions enlisted to prove the male crisis thesis can be argued to exist in some form in Western societies. But do we then take them as combined evidence of a larger crisis in men? Hardly, for as social phenomena each is conditional and contextual. For example, few would argue against the notion that since the end of the Second World War consumerism, as a way of being, has permeated Western culture, if not inspired globalization itself. Following this, it can be accepted that consumerism constructs its own pressures and social consequences, not least a widening poverty gap between rich and poor. But women are equally seduced or, if you like, put at risk by rampant consumerism. Indeed, given most women's less secure material circumstances, they are probably more at risk than men, and certainly there is recent evidence from the European Commission to support this view (European Commission, 2000). Taking the issue of women's successful assault on male privilege, as has already been recognized, during the past three decades or so feminism has become a powerful political discourse impacting on women's subjectivities in numerous ways and with unpredictable consequences for both women and men. But as feminists have long argued, men retain a capacity to resist and threaten this challenge. Even those sociologists not normally associated with pro-feminist scholarship, such as Anthony Giddens, are coming to recognize that many men are now actively resisting women's burgeoning demands for equal rights, and doing so increasingly through recourse to discourses of religious fundamentalism, not only Islamic, but also Christian and Jewish.

The issue of changing masculinities is, however, probably the key one in terms of understanding changing men and a possible crisis in masculinity. One can find numerous examples of how traditional notions of masculinity have moved out of fashion across the Western world. But then, masculinities have always been subject to fashion. Indeed, it can be argued that perceived notions of how males should perform their gender have never been more subject to media and popular interpretation than they are in this global, post-modern age (see Gutterman, ch. 3). Yet, as the studies undertaken by Segal (ch. 10), Wood and Jewkes (ch. 7), Barrett (ch. 4), Donald (ch. 9), and Messner (ch. 14) highlight, despite the evident multiplicity of masculine expression, traditional masculinities and associated values still prevail in most cultural settings. Countless numbers of men still act dominant and 'hard', deny their emotions, resort to violence as a means of self-expression, and seek to validate their masculinity in the public world of work rather the private world of family and relationships. Moreover, such performances not only often go uncriticized, they are in fact lauded by many, both women and other men. There is little evidence yet of the demise of 'laddish culture' in the West, and popular media expressions of this, exemplified by 'hard men' such as Vinnie Jones and Mike Tyson, continue to validate a form of masculinity which not only black and/or working-class men aspire to. Indeed, one only has to look at the increased incidence of Nazi memorabilia being touted in American schools, of the macho posturing of Northern Ireland paramilitaries, and the organized mass rapes of women in former Yugoslavia, to recognize that, in many places, aggressive masculinity is alive and well. Of course, behind the hard veneer of the male 'Nazi', paramilitary, or militiaman, there usually lies a fragile identity and an equally fragile confidence, but nevertheless, the actual performance of such radical masculine expression results in damage to all who come into contact with it. In this respect, while such men may be in some form of emotional or existential crisis, there is little new about this.

As contributors to this volume stress, masculinities are not fixed; they change over time, over space, and, not least, during the lives of men themselves. Having accepted this premise, it is clear that for there to be a crisis of masculinity there would have to be a single masculinity; something solid, fixed, immovable, brittle even. This single masculinity would, by definition, have to be a core masculinity; something which is natural to men and which men can naturally aspire to and hold under most conditions. And this core but brittle masculinity would have to be broken, damaged, or bruised by a combination of consumerism, feminism, post-industrialization, women's rights, and so on. Following this line of thinking, the turn of the millenium must, by definition, be the time when, as a result of a variety of circumstances, men come into crisis. For the factors enlisted by Faludi and others to prove this thesis have never existed prior to now. Which begs the question, is this the first crisis of masculinity that men have suffered?

We put this question, not to seek an answer, but to draw attention to the importance of placing such questions in a historical context. As Kimmel (1987; see also ch. 15), and Whitehead (forthcoming), note, the crisis of masculinity thesis goes back a long way, existing in some form or another for most of the twentieth century. Indeed, public concerns about men's emotional, physical or moral state existed in the US and Europe at least as early as the eighteenth century, coming to inform such movements as the Boy Scouts of America, the particular character of the English public school system, and dominant definitions of race, class and nationhood (see Mangan and Walvin, 1987; Roper and Tosh, 1991; Hantover, 1978; Pleck, 1981; Carby, 1998; Nelson, 1998).

A study of historical debates about men and masculinities reveals an interesting pattern. For it is apparent that whenever larger social and public concerns raise their head (i.e. about possible war, economic recession, rises in crime, educational underachievement, or the moral fabric of a nation) then very quickly the issue of boys/men comes to the fore; usually how to change them, control them, provide them with purpose, or simply avoid the worst excesses of anti-social male behaviour. What emerges, in fact, is a moral panic around men and masculinity, which can quickly turn into a backlash against women and feminism (see Lingard and Douglas, 1999; also Segal, 1999).

Recognizing that Western societies in particular have experienced enormous social, technical, and economic change over the past five decades, one should not be too surprised at the propensity of commentators to declare a crisis in masculinity. For it would be inconceivable that men, individually and as a political category, having for so long been unquestioningly central to political, religious, and economic life, would not be challenged by the major social and cultural disruptions which marked the twentieth century. Yet when taking historical perspectives into account, it can be shown that declarations of a crisis of men and masculinity have been around for over a century. Moreover, recognition of the tedious persistence of traditional (laddish) forms of masculine expression in society should also serve to make us very wary of writing the obituary of masculinity just yet. Many men may need some form of help, but not to lead them back to essentialist retreats: dated, traditionalist and damaging ways of being a man, exemplified by various anti-feminist men's movements, 'hard men', 'macho men', and the Christian Promise Keepers. Despite the welcome interventions of such diverse scholars as John Stoltenberg, Susan Faludi and Anthony Clare, all urging men to reject the 'dying phallus' (Clare, 2000), the 'mandates of manhood' (Stoltenberg, 2000), or their 'illusions of control' (Faludi, 1999), sightings of any resulting 'new man' remain unconfirmed (see McMahon, 2000).

While we take a realistic, if not rather jaundiced, view of the idea that men are in crisis, we do recognize the state of men at the turn of the millennium to be historically significant. For there can be no denying the fact that not only have there been significant social transformations outside the control of any group or individual, but the implications of these changes for men, particularly working-class men, are particularly profound. For example, men can no longer presume to enjoy a secure life-long career; male-dominated industrialization has largely given way to more female-orientated service industries; women are increasingly exercising choice over relationships, divorce, child-bearing and their sexual expression; the very character and notion of the 'family' has shifted dramatically, and is no longer confined to or even dominated by the patriarchal nuclear version; the concept of the male breadwinner family is almost dead, with most dual households now having two income providers; notions of class, having long sustained divisions in masculinity, are now subsumed under often obscure symbolic patterns of consumption and not confined to any specific ethnic or social grouping; and gay sexuality, long the 'Other' which served to define hegemonic masculinity, is no longer confined to the closet, but openly expressed if not celebrated in most Western cities. Add to this potent mixture the simple and self-evident fact that never in history have men been so subject to question, media scrutiny and critically informed scholarship and one gets a direct line to many of the issues and questions which lie at the heart of this book.

In sum, it is important not to fall into the trap of equating changes in men's experiences and opportunities with a crisis in masculinity. Men adapt. Indeed, being human, men are superb at adaptation. This adaptation may occur over a single lifetime, but should be recognized as a continual process which each generation of men (and women) experiences largely unknowingly – though having the capacity to reflect and understand one's experiences certainly helps. In the process of such change, men's notions of masculine self can undergo shifts. This should not surprise us, for what serves to define individuals as males and as men will always be subject to social and cultural specificity. However, despite having the capacity, many men appear to change little over their lifetimes. Indeed, countless men actively resist the changes implied by the gender revolution, recognizing perhaps that, at least materially, they would benefit little from it (Morgan, 1990). Such men often remain locked in a juvenile and crude display of masculinity. This performance as 'masculine subject' (Whitehead, forthcoming; Kerfoot, ch. 13) not only serves men ill emotionally and in their relationships, it can only be sustained and reaffirmed through fraternal groupings, often misogynistic male bonding rituals, rejection of intimacy and an avid denial of the 'Other' – be it women, femininity, or gay sexuality (Messner, ch. 14; Kimmel, ch. 15). Connell describes this crude, but for many men compelling, way of being as 'hegemonic masculinity' (see ch. 1, and also Barrett, ch. 4).

Clearly, far from being in a singular crisis, masculinity is complex, dynamic, powerful, multiple and, not least, political. Recognizing this, and in the process contributing to developing more sophisticated understandings of men and masculinities, are primary aims of this book.

Understanding masculinities

While there are differences between some of the understandings of masculinity which the contributors to this volume utilize, there is a single and important commonality. That is, as a critical sociologist, each contributor rejects the idea that men and masculinities are either locked in a genetic combination, or determined by a fixed, unchangeable, biological set of conditions or factors. In short, each writer argues in some way against a 'Darwinian' explanation for the state of gender relations and human individuality. At a time when it is possible to be seduced into the belief that all human life and its associated complexities can be explained through our genetic coding, it is important to retain a broad but critical perspective on not only gender relations, but sexualities, racial expressions, and ethnic diversities. To do otherwise is to slip into what is undoubtedly for many a comforting view of the human condition – that it is reducible to genetic predispositions. Taken to its extreme, such perspectives lead on to the theory of 'evolutionary psychology', a perspective that is anathema to anti-racist, feminist and pro-feminist scholars. The main arguments against evolutionary psychology are that it ignores diversity amongst women and men; it rests on a limited view of human history; and moreover, it results in justifying men's oppression and marginalization of women and 'Other' men, particularly ethnic minority women and men, and those most disadvantaged in society – the underclass. As Rose and Rose put it:

> For evolutionary psychologists, everything – from men's propensity to rape to our alleged preference for grassy scenery – derives from our mythical origin in the African savanna. In its prioritising of explanations of, for instance, rape as a device for sexually unsuccessful men to propagate their genes, it is completely unable to explain why most men do not rape....We argue that the theory's all-embracing sound-bites are for the most part not just mistaken, but culturally pernicious [not least because] these new fundamentalists assert that their view of human nature should inform the making of social and public policy. (2000a)

There is something of an irony in the fact that, on the one hand, since the 1960s, we have seen sociological perspectives increasingly distancing themselves from notions of determinism (for example, Parsonian structural functionalism), with post-structuralist and post-modern theories coming to prominence during the past decade or so. On the other hand, under the rubric of 'Darwinism', evolutionary perspectives represent a contemporary wave of thinking within medicine, economics, politics, psychology, and psychiatry. In short, while much of sociology has shifted towards a theoretical emphasis on the contingency and multiplicity of identity, power, and the human condition, 'Darwinism' has entered the 'cultural drinking water' (Rose and Rose, 2000a) of the West, in the process seeking to present human behaviour and potential as inevitably limited to pre-fixed genetic impulses (see also Clare, 2000, for discussion).

At a lay level, one can recognize the attraction of biological explanations for understanding gender, for much of our everyday language is permeated with explicit or implicit gender(ed) interpretations. For example, words such as passive, active, sensitive, aggressive, emotional, caring, controlling, warrior, nurse, captain, leader, manager, director, cleaner, virile, frigid, impotent can be read in gendered ways, and interpreted within dualistic but dominant understandings of what it means to be a man or a woman (see Petersen, 1998). Thus language not only informs concepts of masculinity, it is a tool through which to perform, label, and interpret our gender identities (see Kiesling, ch. 6). Language gives meaning to our selves and our lives, without which our ability to locate ourselves in the social web would be missing. However, in resorting to simplistic biological interpretations we are merely replicating the myths of gender and thus reinforcing a 'gender order' (see Connell, chs 1 and 21) within which males are the primary beneficiaries.

It is clearly much harder to grasp the complex dynamics of the social world and to recognize that, while patterns exist, they are not embedded in any natural order of things than it is to resort to stereotypes to 'explain the world'. In part, this is because the multiplicity, contingency and disorder of our everyday existence cannot ever be fully accepted, for to do so would be to place our sense of ontological security at risk (Giddens, 1991). Gender dualisms, such as we see embedded in everyday language, give the illusion of order and thus a certain security. So when we look at men and women, we see first a gendered being, overlaid with culturally dominant representations of race, ethnicity, body and age, and reified through signifying practices (Hall, 1997). The gamut of symbols, myths and ideologically informed practices which ensue from gender representations offer a sense of order, naturalness and timelessness. However, as a gender order, it also creates structural properties inasmuch as it serves to lock human beings, women and men, into political categories. Consequently, the danger with deterministic explanations is that we stop questioning why women and gay men are discriminated against and marginalized in so many situations worldwide. Instead, rather than confront the difficult, personal and political issues, we sidestep them and set our faces against the possibility of real understanding. Ignorance remains, and in that ignorance injustice flourishes.

While the aims of this book are to question and, we hope, enlighten, we are not suggesting that, as men, we ourselves are somehow privileged, different, and thus removed from the conditions of gender that surround us all. Each of us, in his own way, has had to work through – is still working through – the maze of life as men, as sexual beings, and as culturally differentiated in countless ways, not least white academics. We do declare our pro-feminist affiliations, but not to be seen as either superior to or separate from other men. We have come to recognize that we have a male gender; a state of reflexivity that still eludes many men (Middleton, 1992), but we do not claim to see ourselves in some pure, objective fashion. Such is beyond us, as it is beyond all individuals.

It can be argued that for all women and men, but especially critical gender theorists, there are particular ambiguities surrounding one's sense of self and one's understanding of gender, and which arise from attempting to work through the personal tensions ensuing from engagement in the politics of identity (MacInnes, 1998; see also ch. 17). As women and men, academics may well spend countless hours thinking, reading, and writing about gender, but they remain, foremost, women and men; gendered, sexual beings who, like all individuals, have to exist in the social world at some level of interaction. Quite apart from being academics we/they also occupy other 'subject positions' (Gutterman, ch. 3) such as father, mother, husband, wife, lover, son, daughter, parent, and so on. This situation has what Silvia Gherardi (1995) describes as 'schizogenic' characteristics, whereby individuals live out their daily existence always knowing that much of what they do and say is contrary to their deeper intellectual or epistemological learnings.

The ambiguities and complexities around gender also have political implications within organizational life itself. For example, while feminists fight for equal opportunities in organizations, they cannot assume that an increase in the number of women managers or politicians will bring with it cultural shifts towards a more feminine institution. To do so is to fall into the trap of biological determinism. The fact is, we cannot know for certain what changes will be brought about by having more men as primary school teachers, more women politicians, more women directors of multi-national corporations, or more men involved in family life (Morgan, ch. 12). There may well be changes, and one would hope that they were positive, but one should be wary of presuming such. Yet recognizing complexity and difference should not stop us fighting against discrimination, we just need to be clear that what we are fighting against is a culture that privileges men and masculinity, what Brittan (ch. 2) describes as 'masculinism', a dominant ideology or discourse that serves to naturalize male domination.

Many students and researchers who come to engage with critical writings on gender for the first time can be forgiven for going away disappointed at not finding set answers to their pressing questions. Indeed, with the increasing influence of post-structuralist theories on feminist thinking the possibility of finding distinct answers to complex social questions seems as far away as ever. Similarly, within the sociology of masculinity, the increasingly pluralistic character of the scholarship and research speaks not of single 'solutions' to questions surrounding men and masculinity. What it does speak to is difference, diversity, and, at best, identifying patterns of behaviour between, and within, groups of men. So at a macro level, we can recognize that woman and man are political categories and that such categories are politicized and, as a consequence, exist with some degree of opposition. Also, we can recognize that the categories of woman and man are simultaneously self-sustaining inasmuch as without one, the other could not exist. But once we move towards a more nuanced examination of masculine subjectivities, then differences become more apparent and any patterns become more blurred. How, for example, do we interpret the experiences of a gay Chicano male as opposed to a white heterosexual male (see Mirandé, ch. 19), or the 'cool pose' of a black sportsman (Majors, ch. 11) when compared to the masculine performances of white men in white, male-dominated organizations (Collinson and Hearn, ch. 8; Barrett, ch. 4)? As males, each exists within a global, acultural, political gender category, and as males each is likely to benefit, certainly in a material manner, from any prevailing ideology of masculinism which exists within their immediate cultural setting. But their sexuality, race, age, ethnicity, not to mention sense of embodiment, also conspire to influence how they act and think, and how each relates to other men and to women (Messner, ch. 14), indeed how they perceive themselves to be a dominant, powerful gender (Segal, ch. 5).

In coming to an understanding of masculinity we are, in fact, coming to some understanding of the human condition. The challenge for the (pro)-feminist theorist and researcher is to develop insights into how men oppress, exercise power over, and come to enjoy material advantage over women, and other men, but also to set these insights in the context of individual subjectivities and interpretations. In so doing, the critical gender theorist is required to have a foot in two camps. That is, she or he must straddle the space between recognizing macro-conditions, while also having some understanding of how such macro-conditions are lived out, contributed to, and experienced at the level of very different individuals.

Some questions and 'answers'

In order to provide the reader with ease of access to this book, we conclude this introduction by putting together a number of key questions likely to be at the forefront of the mind of any student or researcher concerned to get a purchase on the sociology of masculinity. The aim is to chart a trail of primary reference points, and in so doing avoiding complicating any further that which is already abstruse and often perplexing.

What is the sociology of masculinity?

The sociology of masculinity concerns the critical study of men, their behaviours, practices, values and perspectives. As such, the sociology of masculinity is informed by, and locates itself within, feminist theories. Writers within this genre are understood to be personally/politically aligned with feminist agendas and to have a desire for gender justice. The critical writings on men and masculinity which constitute the sociology of masculinity seek to highlight the ways in which men's powers come to be differentiated, naturalized and embedded across all cultures, political borders and organizational networks. There is, then, a clear wish to change and challenge such power differentials, and, one hopes, change men.

Since its beginnings in the 1950s, the sociology of masculinity has moved through three prominent theoretical waves, in part mirroring similar shifts in the theoretical patterns of feminist thinking. The first of these waves was concerned with the problematics of male role performance and the cost to men of attempting to strictly adhere to dominant expectations of masculine ideology; what Joseph Pleck (1995) has termed 'male gender role "discrepancy"'. The second wave arose in the early 1980s and sought to highlight, not so much the cost to men of patriarchy, but the centrality of male power to dominant ways of being a man. Exemplified by the work of Carrigan, Connell and Lee (1985), second-wave theorizing introduced the concept of 'hegemonic masculinity', and in so doing firmly placed masculinity as a political, multiple, contested, yet powerful concept. The third wave within the sociology of masculinity has been primarily influenced by feminist post-structuralism and theories of post-modernity (see Butler, 1990; Nicholson, 1990). Here the emphasis is on how men's sense of identity is validated through dominant discursive practices of self, and how this identity work connects with (gender) power and resistance. Emphasizing the importance of recognizing differences within and across the political categories of woman and man, third-wave theorizing is increasingly drawing on queer theory, black and Chicano/Latino men's studies, and Foucauldian understandings of the discursive subject (see Petersen, 1998; Whitehead, forthcoming).

What is masculinity?

In line with all the contributors to this volume, the case we make is for recognizing differences between men, and thus seeing masculinities as plural, changing, and historically informed around dominant discourses or ideologies of masculinism. In this respect we cannot answer, in any absolute sense, the question 'What is masculinity?' The nearest that we can get to an 'answer' is to state that masculinities are those behaviours, languages and practices, existing in specific cultural and organizational locations, which are commonly associated with males and thus culturally defined as not feminine. So masculinities exist as both a positive, inasmuch as they offer some means of identity signification for males, and as a negative, inasmuch as they are not the 'Other' (feminine). Masculinities and male behaviours are not the simple product of genetic codings or biological predispositions (see Clatterbaugh, 1990)

Is masculinity totally uninfluenced by biology?

A qualified 'Yes', for although no human behaviour is totally uninfluenced by biology, masculinity reflects social and cultural expectations of male behaviour rather than biology. In short, men are not puppets of their hormones. We do need to recognize, however, that our hormonal state, chromosomal patterns and homeostasis can influence our behaviour. For example, research has indicated links between levels of testosterone in males and dominant and aggressive behaviours. But then, as Anthony Clare notes, 'aggressive behaviour might *cause* higher levels of testosterone' (2000: 22) rather than the other way round. So male aggression is not conditional upon testosterone; young boys with very little testosterone can be aggressive in certain social situations and there is evidence that testosterone levels are not significantly higher in those males who are violent and abusive towards women. Furthermore, females can exhibit dominant and aggressive behaviours, and their testosterone levels are significantly lower than those of males. It is, therefore, important to distinguish between masculinity and hormone-influenced behaviour. Masculinity is a set of fluid social and cultural performances and as such is not a product, in the first instance, of our hormonal state. Aggression and violence are more likely to be carried out by males, but not all males are violent and aggressive (see Hearn, 1998, for discussion).

How can we understand men's power?

Firstly, one can understand power as brute force. It is hard to ignore the fact that most of the means of organized violence and brute force – weapons and the complex knowledge associated with them – are in the hands of men. Secondly, one can understand power as relational and positional, a point underlined by the fact that most positions of power in the public sphere are held by men. This includes business organizations, military organizations, paramilitary organizations (including police and fire prevention), and religious organizations. Relational notions of male power critique gender ideologies in order to explain how, for example, hegemonic masculinity serves to sustain the inequalities which exist between men and women and between different groups of men (see Connell, ch. 1; see also Connell, 1987).

A third concept of power draws attention to the importance of discourse as a means by which power is exercised and resisted, and through which male supremacy and power inequalities become legitimized. Drawing on post-structuralists such as Michel Foucault, third-wave masculinity studies seek to understand the processes by which definitions and discourses reinforce gender inequalities; for example, by positioning men as strong and women as fragile; men as rational, women as emotional; men as disciplined, women as undisciplined; heterosexual men as normal, homosexuals as sick; and so on (see Petersen, 1998, for discussion). Such studies emphasize the necessity to see beyond individual abuses of power and to see power 'as something which circulates' the social web as both a positive and negative force implicated in the process of producing privileged and subordinated discourses and knowledges (see Ramazanoglu, 1993, for discussion). Foucauldian feminists such as Susan Hekman (1990) have argued that dominant discourses informing gender knowledges emphasize and validate particular (maleist) ways of seeing the world, serving to treat this viewpoint as though it represented 'reality'.

Does men's power come from masculinity?

In our view, power and masculinity are relational constructions, processes of ongoing creation and action between individuals and political categories of individuals. Thus discursive or ideological power is not located in a single position and does not require external surveillance and control in order to be sustained and legitimized. Masculine power is largely exercised through self-regulation and self-discipline – a process of 'identity work', one consequence of which is to privilege and validate ways of being male/man/masculine in particular cultural settings. Through taking up and being inculcated with dominant discourses or ideologies of gender, men (and women) contribute in knowing and unknowing ways to both self-identity processes and power inequalities. Individuals may desire to act in ways consistent with gender norms, but in so doing they reproduce male domination and power differentials. To understand how men become powerful, we need to understand how men learn to be masculine, and how dominant discourses of masculinity connect with other forms of power around, for example, class, ethnicity, race, age, religion, culture and nationhood (see Whitehead, forthcoming, for discussion).

Will masculinity ever disappear?

We think this is highly unlikely to happen! At an ontological level, i.e. the individual's sense of being a person, gender plays a pivotal role. All individuals are assigned a sex at birth, and with this sex come the socially dominant scripts and codes of gender. There seems no way of avoiding this. Even if the parents do not want their male child to engage in stereotypical masculine activities (playing with guns, fighting, aggressive posturing, etc.), such activities will be readily available to the child through television, friends, nursery, schooling, and possibly family members. In this way all children are exposed to gender stereo-types, a situation that can never be fully controlled or stopped. What will change to some degree are the stereotypes surrounding gender and sexuality together with those cultural signifying practices which are taken up by individuals as role performances, and thus as part of a deeper desire for gender validation (see Hall, 1997).

Are all men masculine?

If masculinity is a structure of practice that provides resources for con-structing identity, not all men have equal access to the same resources, nor do all men seek these resources. In other words, since masculinity is something that one 'does' rather than something that one 'has', it would be appropriate to say that men 'do' masculinity in a variety of ways and in a variety of settings, depending on the resources available to them. This is true even within hyper-masculine institutions. For example, Bar-rett (ch. 4) documents how men in different jobs within the US military display masculinity in different and often contested ways.

As there are different forms of masculinity, so there is not one hege-monic male type. The (power) relations amongst men produce subordin-ate and marginal masculinities, such as those which surround homo-sexuals and non-white men. Even among gay men, however, varieties of masculine identity exist. Gay men, too, wrestle with contradictory cultural images of masculinity, as Connell (1995) points out in his chapter 'A Very Straight Gay'. Also, there is a growing movement of pro-feminist, heterosexual men who actively seek to undo structures of masculinity (Pease, 2000).

While it is evident that certain behaviours have come to characterize males – sexual and physical assertiveness, competitiveness, aggression – not all men display these traits in the same way. In short, masculinity is rife with contradictions. For example, hegemonic masculinity depends upon notions of compulsive heterosexuality and homophobia reinforced through idealized media images of heroic men. A number of studies explore the cracks and fissures that belie the complications and contradictions embedded in the masculine project. For example, Jefferson (1994) notes that internalized idealized images often do not match men's lived practices, with many men hiding feelings of fear, insecurity, uncertainty. Likewise, Segal (1997) demonstrates that while the pornography industry depicts men as sexually insatiable and powerful, men's experience of sexuality is more complicated and contradictory than popular discourses suggest. Men often experience anxiety about sexual performance, feelings of shame and embarrassment at the thought of sexual incompetence, and humiliation at the prospect of appearing unmanly. Klein (1990) looks at how male bodybuilders attempt to hide weaknesses and vulnerability by elaborating a lifestyle that allows no weaknesses or vulnerability. Clearly, males experience contradictions and difficulties in becoming masculine men. It is not a straightforward, seamless process.

What is the relationship between masculinity and identity?

Discussions as to the relationship between masculinity, identity and gender as social structure have changed somewhat during the various phases of development within the sociology of masculinity. Early influences tended to draw heavily on notions of gender role and its 'strains' or 'discrepancies' for men (Pleck, 1981). Following this, social constructionists argued that gender role theory was inadaquate for exploring male power and failed to fully recognize differences between males (see Kimmel and Messner, 1989; Connell, 1987). Dissatisfied with the lack of critical rigour within much of traditional psychoanalytical theory, Bob Connell turned to a historical exploration of Jungian, Alderian, and orthodox Freudian theories from the perspective of a pro-feminist theorist (Connell, 1994). In a seminal text looking at masculine identity and male dominance, Ian Craib (1987) utilizes object-relations theory and the work of feminist psychoanalyist Nancy Chodorow. And as part of what has come to be seen as the move to a third wave within the sociology of masculinity, Tony Jefferson (1994) engages with Lacanian and Foucauldian analysis in order to theorize masculine subjectivity (see also Frosh, 1994; Middleton, 1992).

The strength of post-structuralist accounts of masculinity, especially those which draw on Lacan and Foucault, is that they offer a means by which to link social action and power relations with identity processes, without, however, falling into a deterministic understanding of power relations as an ideologically inspired, unchanging structure (see Sarup, 1993, for an overview). From a post-structuralist perspective identity is understood as always in process, never finally accomplished. So in this regard, there is no core, grounded, or fixed self, but rather a fluid arrangement of multiple subject positions which together provide the means by which the individual achieves a sense of identity (Rajchman, 1995; Gutterman, ch. 3). The importance of masculinity to this process of identity work is in the validation it can give to this fluid self. So if we accept there is no core self, then socially dominant forms of being a male (masculinities) can be seen to provide an acceptable means by which boys and men may express their gender and thus their sense of identity. In taking up these localized and culturally specific signifying practices, males achieve an association with other males and also a differentiation from the 'Other' – not only women but also those males who appear 'different'. This difference is usually marked through sexual orientation, but can also include forms of embodiment and ethnicity, as well as national and cultural variations of masculine performance.

Because individuals do not have biologically fixed identities, any sense of self can only come about through working to achieve a sense of 'belonging' in the social world. However, 'belonging' is not an automatic process, and so for most men masculine performance is central to achieving entry to, and being accepted within, any particular 'community' of men. This desire for belonging creates, then, both gender and an individual's sense of self. As Bell describes it, 'identity is the effect of performance, and not vice versa' (1999: 3; see also Butler, 1990). It should be noted that such understandings do not assume that males are passive in this process of identity work; this is not simply a case of all-powerful gender socialization. Rather, all individuals are skilled at creating their selves, but within the parameters of their social and cultural experience, factors which are also subject to change.

What is the relationship between masculinity and discourse?

Discourse is more than simply the words and phrases we use. In Foucauldian terms discourses provide the very means by which subjects come to be individuals and come to understand themselves as woman and man

(Sawicki, 1991; Butler, 1990). So we might say that discourses such as 'man as hunter', 'woman as passive', and the 'male sex drive', contain social and cultural assumptions which, once taken up by a person, are presented as 'truths' and as ways of being and relating in the world and to others. In this respect, discourses have identity-enabling properties for they provide guides through the social web for the otherwise fluid and contingent subject (individual). But, more than this, discourses also suggest very strongly to us what can and cannot be spoken at a given time or in a given cultural setting. Discourses are, then, more than just ways of speaking, for they send highly powerful messages in terms of knowledges, what counts as (valid and invalid) knowledge, what is seen as 'truth', and in respect of how individuals should behave in given locales.

If we accept that masculinities and femininities are not biologically given, then we are forced to look at how the social world is formed, framed and enabled in order to get a purchase on gender relations and ways of thinking and performing gender. The concept of discourse provides us with precisely these means, for it highlights not only the power of language, but also how language and practice interact, and how this interaction is taken up by the (discursive) subject as a means of identity validation. The power effects of this identity work are very clearly exposed through discourse. For in speaking of woman as passive, docile and irrational, and of man as active, aggressive and rational, we are engaging with dominant discourses of gender and thus making a contribution to a gender order which, while not unchanging, is powerful in its effects on individuals. However, it should also be noted that dominant and subordinated discourses are in constant movement and outside the power of any group or individual. We are all discursive subjects, without exception. As Foucault puts it: 'discourse transmits and produces power, but it also undermines and exposes it, renders it fragile and makes it possible to thwart it' (1984: 100).

In this way we can see that masculinities exist as discourses – dominant and subordinated ways of thinking, talking and acting as males, and as such provide the very means by which males 'become' men (Whitehead, forthcoming).

What is the relationship between masculinity and sexual expression?

Western civilization has a long history of associating the symbol of the phallus with power. Some theorists have even argued that the male sex drive explains a good portion of male behaviour, including violence, rape, aggressiveness, conflicts and so on. However, Segal (ch. 5) suggests that many of these 'biological' interpretations are in fact culturally reinforcing a certain image of masculinity. Consider, for example, the double standard that permits promiscuous sexuality for men yet forbids it for women. As Connell (1995) points out, this double standard is not about greater desire on the part of men; it has to do with greater power within a gender order that privileges hegemonic masculinity.

Recent studies in masculinity suggest that compulsory heterosexual activity is one key resource for the construction of masculine identity. They suggest that sexual relations with women are often constructed through men. Messner (1992), for example, explores how male peers tell stories of sexual conquest that objectify women, in the process creating bonds between males and policing relationships between men, and between women and men. Similarly, Lyman (1987) writes about men using sexual jokes about women as a way to negotiate relations with one another that serves to separate sex from intimacy.

Why is masculinity conditional upon femininity and vice versa?

Theories of identity have come to value the concept of alterity. Alterity refers to 'otherness', one's status as an outsider. The implication is that identity formation occurs through a process of 'othering' – marking groups as different and excluded. In an odd way, creating identity depends upon defining individuals who are out-group members, often describing us/them in jointly exclusive terms, or binary relations. Definitions of gender achieve meaning within a linguistic system in which (a) differences between genders appear naturalized and (b) women are associated with the marked term; that is, women exist as the unnatural pole that requires an explanation because it departs from the 'norm' (de Beauvoir, 1974).

Ever since classical Greece, we have defined and understood gender as a series of binary polarities. For example, in order to have a paternalistic masculinity, it is necessary to have an image of women in need of protection from the harsh world of business and politics. In order to define hegemonic masculinity as strong, wilful, controlling, determined and competent, it is necessary to see femininity as fragile, incompetent, angelic, precious. Bordo (1993) discusses how the image of woman as ministering angel, sweet, frail, gentle, domestic, without intensity, is necessary to sustain an image of men as cool, strong, effortlessly confident, under calm control.

The embodiment of differences between and across the categories of woman and man are turned into ideological fictions and thus politicized (Silverman, 1992). Thus gays are 'othered' by being described in feminine terms. Petersen (1998) demonstrates how discourses on homosexuality create a linguistic dichotomy that redefines and sustains the category of the normal man, explicitly delineating what proper men do, and how proper men should live. In this way, we can see how gay male sexuality is turned into a political category that serves to reify the 'naturalness' of compulsory heterosexuality (see Edwards, 1994; Weeks, 1985).

Once we give up the notion of biological determinism and explore the constructive nature of gender, we begin to see the way in which these ideological markings are constructed in dynamic fashion. Gender is historically and socially constituted, is dynamic and ruled by changing conventions and expectations. Constructionist theories claim that the construction of gender as dichotomous, in a way that mirrors biological differences, is a fiction that requires an active doing and an active learning (Lorber and Farrell, 1991). Thus no matter how definitions of masculinity change, they are always in contrast to some definition of femininity and always elevated over this. In this way, as Kimmel (ch. 15) demonstrates, anti-femininity lies at the heart of masculinity.

REFERENCES

Bell, V. (1999) Performativity and Belonging: An Introduction. *Theory, Culture and Society*, 16: 2, pp. 1–10.

Bly, R. (1990) *Iron John: A Book about Men*. Reading, MA: Addison-Wesley.

Bordo, S. (1993) *Unbearable Weight: Feminism, Western Culture and the Body*. Berkeley, CA: University of California.

Bowker, L. H. (ed.) (1998) *Masculinities and Violence*. Thousand Oaks: Sage.

Brod, H. and Kaufman, M. (eds) (1994) *Theorizing Masculinities*. Thousand Oaks: Sage.

Butler, J. (1990) *Gender Trouble: Feminism and the Subversion of Identity*. New York: Routledge.

Carby, H. V. (1998) *Race Men*. Cambridge, MA: Harvard University Press.

Carrigan, T., Connell, R. W. and Lee, J. (1985) Toward a New Sociology of Masculinity. *Theory and Society*, 14, pp. 551–604.

Clare, A. (2000) *On Men: Masculinity in Crisis*. London: Chatto & Windus.

Clatterbaugh, K. (1990) *Contemporary Perspectives on Masculinity: Men, Women, and Politics in Modern Society*. Boulder, CO: Westview Press.

Collinson, D. L. and Hearn, J. (eds) (1996) *Men as Managers, Managers as Men*. London: Sage.

Connell, R. W. (1987) *Gender and Power*. Cambridge: Polity.

Connell, R. W. (1994) Psychoanalysis on Masculinity, in H. Brod and M. Kaufman (eds), *Theorizing Masculinities*. Thousand Oaks: Sage.

Connell, R. W. (1995) *Masculinities*. Cambridge: Polity.

Cornwall, A. and Lindisfarne, N. (eds) (1994) *Dislocating Masculinity: Comparative Ethnographies*. London: Routledge.

Craib, I. (1987) Masculinity and Male Dominance. *The Sociological Review*, 35: 4, pp. 721–43.

Creighton, C. (1999) The Rise and Decline of the 'Male Breadwinner Family' in Britain. *Cambridge Journal of Economics*, 23: 5, pp. 519–41.

David, D. and Brannon, R. (eds) (1976) *The Forty-Nine Percent Majority: The Male Sex Role*. Reading, MA: Addison-Wesley.

de Beauvoir, S. (1974) *The Second Sex*. Trans. and ed. H. M. Parshley. New York: Vintage Books.

Donaldson, M. (1993) What is Hegemonic Masculinity? *Theory and Society*, 22, 634–57.

Edley, N. and Wetherall, M. (1995) *Men in Perspective: Practice, Power and Identity*. London: Prentice Hall/Harvester Wheatsheaf.

Edwards, T. (1994) *Erotics & Politics*. London: Routledge.

European Commission (2000) *Building an Inclusive Europe*. Brussels.

Faludi, S. (1999) *Stiffed: The Betrayal of the Modern Man*. London: Chatto & Windus.

Farganis, S. (1994) *Situating Feminism: From Thought to Action*. Thousand Oaks: Sage.

Foucault, M. (1984) *The History of Sexuality*, vol. 1: *An Introduction*. London: Penguin.

Franks, S. (1999) *Having None of It: Women, Men and the Future of Work*. London: Granta Books.

Frosh, S. (1994) *Sexual Difference: Masculinity and Psychoanalysis*. London: Routledge.

Gherardi, S. (1995) *Gender, Symbolism and Organizational Cultures*. London: Sage.

Giddens, A. (1991) *Modernity and Self-Identity: Self and Society in the Late Modern Age*. Cambridge: Polity.

Giddens, A. and Hutton, W. (2000) *In Conversation*, in W. Hutton and A. Giddens (eds), *On The Edge: Living with Global Capitalism*. London: Jonathan Cape.

Hacker, H. M. (1957) The New Burdens of Masculinity, *Marriage and Family Living*, 3, pp. 227–33.

Hall, S. (ed.) (1997) *Representation: Cultural Representations and Signifying Practices*. London: Sage, in association with the Open University.

Hantover, J. P. (1978) The Boy Scouts and the Validation of Masculinity. *Journal of Social Issues*, 34: 1, pp. 184–95.

Hartley, R. E. (1959) Sex-Role Pressures and the Socialization of the Male Child. *Psychological Reports*, 5, pp. 457–68.

Hearn, J. (1998) *The Violences of Men*. London: Sage.

Hekman, S. J. (1990) *Gender and Knowledge: Elements of a Postmoderm Feminism*. Cambridge: Polity.

Hochschild, A. (1989) *The Second Shift*. New York: Avon.

Horrocks, R. (1994) *Masculinity in Crisis*. London: Macmillan.

Jackson, D. (1990) *Unmasking Masculinity*. London: Unwin Hyman.

Jefferson, T. (1994) Theorising Masculine Subjectivity, in T. Newburn and E. Stanko (eds), *Just Boys Doing Business? Men, Masculinities and Crime*. London: Routledge.

Jefferson, T. (1998) Muscle, 'Hard Men' and 'Iron' Mike Tyson: Reflections on Desire, Anxiety and the Embodiment of Masculinity. *Body and Society*, 4: 1, pp. 77–98.

Kimmel, M. S. (1987) The Contemporary 'Crisis' of Masculinity in Historical Perspective, in H. Brod (ed.), *The Making of Masculinities*. Boston, MA: Allen & Unwin.

Kimmel, M. S. (ed.) (1995) *The Politics of Manhood*. Philadelphia: Temple University Press.

Kimmel, M. S. and Messner, M. A. (1989) Introduction, in M. S. Kimmel and M. A. Messner (eds), *Men's Lives*. New York: Macmillan.

Klein, A. M. (1990) Little Big Man: Hustling, Gender, Narcissism, and Body-building Subculture, in M. A. Messner and D. F. Sabo (eds), *Sport, Men, and the Gender Order*. Champaign, III: Human Kinetics.

Lingard, B. and Douglas, P. (1999) *Men Engaging Feminisms: Pro-Feminism, Backlashes and Schooling*. Buckingham: Open University Press.

Lorber, J. and Farrell, S. A. (eds) (1991) *The Social Construction of Gender*. London: Sage.

Lyman, P. (1987) The Fraternal Bond as a Joking Relationship: A Case Study of the Role of Sexist Jokes in Male Group Bonding, in M. S. Kimmel (ed.), *Changing Men*. Newbury Park: Sage.

Mac an Ghaill, M. (1994) *The Making of Men*. Buckingham: Open University Press.

MacInnes, J. (1998) *The End of Masculinity*. Buckingham: Open University Press.

Mangan, J. A. and Walvin, J. (1987) *Manliness and Morality: Middle Class Masculinity in Britain and America*. Manchester: Manchester University Press.

McMahon, A. (2000) *Taking Care of Men: Sexual Politics in the Public Mind*. Cambridge: Cambridge University Press.

Messner, M. A. (1992) *Power at Play*. Boston, MA: Beacon Books.

Messner, M. A. (1997) *Politics of Masculinities: Men in Movements*. Thousand Oaks: Sage.

Middleton, P. (1992) *The Inward Gaze: Masculinity and Subjectivity in Modern Culture*. London: Routledge.

Morgan, D. H. J. (1990) Issues of Critical Sociological Theory: Men in Families, in J. Sprey (ed.), *Fashioning Family Theory*. London: Sage.

Nelson, D. D. (1998) *National Manhood: Capitalist Citizenship and the Imagined Fraternity of White Men*. London: Duke University Press.

Nicholson, L. J. (ed.) (1990) *Feminism/Postmodernism*. New York: Routledge.

Office of National Statistics (2000) *Social Trends 30*. London: HMSO.

Pease, B. (2000) *Recreating Men: Postmodern Masculinity Politics*. London: Sage.

Petersen, A. (1998) *Unmasking the Masculine*. London: Sage.

Pleck, J. H. (1976) The Male Sex Role: Problems, Definitions, and Sources of Change. *Journal of Social Issues*, 32, pp. 155–64.

Pleck, J. H. (1981) *The Myth of Masculinity*. Cambridge, MA: MIT Press.

Pleck, J. H. (1995) The Gender Role Strain Paradigm: An Update, in R. F. Levant and W. S. Pollack (eds), *A New Psychology of Men*. New York: Basic Books.

Rajchman, J. (ed.) (1995) *The Identity in Question*. New York: Routledge.

Ramazanoglu, C. (ed.) (1993) *Up Against Foucault*. London: Routledge.

Rendall, J. (1985) *The Origins of Modern Feminism: Women in Britain, France and the United States, 1780–1860*. London: Macmillan.

Roper, M. (1994) *Masculinity and the British Organization Man Since 1945*. Oxford: Oxford University Press.

Roper, M. and Tosh, J. (eds) (1991) *Manful Assertions: Masculinities in Britain Since 1800*. London: Routledge.

Rose, H. and Rose, S. (2000a) All-Inclusive Intellectual Myth. *The Times Higher Educational Supplement*, 14 July 2000.

Rose, H. and Rose, S. (eds) (2000b) *Alas, Poor Darwin: Arguments Against Evolutionary Psychology*. London: Jonathan Cape.

Rutherford, J. (1992) *Men's Silences: Predicaments in Masculinity*. London: Routledge.

Sabo, D. (1985) Sport, Patriarchy, and Male Identity: New Questions about Men and Sport. *Arena Review*, 9, pp. 1–30.

Sarup, M. (1993) *Post-structuralism and Postmodernism*. 2nd edn. New York: Harvester Wheatsheaf.

Sawicki, J. (1991) *Disciplining Foucault: Feminism, Power, and the Body*. New York: Routledge.

Segal, L. (1997) *Slow Motion: Changing Masculinities, Changing Men*. London: Virago.

Segal, L. (1999) *Why Feminism?* Cambridge: Polity.

Seidler, V. (1994) *Unreasonable Men: Masculinity and Social Theory*. London: Routledge.

Silverman, K. (1992) *Male Subjectivity at the Margins*. New York: Routledge.

Stoltenberg, J. (2000) *The End of Manhood: Parables on Sex and Selfhood*. London: UCL Press.

Tolson, A. (1977) *The Limits of Masculinity*. London: Tavistock.

Tong, R. (1993) *Feminist Thought: A Comprehensive Introduction*. London: Routledge.

Weeks, J. (1985) *Sexuality and its Discontents*. London: Routledge.

Whitehead, S. (forthcoming) *Men and Masculinities: Key Themes and New Directions in the Sociology of Masculinity*. Cambridge: Polity.

Part I
Defining and
Locating
Masculinities

This opening section presents key definitions and perspectives within the sociology of masculinity which inform, to some degree, all the subsequent chapters in this volume. The nature/nurture debate, masculinity as ideology, male power, the gender order, hegemonic masculinity, and masculine identity and subjectivity are all discussed. While the three chapters do differ somewhat in their theoretical persuasion, they are unified in their dismissal of any understanding that masculinity is a singular, biological, inevitable, core construct of males.

R. W. Connell, in the opening chapter 'The Social Organization of Masculinity', challenges any comfortable notion we might have that masculinity is either a coherent, monolithic system, or a 'character type'. In so doing, Connell's piece sets the tone for the entire book in that he defines masculinity as a configuration of practice within a system of gender relations. Connell makes the point that masculinity is inherently relational and does not exist except in contrast to femininity. Therefore, to understand masculinity we must first understand something of the historical dynamics of the gender order. In this chapter, Connell revisits the four common approaches which present masculinity as essential to men: socio-biological theories; positivist approaches typified in masculinity/femininity scales; normative definitions depicted in the media and expressed in sex role theory; and semiotic approaches that frame masculinity and femininity as symbolic contrasts. Connell proposes that we must understand gender, and specifically masculinity, as a **structure of social practice**, one that is reproduced within historical situations through daily actions. The implication is that if we take a dynamic view of the process of gender and think of masculinity and femininity as gender projects, we now begin to see the fractured and shifting nature of gender identity. From this perspective, one that is further explored in following chapters, it can be seen that there are multiple masculinities, often marked by internal contradictions and historical disruptions. However, these multiple masculinities are not necessarily equally valued or powerful across the social web. Connell goes on to outline the dynamics of **hegemonic masculinity** while emphasizing the importance of relations among men that produce subordinated and marginalized masculinity projects. Connell concludes that the gender order is far from stable. Indeed, the modern gender order appears to be experiencing something of a legitimacy crisis, in part arising from the influence of feminism and global struggles for gender equality.

Arthur Brittan's chapter, 'Masculinities and Masculinism', directly challenges biological accounts that posit one, singular, masculine nature. In so doing, Brittan offers a means by which to understand something of the power effects of dominant forms of masculinity. Gender norms, and specifically masculine norms, go through cultural and historical transformations producing multiple and variant masculinities. Thus, Brittan reminds us that biological 'facts' are inevitably mediated by social, cultural values. In understanding the place of masculinity in gender, Brittan proposes that we distinguish between masculinities and the **dominant ideology of masculinism**. In introducing the concept of masculinism, Brittan defines it as a core ideology underpinning male power; a belief system that is resistant to the vagaries of fashion and social change. Brittan proceeds to discuss the concept of masculinism in some detail, emphasizing that while men do not collectively 'form committees to ensure their domination', the ideology of masculinism presents male power as given. So, in this respect, Brittan advances the debates within the sociology of masculinity quite significantly, in that he argues for seeing masculinities as non-biological, plural and changing, but connected to a larger ideology which operates in the service of males by positing male–female differences as natural and, thus, unchangeable.

In chapter 3, 'Postmodernism and the Interrogation of Masculinity', David Gutterman continues the critique of the Enlightenment concept of a unitary, transcendent subject. Gutterman argues that while an individual's identity may appear in simple binary categories (like man and woman, heterosexual and homosexual), identity should be recognized as multiple, contradictory, contingent, precarious and temporary. Binary notions of gender identity have become ossified and naturalized in most societies, in the process coming to have a direct bearing on social values and systems. However, while gender identities may, in common-sense terms, be understood as stable, they are, on the contrary, highly unstable and contingent on numerous social and cultural variables. Gutterman goes on to note that sometimes these contingencies become branded and it appears that we have little power to challenge or reshape them. In presenting a case for recognizing masculinities as dynamic processes with political possibilities, Gutterman explores the notion of identity as performance. Drawing on post-structuralist and post-modern perspectives, he argues that **identity is something that one does rather than what one is or one has**. Individuals have at their disposal, through discursive subject positions, a vast array of scripts available to them as members of a culture, community, or group. However, these scripts or discourses are never totalized or absolute. As examples, Gutterman cites two places where strong, traditional scripts are being challenged: through gay male gender identities and the subjectivities and practices of pro-feminist men. By offering counter-expressions of masculine performance, gay men and pro-feminist men challenge the naturalness of the division of feminism and masculinism while dismantling categories from positionings as the 'Other'. Yet while acknowledging the positive political possibilities that can ensue from challenges to traditional masculine identities, Gutterman warns that counter-performances of gender identity can, themselves, be construed as having a natural, stable core.

1

The Social Organization of Masculinity

R. W. Connell

The main currents of twentieth-century research have failed to produce a coherent science of masculinity. This does not reveal the failure of the scientists so much as the impossibility of the task. 'Masculinity' is not a coherent object about which a generalizing science can be produced. Yet we can have coherent knowledge about the issues raised in these attempts. If we broaden the angle of vision, we can see masculinity, not as an isolated object, but as an aspect of a larger structure.

This demands an account of the larger structure and how masculinities are located in it. The task of this chapter is to set out a framework based on contemporary analyses of gender relations. This framework will provide a way of distinguishing types of masculinity, and of understanding the dynamics of change.

First, however, there is some ground to clear. The definition of the basic term in the discussion has never been wonderfully clear.

Defining masculinity

All societies have cultural accounts of gender, but not all have the concept 'masculinity'. In its modern usage the term assumes that one's behaviour results from the type of person one is. That is to say, an unmasculine person would behave differently: being peaceable rather than violent, conciliatory rather than dominating, hardly able to kick a football, uninterested in sexual conquest, and so forth.

This conception presupposes a belief in individual difference and personal agency. In that sense it is built on the conception of individuality that developed in early-modern Europe with the growth of colonial empires and capitalist economic relations.

But the concept is also inherently relational. 'Masculinity' does not exist except in contrast with 'femininity'. A culture which does not treat women and men as bearers of polarized character types, at least in principle, does not have a concept of masculinity in the sense of modern European/American culture.

Historical research suggests that this was true of European culture itself before the eighteenth century. Women were certainly regarded as different from men, but different in the sense of being incomplete or inferior examples of the same character (for instance, having less of the faculty of reason). Women and men were not seen as bearers of qualitatively different characters; this conception accompanied the bourgeois ideology of 'separate spheres' in the nineteenth century.[1]

In both respects our concept of masculinity seems to be a fairly recent historical product, a few hundred years old at most. In speaking of masculinity at all, then, we are 'doing gender' in a culturally specific way. This should be borne in mind with any claim to have discovered transhistorical truths about manhood and the masculine.

Definitions of masculinity have mostly taken our cultural standpoint for granted, but have followed different strategies to characterize the type of person who is masculine. Four main strategies have been followed; they are easily distinguished in terms of their logic, though often combined in practice.

Essentialist definitions usually pick a feature that defines the core of the masculine, and hang an account of men's lives on that. Freud flirted with an essentialist definition when he equated masculinity with activity in contrast to feminine passivity – though he came to see that equation as oversimplified. Later authors' attempts to capture an essence of masculinity have been colourfully varied: risk-taking, responsibility, irresponsibility, aggression, Zeus energy... Perhaps the finest is the sociobiologist Lionel Tiger's idea that true maleness, underlying male bonding and war, is elicited by 'hard and heavy phenomena'.[2] Many heavy-metal rock fans would agree.

The weakness in the essentialist approach is obvious: the choice of the essence is quite arbitrary. Nothing obliges different essentialists to agree, and in fact they often do not. Claims about a universal basis of masculinity tell us more about the ethos of the claimant than about anything else.

Positivist social science, whose ethos emphasizes finding the facts, yields a simple definition of masculinity: what men actually are. This definition is the logical basis of masculinity/femininity (M/F) scales in psychology, whose items are validated by showing that they discriminate statistically between groups of men and women. It is also the basis of those ethnographic discussions of masculinity which describe the pattern of men's lives in a given culture and, whatever it is, call the pattern masculinity.[3]

There are three difficulties here. First, as modern epistemology recognizes, there is no description without a standpoint. The apparently neutral descriptions on which these definitions rest are themselves underpinned by assumptions about gender. Obviously enough, to start compiling an M/F scale one must have some idea of what to count or list when making up the items.

Second, to list what men and women do requires that people be already sorted into the categories 'men' and 'women'. This, as Suzanne Kessler and Wendy McKenna showed in their classic ethnomethodological study of gender research, is unavoidably a process of social attribution using common-sense typologies of gender. Positivist procedure thus rests on the very typifications that are supposedly under investigation in gender research.

Third, to define masculinity as what-men-empirically-are is to rule out the usage in which we call some women 'masculine' and some men 'feminine', or some actions or attitudes 'masculine' or 'feminine' regardless of who displays them. This is not a trivial use of the terms. It is crucial, for instance, to psychoanalytic thinking about contradictions within personality.

Indeed, this usage is fundamental to gender analysis. If we spoke only of differences between men as a bloc and women as a bloc, we would not need the terms 'masculine' and 'feminine' at all. We could just speak of 'men's' and 'women's', or 'male' and 'female'. The terms 'masculine' and 'feminine' point beyond categorical sex difference to the ways men differ among themselves, and women differ among themselves, in matters of gender.[4]

Normative definitions recognize these differences and offer a standard: masculinity is what men ought to be. This definition is often found in media studies, in discussions of exemplars such as John Wayne or of genres such as the thriller. Strict sex role theory treats masculinity precisely as a social norm for the behaviour of men. In practice, male sex role texts often blend normative with essentialist definitions, as in Robert Brannon's widely quoted account of 'our culture's blueprint of manhood': No Sissy Stuff, The Big Wheel, The Sturdy Oak and Give 'em Hell.[5]

Normative definitions allow that different men approach the standards to different degrees. But this soon produces paradoxes, some of which were recognized in the early Men's Liberation writings. Few men actually match the 'blueprint' or display the toughness and independence acted by Wayne, Bogart or Eastwood. (This point is picked up by film itself, in spoofs such as *Blazing Saddles* and *Play it Again, Sam*.) What is 'normative' about a norm hardly anyone meets? Are we to say the majority of men are unmasculine? How do we assay the toughness needed to resist the norm of toughness, or the heroism needed to come out as gay?

A more subtle difficulty is that a purely normative definition gives no grip on masculinity at the level of personality. Joseph Pleck correctly identified the unwarranted assumption that role and identity correspond. This assumption is, I think, why sex role theorists often drift towards essentialism.

Semiotic approaches abandon the level of personality and define masculinity through a system of symbolic difference in which masculine and feminine places are contrasted. Masculinity is, in effect, defined as not-femininity.

This follows the formulae of structural linguistics, where elements of speech are defined by their differences from each other. The approach has been widely used in feminist and poststructuralist cultural analyses of gender and in Lacanian psychoanalysis and studies of symbolism. It yields more than an abstract contrast of masculinity and femininity, of the kind found in M/F scales. In the semiotic opposition of masculinity and femininity, masculinity is the unmarked term, the place of symbolic authority. The phallus is master-signifier, and femininity is symbolically defined by lack.

This definition of masculinity has been very effective in cultural analysis. It escapes the arbitrariness of essentialism and the paradoxes of positivist and normative definitions. It is, however, limited in its scope – unless one assumes, as some postmodern theorists do, that discourse is all we can talk about in social analysis. To grapple with the full range of issues about masculinity we need ways of talking about relationships of other kinds too: about gendered places in production and consumption, places in institutions and in natural environments, places in social and military struggles.[6]

What can be generalized is the principle of connection. The idea that one symbol can only be understood within a connected system of symbols applies equally well in other spheres. No masculinity arises except in a system of gender relations.

Rather than attempting to define masculinity as an object (a natural character type, a behavioural average, a norm), we need to focus on the processes and relationships through which men and women conduct gendered lives. 'Masculinity', to the extent the term can be briefly defined at all, is simultaneously a place in gender relations, the practices through which men and women engage that place in gender, and the effects of these practices in bodily experience, personality and culture.

Gender as a structure of social practice

[...] Gender is a way in which social practice is ordered. In gender processes, the everyday conduct of life is organized in relation to a reproductive arena, defined by the bodily structures and processes of human reproduction. This arena includes sexual arousal and intercourse, childbirth and infant care, bodily sex difference and similarity.

I call this a 'reproductive arena' not a 'biological base' to emphasize that we are talking about a historical process involving the body, not a fixed set of biological determinants. Gender is social practice that constantly refers to bodies and what bodies do, it is not social practice reduced to the body. Indeed reductionism presents the exact reverse of the real situation. Gender exists precisely to the extent that biology does *not* determine the social. It marks one of those points of transition where historical process supersedes biological evolution as the form of change. Gender is a scandal, an outrage, from the point of view of essentialism. Sociobiologists are constantly trying to abolish it, by proving that human social arrangements are a reflex of evolutionary imperatives.

Social practice is creative and inventive, but not inchoate. It responds to particular situations and is generated within definite structures of social relations. Gender relations, the relations among people and groups organized through the reproductive arena, form one of the major structures of all documented societies.

Practice that relates to this structure, generated as people and groups grapple with their historical situations, does not consist of isolated acts. Actions are configured in larger units, and when we speak of masculinity and femininity we are naming configurations of gender practice.

'Configuration' is perhaps too static a term. The important thing is the *process* of configuring practice. (Jean-Paul Sartre speaks in *Search for a Method* of the 'unification of the means in action'.) Taking a dynamic view of the organization of practice, we arrive at an understanding of masculinity and femininity as *gender projects*. These are processes of configuring practice through time, which transform their starting-points in gender structures.[7] [...]

We find the gender configuring of practice however we slice the social world, whatever unit of analysis we choose. The most familiar is the individual life course, the basis of the common-sense notions of masculinity and femininity. The configuration of practice here is what psychologists have traditionally called 'personality' or 'character'. [...]

Such a focus is liable to exaggerate the coherence of practice that can be achieved at any one site. It is thus not surprising that psychoanalysis, originally stressing contradiction, drifted towards the concept of 'identity'. Post-structuralist critics of psychology such as Wendy Hollway have emphasized that gender identities are fractured and shifting, because multiple discourses intersect in any individual life.[8] This argument highlights another site, that of discourse, ideology or culture. Here gender is organized in symbolic practices that may continue much longer than the individual life (for instance: the construction of heroic masculinities in epics; the construction of 'gender dysphorias' or 'perversions' in medical theory).

Social science has come to recognize a third site of gender configuration, institutions such as the state, the workplace and the school. Many find it difficult to accept that institutions are substantively, not just metaphorically, gendered. This is, nevertheless, a key point.

The state, for instance, is a masculine institution. To say this is not to imply that the personalities of top male office-holders somehow seep through and stain the institution. It is to say something much stronger: that state organizational practices are structured in relation to the reproductive arena. The overwhelming majority of top office-holders are men because there is a gender configuring of recruitment and promotion, a gender configuring of the internal division of labour and systems of control, a gender configuring of policymaking, practical routines, and ways of mobilizing pleasure and consent.[9]

The gender structuring of practice need have nothing biologically to do with reproduction. The link with the reproductive arena is social. This becomes clear when it is challenged. An example is the recent struggle within the state over 'gays in the military', i.e., the rules excluding soldiers and sailors because of the gender of their sexual object-choice. In the United States, where this struggle was most severe, critics made the case for change in terms of civil liberties and military efficiency, arguing in effect that object-choice has little to do with the capacity to kill. The admirals and generals defended the status quo on a variety of spurious grounds. The unadmitted reason was the cultural importance of a particular definition of masculinity in maintaining the fragile cohesion of modern armed forces.

It has been clear since the work of Juliet Mitchell and Gayle Rubin in the 1970s that gender is an internally complex structure, where a number of different logics are superimposed. This is a fact of great importance for the analysis of masculinities. Any one masculinity, as a configuration of practice, is simultaneously positioned in a number of structures of relationship, which may be following different historical trajectories. Accordingly masculinity, like femininity, is always liable to internal contradiction and historical disruption.

We need at least a three-fold model of the structure of gender, distinguishing relations of (a) power, (b) production and (c) cathexis (emotional attachment). This is a provisional model, but it gives some purchase on issues about masculinity.[10]

(a) *Power relations* The main axis of power in the contemporary European/American gender order is the overall subordination of women and dominance of men – the structure Women's Liberation named 'patriarchy'. This general structure exists despite many local reversals (e.g., woman-headed households, female teachers with male students). It persists despite resistance of many kinds, now articulated in feminism. These reversals and resistances mean continuing difficulties for patriarchal power. They define a problem of legitimacy which has great importance for the politics of masculinity.

(b) *Production relations* Gender divisions of labour are familiar in the form of the allocation of tasks, sometimes reaching extraordinarily fine detail. (In the English village studied by the sociologist Pauline Hunt, for instance, it was customary for women to wash the inside of windows, men to wash the outside.) Equal attention should be paid to the economic consequences of gender divisions of labour, the dividend accruing to men from unequal shares of the products of social labour. This is most often discussed in terms of unequal wage rates, but the gendered character of capital should also be noted. A capitalist economy working through a gender division of labour is, necessarily, a gendered accumulation process. So it is not a statistical accident, but a part of the social construction of masculinity, that men and not women control the major corporations and the great private fortunes. Implausible as it sounds, the accumulation of wealth has become firmly linked to the reproductive arena, through the social relations of gender.[11]

(c) *Cathexis* Sexual desire is so often seen as natural that it is commonly excluded from social theory. Yet when we consider desire in Freudian terms, as emotional energy being attached to an object, its gendered character is clear. This is true both for heterosexual and homosexual desire. (It is striking that in our culture the non-gendered object choice, 'bisexual' desire, is ill-defined and unstable.) The practices that shape and realize desire are thus an aspect of the gender order. Accordingly we can ask political questions about the relationships involved: whether they are consensual or coercive, whether pleasure is equally given and received. In feminist analyses of sexuality these have become sharp questions about the connection of heterosexuality with men's position of social dominance.[12]

Because gender is a way of structuring social practice in general, not a special type of practice, it is unavoidably involved with other social structures. It is now common to say that gender 'intersects' – better, interacts – with race and class. We might add that it constantly interacts with nationality or position in the world order.

This fact also has strong implications for the analysis of masculinity. White men's masculinities, for instance, are constructed not only in relation to white women but also in relation to black men. Paul Hoch in *White Hero, Black Beast* more than a decade ago pointed to the pervasiveness of racial imagery in Western discourses of masculinity. White fears of black men's violence have a long history in colonial and post-colonial situations. Black fears of white men's terrorism, founded in the history of colonialism, have a continuing basis in white men's control of police, courts and prisons in metropolitan countries. African-American men are massively over-represented in American prisons, as Aboriginal men are in Australian prisons. This situation is strikingly condensed in the American black expression 'The Man', fusing white masculinity and institutional power. As the black rap singer Ice-T put it,

> It makes no difference whether you're in or out. The ghetto, the Pen, it's all institutionalized. It's being controlled by the Man...Ever since 1976, they stop trying to rehabilitate Brothers. Now it's strictly punishment. The Man's answer to the problem is not more education – it's more prisons. They're saying let's not educate them, let's lock them the fuck up. So when you come outta there you're all braindead, so yeah it's a cycle.[13]

Similarly, it is impossible to understand the shaping of working-class masculinities without giving full weight to their class as well as their gender politics. This is vividly shown in historical work such as Sonya Rose's *Limited Livelihoods*, on industrial England in the nineteenth century. An ideal of working-class manliness and self-respect was constructed in response to class deprivation and paternalist strategies of management, at the same time and through the same gestures as it was defined against working-class women. The strategy of the 'family wage', which long depressed women's wages in twentieth-century economies, grew out of this interplay.[14]

To understand gender, then, we must constantly go beyond gender. The same applies in reverse. We cannot understand class, race or global inequality without constantly moving towards gender. Gender relations are a major component of social structure as a whole, and gender politics are among the main determinants of our collective fate.

Relations among masculinities: hegemony, subordination, complicity, marginalization

With growing recognition of the interplay between gender, race and class it has become common to recognize multiple masculinities: black as well as white, working-class as well as middle-class. This is welcome, but it risks another kind of oversimplification. It is easy in this framework to think that there is *a* black masculinity or *a* working-class masculinity.

To recognize more than one kind of masculinity is only a first step. We have to examine the relations between them. Further, we have to unpack the milieux of class and race and scrutinize the gender relations operating within them. There are, after all, gay black men and effeminate factory hands, not to mention middle-class rapists and cross-dressing bourgeois.

A focus on the gender relations among men is necessary to keep the analysis dynamic, to prevent the acknowledgement of multiple masculinities collapsing into a character typology, as happened with Fromm and the *Authoritarian Personality* research. 'Hegemonic masculinity' is not a fixed character type, always and everywhere the same. It is, rather, the masculinity that occupies the hegemonic position in a given pattern of gender relations, a position always contestable.

A focus on relations also offers a gain in realism. Recognizing multiple masculinities, especially in an individualist culture such as the United States, risks taking them for alternative lifestyles, a matter of consumer choice. A relational approach makes it easier to recognize the hard compulsions under which gender configurations are formed, the bitterness as well as the pleasure in gendered experience.

With these guidelines, let us consider the practices and relations that construct the main patterns of masculinity in the current Western gender order.

Hegemony

The concept of 'hegemony', deriving from Antonio Gramsci's analysis of class relations, refers to the cultural dynamic by which a group claims and sustains a leading position in social life. At any given time, one form of masculinity rather than others is culturally exalted. Hegemonic masculinity can be defined as the configuration of gender practice which embodies the currently accepted answer to the problem of the legitimacy

of patriarchy, which guarantees (or is taken to guarantee) the dominant
position of men and the subordination of women.[15]

This is not to say that the most visible bearers of hegemonic masculinity are always the most powerful people. They may be exemplars, such as
film actors, or even fantasy figures, such as film characters. Individual
holders of institutional power or great wealth may be far from the
hegemonic pattern in their personal lives. (Thus a male member of a
prominent business dynasty was a key figure in the gay/transvestite social
scene in Sydney in the 1950s, because of his wealth and the protection
this gave in the cold-war climate of political and police harassment.)[16]

Nevertheless, hegemony is likely to be established only if there is some
correspondence between cultural ideal and institutional power, collective
if not individual. So the top levels of business, the military and government provide a fairly convincing *corporate* display of masculinity, still
very little shaken by feminist women or dissenting men. It is the successful claim to authority, more than direct violence, that is the mark of
hegemony (though violence often underpins or supports authority).

I stress that hegemonic masculinity embodies a 'currently accepted'
strategy. When conditions for the defence of patriarchy change, the bases
for the dominance of a particular masculinity are eroded. New groups
may challenge old solutions and construct a new hegemony. The dominance of *any* group of men may be challenged by women. Hegemony,
then, is a historically mobile relation. Its ebb and flow is a key element of
the picture of masculinity.

Subordination

Hegemony relates to cultural dominance in the society as a whole.
Within that overall framework there are specific gender relations of
dominance and subordination between groups of men.

The most important case in contemporary European/American society
is the dominance of heterosexual men and the subordination of homosexual men. This is much more than a cultural stigmatization of
homosexuality or gay identity. Gay men are subordinated to straight
men by an array of quite material practices.

These practices were listed in early Gay Liberation texts such as
Dennis Altman's *Homosexual: Oppression and Liberation*. They have
been documented at length in studies such as the NSW Anti-Discrimination Board's 1982 report *Discrimination and Homosexuality*. They are
still a matter of everyday experience for homosexual men. They include
political and cultural exclusion, cultural abuse (in the United States gay

men have now become the main symbolic target of the religious right), legal violence (such as imprisonment under sodomy statutes), street violence (ranging from intimidation to murder), economic discrimination and personal boycotts. It is not surprising that an Australian working-class man, reflecting on his experience of coming out in a homophobic culture, would remark: 'You know, I didn't totally realize what it was to be gay. I mean it's a bastard of a life.'[17]

Oppression positions homosexual masculinities at the bottom of a gender hierarchy among men. Gayness, in patriarchal ideology, is the repository of whatever is symbolically expelled from hegemonic masculinity, the items ranging from fastidious taste in home decoration to receptive anal pleasure. Hence, from the point of view of hegemonic masculinity, gayness is easily assimilated to femininity. And hence – in the view of some gay theorists – the ferocity of homophobic attacks.

Gay masculinity is the most conspicuous, but it is not the only subordinated masculinity. Some heterosexual men and boys too are expelled from the circle of legitimacy. The process is marked by a rich vocabulary of abuse: wimp, milksop, nerd, turkey, sissy, lily liver, jellyfish, yellow-belly, candy ass, ladyfinger, pushover, cookie pusher, cream puff, mother-fucker, pantywaist, mother's boy, four-eyes, ear-'ole, dweeb, geek, Milquetoast, Cedric, and so on. Here too the symbolic blurring with femininity is obvious.

Complicity

Normative definitions of masculinity, as I have noted, face the problem that not many men actually meet the normative standards. This point applies to hegemonic masculinity. The number of men rigorously practising the hegemonic pattern in its entirety may be quite small. Yet the majority of men gain from its hegemony, since they benefit from the patriarchal dividend, the advantage men in general gain from the overall subordination of women.

Accounts of masculinity have generally concerned themselves with syndromes and types, not with numbers. Yet in thinking about the dynamics of society as a whole, numbers matter. Sexual politics is mass politics, and strategic thinking needs to be concerned with where the masses of people are. If a large number of men have some connection with the hegemonic project but do not embody hegemonic masculinity, we need a way of theorizing their specific situation.

This can be done by recognizing another relationship among groups of men, the relationship of complicity with the hegemonic project. Masculinities constructed in ways that realize the patriarchal dividend, without the tensions or risks of being the frontline troops of patriarchy, are complicit in this sense.

It is tempting to treat them simply as slacker versions of hegemonic masculinity – the difference between the men who cheer football matches on TV and those who run out into the mud and the tackles themselves. But there is often something more definite and carefully crafted than that. Marriage, fatherhood and community life often involve extensive compromises with women rather than naked domination or an uncontested display of authority.[18] A great many men who draw the patriarchal dividend also respect their wives and mothers, are never violent towards women, do their accustomed share of the housework, bring home the family wage, and can easily convince themselves that feminists must be bra-burning extremists.

Marginalization

Hegemony, subordination and complicity, as just defined, are relations internal to the gender order. The interplay of gender with other structures such as class and race creates further relationships between masculinities.

New information technology became a vehicle for redefining middle-class masculinities at a time when the meaning of labour for working-class men was in contention. This is not a question of a fixed middle-class masculinity confronting a fixed working-class masculinity. Both are being reshaped, by a social dynamic in which class and gender relations are simultaneously in play.

Race relations may also become an integral part of the dynamic between masculinities. In a white-supremacist context, black masculinities play symbolic roles for white gender construction. For instance, black sporting stars become exemplars of masculine toughness, while the fantasy figure of the black rapist plays an important role in sexual politics among whites, a role much exploited by right-wing politics in the United States. Conversely, hegemonic masculinity among whites sustains the institutional oppression and physical terror that have framed the making of masculinities in black communities.

Robert Staples's discussion of internal colonialism in *Black Masculinity* shows the effect of class and race relations at the same time. As he argues, the level of violence among black men in the United States can only be understood through the changing place of the black labour force in American capitalism and the violent means used to control it. Massive unemployment and urban poverty now powerfully interact with institutional racism in the shaping of black masculinity.[19]

Though the term is not ideal, I cannot improve on 'marginalization' to refer to the relations between the masculinities in dominant and subordinated classes or ethnic groups. Marginalization is always relative to the *authorization* of the hegemonic masculinity of the dominant group. Thus, in the United States, particular black athletes may be exemplars for hegemonic masculinity. But the fame and wealth of individual stars has no trickle-down effect; it does not yield social authority to black men generally.

The relation of marginalization and authorization may also exist between subordinated masculinities. A striking example is the arrest and conviction of Oscar Wilde, one of the first men caught in the net of modern anti-homosexual legislation. Wilde was trapped because of his connections with homosexual working-class youths, a practice unchallenged until his legal battle with a wealthy aristocrat, the Marquess of Queensberry, made him vulnerable.[20]

These two types of relationship – hegemony, domination/subordination and complicity on the one hand, marginalization/authorization on the other – provide a framework in which we can analyse specific masculinities. (This is a sparse framework, but social theory should be hardworking.) I emphasize that terms such as 'hegemonic masculinity' and 'marginalized masculinities' name not fixed character types but configurations of practice generated in particular situations in a changing structure of relationships. Any theory of masculinity worth having must give an account of this process of change.

Historical dynamics, violence and crisis tendencies

To recognize gender as a social pattern requires us to see it as a product of history, and also as a *producer* of history. I define gender practice as onto-formative, as constituting reality, and it is a crucial part of this idea that social reality is dynamic in time. We habitually think of the social as less real than the biological, what changes as less real than what stays the same. But there is a colossal reality to history. It is the modality of human life, precisely what defines us as human. No other species produces and lives in history, replacing organic evolution with radically new determinants of change.

To recognize masculinity and femininity as historical, then, is not to suggest they are flimsy or trivial. It is to locate them firmly in the world

of social agency. And it raises a string of questions about their histor-
icity.

The structures of gender relations are formed and transformed over
time. It has been common in historical writing to see this change as
coming from outside gender – from technology or class dynamics, most
often. But change is also generated from within gender relations. The
dynamic is as old as gender relations. It has, however, become more
clearly defined in the last two centuries with the emergence of a public
politics of gender and sexuality.

With the women's suffrage movement and the early homophile movement, the conflict of interests embedded in gender relations became
visible. Interests are formed in any structure of inequality, which necessarily defines groups that will gain and lose differently by sustaining or by
changing the structure. A gender order where men dominate women
cannot avoid constituting men as an interest group concerned with
defence, and women as an interest group concerned with change. This
is a structural fact, independent of whether men as individuals love or
hate women, or believe in equality or abjection, and independent of
whether women are currently pursuing change.

To speak of a patriarchal dividend is to raise exactly this question of
interest. Men gain a dividend from patriarchy in terms of honour, prestige and the right to command. They also gain a material dividend. In the
rich capitalist countries, men's average incomes are approximately
double women's average incomes. (The more familiar comparisons, of
wage rates for full-time employment, greatly understate gender differences in actual incomes.) Men are vastly more likely to control a major
block of capital as chief executive of a major corporation, or as direct
owner. For instance, of 55 US fortunes above $1 billion in 1992, only five
were mainly in the hands of women – and all but one of those as a result
of inheritance from men.

Men are much more likely to hold state power: for instance, men are
ten times more likely than women to hold office as a member of parliament (an average across all countries of the world). Perhaps men do most
of the work? No: in the rich countries, time-budget studies show women
and men work on average about the same number of hours in the year.
(The major difference is in how much of this work gets paid.)[21]

Given these facts, the 'battle of the sexes' is no joke. Social struggle
must result from inequalities on such a scale. It follows that the politics of
masculinity cannot concern only questions of personal life and identity. It
must also concern questions of social justice.

A structure of inequality on this scale, involving a massive disposses-
sion of social resources, is hard to imagine without violence. It is,
overwhelmingly, the dominant gender who hold and use the means of

violence. Men are armed far more often than women. Indeed under many gender regimes women have been forbidden to bear or use arms (a rule applied, astonishingly, even within armies). Patriarchal definitions of femininity (dependence, fearfulness) amount to a cultural disarmament that may be quite as effective as the physical kind. Domestic violence cases often find abused women, physically able to look after themselves, who have accepted the abusers' definitions of themselves as incompetent and helpless.[22]

Two patterns of violence follow from this situation. First, many members of the privileged group use violence to sustain their dominance. Intimidation of women ranges across the spectrum from wolf-whistling in the street, to office harassment, to rape and domestic assault, to murder by a woman's patriarchal 'owner', such as a separated husband. Physical attacks are commonly accompanied by verbal abuse of women (whores and bitches, in recent popular music that recommends beating women). Most men do not attack or harass women; but those who do are unlikely to think themselves deviant. On the contrary they usually feel they are entirely justified, that they are exercising a right. They are authorized by an ideology of supremacy.

Second, violence becomes important in gender politics among men. Most episodes of major violence (counting military combat, homicide and armed assault) are transactions among men. Terror is used as a means of drawing boundaries and making exclusions, for example, in heterosexual violence against gay men. Violence can become a way of claiming or asserting masculinity in group struggles. This is an explosive process when an oppressed group gains the means of violence – as witness the levels of violence among black men in contemporary South Africa and the United States. The youth gang violence of inner-city streets is a striking example of the assertion of marginalized masculinites against other men, continuous with the assertion of masculinity in sexual violence against women.[23]

Violence can be used to enforce a reactionary gender politics, as in the recent firebombings and murders of abortion service providers in the United States. It must also be said that collective violence among men can open possibilities for progress in gender relations. The two global wars [in the twentieth] century produced important transitions in women's employment, shook up gender ideology, and accelerated the making of homosexual communities.

Violence is part of a system of domination, but is at the same time a measure of its imperfection. A thoroughly legitimate hierarchy would have less need to intimidate. The scale of contemporary violence points to crisis tendencies (to borrow a term from Jürgen Habermas) in the modern gender order.

The concept of crisis tendencies needs to be distinguished from the colloquial sense in which people speak of a 'crisis of masculinity'. As a theoretical term 'crisis' presupposes a coherent system of some kind, which is destroyed or restored by the outcome of the crisis. Masculinity, as the argument so far has shown, is not a system in that sense. It is, rather, a configuration of practice *within* a system of gender relations. We cannot logically speak of the crisis of a configuration; rather we might speak of its disruption or its transformation. We can, however, logically speak of the crisis of a gender order as a whole, and of its tendencies towards crisis.[24]

Such crisis tendencies will always implicate masculinities, though not necessarily by disrupting them. Crisis tendencies may, for instance, provoke attempts to restore a dominant masculinity. Michael Kimmel has pointed to this dynamic in turn-of-the-century United States society, where fear of the women's suffrage movement played into the cult of the outdoorsman. Klaus Theweleit in *Male Fantasies* traced the more savage process that produced the sexual politics of fascism in the aftermath of the suffrage movement and German defeat in the Great War. More recently, Women's Liberation and defeat in Vietnam have stirred new cults of true masculinity in the United States, from violent 'adventure' movies such as the *Rambo* series, to the expansion of the gun cult and what William Gibson in a frightening recent study has called 'paramilitary culture'.[25]

To understand the making of contemporary masculinities, then, we need to map the crisis tendencies of the gender order. This is no light task! But it is possible to make a start, using as a framework the three structures of gender relations defined earlier in this chapter.

Power relations show the most visible evidence of crisis tendencies: a historic collapse of the legitimacy of patriarchal power, and a global movement for the emancipation of women. This is fuelled by an underlying contradiction between the inequality of women and men, on the one hand, and the universalizing logics of modern state structures and market relations, on the other.

The incapacity of the institutions of civil society, notably the family, to resolve this tension provokes broad but incoherent state action (from family law to population policy) which itself becomes the focus of political turbulence. Masculinities are reconfigured around this crisis tendency both through conflict over strategies of legitimation, and through men's divergent responses to feminism. While the tension leads some men to the cults of masculinity just mentioned, it leads others to support feminist reforms.[26]

Production relations have also been the site of massive institutional changes. Most notable are the vast postwar growth in married women's employment in rich countries, and the even vaster incorporation of women's labour into the money economy in poor countries.

There is a basic contradiction between men's and women's equal contribution to production, and the gendered appropriation of the products of social labour. Patriarchal control of wealth is sustained by inheritance mechanisms, which, however, insert some women into the property system as owners. The turbulence of the gendered accumulation process creates a series of tensions and inequalities in men's chances of benefiting from it. Some men, for instance, are excluded from its benefits by unemployment; others are advantaged by their connection with new physical or social technologies.

Relations of cathexis have visibly changed with the stabilization of lesbian and gay sexuality as a public alternative within the heterosexual order. This change was supported by the broad claim by women for sexual pleasure and control of their own bodies, which has affected heterosexual practice as well as homosexual.

The patriarchal order prohibits forms of emotion, attachment and pleasure that patriarchal society itself produces. Tensions develop around sexual inequality and men's rights in marriage, around the prohibition on homosexual affection (given that patriarchy constantly produces homosocial institutions) and around the threat to social order symbolized by sexual freedoms.

This sketch of crisis tendencies is a very brief account of a vast subject, but it is perhaps enough to show changes in masculinities in something like their true perspective. The canvas is much broader than images of a modern male sex role, or renewal of the deep masculine, imply. Economy, state and global relationships are involved as well as households and personal relationships.

The vast changes in gender relations around the globe produce ferociously complex changes in the conditions of practice with which men as well as women have to grapple. No one is an innocent bystander in this arena of change. We are all engaged in constructing a world of gender relations. How it is made, what strategies different groups pursue, and with what effects, are political questions. Men no more than women are chained to the gender patterns they have inherited. Men too can make political choices for a new world of gender relations. Yet those choices are always made in concrete social circumstances, which limit what can be attempted; and the outcomes are not easily controlled.

To understand a historical process of this depth and complexity is not a task for *a priori* theorizing. It requires concrete study; more exactly, a range of studies that can illuminate the larger dynamic.

NOTES

1 Bloch 1978 outlines the argument for the Protestant middle classes of England and North America. Laqueur 1990 offers a more sweeping argument on similar lines about views of the body.

2 Tiger 1969: 211. Tiger goes on to suggest that war may be part of 'the masculine aesthetic', like driving a racing car at high speed . . . The passage is still worth reading; like Bly's *Iron John*, a stunning example of the muddled thinking that the question of masculinity seems to provoke, in this case flavoured by what C. Wright Mills once called 'crackpot realism'.

3 The deeply confused logic of M/F scales was laid bare in a classic paper by Constantinople 1973. Ethnographic positivism on masculinity reaches a nadir in Gilmore 1990, who swings between normative theory and positivist practice.

4 Kessler and McKenna 1978 develop the important argument about the 'primacy of gender attribution'. For an illuminating discussion of masculine women, see Devor 1989.

5 Easthope 1986; Brannon 1976.

6 A strictly semiotic approach in the literature on masculinity is not common; this approach is found mostly in more general treatments of gender. However, Saco 1992 offers a very clear defence of the approach, and its potential is shown by the collection in which her paper appears, Craig 1992.

7 Sartre 1968: 159–60.

8 Hollway 1984.

9 Franzway et al. 1989, Grant and Tancred 1992.

10 Mitchell 1971, Rubin 1975. The three-fold model is spelt out in Connell 1987.

11 Hunt 1980. Feminist political economy is, however, under way, and these notes draw on Mies 1986, Waring 1988, Armstrong and Armstrong 1990.

12 Some of the best writing on the politics of heterosexuality comes from Canada: Valverde 1985, Buchbinder et al. 1987. The conceptual approach here is developed in Connell and Dowsett 1992.

13 Interview with Ice-T in *City on a Hill Press* (Santa Cruz, CA), 21 Jan. 1993; Hoch 1979.

14 Rose 1992, ch. 6 especially.

15 I would emphasize the dynamic character of Gramsci's concept of hegemony, which is not the functionalist theory of cultural reproduction often portrayed. Gramsci always had in mind a social struggle for leadership in historical change.

16 Wotherspoon 1991 (chapter 3) describes this climate, and discreetly does not mention individuals.

17 Altman 1972; Anti-Discrimination Board 1982. Quotation from Connell, Davis and Dowsett 1993: 122.

18 See, for instance, the white US families described by Rubin 1976.

19   Staples 1982. The more recent United States literature on black masculinity, e.g., Majors and Gordon 1994, has made a worrying retreat from Staples's structural analysis towards sex role theory; its favoured political strategy, not surprisingly, is counselling programs to resocialize black youth.
20   Ellmann 1987.
21   For patterns of wealth, see the survey of US millionaries by *Forbes* magazine, 19 October 1992. On parliaments, see 1993 survey by Inter-Parliamentary Union reported in *San Francisco Chronicle* 12 September 1993, and United Nations Development Programme 1992: 145. The results of time-budget studies may surprise some readers; see Bittman 1991.
22   The argument here draws on Russell 1982, Connell 1985, Ptacek 1988, Smith 1989.
23   Messerschmidt 1993: 105–17.
24   For the general concept of crisis tendencies, see Habermas 1976, O'Connor 1987; for its relevance to gender, Connell 1987: 158–63.
25   Kimmel 1987; Theweleit 1987; Gibson 1994.
26   A response documented in great detail by Kimmel and Mosmiller 1992.

REFERENCES

Altman, Dennis. 1972. *Homosexual: Oppression and Liberation.* Sydney: Angus & Robertson.

Anti-Discrimination Board, New South Wales. 1982. *Discrimination and Homosexuality.* Sydney: Anti-Discrimination Board.

Armstrong, Pat and Hugh Armstrong. 1990. *Theorizing Women's Work.* Toronto: Garamond Press.

Bittman, Michael. 1991. *Juggling Time: How Australian Families Use Time.* Canberra: Commonwealth of Australia, Office of the Status of Women.

Bloch, Ruth H. 1978. 'Untangling the roots of modern sex roles: a survey of four centuries of change'. *Signs* 4: 237–52.

Bly, Robert. 1990. *Iron John: A Book About Men.* Reading, MA: Addison-Wesley.

Brannon, Robert. 1976. 'The male sex role: our culture's blueprint of manhood, and what it's done for us lately'. pp. 1–45 in *The Forty-Nine Percent Majority: The Male Sex Role*, ed. Deborah S. David and Robert Brannon. Reading, MA: Addison-Wesley.

Buchbinder, Howard, Varda Burstyn, Dinah Forbes and Mercedes Steedman. 1987. *Who's On Top? The Politics of Heterosexuality.* Toronto: Garamond Press.

Connell, R. W. 1985. 'Masculinity, violence and war'. pp. 4–10 in *War/Masculinity*, ed. Paul Patton and Ross Poole. Sydney: Intervention.

—— 1987. *Gender and Power: Society, the Person and Sexual Politics.* Cambridge: Polity.

Connell, R. W., M. Davis and G. W. Dowsett. 1993. 'A bastard of a life: homosexual desire and practice among men in working-class milieux'. *Australian and New Zealand Journal of Sociology* 29: 112–35.

Connell, R. W. and G. W. Dowsett, eds. 1992. *Rethinking Sex: Social Theory and Sexuality Research*. Melbourne: Melbourne University Press.

Constantinople, Anne. 1973. 'Masculinity-femininity: an exception to a famous dictum?' *Psychological Bulletin* 80: 389–407.

Craig, Steve, ed. 1992. *Men, Masculinity and the Media*. Newbury Park, CA: Sage.

Devor, Holly. 1989. *Gender Blending: Confronting the Limits of Duality*. Bloomington and Indianapolis: Indiana University Press.

Easthope, Anthony. 1986. *What a Man's Gotta Do: The Masculine Myth in Popular Culture*. London: Paladin.

Ellmann, Richard. 1987. *Oscar Wilde*. London: Hamish Hamilton.

Franzway, Suzanne, Dianne Court and R. W. Connell. 1989. *Staking a Claim: Feminism, Bureaucracy and the State*. Sydney: Allen & Unwin; Cambridge: Polity.

Gibson, James William. 1994. *Warrior Dreams: Paramilitary Culture in Post-Vietnam America*. New York: Hill & Wang.

Gilmore, David D. 1990. *Manhood in the Making: Cultural Concepts of Masculinity*. New Haven: Yale University Press.

Grant, Judith and Peta Tancred. 1992. 'A feminist perspective on state bureaucracy'. pp. 112–28 in *Gendering Organizational Analysis*, ed. Albert J. Mills and Peta Tancred. Newbury Park, CA: Sage.

Habermas, Jürgen. 1976. *Legitimation Crisis*. London: Heinemann.

Hoch, Paul. 1979. *White Hero, Black Beast: Racism, Sexism and the Mask of Masculinity*. London: Pluto Press.

Hollway, Wendy. 1984. 'Gender difference and the production of subjectivity'. pp. 227–63 in *Changing the Subject*, ed. J. Henriques et al. London: Methuen.

Hunt, Pauline. 1980. *Gender and Class Consciousness*. London: Macmillan.

Kessler, Suzanne, J. and Wendy McKenna. 1978. *Gender: An Ethnomethodological Approach*. New York: Wiley.

Kimmel, Michael S. 1987. 'Rethinking "masculinity": new directions in research'. pp. 9–24 in *Changing Men: New Directions in Research on Men and Masculinity*, ed. Michael S. Kimmel. Newbury Park, CA: Sage.

Kimmel, Michael S. and Thomas E. Mosmiller, eds. 1992. *Against the Tide: Pro-Feminist Men in the United States, 1776–1990, a Documentary History*. Boston: Beacon Press.

Laqueur, Thomas W. 1990. *Making Sex: Body and Gender from the Greeks to Freud*. Cambridge, MA: Harvard University Press.

Majors, Richard G. and Jacob U. Gordon. 1994. *The American Black Male: His Present Status and his Future*. Chicago: Nelson-Hall.

Messerschmidt, James W. 1993. *Masculinities and Crime: Critique and Reconceptualization of Theory*. Lanham, MD: Rowman & Littlefield.

Mies, Maria. 1986. *Patriarchy and Accumulation on a World Scale: Women in the International Division of Labour*. London: Zed Books.

Mitchell, Juliet. 1971. *Woman's Estate*. Harmondsworth: Penguin.

O'Connor, James. 1987. *The Meaning of Crisis: A Theoretical Introduction*. Oxford: Blackwell.

Ptacek, James. 1988. 'Why do men batter their wives?' pp. 133–57 in *Feminist Perspectives on Wife Abuse*, ed. Kersti Yllö and Michele Bograd. Newbury Park, CA: Sage.

Rose, Sonya O. 1992. *Limited Livelihoods: Gender and Class in Nineteenth-Century England*. Berkeley: University of California Press.

Rubin, Gayle. 1975. 'The traffic in women: notes on the "political economy" of sex'. pp. 157–210 in *Toward an Anthropology of Women*, ed. Rayna R. Reiter. New York. Monthly Review Press.

Rubin, Lillian B. 1976. *Worlds of Pain: Life in the Working-Class Family*. New York: Basic Books.

Russell, Diana E. H. 1982. *Rape in Marriage*. New York: Macmillan.

Saco, Diana. 1992. 'Masculinity as signs: poststructuralist feminist approaches to the study of gender'. pp. 23–39 in *Men, Masculinity and the Media*, ed. Steve Craig. Newbury Park, CA: Sage.

Sartre, Jean Paul. 1968 [1960]. *Search for a Method*. New York: Vintage.

Smith, Joan. 1989. *Misogynies*. London: Faber & Faber.

Staples, Robert. 1982. *Black Masculinity: The Black Male's Role in American Society*. San Francisco: Black Scholar Press.

Theweleit, Klaus. 1987. *Male Fantasies*. Cambridge: Polity.

Tiger, Lionel. 1969. *Men in Groups*. New York: Random House.

United Nations Development Programme. 1992. *Human Development Report*. New York: Oxford University Press.

Valverde, Mariana. 1985. *Sex, Power and Pleasure*. Toronto: Women's Press.

Waring, Marilyn. 1988. *Counting for Nothing: What Men Value and What Women are Worth*. Wellington: Allen & Unwin and Port Nicholson Press.

Wotherspoon, Gary. 1991. *City of the Plain: History of a Gay Sub-culture*, Sydney: Hale & Iremonger.

2

Masculinities and Masculinism

Arthur Brittan

Most discussions of masculinity tend to treat it as if it is measurable. Some men have more of it, others less. Those men who appear to lack masculinity are, by definition, sick or genetically inadequate. Gay men, for example, are often regarded as men who lack a proper hormonal balance, and who consequently are not 'real' men. This assumption – that we can know and describe men in terms of some discoverable dimension – is problematic because it suggests that masculinity is timeless and universal.

My aim is to examine this assumption. My position is that we cannot talk of masculinity, only masculinities. This is not to claim that masculinity is so variable that we cannot identify it as a topic. I am not in favour of a doctrinaire relativism which would make it an almost impossible object of study. It seems to me that any account of masculinity must begin with its place in the general discussion of gender. Since gender does not exist outside history and culture, this means that both masculinity and femininity are continuously subject to a process of reinterpretation. The way men are regarded in late twentieth-century England is obviously different from the way that they were regarded in the nineteenth century. Moreover, versions of masculinity may vary over a limited time scale. In this respect, Ehrenreich (1983) has documented the changes in American men's attitudes to marriage from the fifties to the eighties.

> In the 1950s ... there was a firm expectation ... that required men to grow up, marry and support their wives. To do anything else was less than grown-up, and the man who willfully deviated was judged to be somehow 'less than a man'. This expectation was supported by an enormous weight of expert opinion, moral sentiment and public bias, both within popular

culture and the elite centres of academic wisdom. But by the end of the 1970s and the beginning of the 1980s, adult manhood was no longer burdened with the automatic expectation of marriage and breadwinning. The man who postpones marriage even into middle age, who avoids women who are likely to become financial dependents, who is dedicated to his own pleasures, is likely to be found not suspiciously deviant but 'healthy'. And this judgement, like the prior one, is supported by expert opinion and by the moral sentiments and biases of a considerable sector of the American middle class. (Ehrenreich, 1983, pp. 11–12)

If the 'breadwinner ethic' has indeed collapsed among large sections of middle-class American men, then is there any point in talking about masculinity in terms of a generalized category? If men are now dedicated to the cultivation of their own pleasures, does it make much sense even to attempt to theorize about masculinity? Does the concept 'masculinity' have any meaning at all when it seems to change from moment to moment? Surely this is not what is being suggested by Ehrenreich. The fact that men are rebelling against their role as breadwinners does not entail the undermining of their dominance in the political and economic spheres. Nor, for that matter, does it imply that they have surrendered authority in the family or household. What has changed is not male power as such, but its form, its presentation, its packaging. In other words, while it is apparent that styles of masculinity may alter in relatively short time spans, the substance of male power does not. Hence, men who run away from family involvements are not signalling their general abdication of power; all they are doing is redefining the arena in which that power is exercised.

The fact that masculinity may appear in different guises at different times does not entitle us to draw the conclusion that we are dealing with an ephemeral quality which is sometimes present and sometimes not. In the final analysis, how men behave will depend upon the existing social relations of gender. By this I mean the way in which men and women confront each other ideologically and politically. Gender is never simply an arrangement in which the roles of men and women are decided in a contingent and haphazard way. At any given moment, gender will reflect the material interests of those who have power and those who do not. Masculinity, therefore, does not exist in isolation from femininity – it will always be an expression of the current image that men have of themselves in relation to women. And these images are often contradictory and ambivalent.

Masculinity, from this point of view, is always local and subject to change. Obviously, some masculinities are long-lived, whilst others are as ephemeral as fads in pop music. However, what does not easily change is the justification and naturalization of male power; that is, what remains relatively constant in the masculine ideology, masculinism or heterosexualism. What I am proposing here is that we must distinguish between three concepts which often tend to be confused in the literature as well as in political and everyday discourse, namely masculinity, masculinism and patriarchy.

Masculinity refers to those aspects of men's behaviour that fluctuate over time. In some cases these fluctuations may last for decades – in others it may be a matter of weeks or months. For example, if we look at the fashion in male hairstyles over the past 20 years or so, wc find that they range from the shoulder length vogue of the sixties, to the punk cuts of the late seventies and early eighties. During the same period men have experimented with both macho and androgynous styles of self-presentation. At the same time, we have been bombarded with stories about role reversals in marriage and the home. Men are now 'into' fatherhood. They look after their children, they sometimes change nappies and, in some cases, they stay at home and play the role of houseperson. The speed of these changes, it is sometimes suggested, has led to a crisis in masculinity. The implication here is that male identity is a fragile and tentative thing with no secure anchorage in the contemporary world. Such fragility makes it almost impossible to talk about masculinity as though it had some recognizable substantive basis. And yet, in everyday and academic discourse, we find that men are commonly described as aggressive, assertive, independent, competitive, insensitive and so on. These attributions are based on the idea that there is something about men which transcends their local situation. Men are seen as having natures which determine their behaviour in all situations.

Indeed, the habit of attributing some kind of exalted power to masculinity is so ingrained in our culture that it makes it very difficult to give credence to those explanations which stress its contextuality. This is precisely the point. Those people who speak of masculinity as an essence, as an inborn characteristic, are confusing masculinity with masculinism, the masculine ideology. Masculinism is the ideology that justifies and naturalizes male domination. As such, it is the ideology of patriarchy. Masculinism takes it for granted that there is a fundamental difference between men and women, it assumes that heterosexuality is normal, it accepts without question the sexual division of labour, and it sanctions the political and dominant role of men in the public and private spheres. Moreover, the masculine ideology is not subject to the vagaries of fashion – it tends to be relatively resistant to change. In general, masculinism gives primacy to the belief that gender is not negotiable – it does not accept evidence from feminist and other sources that the relationships between men and women are political and constructed nor, for that matter, does it allow for the possibility that lesbianism and homosexuality are not forms of deviance or abnormality, but are alternative forms of gender commitment.

Masculinism as a dominant ideology

However, I am not for one moment suggesting that the connection between masculinism and masculinity is tenuous. This would be absurd. If, for example, we look at the exaggerated politeness of male behaviour in some middle-class contexts, and then we observe the more direct male assertiveness in a working-class environment, this does not entitle us to draw the conclusion that middle-class and working-class masculinity are qualitatively different. Alternatively, if we examine the behaviour of men cross-culturally and discover that the number of ways of 'being a man' appears to be flexible and varied, it is then wrong to assume that this variation undermines male domination. Just as there is a large number of styles and behaviours associated with class relations so there is an almost infinite number of styles and behaviours associated with gender relations. Working-class life in the north of England is not a carbon copy of working-class behaviour in the south. This is not to say that the specificity of working-class life in different parts of Britain cannot be subsumed under the rubric of a more general view of class. Similarly, the fact that men have a multitude of ways of expressing their masculinity in different times and places does not mean that these masculinities have nothing to do with male dominance.

I realize that there are problems in talking about masculinism as a dominant ideology. To assume this is to accept without reservation that a dominant group's ideology is inevitably imposed upon everybody else. In the case of the masculine ideology, this is to claim that men have a collective ideology which they collectively force women to accept as being natural and inevitable. This implies that men constitute a class, and that they maximize their class interest. Now this is a vulgar version of ideology. It proposes that ideology is some kind of monolithic worldview which is used by a ruling group to justify and legitimate its claims to rule. By no stretch of the imagination can men be considered to be a class in this sense. One has only to look at the position of black and white men in Britain, or in the United States, to establish that their membership of a common class is problematic. Of course, it is true that black and white male workers may occupy the same class location, but this does not mean that they constitute a homogeneous class. Furthermore, it may be asked, in what ways do white working-class men have the same interests as black men workers in a country like South Africa? To assert that these men are a class sharing a common ideology poses all sorts of difficulty.

Accordingly, the proposition that masculinism is the ideology that justifies and naturalizes male domination needs to be qualified. Granted that men collectively do not form committees to ensure their continued domination, and that men themselves are exploited and dominated by other men, we can nevertheless still speak of a set of gender relations in which the power of men is taken for granted, not only in the public but in the domestic sphere as well. Masculinism is reproduced and reaffirmed in the household, in the economy and in the polity. Even when there is a great deal of gender and sexual experimentation, as was the case in the sixties and the early seventies, masculinism was never under real attack because gender relations remained relatively constant. The great amount of attention given to the increased participation of men in household chores and the emphasis on 'democratic' family relation-ships did not, in any marked way, alter these gender relations. Despite the feminist analysis and demystification of patriarchy, the masculine ideology remains intact, as evidenced by the successful counter-campaign of the New Right in the United States and Britain.

REFERENCES

Ehrenreich, Barbara. 1983: *The Hearts of Men: American Dreams and the Flight from Commitment*. London: Pluto Press.

3

Postmodernism and the Interrogation of Masculinity

David S. Gutterman

The form is fluid, but the meaning even more so.

Nietzsche, *On the Genealogy of Morals*,
Second Essay, Section 12

Shifting subjects, indeterminate identities, ascribing agency

Over the last hundred years, the Enlightenment concept of the transcendent subject (existing before and beyond the social realm) has been critiqued by theorists who maintain that subjects are culturally constituted. This shift has roots in Nietzsche's (1967) pronouncement in *On the Genealogy of Morals* that 'there is no "being" behind doing, effecting, becoming; "the doer" is merely a fiction added to the deed – the deed is everything' (p. 45). This 'deed' that constitutes individuals is often seen as social forces – from one's relation to the mode of production (in the Marxist tradition) to the public discourses that produce social systems of value (a perspective most often associated with postmodernism). Michel Foucault, a leading proponent of this latter direction of analysis, instructs that systems of power in a given society produce social subjects discursively. 'The individual,' Foucault (1980) writes, 'is an effect of power' (p. 98).

If the social subject is discursively 'produced' by 'relations of power' (Foucault, 1988, p. 118), then a subsequent question is whether the subject represents the productive work of any one discourse or a pleni-tude of discourses. As Teresa de Lauretis argues, feminism and feminist theory have been, and must continue to be, critical sites of argument and discussion with regard to this issue of singularly or multiply constructed subjects. For example, conflicts within feminism between African Amer-ican and white women concerning representatives and goals have illus-trated that individuals are produced by a variety of discourses. Therefore the category of 'women' will reflect differences between and among women of, for example, varying races, ages, classes, and sexualities. Indeed, rather than perceiving an individual in relation to a singular subject position, an individual ought to be recognized as being produced by a multitude of discourses. As Chantal Mouffe (1992) has asserted:

> We can then conceive the social agent as constituted by an ensemble of 'subject positions' that can never be totally fixed in a closed system of differences, constructed by a diversity of discourses among which there is no necessary relation but a constant movement of overdetermination and displacement. The identity of such a multiple and contradictory subject is therefore always contingent and precarious, temporarily fixed at the inter-section of those subject positions and dependent on specific forms of identification. (p. 372)

Mouffe's conception of a 'multiple and contradictory subject . . . contin-gent and precarious' has critical social and political implications. For now, suffice it to say that understandings of subjects produced by a multiplicity of discourses will necessarily lead to internal conflict and contradiction. These conflicts in turn create an arena where the governing conceptions of a particular discourse suffer a sort of slippage wherein predominant roles and values lose their claims to absolute authority and subsequently can be altered. Barbara Herrnstein Smith (1988) refers to the resulting personal heterogeneity as 'our irreducible *scrappiness*' (p. 148).

Furthermore, one can think of this multiply constituted subject as having a multiplicity of identities. Accordingly, it is critical to examine the process of identification or identity formation by which individuals come to identify themselves and be identified by others. A framework of oppositional binarisms has historically provided the governing logic of identity formation in the West. This framework has grounded identity in a series of either/or categories within which individuals are expected to exist. Within these governing categories, Iris Marion Young (1990) asserts, 'Any move to define an identity, a closed totality, always depends on excluding some elements, separating the pure from the impure' (p. 303). In this manner, individual identity says as much about who one is not, as it does about who one is.

The hazards of perceiving identity within such a framework of closed boxes of purity are manifold, particularly around the perception of difference. William Connolly (1991) asserts, 'An identity is established in relation to a series of differences that have become socially recognized. These differences are essential to its being. . . . Identity requires difference in order to be, and converts difference into otherness in order to secure its own self-certainty' (p. 64). For example, the axis that serves as the fundamental basis of gender identity in the West clearly functions along this organization of the same/different. The perception that men and women are 'opposite sexes' (with accompanying 'genders' – masculine/feminine) creates the expectation that one is either a man or a woman and that these two categories are essentially disparate. This sense of difference then becomes the demarcation of otherness when gradations of value are placed on the two distinct domains.

In Western culture, of course, that which is usually associated with men (activity, culture, reason) is usually held in higher esteem than that which is associated with women (passivity, nature, emotion). I say 'usually' here for I want to assert that within broad cultural paradigms there are often localized situations where gendered attributes can be reversed. This inversion transpires in terms both of identity (i.e., women who drag men to the opera are sometimes seen as the bearers of culture) and of value (i.e., when male aggressiveness intersects with African-Americans in society, the assertive, forceful qualities of those men are demonized rather than valorized by portions of the white American population). In negotiating the obstacles to opening closed binary systems (grounded on difference as otherness), it is crucial to remember that not only are cultural norms socially constructed but so too are the values attached to those norms.

I accept that identity formation is relational (i.e., what I am or claim to be is rooted in making distinctions from what I am not). However, I also believe that this recognition of difference does not need to be perceived as indicative of otherness, or, in Connolly's words, 'evil.' Indeed, the goal I am advocating is an intervention in the process where difference is transformed into otherness or evil. Connolly suggests that the crucial step is moving away from the teleological project of trying to master the world and our 'selves.' That is, the effort to position oneself as a transcendent subject necessitates investment in difference. This difference implicitly challenges the claim to transcendency for it entails an eternal oppositional entity or identity. The transcendency is falsely maintained by inscribing difference with a negative cultural valuation in order to limit the capacity of 'different' beings to become subjects. The critical step in the process of acknowledging and celebrating difference is a recognition of contingency – of the instability of our 'selves' and the world. Connolly (1991) defines contingency as follows:

By contrast to the necessary and the universal, it means that which is changeable and particular; by contrast to the certain and constant, it means that which is uncertain and variable; by contrast to the self-subsistent and causal, it means that which is dependent and effect; by contrast to the expected and regular, it means that which is unexpected and irregular; and by contrast to the safe and reassuring, it means that which is dangerous, unruly, and obdurate in its danger. (p. 28)

This definition of contingency provides a foundation from which one can understand both 'individual scrappiness' and the complex identity of social groups. An appreciation of contingency enables an appreciation of difference. As Connolly (1991) explains, 'The one who construes her identity to be laced with contingencies, including branded contingencies, is in a better position to question and resist the drive to convert difference into otherness to be defeated, converted or marginalized' (p. 180).

The notion of 'branded contingencies' is an important one. I believe Connolly is suggesting here that specific facets of personal identity can be discursively inscribed on individuals so forcefully that an individual may have very little power or space in which to discursively challenge or reshape that particular aspect of his or her social persona. In a fascinating discussion of the socialization of her son, Kathy Ferguson (1993) addresses the process by which contingent identities are branded on to social subjects. Determined to raise her son in a nonstereotypical fashion, Ferguson paid careful attention to the adjectives she appended to the word *boy*: 'I told him often that he is a sweet boy, a gentle boy, a beautiful boy, as well as a smart and strong boy' (p. 128). She could not, however, escape the gendered implications of the word *boy*. Indeed, when examining the cultural construction of identity, I believe it is useful to conceive words like *boy* not as nouns but rather as adjectives that describe a subject. By doing so one can more easily and deeply appreciate the contingency of the meanings attached to the word *boy*. Being a boy is different in different cultures/families/contexts and will mean different things to individuals as they grow older.

In the United States, where gender, racial, and sexual identities are so emphatically marked on individuals, there is often little discursive space to challenge these aspects of one's identity. I am reminded here of a line from Marlon Riggs' (1989) film *Tongues Untied* in which Riggs states, 'Cornered by identities I never wanted to claim, I ran – fast – hard – deep – inside myself.' In this case, Riggs was categorized and defined as the 'governing culture' recognized his (racial) difference, branded the cultural meanings attached to race (gender and sexuality) onto him, and turned them into otherness. However, as Riggs recognizes the contingent, unstable state of the identities branded onto him, he is able to resist the limits placed on him by others while reveling in difference.

The metaphor of performance provides an explanatory framework for understanding the contingency of identity. Performance here should by no means be construed to signify falseness or unrealness. Rather, I am suggesting that 'identity is something one *does*, an active corralling of practices, events, desires, contingencies, a regulatory semiotic and material operation' (Ferguson, 1993, p. 159). As members of any particular culture, community, or group, individuals are given a vast array of scripts that together constitute them as social subjects. Some scripts are branded onto individuals more emphatically than others. However, as we see in *Tongues Untied*, recognizing that identity is contingent, is a performance, provides the potential for rewriting the scripts of individual (and group) identity. The notion of rewriting leads to the critical question of agency.

A common critique of the postmodern subject is that by sacrificing stability and unity one also sacrifices agency. The transcendent subject was traditionally perceived as a fundamental precursor to agency. So, for example, the feminist movement initially focused on establishing a notion of woman that could serve as a prediscursive subject and thus enable women to attain political agency. Indeed, many feminist theorists respond skeptically to postmodern reconceptions of the social subject, asking, in the words of Nancy Hartsock (1990), 'Why is it that just at the moment when so many of us who have been silenced begin to demand the right to name ourselves, to act as subjects rather than objects of history, that just then the concept of subjecthood becomes problematic?' (p. 163). As Hartsock's question indicates, this question of agency must be answered if postmodernism is to be able to support and sustain (no matter how ungrounded the ground) a politics of social change – a need obviously central to social movements seeking to reframe the implications of differences of sex, race, sexuality, and so forth.

Judith Butler (1992) answers this question of agency in a world of postmodern subjects by stating:

> We may be tempted to think that to assume the subject in advance is necessary in order to safeguard the agency of the subject. But to claim that the subject is constituted is not to claim that the subject is determined. On the contrary, the constituted character of the subject is the very precondition of its agency. (p. 12)

That is, although subjects are constituted, the process and content of their constitution provide the foundation for reformulating the terms of discourse which produce subjects. As Joan Scott (1993) has stated:

Treating the emergence of a new identity as a discursive event is not to introduce a new form of linguistic determinism, nor to deprive subjects of agency. It is to refuse a separation between 'experience' and language and to insist instead on the productive quality of discourse. Subjects are constituted discursively, but there are conflicts among discursive systems, contradictions within any one of them, multiple meanings possible for the subjects they deploy. And subjects do have agency. They are not unified autonomous individuals exercising free will, but rather subjects whose agency is created through situations and statuses conferred upon them. (p. 409)

Postmodern theories of subjectivity, identity, and agency, then, can be useful not only for rethinking governing cultural values but also as a framework for actively seeking social change. Indeed, postmodernism's focus on instability, multiplicity, and contingency, as well as its subsequent celebration of difference, provides an extraordinary basis for interrogating the cultural scripts of normative masculinity. For the remainder of this chapter, I will first focus on two places of resistance to governing scripts of masculinity – the question of gay male gender identity and the efforts of profeminist men. I will then discuss two different strategies that can be employed in efforts for social change (including struggles to reimagine masculinity) – identity politics and coalition politics.

Resistance to the heterosexual matrix and normative masculinity

The social construction of masculinity in Western culture provides a fascinating (and disturbing) example of the ways the 'drive to convert difference to otherness' has functioned. Masculinity (and femininity) has long served as crucial social marker of individual identity. Masculinity has largely been produced and sustained by interwoven discourses of sexuality and gender – discourses themselves rooted in dualistic configurations. As Jeffrey Weeks (1985) has written, 'masculinity or the male identity is achieved by the constant process of warding off threats to it. It is precariously achieved by the rejection of femininity and homosexuality' (p. 190). This definition of masculinity as a category maintained by making strict polar distinctions of gender and sexuality is consistent with the concept of the 'heterosexual matrix' that Judith Butler maintains governs Western culture today. Drawing from the works of Monique Wittig and Adrienne Rich, Butler (1990) defines the heterosexual matrix as:

> [A] hegemonic discursive/epistemic model of gender intelligibility that assumes that for bodies to cohere and make sense there must be a stable sex expressed through a stable gender (masculine expresses male, feminine expresses female) that is oppositionally and hierarchically defined through the compulsory practice of heterosexuality. (p. 151, n. 6)

In other words, the cultural demand for heterosexuality creates the need for clear markers of gender so that sexual partners can be 'correctly' chosen. In this way discourses of (hetero) sexuality establish the categories of gender, and these categories enable the perpetuation of that system of sexuality. Because this system is 'oppositionally and hierarchically defined' any aberration from either the category of gender or that of normative heterosexuality is met with efforts to silence, change, or destroy the differences. This process epitomizes how gender is used to maintain heterosexuality, which is itself a 'contingency branded into' men and women in our culture (Connolly, 1991, p. 176).

The concept of the heterosexual matrix (as well as Weeks' formulation of normative masculinity) illustrates how the discourses of gender and sexuality are entangled and mutually sustaining/informing. However, I agree with Eve Sedgwick (1990) that 'gender and sexuality represent two analytic axes that may productively be imagined as being as distinct from one another as, say, gender and class, or class and race. Distinct, that is to say, no more than minimally, but nonetheless usefully' (p. 30). I believe that the importance of this separation lies in the consequent freedom to reimagine sexuality apart from gender. This freedom is 'useful' for it can lead to a cultural valuation of sexual practices and perspectives that are only indirectly informed by gender. For example, as Samira Kawash (1993) points out, if the gender of a person's sexual object choice is given priority, cultural notions of sexuality will revolve around the axis of the same (homo)/different (hetero) binary (p. 28). One example of the ramifications in Western culture of this configuration of sexuality is the way '[i]t delegitimates non-gender-exclusive desires. Current struggles over the "authenticity" of bisexuality illustrate this effect: if the world is divided into "same" and "different," "homo" and "hetero," then bisexuality is something which cannot exist, and individuals claiming a bisexual identity are confused or in a state of transition' (p. 28).

In *Epistemology of the Closet*, Eve Sedgwick (1990) presents a brief list of alternate ways of thinking about sexuality that offers clues into the possible openings provided by distinguishing between sexuality and gender. 'To some people, the nimbus of "the sexual" seems scarcely to extend beyond the boundaries of discrete genital acts; to others, it enfolds them loosely or floats virtually free of them; many people have their richest mental/emotional involvement with sexual acts that they don't do, or even don't *want* to do' (pp. 25–6). Among other potential openings is the denaturalizing of the relationship between sexuality, reproduction, and motherhood. The political implications of the fracturing of that triad are manifold – not the least of which is the proliferation of nonnormative heterosexual parental and familial structures. Ultimately rethinking the relationship and the distinctions between sexuality, gender, and the heterosexual matrix enables a reimagination of masculinity that is open to a cornucopia of contingent, shifting identities.

Gay male gender identity

Gay male gender identity is an area where the scripts of the heterosexual matrix and normative masculinity are being interrogated and rewritten. This issue invites conflicting forces of cultural discourses and personal identity. The cultural discourse on gender in the United States today still revolves around fairly clear notions of what it means to be male, and sexuality is a central facet of male gender identity. Sexual acts and desires – a sense of the 'erotic' as D'Emilio and Freedman put it – have been a crucial element of the identity of many gay men (D'Emilio & Freedman, 1988, p. 323). The conflicts between individual nonnormative sexuality and cultural conceptions of normative maleness create interesting places of slippage where the standards of gender are undermined or contested. For instance, some facets of gay male culture in the United States are rooted in a 'self-conscious "effeminacy"' whereby gay men adopt mannerisms most often associated in our culture with women (Weeks, 1985, p. 190). The disposition has 'played with gender definitions as they existed, accepting the limits of the apparently natural dichotomies, but in doing so sought to subvert them, treat them as inevitable but ridiculous' (Weeks, 1985, p. 191). This effeminacy achieves its clearest manifestation in drag and 'genderfuck.'

Clothes and other accompanying accoutrements are commonly used to signify gender (and, at times, sexual) identity. How a person dresses says much about self-definition and identity formation. One self-identified 'drag queen,' Christopher Lonc (1991), explained his dress as follows: 'It is my choice not to be a man, and it is my choice to be beautiful. I am not a female impersonator; I don't want to mock women. I want to criticize and to poke fun at the roles of women and of men too. I want to show how not-normal I can be' (p. 225). This self-expression thus also serves as a political force of destabilization. As Judith Butler (1990) states, 'In imitating gender, drag implicitly reveals the imitative structure of gender itself – as well as its contingency' (p. 137). Furthermore, the entanglements of the relationship between sexuality and gender in the culture can also be seen in drag. For instance, Lonc (1991) discusses how he initially adopted the 'passive' role of a 'woman' in sex in an effort to 'mimic straight society' but eventually was able to adopt an active role in sex. He explains:

> Looking back I can see that I did it because I too was trapped into thinking that the appearance of a person completely defined their sexual prefer-ence... [but after taking an active role in sex] I felt the fallacy of the traditional men's role... versus the traditional female role. I think it also made me understand drag and genderfuck more because it made visible and experiential the nonsense of clear-cut opposites. It made me see that what I had assumed were mutually exclusive roles were the same thing. (p. 226)

Both the entrenchment and the fragility of the binaristic logic that frames the predominant cultural notions of sexual and gender identity categories are evident in this testimony. The acknowledgment of this fragility is critical for the recognition of the overriding fluidity of sexual and gender identity.

The fluidity and instability of the discourses of sexuality and gender (as well as the relationship between these discourses) can also be seen in what Weeks (1985) calls, 'the macho-style amongst gay men' (p. 191). The emphasis on physical strength, blue jeans, muscle shirts, tank tops, motorcycles, and other conventional characteristics of normative male gender identity is frequent in gay culture. For example, the commonal-ities in gay male pornography and heterosexual male pornography with regard to the focus on sexual performance, size of the penis, and perpet-ual male sexual desire reflect similarities in male gender roles and behavior. Moreover, a weight room, spa, or other physically-oriented environment often serves as a place for men to meet in gay male pornog-raphy. The adoption of such characteristics can be read as an effort at destabilizing predominant cultural constructions of masculinity. As Richard Dyer explains:

> By taking the signs of masculinity and eroticising them in a blatantly homosexual context, much mischief is done to the security with which 'men' are defined in society, and by which their power is secured. If that bearded, muscular beer drinker turns out to be a pansy, how ever are they going to know the 'real' men any more? (Dyer, as quoted in Weeks, 1985, p. 191)

Given this emphasis on conventional male gender characteristics, Weeks maintains that gay people have increasingly 'defined themselves less as gender deviants and more as variants in terms of [sexual] object choice.' As a result, '*sexual* identity, at least in the lesbian or gay subcultures of the west, has broken free from *gender* identity' (Weeks, 1985, p. 191). I do not agree with Weeks' conclusion that sexual identity for gay people is now independent of considerations of gender. Rather, as I have been arguing, sexual and gender identities are fluid, unstable, contingent, distinct, but also entangled. If there is a 'break' as Weeks puts it concerning the identity of 'macho' gay men, I would suggest that in this case male gender identity has broken free from the imperative of heterosexuality. This break is a space where the performative character of gender identity can clearly be seen – witness 'genderfuck' and the 'troublesome' (to the dominant culture) tangle of normative masculine gender identity and nonnormative sexuality. This break is a space where the scripts of normative masculinity can give way to a proliferation of masculinities.

The subversive potential of profeminist men

Another example of the way cultural scripts can be rewritten can be seen in the efforts of profeminist men. As Weeks explains, to be a 'man' in our culture one is supposed to stalwartly reject homosexuality and what is considered feminine. Profeminist men not only resist these scripts but also move beyond the acceptance of that which is constructed as feminine to engage and involve themselves in feminist principles and actions. Indeed, rather than creating new categories of masculinity and femininity, or heterosexuality and homosexuality, at their best profeminist men challenge the 'naturalness' of these divisions. Profeminists are often most effective when they use their culturally privileged status as men as a platform from which to disrupt categories of sexual and gender identity. (The privileges of race, class, education, etc., of course, also provide some profeminist men with access to other platforms.) This is often a delicate balancing act, but by contextualizing and critiquing the closed category of male, heterosexual identity, profeminist men pose a unique predicament for cultural discourses of power. Much as heterosexual transvestites and macho gay men are especially disturbing to normative standards of masculinity, the slipperiness of profeminist men provides them with opportunities to be extraordinarily subversive. Thus, whereas women and gay men often are forced to seek to dismantle the categories of gender and sexuality from culturally ordained positions of the 'other,' profeminist men can work to dismantle the system from positions of power by challenging the very standards of identity that afford them normative status in the culture.

One illustration of this subversiveness is the ability of profeminist men to gain access to audiences of men who otherwise would be hostile to feminist women or gay and lesbian individuals. I believe that engaging heterosexual men in the ongoing discussion concerning the instability of categories of sexuality and gender, as well as various issues such as rape, sexual harassment, and homophobia, is critical for the continuing success of feminist and gay and lesbian movements. Diverse yet complementary strategies need to be employed to meet this end. This process of gaining access to male audiences is, however, quite complex. If profeminist men openly and confrontationally display their political allegiance when speaking about sexuality and gender issues to nonfeminist men, they often face the same hostility as feminist women (if not more hostility because of violating an unspoken, assumed 'brotherhood'). One strategy for gaining access to nonfeminist men is for profeminist men to 'pass' as 'normal' (nonfeminist) men. Such behavior is similar to selectively being closeted. Eve Sedgwick's comments about the destabilizing potential of 'relations of the closet' are particularly poignant here. She states, 'relations of the closet – the relations of the known and the unknown, the explicit and the inexplicit around homo/heterosexual definition – have the potential for being peculiarly revealing... "Closeted-ness" is itself a performance...' (Sedgwick, 1990, p. 3). Viewing 'closeted-ness as performance' enables one to recognize the instability of closeted positions.

The metaphor of cross-dressing provides another way of conceiving this sort of ambiguity that profeminist men can create and utilize. In Western culture two basic presumptions about men are that they are straight and that they are not feminist. Men who seek to destabilize notions of sexual and gender identity (including these two presumptions) will often position themselves against these two normative markers of masculinity (i.e., as queer and/or feminist). But by 'cross-dressing as normal men' (and here I mean cross-dressing both in physical appearance and in overt attitude), these profeminist men can 'pass' as 'normal men' and can then move among other men, strategically subverting social demarcations of sexuality and gender. In one typical scenario a profeminist man can pass long enough to be heard by nonfeminist men and then frame the discourse in such a way that questions designed to destabilize cultural constructions of sexuality and gender are prominently entertained. Undoubtedly raising these questions will reveal the profeminist man's political beliefs, but by this time the crucial first step of gaining access to nonfeminist men will have been achieved. Moreover, this public expression of feminist beliefs by profeminist men will also be disruptive of governing attitudes to sexuality and gender in much the same way as macho gay men. To paraphrase Richard Dyer: If that man in the corner is drinking beer and talking about basketball and then starts espousing feminist ideas, how can one tell who the 'real men' are anymore?

Indeed, I believe that given cultural presumptions of normative behavior, individuals are all often moving in and out of closets, are all often 'cross-dressing' based on cultural norms and expectations. This consequence of cultural presumptions of normalcy ought to be utilized in efforts to destabilize categories of sexuality and gender. As Judith Butler (1990) says:

> Inasmuch as 'identity' is assured through the stabilizing concepts of sex, gender and sexuality, the very notion of 'the person' is called into question by the cultural emergence of those 'incoherent' or 'discontinuous' gendered beings who appear to be persons but who fail to conform to the gendered norms of cultural intelligibility by which persons are defined. (p. 17)

Profeminist men can actively become such 'incoherent and discontinuous gendered beings' by adopting a strategy I will call the 'politics of ambiguity.' By utilizing the fluidity of identity and the shield provided by cultural presumptions of normalcy, profeminist men can thereby gain access to other men and then reveal the 'rewrites' they have made in the cultural scripts of masculinity, as well as encourage, challenge, and nurture other men to rewrite the scripts of their own identity.

Strategies for change: identity politics and coalition politics

I am not content to discuss theoretical aspects of identity without addressing the political and activist implications of postmodern subjectivity. Accordingly, I want to conclude this chapter by examining two different strategies often employed in efforts for social change: identity politics and coalition politics. Identity politics is generally organized around subject positions or identity markers that are prominent demarcations of difference in a given culture. These demarcations of difference are so central to the organization and value systems of a culture that they become naturalized and thus perceived as stable categories (or 'forms' in the words of Nietzsche) with stable meanings. For instance, although sexuality has long played a central role in the constitution of identity in the West, Eve Sedgwick (1990) argues that:

> What was new from the turn of the century was the world-mapping by which every given person, just as he or she was necessarily assignable to a

male or a female gender, was now considered necessarily assignable as well
to a homo- or hetero-sexuality, a binarized identity that was full of implications, however confusing...[and] that left no space in the culture
exempt from the potent incoherences of homo/heterosexual definition.
(p. 2)

That is, the binary of heterosexual/homosexual has in the past hundred
years become an ossified marker of identity and difference. With this
broad change in mind, it is important to recognize that the more central
an element is to a system in power (in this case sexuality as a component
of individual identity) and the more fundamental that system is in the
grander scheme of structures of cultural order (categories of 'sexed'
people in the United States), the more the 'deviant' identification or
behavior will be contested and ostracized. Thus as sexuality became a
more central element of individual identification, the boundaries between
normative sexuality and aberrant sexuality became more precisely de-
marcated. In this case, the vast multiplicity of sexuality became reduced
to heterosexual (normative, extremely highly valued) and homosexual
(deviant, negative cultural valuation) – categories that are presumed to be
stable in U.S. culture.

Given the increasing centrality of sexuality as a defining element of
individual identity and the constitution of the social subject, it is no
surprise that identity politics has been central in feminist and gay movements. For example, Jeffrey Escoffier (1985) asserts, 'The fundamental
ambivalence of homosexuals originating in their being raised to be heterosexuals made the discursive process of identity formation central to gay
and lesbian politics' (pp. 119–20). The centrality of identity politics in gay
activism in the United States today is illustrated by the emphasis placed on
'coming out' (and to some extent 'outing') as a critical political strategy.
Beyond the political ramifications, 'Coming out of the closet was incorporated into the basic assumptions of what it meant to be gay. As such, it came
to represent not simply a single act, but the adoption of an identity in
which the erotic played a central role' (D'Emilio & Freedman, 1988,
p. 323). In *Epistemology of the Closet*, Eve Sedgwick (1990) mentions a
'T-shirt that ACT-UP sells in New York bearing the text, "I am out,
therefore I am"' (p. 4). This play on Descartes's dictum concerning the
essential constitutive facet of the human subject illustrates the manner
in which coming out is perceived as central to individual identity. The
centrality of coming out is reinforced by the political statement made by
the wearer of the T-shirt, demonstrating the importance of identity politics
in the strategies employed by many gay activists.

However, a danger lies in the assumptions often made in politics
grounded on identity. Just as it is important to question whether 'think-

ing' is a fixed state on which to ground human subjectivity, in this case one must address the stability of 'being out.' Indeed, being out has highly contingent implications – meaning different things to different people and different things to the same person in different contexts. Moreover, just as ' "closeted-ness" is a performance' (Sedgwick, 1990, p. 3), so too is being out – and as such, there are a multiplicity of scripts available to be performed and even more to be written.

Examining the problems of grounding social movements on identity politics, feminist theorist Christina Crosby (1992) asserts that such formulations run the risk of not interrogating the stability of identity itself. Crosby cautions against assuming 'that ontology is the ground of epistemology, that who I am *determines* what and how I know' (p. 137, emphasis added). Remember Judith Butler's earlier assertion that the social subject is constituted but *not* determined by cultural forces. This distinction is critical and cannot be overstated. As a result, identity politics is never innocent or complete. For as Donna Haraway (1991) makes clear, 'We are never [even] immediately present to ourselves,' and thus any politics grounded predominantly on a presumed stable aspect of individual identity will be limited in its ability to create fundamental changes in social discourse and thus the systems and institutions of social power (p. 192). So the acknowledgment that identities are partial and unstable must be continually foregrounded to avoid an identity politics that remains rooted in value-laden demarcations of self and other. By maintaining an awareness that the self is unstable and partial, one can escape from closing categories of identity and subjectivity definition; rather, a fluidity is maintained that ideally will allow for a pleasurable disunity, a proliferation of difference.

This fluidity is crucial for a political strategy that is also central to struggles for social change: coalition politics. Coalition politics is rooted in the capacity of individuals and groups to come together in order to achieve a common goal. However, the members of the coalition, as well as the goal itself, are neither unified nor stable. Much as individual subjectivity is contingent and multiple, so too is the subjectivity of a coalition. Much as a stable subject is not needed for personal agency, so too is coalitions' capacity for action drawn from the multiple discourses and identities that constitute its subjectivity. Coalitions 'are not utterly groundless, but their grounds are shifting, provisional, passionately felt yet unreliable. Coalition politics makes sense for mobile subjectivities, which can feel empathy with many different perspectives but find themselves fully at home in none' (Ferguson, 1993, p. 178). Acceptance of such a formulation enables a group to come together across differences to struggle for a common goal.

The recognition that mobile subjectivities do not provide a place where one can be 'home' is vital for postmodern concepts of the subject and coalition politics. Describing postmodern 'eccentric subjects,' Teresa de Lauretis (1990) asserts that such subjectivities entail 'leaving or giving up a place that is safe, that is "home" – physically, emotionally, linguistically, epistemologically – for another place that is unknown and risky... a place of discourse from which speaking and thinking are at best tentative, uncertain, unguaranteed' (p. 138). Similarly, Bernice Johnson Reagon (1983), in her classic speech on coalition politics, states: 'Coalition work is not work done in your home. Coalition work has to be done in the streets. And it is some of the most dangerous work you can do. And you shouldn't look for comfort.... In a coalition you have to give, and it is different from your home' (p. 359).

So, one is faced with the question of who is prepared and able to take such risks. These risks are ameliorated if the contingency and fluidity of identity are recognized. As I have argued, gay/bisexual and profeminist men who interrogate and rewrite the cultural scripts of masculinity are often aware of the fluidity of identity. By perceiving themselves as 'mobile subjectivities... [which] are ambiguous: messy, multiple, unstable but persevering' (Ferguson, 1993, p. 154), such individuals are able to honor and profit from the differences they will be sure to encounter in a coalition (as well as in themselves). Moreover, the appreciation of difference enables a coalition, for example, not to try to figure out what *a* new cultural script for masculinity ought to be. Instead, the coalition could focus on destabilizing and denaturalizing the scripts in place and create the space for a variety of different masculinities to be performed. Focusing on the creation of such space is consistent with the recognition that 'in coalition politics acceptance of incompleteness is crucial' (Ferguson, 1993, p. 35). If individuals embrace such ambiguity, they can perform fluidly – and work in coalitions with others – in a contingent world.

REFERENCES

Butler, J. (1990). *Gender trouble: Feminism and the subversion of identity*. New York: Routledge.

Butler, J. (1992). Contingent foundations: Feminism and the question of 'postmodernism.' In J. Butler & J. W. Scott (Eds.), *Feminists theorize the political* (pp. 3–21). New York: Routledge.

Connolly, W. E. (1991). *Identity\difference: Democratic negotiations of political paradox*. Ithaca, NY: Cornell University Press.

Crosby, C. (1992). Dealing with difference. In J. Butler & J. W. Scott (Eds.), *Feminists theorize the political* (pp. 130–43). New York: Routledge.

de Lauretis, T. (1990). Eccentric subjects: Feminist theory and historical consciousness. *Feminist Studies 16* (1), 115–150.

D'Emilio, J., & Freedman, E. B. (1988). *Intimate matters: A history of sexuality in America*. New York: Harper & Row.

Escoffier, J. (1985, July–October). Sexual revolution and the politics of gay identity. *Socialist Review*, Numbers 81 & 82, *15* (4 & 5), 119–53.

Ferguson, K. E. (1993). *The man question: Visions of subjectivity in feminist theory*. Berkeley: University of California Press.

Foucault, M. (1980). Two lectures. In C. Gordon (Ed.), *Power/knowledge: Selected interviews and other writings* (pp. 78–100). New York: Pantheon.

Foucault, M. (1988). Power and sex. In L. D. Kritzman (Ed.), *Politics, philosophy, culture: Interviews and other writings, 1977–1984* (pp. 110–124). New York: Routledge.

Haraway, D. (1991). *Simians, cyborgs and women: The reinvention of nature*. New York: Routledge.

Hartsock, N. (1990). Foucault on power: A theory for women? In L. Nicholson (Ed.), *Feminism/postmodernism* (pp. 157–175). New York: Routledge.

Kawash, S. (1993). Feminism, desire and the problem of sexual identity. In C. M. Baker (Ed.), *Proceedings from 'Engendering Knowledge/Engendering Power: Feminism as Theory and Practice'* (pp. 27–30). Durham, NC: Duke University Women's Studies Program.

Lonc, C. (1991). Genderfuck and its delights. In W. Leyland (Ed.), *Gay roots: Twenty years of gay sunshine: An anthology of gay history, sex, politics, and culture* (pp. 224–227). San Francisco: Gay Sunshine Press.

Mouffe, C. (1992). Feminism, citizenship and radical democratic politics. In J. Butler & J. W. Scott (Eds.), *Feminists theorize the political* (pp. 369–384). New York: Routledge.

Nietzsche, F. (1967). *On the genealogy of morals and ecce homo* (W. Kaufmann & R. J. Hollingdale, Trans.). New York: Vintage.

Reagon, B. J. (1983). Coalition politics: Turning the century. In B. Smith (Ed.), *Home girls* (pp. 356–368). New York: Kitchen Table Women of Color Press.

Riggs, M. (Producer, Director, Photographer, & Editor). (1989). *Tongues untied* [Video]. San Francisco: Frameline.

Scott, J. W. (1993). The evidence of experience. In H. Abelove, M. A. Barale, & D. M. Halperin (Eds.), *The lesbian and gay studies reader* (pp. 397–415). New York: Routledge.

Sedgwick, E. K. (1990). *Epistemology of the closet*. Berkeley: University of California Press.

Smith, B. H. (1988). *Contingencies of value: Alternative perspectives for critical theory*. Cambridge, MA: Harvard University Press.

Weeks, J. (1985). *Sexuality and its discontents: Meanings, myths & modern sexualities*. London: Routledge & Kegan Paul.

Young, I. M. (1990). The ideal of community and the politics of difference. In L. Nicholson (Ed.), *Feminism/postmodernism* (pp. 300–323). New York: Routledge.

Part II
Power,
Oppression and
Dominance

Across the global social web the consequences of male power, oppression and dominance continue to be manifest and apparent in countless situations. Recognizing such, a central aim of feminist and pro-feminist studies is to expose, explore and subject to critical scrutiny the power of men and the power effects of gender. However, as the chapters in part II reveal, despite having oppressive characteristics, the exercise of power by men is not without ambiguity, nor does it go unresisted. The chapters look at male power in the contexts of hegemonic masculinity, identity construction, sexuality, language, and violence.

Frank J. Barrett's chapter explores the construction of masculinity as power within one hyper-masculine institution – the US navy. Barrett shows how masculine identity construction depends to a large extent on the identity resources available within different organizational hierarchies. By exploring the complex interaction between individuals and groups of men, he reveals masculinity as both multiple and potentially oppressive. The power dynamics of masculinity require, in this organizational site, US naval officers to subscribe to a **hegemonic masculine ideal**.

Hegemonic masculinity in the US navy is achieved by exhibiting perseverance, toughness, refusal to quit, and courage in the face of often gruelling tests. Naval officers attempt to secure a masculine identity in comparison and contrast to a series of 'Others': those deemed weaker, less able, feminine or less masculine. Under these assumptions, masculine identity must be continually tested and demonstrated, thus making the officer continually vulnerable to failure. By revealing subtle contrasts in the masculine performances of aviators, supply officers, and surface warfare officers, Barrett's research shows how strategies of (masculine) differentiation depend on constant comparison to different sub-(naval) specialties as a way to achieve identity. Not only that, such performances also depend upon the continual contrast to definitions of femininity. In short, the organization of the US navy can be seen to be designed to create chronic testing that continually marks those who pass these tests in terms of traditional masculinity and serves to separate the weak from the strong. Thus, despite its inherent fragility and contradictions, masculinity in this organizational setting is presented as, and validated through, the exercise of power over self and others and by the constant reaffirmation of what it means to be a (man) US naval officer.

There has long been a popular conception that much of male behaviour, especially competitive and dominating behaviour, can be explained by the male sex drive. In 'The Belly of the Beast: Sex as Male Domination', Lynne Segal questions this commonly accepted depiction of male sexuality. She challenges the view that forms of oppressive social behaviour, including racism, fascism and imperialism, can be explained by male sexuality. The notion that male sexuality is a raging beast dominating social and cultural realities permeates Western civilization, not least through the numerous images and myths that equate the symbol of the phallus with power. Early psychoanalytical studies of sex have contributed to this simplification, depicting male sexuality as an overpowering instinct. Similarly, popular media images continue to picture men as having insatiable sexual appetites.

Segal argues, however, that the lived experience of male sexuality is often fragile and in contradiction with dominant ideologies, and that heterosexual masculine performances do not themselves grant men power over women. Segal cites literature that explores how men's lived experience of their own sexuality does not resemble these depictions of power-wielding. On the contrary, men often admit to feelings of confusion, insecurity, ineptness, and the fear of failure associated with their sexuality. As pornographic imagery furthers the depiction of men as sexually insatiable and powerful, men's own anxiety about sexual performance increases, while reported sexual attacks on women increase in number. What we see upon closer inspection is that male sexuality, like masculinity, is not a singular, unchanging thing, but a set of embodied practices caught up in myth and counter-myth. Segal suggests that the ideologies and 'truths' which present male sexuality as predatory and overpowering themselves contribute to the conditions and expectations of male power and dominance. In concluding, Segal argues that it is necessary to **transform the meanings attached to sexuality**, that is, if we are to disrupt and weaken the relationship between male sexuality and dominance.

If men are not born with masculine identities intact, how are they socialized to assume positions of power? Since men are often socialized to expect to fill leadership roles, how do men prepare themselves to act in ways others construe as powerful? Scott Kiesling, in 'Power and the Language of Men', begins to address these questions. He reminds us that power and identity are social accomplishments. Men learn the appropriate language and appropriate displays that are the resources of identity creation – including certain ways of speaking and acting, and certain expressive demeanours.

Kiesling explores one prominent institution that shapes young men's behaviour: a college fraternity. This site provides an excellent vignette to demonstrate how men employ ideological resources to present a competitive, confident identity within a hierarchic society. Kiesling demonstrates the different discourse strategies men use to orient themselves towards different processes of power as they take turns speaking at a fraternity election meeting. Each is under pressure to display a powerful identity. Each chooses a different ideological approach, ranging from structural to demeanour power. Kiesling's analysis demonstrates that men learn norms and customs that allow them to act with a certain masculine demeanour. When rituals such as rushes and initiations create bonds between men who 'pledge' their membership, Kiesling hints that they are joining more than a fraternity. Perhaps they are preparing themselves for roles in a hierarchic, male-dominated world in which, if they are to join it, these young men must be **prepared to wield masculine displays of power and dominance**. As we witness these men adopting idealized forms of male roles, ranging from structural power to resistance efforts, we can appreciate the ways in which male power relies upon public displays that are more precarious than we might have imagined.

From an American fraternity house we move to a different cultural setting to explore a disturbing way that power relations are manifested – male violence against women. Katharine Wood and Rachel Jewkes, in a very compelling piece, 'Violence, Rape, and Sexual Coercion: Everyday Love in a South African Township', suggest that masculine displays of power are not limited to discourse strategies or displays of demeanour but have a very physical and oppressive dimension. Their research reveals the way in which **male power and oppression is exercised through the practice of heterosexual relationships**. Based on a poignant analysis of informants' narratives, the authors demonstrate that violence and assault are a regular feature of sexual relationships within a South African township. These stories depict sex as a male-driven, compulsive activity that includes, but is not limited to, physical assault and control of women's and young girls' lives. This male control is exercised through sexuality and includes the males' prerogative to define the conditions and timing of sex. This extreme disempowerment has dramatic implications for the health and well-being of these women. Moreover, as the authors note, there are important implications for programmes for HIV prevention and AIDS research. The women's narratives suggest they are often unable to negotiate the timing of sex and the conditions under which it occurs, and that many feel powerless to protect themselves against pregnancy or AIDS. Social change programmes need to be aware of the context of abuse that surrounds these sexual partnerships. Such change programmes, if they are to have an effect, must do more than intervene to educate women. They also must educate young and adult males in order to have any impact on this form of male oppression.

4

The Organizational Construction of Hegemonic Masculinity: The Case of the US Navy

Frank J. Barrett

Following the growth of women's studies and feminist approaches to research, an interest in the critical study of men – in 'Naming Men as Men' (Collinson and Hearn 1994) – has emerged. Studies of masculinity in various social institutions have problematized the construction of masculinity and have made men visible as a social category. This includes the study of men and crime (Messerschmidt 1993); men in the printing press industry (Cockburn 1983); men in financial service institutions (Kerfoot and Knights 1993); male engineers on the shop floor (Collinson 1988) and studies of sports and masculinity (Messner 1992; Messner and Sabo 1990; Klein 1993).

The military is a prime candidate for the study of masculinity, not only because it is an institution populated with men, but also because it plays a primary role in shaping images of masculinity in the larger society (Connell 1992; Morgan 1994). Following Arkin and Dobrofsky (1978), 'The military has socialized millions of men according to some traditional blueprint. As such the dominant adult male role model could largely be the product of the military, particularly in as much as those who are thus socialized have returned to society' (p. 167).

Militaries around the world have defined the soldier as an embodiment of traditional male sex role behaviors. From recruiting posters that seek 'a few good men' to popular media images of John Wayne fearlessly leading the troops in a World War II battle, Tom Cruise as a 'top gun' pilot, or Sylvester Stallone as Rambo single-handedly rescuing American prisoners of war, there has long been an association between the military and images of masculinity.

This study applies some of the analytic insights of critical men's studies to understand the construction of masculinity within the US Navy. This article explores how the Navy reproduces an ideology of hegemonic masculinity and how male officers' concrete practices and choices construct an order of gender relations. After reviewing a few of the core themes in the new critical men's study, I will deconstruct the notion of monolithic masculinity associated with the military and explore a number of alternative masculine discourses and identities that male officers construct in this culture. In particular, I will show how the various constructions of masculinity vary across job specialties. In doing so, I will argue that these versions of masculinity are relationally constructed through associations of difference. I seek to show how definitions of masculinity emerge within collective practices, definitions that reside as much within organizational patterns and practices as within individual personalities. Finally, I explore some of the contradictions within the Navy's gender regime. The view here is that gender is an actively constructed social accomplishment. Following Morgan's (1994) call to study a range of masculinities within the military, this study reveals that the link between masculinity, violence, and the military is more complex than the image of 'man the warrior' might suggest.

The gender order and masculine hegemony

From the perspective of social constructionism, there is an important distinction between the categories of sex and gender. Sex refers to the biological categories 'male' and 'female'. But gender is a social organizing principle, a human invention like language, that organizes life in culturally patterned ways. Gender is an institution that structures social relationships and upholds and reproduces rules and patterns of expectation. Most of us learn to comply with these rules and experience them as natural and common sense. However, these structures have no validity other than through the daily practices and actions that people engage in. Human beings are agents, whose actions and practices either accomplish or challenge the taken-for-granted gender norms and expectations. Human beings actively accomplish, or 'do gender' (West and Zimmerman 1987) continuously – in the way we talk, walk, shake hands, and dress. But we 'do' these activities within the context of larger social patterns. Hence, the relationship between individual practices and larger social structures is recursive. Following Lorber (1994), 'The social reproduction of gender in individuals reproduces the gendered societal structure; as individuals act out gender norms and expectations in face-to-face interaction, they are constructing gendered systems of dominance and power' (p. 6).

The concept 'masculinity', then, is not a genetic instinct or a stable role set (see Connell 1987). Masculinity is embedded within an ensemble of social practices, symbols, discourses, and ideologies associated with the category of 'man'. In a landmark article, Carrigan, Connell, and Lee (1985) called for further study of a range of masculinities differentiated by structures of power dynamics, by different rules of emotional attachment, and by different rules regarding the division of labor. The term 'hegemony' originates with Gramsci's notion of class relations and refers to the dynamic process by which groups create and sustain power, how 'normal' definitions and taken-for-granted expressions come to define situations. Hegemony goes beyond the material holding of power and refers to the *process* by which 'normal' and ideal definitions emerge, how the terms of morality surface and persuade.

The term 'hegemonic masculinity' refers to a particular idealized image of masculinity in relation to which images of femininity and other masculinities are marginalized and subordinated. The hegemonic ideal of masculinity in current Western culture is a man who is independent, risk-taking, aggressive, heterosexual, and rational (Connell 1995). It is important to recognize that hegemonic masculinity is not the same as stereotypical sex roles, however. Critical men's studies refer to a dynamic conception of a gender order (Connell 1987; Messner and Sabo 1990) as a structure of social relations that are historically variable. Rotundo (1993), for example, traces the historical changes in American images of masculinity. Roper and Tosh (1991) trace the changing images of masculinity in England since the 19th century. These studies emphasize how hegemonic versions of masculinity achieve meaning within patterns of difference. They examine contrasting dichotomies such as reason/ feeling, and mind/body, as well as various constructions of the 'other', contrasting images of masculinity with images of the child and the feminine (Roper and Tosh 1991).

Masculine hegemony refers not only to the various groupings of men and the ideals they uphold. It refers also to the process by which these groups and ideals form, the organizational situations and constraints that shape and construct these ideals and groups. Cockburn's (1983) study of British printing press workers illustrates this process: when new technology changed work procedures, systematic efforts were made to exclude women from the trade and to marginalize other categories of younger and unskilled men in order to sustain a definition of printing as a 'masculine' occupation. Messner's (1992) study of professional athletes and Klein's (1993) ethnographic study of professional body builders reveal that men produce a variety of masculinities as they struggle toward the hegemonic ideal that few of them can attain, and even fewer can sustain, in the face of such obstacles as competition, failure, injury, or retirement. Kerfoot and Knights (1993) demonstrate how paternalistic and competitive masculine discourses within the UK financial service industry reproduce a variety of masculinizing practices and identity maintenance strategies. Messerschmidt (1993) studies how criminal actions are one form of accomplishing masculinity that varies by class differences, from accommodating to opposition masculinities as a means to secure identity. These studies deconstruct a monolithic image of masculinity and outline a variety of alternative masculinities and strategies various groups of men use to create, negotiate, and maintain a masculine identity.

In many of these studies, subjectivity and identity are essential themes. Power relations, discourses, ideologies, and practices produce multiple and sometimes contradictory masculine identities (Collinson and Hearn 1994). Many of these studies discuss the precarious nature of masculine identities that must be achieved, negotiated, and contested in day-to-day interaction (Kerfoot and Knights 1993). Because every gender regime has internal contradictions between ideology and practice, a relational theory of masculinity must identify how men work through these contradictions and challenges to achieving a secure identity. For example, if the hegemonic ideal of masculinity involves an image of rugged heterosexuality, independence, and toughness, how do these men carve out an identity in an organizational world in which much day-to-day work neither demands nor allows for these displays?

[. . .]

Constructing masculinity in the US Navy

1 Masculinity as discipline, perseverance, and toughness

Various studies of military training reveal that the military persuasively bounds off the recruit from civilian life in an effort to socialize 'boys to be men'. Recruits learn the value of appearance, cleanliness, exacting detail, and respect for rank and tradition. They come to value conformity and obedience, and learn display rules for exhibiting aggression and courage in the face of risk. Like Goffman's notion of a total institution (Goffman 1961), socialization is pervasive: recruits are 'cut off from the wider society', and live in an enclosed 'formally administered round of life' (p. xiii). Lovell's (1964) study of the professional socialization of cadets at West Point and Zurcher's (1967) study of recruits' nine week indoctrination in Navy basic training (boot camp), discuss the deliberate efforts to shape recruits into becoming what Janowitz (1960) calls 'professionals in violence' (p. 3). From small rituals such as shaving heads and discarding civilian clothes for uniforms, to warrior initiation rites, violent drill instructors, hazing rituals, sex education films on the harms of venereal disease, recruits learn that there is 'a cult of toughness and masculinity traditionally associated with making soldiers out of civilians'. They are taught that the proper response to tests they face is to exhibit 'courage, endurance, toughness, and lack of squeamishness' (Stouffer et al. 1949, p. 156).

Throughout all communities in the Navy, the image of masculinity that is perpetuated involves physical toughness, the endurance of hardships, aggressiveness, a rugged heterosexuality, unemotional logic, and a refusal to complain. And yet it is never assumed that such character traits are permanent. Indeed, the Navy creates structures and routines that call for continual testing of these qualities. This is a culture that chronically creates trials that separate the 'weak' from the rest. From the first day of training, the culture creates a testing ground that creates boundaries of inclusion around those who exhibit strength, endurance and competence. Passing these early tests is a sign that one is capable of perseverance and toughness. One lieutenant, John Baker, came from a working class background and joined the Navy after college because it offered a good career opportunity. He found the experience of Basic Training to be challenging, but affirming: 'At OCS [Officers Candidate School], it was very demanding, it required a lot of discipline. I loved it. We started with 23 and ended with eight. We got very close. I'm a person who doesn't quit.'

Many officers echoed the feelings of Lt. Baker, who embraces the experience of 'not quitting', of exhibiting the rugged discipline that separated a select group from those who quit. Lt. Tom Knorr grew up in Kansas and graduated from college with a degree in engineering. While in college, he volunteered for a few years as a paramedic. He felt a lack of direction in his life. An influential moment occurred when he saw the movie, 'An Officer and a Gentleman' and saw the military as a career that would give his life discipline and direction. In particular, he decided to become a pilot because 'In a jet you're the one in charge'. He learned very quickly that Officers Candidate School (OCS) would not be easy.

[OCS] was tough, but there was no way I would quit. I cut all my ties to the past when I left. I figured, I'm at OCS now, I can't quit. If I quit and went back home after six months people would wonder why, they'd think I was a quitter. I couldn't face those questions. They overload you at OCS. Every day you have two hours of physical training. Mentally you're thrown in situations you're not familiar with. You're stripped of your identity. You either make it or you don't survive. Some people quit. I wasn't going to quit. Even if I was last, no one would call me a quitter. What we learned to say was, you can strip everything away, but you can't touch my pride.

Masculinity achieves meaning within patterns of differences. If success for men is associated with 'not quitting' in the face of hardships, femininity becomes associated with quitting, complaining, and weakness. This follows Kimmel's (1994) notion that definitions of masculinity depend on changing definitions of women and gay men who serve as the 'others' against which heterosexual men construct and project an identity. In fact, there is a tradition in the military of reserving the labels associated with femininity for the 'other' (Enloe 1990; Strange 1983; Jeffords 1989). In many of the world's armies, for example, it is a tradition to insult a potential or defeated enemy by calling him a 'woman' (Enloe 1990; Strange 1983). During the Vietnam War, US Marines often depicted the South Vietnamese Army as 'faggots' because they were reluctant to engage in combat (Levy 1992). Association of fear, passivity, and the feminine was sometimes extended to American soldiers who were afraid to fight in World War II (Gray 1959). In basic training, drill instructors sometimes called marine recruits 'faggots' to imply that they lack the aggression associated with masculinity (Levy 1992).

The subjects for this study confirmed this. They reported that, from the first day of training, recruits who complain or do not keep up with the others are the targets of gendered insults: they are called girls, pussies, weenies, and wimps by the instructors. Often, while marching, the instructor leads the men in songs that demean women as weak and feeble.

However, in the 1990s, more women were being integrated into the Navy, creating a challenge to the traditional image of the male warrior. If these grueling tests separate the men from the boys, what does it mean if a woman can pass them? One way that men transform this contradiction is through constructions of women as physically weak and unable to do what men do.

The association between weakness and women was reproduced in stories that officers told about women officers during training. Every officer interviewed had some story to tell about women who could not endure the hardships associated with military life. One officer remarked

that women cannot tolerate the same stress that he and his male colleagues can:

> We do this fitness test – you have to hang from a bar. Some women hang
> there and just quit when it hurts instead of enduring the pain for 45 seconds
> or so. They'd just stop when it hurt. In boot camp you have to endure the
> pain or you go home. That's why women can't do combat.

Many of the officers spoke in metaphors of surrender and relinquishment
when discussing women. They talked about women who 'folded', who
'gave in' or 'fell out', expressions that invoke an image of someone
collapsing from the weight of something they cannot handle. Like helicopter pilot Lt. Ted Smith, many officers recalled that the women had to
be given easier physical tests:

> In flight school we had this obstacle course. We thought we were in great
> shape, but running in sand is tough. You have to go over this 6 foot wall.
> The women didn't have to do any of that. They could run around the wall.
> Men who couldn't do it had to go back and do it over.

Many men told stories about women who 'got off easy'. One officer
discussed the difference between the men who endured and the women
who 'fell out'.

> Some good [male] officers [came] out of there. The good ones were up
> front, intelligent, had good physical prowess, didn't fall out on marches.
> They didn't have to be brought in on a truck like some of the women. They
> [the women] just lose credibility when they fall out on physical exercises.
> They lined the roads.

The 'good ones' achieves a meaning of 'up front', 'intelligent', physically
powerful through a gendered contrast to the women who surrendered to
the stress of the OCS tests. By engaging in a collective interpretive
practice, the men reach a consensus that what constitutes pride is associated with 'not quitting'. Passing these tests constitutes membership in an
élite, seemingly homogenous group.

> You succeed or fail as a unit. There's a lot of stress. Like one day, you're
> doing trench assault. It's hot and humid. One of the colonels would say,
> 'That's horrible. Do it again.' You're tired, you've been crawling for
> hundreds of yards...When you're done, you have a beer together and
> say, 'Look what we just did'. We live or die together. We put our lives
> into each other's hands.

Many officers described such ritualized collective celebration as occasions to re-live the experience. The colonel's humiliating exhortations are superseded by the group's re-affirmation: they talk to each other in codes that only a select group could understand, to remind one another that *they did it, they did not quit.* Those men who drop out of the training and those who appear unable to pass these grueling tests help define those who do pass as strong, competent, reliable, members of an exclusive club. Lt. Smith continued: 'This is like a big boys club. It's the varsity...There's a status to being here. You know that other guys...passed the same tests. They're with you. They're your peers. It's a boys club. It's the élite. You earned it.' The telling and retelling of stories, the collective sense making that produces a communal feeling, maintains the boundaries and legitimates the status of those who pass the tests. By reproducing stories of women who quit or 'stop when it hurts', the integration of women into the Navy is less likely to dilute the tough image associated with the ideology of masculinity.

One privilege of membership includes the freedom to continue aggressive and crude language, to go beyond barriers of a more 'civil' society. Within an all male group, the men are permitted to 'be like boys', to swear, tease one another. The officer above continued: 'If you make a mistake, others heckle you, needle you. There are no barriers, you're free to be rude to each other. It's part of the boys club. But with women, you have to be a gentleman, you feel ill at ease. You can't do that stuff.' Having to be 'a gentleman' around women invokes a patriarchal masculinity (Kerfoot and Knights 1993) and differentiates men from women, furthering the sense that women are 'soft' and need to be protected from the 'hard' rudeness and incivility that the other men can tolerate. Engaging in 'improper' behavior is a socially differentiated staging area that constitutes friendship, status, and self-identity. As in Fine's (1986) study of the 'dirty play of little boys', this behavior does not represent a personal, destructive impulse as much as a 'showing off' in the presence of others (Fine, p. 140). Like the men in Collinson's (1988) study of engineering culture, these men secure a masculine identity and achieve group acceptance by tolerating degrading and humiliating remarks.

2 Naval aviators: masculinity as taking risks in the face of danger

The specialty that evokes the highest status among naval officers is aviation. Nicknamed 'fly boys' and 'airedales', pilots come closest to embodying the ideal of hegemonic masculinity. They represent aggressiveness, technical mastery of complex machinery, courage, and autonomy – a traditional preserve of men (Hacker 1989; Cockburn 1985). As one pilot said, 'At the age of 26 I was flying this multi-million dollar aircraft on my own. I had all this technology in my hands.' In addition pilots have a reputation for boldness, irreverence, aggressive heterosexual activity. There are numerous stories about aviators attending wild, drunken parties, engaging in anonymous heterosexual relations. Each of the aviators interviewed confirmed that his life is marked by a degree of recklessness and wildness and each attributed this risk-taking behavior to the danger associated with flying. Many echoed the words of one pilot who said: 'Each time we go out, we never know if we'll be back . . . So, we live for today. We do tend to be wild and take more risks. It's a mortality thing.' After a recent fatal crash of an F-18 jet, one pilot joked: 'We're aviators. We laugh in the face of death.'

All of the aviators discussed the thrill they experience when flying. In particular, they enjoy the moments of autonomy, the freedom to leave the base or the ship and fly through open space. Lt. Hanks, navigator aboard an anti-submarine aircraft said:

> We'd launch at 5 a.m. chasing subs. It was exciting. Decisions are made based on data you feed back. We'd be out for 6 hours, turn off the radar, the ship didn't know where we were. We climbed above the clouds. It was fun, like a video game in real life. It was awesome.

For those who engaged in combat, the experiences were unforgettable. The three officers interviewed who had flown in combat missions recalled them as the most intense experiences of their lives:

> Flying combat in the Gulf was an incredible high. It cheapens the experience to even talk about it. I was totally in tune with my surroundings . . . It was synergy . . . We flew at 10 feet (above ground) because of all the oil smoke, so we were going at over 110 miles an hour at 10 feet above the ground . . . One day we flew the entire length and breadth of Kuwait in one day. You could see the incredible devastation, the burned out tanks, the bodies. It was awesome . . . If you hit a telephone wire, you were dead. So I was totally in tune with my surroundings. I was the right guy at the right time. I was very scared. It was like a great video game and I had the keys to the car.

This aviator's feelings of transcendence and vitality render this experience almost inexpressible ('it cheapens it to even talk about it'). This is language usually reserved for the sacred. The passion and intensity surrounding this passage echo Gray's (1959) recollections of combat in World War II in which he recalls the experience of being completely outside himself, feeling 'ecstasy', 'powerful fascination', in language that borders on eroticism. Following Hacker (1989) and Game and Pringle (1983) such feelings of power associated with operating 'hard' technology mark this as an area of male preserve. Following Connell's (1995) notion that masculinity practices serve as ideologies that blur contradictions, the erotic pleasure the pilots find in 'playing' these real-life high-tech video games displaces their awareness that people are being killed and maimed.

The élite status of the aviators is institutionalized. Their specialty is, in fact, the highest paid in the Navy. In addition to receiving a special $250 monthly stipend, called 'flight pay', above the base salary commensurate with their rank, after five years they receive an additional $650 per month, a bonus that increases incrementally with tenure. Other naval officers single out jet pilots as the Navy's élite, the object of jealousy and resentment from surface warfare officers who feel that they live under much harsher conditions than do the 'airedales'. Being considered the élite comes at a price: aviators find themselves under intense scrutiny. Only those who pass highly competitive aptitude and physical exams are considered for flight school. Even after an officer is selected to attend flight school, there is a 'weeding out' process. Aviators recall stories of flight instructors who deliberately try to challenge the student pilots, to 'stress (us) beyond our capacity' as one put it, 'to see if you can take it'. Students are taught a given number of maneuvers each day, and then are regularly tested to see if they can correctly perform the maneuvers, at first in simulators and later in a training aircraft. Every training flight is graded by an instructor, who often yells at and belittles students who make errors. A failure to adequately perform a maneuver is called a 'down'. Every time a student receives a 'down', he must appear before an attrition board made up of senior training officers in his squadron, who question him about his knowledge of flight procedures and determine if the student is fit to fly. Because the performance is so public, failing a flight test is humiliating. Few officers were willing to discuss the experience of failure in much detail, but those who did recalled these moments as very painful and isolating. One pilot recalled that his wife had just given birth to a new baby and he was very nervous. 'I was a bundle of nerves that day, our first child had just been born. We went flying and I did awful. He broadcast over the radio in front of everyone, so they could all hear it, 'We have a down.' It was a kick in the ass.' Following this incident, this officer went to his room and 'had a tantrum', destroying the room in a 'fit of anger and frustration'. He recalled it as one of the most humiliating and painful experiences of his life. One of the contradictions inherent in this masculine culture is that, while the organization creates experiences of inevitable failure, there is no legitimate way for members to justify failure.

Flight instructors and attrition boards, in addition to testing for knowledge of maneuvers, also appraise the students' mental and emotional disposition. Capacity to analytically and rationally function under conditions of considerable stress is one of the requirements for surviving flight school. 'Flight school is a weeding out process. A lot of instructors are dicks. They want to see how much you can take. They ask you to do these maneuvers and if you blow it, they start screaming at you right there in the airplane.' The 'tough ones' learn to deal with these belittling gestures. One aviator, Lt. Cdr. McCorkle, a former college football star and an F-18 attack pilot, described how he handled the pressure by framing his instructors' 'tantrums' as 'a game'.

> Maybe it was because I was used to getting yelled at in football practice by the coach, or getting yelled at by the upperclassmen at the naval academy, but I just took it as a game. Some guys couldn't take it, they'd fold. You just learn to keep your mouth shut and take it. You're steaming on the inside.

Previous masculinizing practices, in particular having a football coach who belittled and ridiculed the players, provided an anticipatory socialization for Lt. Cdr. McCorkle. In playing sports, judgement under pressure, stoic courage, endurance of pain, and controlling emotion are all considered signs of manhood (Whitson 1990). Lt. Cdr. McCorkle's language is strikingly similar to that of male athletes who learn 'to take orders, to take pain, to 'take out' the opponents' (Sabo 1992, p. 160).

Successful pilots are the ones who demonstrate that they can 'take it' without flinching, that they can continue to think analytically and suppress emotions. Lt. Cdr. McCorkle described flying 300 miles off the coast of Japan at night, 250 miles from his aircraft carrier when his electrical systems began to malfunction. He had no instruments to track his velocity speed or altitude and had to perform various emergency procedures simultaneously to save the aircraft and return safely. In his words, 'Emotions are out of place. You have to keep thinking and stay focused or you lose the aircraft. Every second is precious.'

Organizational practices reinforce the status hierarchy that marks the risk-takers as élite. Upon graduating from flight school, each officer is continuously ranked against his/her peers. Those ranked highest receive priority in choosing the aircraft they wish to specialize in. They can choose jets, propeller planes, or helicopters, each with a different mission.

As Foucault (1977) points out, power relations are embedded in processes of categorization and differentiation. Jet fighter pilots are seen as the most masculine and most prestigious. (Even among aviators, there is a status hierarchy based on risk taking and gender. Jet pilots refer to helicopter pilots as 'wimps'.) Even after the pilot receives his wings, the system of ranking and surveillance continues. For a jet pilot, successfully completing an aircraft carrier landing is an important rite of passage. This is known as a 'trap' or an 'arrested landing' because the plane's momentum is halted by a wire across the carrier, a very dangerous operation, especially when landing at night. Each final approach and carrier landing is graded by the LSO (landing signal officer) on a scale of 0 to 5. At the end of each tour of duty, patches (which are later attached to uniforms for all to see) are awarded to the five highest rated pilots in each squadron.

The surveillance goes beyond formal ranking. When a carrier is underway, all flight deck activity is filmed and telecast in the officers' wardroom. The pilots who are not flying that day often gather to watch the approaches and landings and talk about their colleagues' performance. Pilots who handle their approach well are lauded, just as those who make a 'shaky' approach often find themselves the target of jokes and teasing. One officer said, 'Every time you come in, your buddies are watching you land, talking about if it's good form or not'. Statistics are tracked in a log book: how many hours of flight each pilot has; how many 'traps' and 'cats' (a euphemism for being catapulted off the carrier at takeoff); how many flight hours; how many combat hours. These statistics are posted on each pilot's fitness report and become a source of bragging rights.

3 Masculinity and the surface warfare officer: enduring hardship and calmly demonstrating competence in the face of pressure

Naval officers who operate surface ships – destroyers, aircraft carriers – make up the largest community in the US Navy. When life at sea is referred to as 'a man's job', the implication is that only rugged, robust characters can thrive in such conditions. This is no life for the frail and weak. When discussing life on board ships, the officers described the physical conditions as stark and severe. An officer shares a tiny room with one other officer, usually of equal rank. The bed is barely wide or long enough to hold a body. One officer described the formidable conditions:

> You run out of fresh milk ... You're drinking powdered milk, powdered eggs ... You have to decide to store people and bullets or eggs. The water is a problem. You have to make your own on the ship ... The boilers need water to make steam. They get it before we get it to drink or take showers.

They often just shut off the water controls. A 'navy shower' is one that takes two minutes . . . Plus the ship is rocking so you're slipping and sliding.

Life is described as physically strenuous and mentally exhausting. While at sea officers rarely get adequate sleep. In addition to their daily tasks ensuring that the engineering, electrical, and weapons systems on board ship are in full operation, officers also must take turns standing watch on the bridge at night. Many said that if they average four hours sleep per night, they are lucky. It is not unusual for an officer to be awake for 48 hours straight. This endurance is seen as commendable. One officer said, 'For two years on ship I think I never slept. I'd go 48 hours with no sleep. But that's a sign of endurance. The XO says to me, "Now there's a man".' Another officer gave this description: 'You stand watch about every three days. You get up at 2:30 in the morning and stand watch till 4 a.m. It's pitch black on the bridge . . . The sound of the engine rumbling, it's very hypontizing. If you fall asleep and someone catches you, you get written up.'

Many officers told stories of being subjected to a series of tests and observations during their early careers at sea. In what they referred to as 'baptism by fire', they are 'thrown into messes', difficult situations and maneuvers. Many of the men called these experiences 'deliberate set ups' in which their superiors put them through challenging situations 'just to see if (we) blow it'. A few echoed the experience of this officer, who described an early experience as a young ensign on board his first ship:

My first ship, the CO stuck me up on the bridge. I was the steering control. I gave the commands, I'd tell them the speed, the course change, place the ship in position. It takes absolute concentration. I was scared to death, the ships could collide. It's part of the training. He sticks you up there to see if you blow it. The CO deliberately set up experiences like that. I qualified as a quarterdeck watch officer, the ceremonial watch on bridge for honors, ceremonies, that kind of thing . . . The CO said I was the finest ensign ever. When the second CO took over he asked the first 'who should I trust to drive this ship?' and the first one said it was me. I had the honor of driving the ship out for the brand new CO. The second CO asked me to stay. I was gung ho.

This officer and his colleagues know the symbolic significance of standing on the bridge and steering the ship through the open ocean. It embodies the totalizing power of technology, an experience traditionally reserved for men (see Hacker 1989). And yet, this is not a task that is simply to be enjoyed. Many things could go wrong. Errors are highly consequential in this culture; much of the territory through which these officers must navigate, both literally and metaphorically, is marked by lurking dangers:

if the ships collide, careers would be terminated. Anxiety runs high, and yet it is necessary to maintain 'absolute concentration', to prevent feelings of fear from interfering with performing the complex maneuvers correctly. The rewards for executing these tactics are highly public and coveted. Not only does the young ensign successfully achieve a 'qualification' to serve as quarterdeck officer, but he also becomes the officer in charge of piloting the ship during ceremonial operations, including the 'honor' of driving the ship out for the new CO. Masculinity in this culture is very public, but never secure. It must be continually demonstrated.

If passing these trials is a chance to display competence, they pale in comparison to the opportunity to excel under conditions of a *real* incident. Even under these conditions, however, one knows that one is the object of surveillance and evaluation, which even further magnifies their significance. Lieutenant Junior Grade (Lt. J. G.) Ricky, was a 26 year-old division officer on a ship in the Gulf for six months. One day he was officer on deck, in charge of driving the ship in the gulf, when he received a report that there were 14 people stranded in the water. (They were later discovered to be 14 Iranians escaping from their homeland.) The ship was cruising off the coasts of Kuwait and Iran. Ricky describes the story in vivid detail:

> We were off the edge of a mine field along the cost of Kuwait. We were entering a dangerous zone and it was my show to run. The CO came up but he sat back and watched and let me handle things. The captain wanted me to be the officer and junior officer on deck – to drive the ship and run the rescue effort because the junior officer had made a minor mistake earlier.

One failure is enough to create a reputation in this culture. When a real crisis emerges, the CO decides not to rely on this lieutenant's colleague, who had made a 'minor mistake' earlier. Everyone who is on deck at this moment knows that these are events that shape careers. This is the *real thing*, the opportunity to either shine or fail. But the other junior officer, having failed to demonstrate the ability to function competently under pressure, will not get the chance. Lieutenant J. G. Ricky went on to describe the intensity of the action – the complex, simultaneous events that he had to control.

> I ordered the second engine full speed and called the CO. I called the [rescue] boat crew. You call the boat, the engineering plant, the combat info center, the radars. Tell them what to do ... I'm in direct contact with the helo [helicopter]. I call flight quarters – make sure the winds are correct so the helo can land. They had a search and rescue swimmer on board. He had to land the helo while doing 25 knots. It was a very fast speed trying to

get a search and rescue out. I was getting constant status reports, coordinated everything. The CO said you've got it under control... He let me handle the show... We got all 14 of them out. It was high viz [high visibility] big time.

The experience of power and total control, the cool rationality engaged in the physical operation of levers, balances, dials, and switches are occasions for the display of mastery. (These experiences have traditionally been withheld from women [Hacker 1989].) The excitement associated with the possibility of danger and failure heighten the senses: something could go very wrong. He's displaying discipline and technical skill, coordination and agility of physical movements, rational processing of complex information under conditions of extreme stress. These are the qualities that define the terms of the gender hierarchy – not only between men and women but between groups of men. Not everyone on the bridge is seen as capable of executing these maneuvers. The lieutenant is under constant surveillance by his CO. The contrast between the 'real' experience and the drudgery of daily life on ship makes this significant.

Before that it was just back and forth along the coast of Kuwait. The crew was excited. It lifted everybody's spirits, we actually did something. I did a really good job. There were a thousand things going on and I didn't miss a beat. The other officers came up and patted me on the back and said 'good job'. The CO was excited too... He got on the intercom system for the whole ship and announced BZ (Bravo Zulu) to Lt. J. G. Ricky for handling this. He congratulated all the crews, but me personally... The admiral who was the task force commander sent a BZ letter to the ship. It was a big time for us.

The Navy has an elaborate system of awards and rituals that reinforce the value of demonstrating mastery, especially successful performance under pressure. In part because of the letters of commendation from the Admiral that followed this incident, and others like it, the captain of the ship was promoted, the lieutenant above was promoted, and other officers involved in the operation were highly commended. These organizational practices – surveillance, testing, recording, keeping career records – begin to shape and guide the passions of these men. They yearn for the opportunity to demonstrate prowess under pressure.

Some of the officers interviewed said that these testing experiences should be a masculine preserve. They expressed concern that women could not 'take it', could not tolerate the grueling conditions that the men suffer through. They fear that if women assume combat positions, they will be unable to handle the pressure. One officer, discussing the challenge of taking command of a ship underway said, 'The first time some woman gets up there and cries because she can't stand the pressure, that's it. It's over for her and any other woman who tries to come up there'. A helicopter pilot recalled that when he was instructing a female student pilot on a maneuver, she lost one of the checkpoints and was unable to find her way.

> What would a man do? You'd just go back to the last check point until you find your way again. But she just lost it. She started crying and said 'I'm lost. I'm lost.' I took over the controls, but boy I laid into her when we got back. You can't do that. You have to separate your emotions and stay focused. That's what I worry about with women.

Many echoed the attitude of this officer, who has served on ships for 10 of his 15 years in the Navy: 'I'm tired of these women officers who are prissy bitches...with hang nails...They don't pull their load. They might do special things for the CO on the side. I remember one would leave a shirt button undone and rub her breasts all over you.'

4 Supply officers: masculinity as technical rationality

With the advent of new technology, there is an increase in non-combatants and support services in militaries (Connell 1992). This has produced a new kind of masculinity, the professionalized calculative rationality. Seidler's (1989) study of the connection between masculinity, disembodied reason, and bureaucratic efficiency also supports this conclusion.

Supply officers are considered 'non-operational support' and occupy the lowest status in the Navy. They have fewer opportunities to demonstrate courage, autonomy, and perseverance, the hallmark of the hegemonic ideal in this culture. The gendered nature of this status hierarchy is expressed in the derogatory terms used to describe supply officers. Combat specialists often refer to them as 'supply pussies' or 'suppo weenies'. One jet pilot described how the supply corps is viewed by aviators.

> The supply community is seen as rejects. They're suppo weenies. They couldn't be aviators, couldn't do submarines. There's usually one or two of them on a ship and they're separate from the surface guys. They have nothing in common with them. They're always ostracized and different. There's no glory in their jobs...They have no fun. They do all these work-ups that go on forever.

Another aviator described the supply community:

> The supply guys are by themselves. They act like little dicks. You depend on
> them. They see themselves as lower on the totem pole so they act like little
> jerks to compensate for their inferior feelings. They don't want to share
> their knowledge of the support system so people can't get around them.

This is a fairly common appraisal of supply officers. The metonomy of
small genitalia connotes a lack of virility and power in this culture.
There's some irony in this. They do have power; as this aviator said,
'you depend on them'. And some officers feel that supply officers over-
compensate for feelings of inferiority with regard to combat specialists by
displaying power in other ways, such as withholding the flow of supplies
and the appropriation of funds. As a consequence, the line officers are
often careful to 'stay on their good side'. As one said, 'The suppo could
be your best friend if you really need something'.

The conferral of lower status is not lost on the supply community. As
one supply officer said:

> Supply officers are considered staff. We are never allowed to command the
> vessel... [or] to be risk takers. If you fly you get to deviate from the
> guidelines. They [aviators] get to be more autonomous. We're like CPAs
> [certified public accountants]. We have to follow these rules and laws, not
> these general guidelines like the pilots. It looks boring.

Unlike aviators and surface warfare officers, supply officers are not
permitted the traditional masculine experiences: the opportunity to
take risks, to command and be in charge, and to be autonomous.

Supply officers employ a number of strategies of self-differentiation, a
way to demonstrate their competence. One way is to achieve a superior
ranking. Like all department heads, the supply officer is ranked
against other officers on the ship. Also, as a result of bi-annual inspections, each supply department is rated against other ships' supply
departments within the fleet. This becomes an important way to distinguish oneself, to stand out from the others. One supply officer reported
that his peak experience in the Navy was receiving recognition for
running the top-rated supply department of all the ships within his
fleet.

> On one ship I headed, we gained fleet-wide notoriety for the ship. We
> caused the engineering department to pale in comparison... All my junior
> people got promoted as a result... We were rated the best boat in the
> Pacific fleet. All the supply and food operations were rated the best. It's a
> very coveted award.

The job of a supply officer is often one of material tracking, fiscal accounting, and administrative planning. The supply officer needs to know the status of every piece of equipment and every material part under his watchful eye. Inventory inspections occur approximately once every six months and the supply officer is rated on how well he accounts for his equipment. Also, the supply corps is responsible for food operations on board ship. One supply officer described his job this way: 'Every day you check the inventory. Sometimes there's 22,000 line items that have to be checked... You have to make sure the food service spaces are immaculate.'

Given that they keep the squadron well-supplied, many supply officers echo the feelings of this officer, who argues that his job is indispensable: 'Where would they be without us?' Many said that they deliberately chose the supply corps because it is excellent preparation for a career in the civilian sector. 'To manage $16 million when you're 25 years old – to have to balance to the penny – jet pilots can't do that'. Many are like this officer, a graduate of the Naval Academy who wanted to become a pilot, but due to football injuries was not permitted to assume a combat specialty. He draws on masculine themes of rationality and responsibility as a source of identity.

> The good suppo officer sees himself as a vital link. Okay, tomorrow you tell me how your life is without supply. They say, 'You're just a chop' ['chopping on paper' is a demeaning reference to filling out forms and doing paperwork]... They say [you're a suppo officer] because you're not physically qualified... I did this because it's a good business move for after my Navy career. I get to manage people. I get to run information systems. It prepares me for the business world later – after I retire.

This tone of apology and justification was heard from many of the non-combat males in support communities. This officer differentiates his status in an area where he is able to exert control. For men like this, it is impossible to ignore the hegemonic masculine ideal of control, autonomy, and authority. They may not fly a jet or command a ship, but they control people and information systems. The search for a stable masculine identity is embedded in a theme of upward mobility. This preoccupation with hierarchical advancement and competition for career progress is a common theme of middle-class men in organizations (Collinson and Hearn 1994) and was commonly heard among supply officers.

Conclusion

Critical men's studies view masculinity as dynamic patterns of ideologies and practices constructed in interaction. In this vein, Coltrane (1994) argued for comparative studies that challenge a 'falsely universalizing concept of gender'. However, Collinson and Hearn (1994) warn against treating multiple masculinities as another set of static categories. Instead, they encourage the study of the dynamic, shifting, and contradictory character of gender relations. Specifically, they contend, it is important to attend to the construction of unities, differences, and interrelationships between men. For this reason, it is important to pay attention to men's location within the structure of the gender order.

In this chapter, I have taken such a relational perspective on the construction of gender and explored alternative masculinities within the US Navy. There are a number of different strands of hegemonic masculinity that these officers can draw upon to secure masculine identity. These themes include: risk taking; discipline; excitement associated with operation of powerful technology; tolerance of degradation; stoic endurance of hardship; tenacity and perseverance in the face of difficult physical trials; rational calculation; absence of emotion; and technological mastery. While this article has focused on differences between occupational specialties, there are also variations within these groups, a theme to be addressed elsewhere. To illustrate, risk taking is a high value in this culture and not the exclusive privilege of aviators. One supply officer said, for example, 'If there's a fire on board ship, I want the CO to know that I'll risk climbing in there to save someone just like anybody else'. However, these officers' discourses are constrained and facilitated by the resources available within various communities. While aviators have more opportunities to display risk taking, surface warfare officers have opportunities to demonstrate physical hardships and grueling work schedules, and supply officers frequently have more opportunity to display rational calculation and responsibility for resources. By focusing on the themes within each organizational community, I have drawn attention to the importance of organizational position in constructing a masculine strategy.

Besides the opportunities and limitations nested within organizational positions, these officers attempt to secure a masculine identity in contrast to others. Aviators are seen as 'the élite' in relation to surface warfare officers and supply officers, who suffer harsh conditions and bureaucratic surveillance but who rarely experience the autonomy, the thrill and the glory of high-tech flying. Surface warfare officers consider their jobs 'manly' because they survive more rugged conditions and endure more intense competition than do other officers. Supply officers often distinguish themselves as technical specialists preparing for a successful business career.

However, one cannot overlook how masculine hegemony becomes a successful strategy for subordinating women. All of the masculinities achieve meaning in contrast to definitions of feminity. In men's interviews, women are depicted as emotionally unstable, less able to endure physical challenges, and unable to tolerate the harsh conditions of ship life. This is consistent with western masculine socialization, in which boys learn that being a man has no other definition than not being a woman: 'This notion of anti-femininity lies at the heart of contemporary and historical conceptions of manhood, so that masculinity is defined more by what one is not rather than what one is' (Kimmel 1994, p. 126). One recent review of research on women's increased participation in militaries of western nations concludes that in addition to experiencing limited career opportunities, women are often depicted as 'innately unsuited', lacking aggression, discipline, and commitment (Chandler et al. 1995). The authors suggest that this construction may have consequences for American naval women now able to serve on board surface ships – perhaps they will be limited to peripheral support tasks or 'women-friendly' tasks such as supply and communications.

There is a contradiction between the masculine display of rugged individualism/autonomy and the subordination and surveillance to which all military personnel are subject. These officers are hardly free and autonomous, a traditionally core feature of masculine hegemony. Officers must find other modes of expression of non-conformity, which might explain some of the wild, 'uncivil' behavior that occurs at social events and parties, including the scandalous sexual escapades that occurred at the 1991 Tailhook convention (*Tailhook Report* 1993). This also might explain the intensity with which women are 'othered'. Discipline, obedience, compliance, and exacting detail, ideals that are depicted as 'tough' and masculine, depend upon contrasting images of the feminized 'other' – being undisciplined, scattered, emotional, unreliable. Homosexuals have also been 'othered' using these terms. For years, one of the core arguments for excluding homosexuals from military service was their lack of discipline and unreliability – it was feared that they would be a security risk (Herek 1993, 1990). The argument here is that the more the masculine theme of discipline and endurance is emphasized, the less important it is to exhibit autonomy and independent control. One way to emphasize discipline, endurance, and rationality as masculine traits is to depict lack of discipline, unreliability, and emotion as feminine.

There is another contradiction at the heart of this culture that suggests attempts to achieve a secure masculine identity create conditions that undermine the possibility of such an achievement. The military life is very demanding. Every officer, at some point(s) in his career, is likely to experience degradation and humiliation that often accompany continual surveillance, testing, ranking, grueling life conditions, and the constant possibility of failure. This study suggests that their investment in masculine discourse is a strategy they employ to compensate for these negative experiences: one way to overcome subjective insecurity is to re-interpret the tolerance of grueling conditions and constant surveillance as manly experiences. ('This is so awful and painful that most can't tolerate it, but I've shown I can take it'.)

But as Collinson (1992) demonstrated in his study of masculinity among manual laborers, such efforts are precarious. Depending on external confirmation – the approval of a commanding officer, the awarding of a surface warfare pin, promotion, the accolades of peers – to affirm and re-affirm to themselves and others who and what they are, is potentially self-defeating. Preoccupation with differentiating self and discounting others creates an enduring sense of subjective insecurity. This persistent sense of fragility and precariousness generates a greater need to display worth. Such defensive posturing – differentiating self by out-performing others, validating self by negating others – is not only unlikely to lead to the achievement of a secure identity, it creates the very social conditions that drive men to strive for a chance to demonstrate exceptionality. These officers are chronically aware that their peers are eager to surpass them. The achievement of masculinity in this culture is never secure. It must be continually confirmed and exhibited. This follows Collinson's conclusion that a culture that encourages continual comparison 'recreates the social insecurity it is intended to transcend' (1992, p. 97).

The military is a gendered institution. Its structure, practices, values, rites, and rituals reflect accepted notions of masculinity and femininity. But it is also a gendering institution. It helps to create gendered identities. This chapter discusses the various power struggles and obstacles that surround men's practices, as well as the multiple strategies of assertion and differentiation male officers enact in attempts to secure a masculine identity. Since upholding a hegemonic ideal of masculinity takes collective effort, a second focus of this study has been the organizational rules, practices, and structures, particularly the systems of ranking and testing, that contribute to the construction of the hegemonic ideal.

ACKNOWLEDGEMENT

I would like to acknowledge the suggestions of Bob Connell and three anonymous reviewers. I would also like to acknowledge Norm Fitzpatrick and Doug Borrebach who assisted in the collection of data.

REFERENCES

Arkin, W. and Dobrofsky, L. (1978) Military socialization and masculinity. *Journal of Social Issues*, 34,1, 151–68.

Carrigan, T., Connell, B. and Lee, J. (1985) Toward a new sociology of masculinity. *Theory and Society*, 5,4.

Chandler, J., Bryant, L. and Bunyard, T. (1995) Women in military occupations. *Work, Employment and Society*, 9,1, 123–35.

Cockburn, C. (1983) *Brother: Male Dominance and Technological Change*. London: Pluto Press.

Cockburn, C. (1985) *Machinery of Dominance*. Boston: Northeastern University Press.

Collinson, D. (1988) Engineering humour: masculinity, joking and conflict in shopfloor relations. *Organization Studies*, 9,2, 181–99.

Collinson, D. (1992) *Managing the Shopfloor*. Berlin: Walter de Gruyter.

Collinson, D. and Hearn, J. (1994) Naming men as men: implications for work organization and management. *Gender, Work and Organization*, 1,1, 2–22.

Coltrane, S. (1994) Theorizing masculinities in contemporary social science. In H. Brod and M. Kaufman (eds.), *Theorizing Masculinities*. pp. 39–60. Thousand Oaks, Calif.: Sage.

Connell, R. (1987) *Gender and Power*. Berkeley: University of California Press.

Connell, R. (1995) *Masculinities*. Berkeley: University of California Press.

Connell, R. W. (1992) Masculinity, violence, and war. In M. Kimmel and M. Messner (eds.), *Men's Lives*, pp. 176–83. New York: Macmillan.

Enloe, C. (1990) *Bananas, Beaches, and Bases*. Berkeley: University of California Press.

Fine, G. (1986) The dirty play of little boys. *Society*, 24,1 (Nov.).

Foucault, M. (1977) *Discipline and Punish*. London: Allen Lane.

Game, A. and Pringle, R. (1983) *Gender at Work*. Sydney: Allen and Unwin.

Goffman, E. (1961) *Asylums*. New York: Doubleday.

Gray, J. (1959) *The Warriors*. New York: Harper and Row.

Hacker, S. (1989) *Power, Pleasure, and Technology*. New York: Routledge.

Herek, G. (1990) Gay people and government security clearances. *American Psychologist*, 45,9, 1035–42.

Herek, G. (1993) Sexual orientation and military service: a social science perspective. *American Psychologist*, 48,5, 538–49.

Janowitz, M. (1960) *The Professional Soldier*. New York: Free Press.

Jeffords, (1989) *The Remasculinization of America*. Berkeley: University of California Press.

Kerfoot, D. and Knights, D. (1993) Management, masculinity and manipulation: from paternalism to corporate strategy in financial services in Britain. *Journal of Management Studies*, 30,4, 659–67 (July).

Kimmel, M. (1994) Masculinity as homophobia: fear, shame, and silence in the construction of gender identity. In H. Brod and M. Kaufman (eds.), *Theorizing Masculinities*, pp. 119–41. Thousand Oakes: Sage.

Klein, A. (1993) *Little Big Men*. New York: State University of New York Press.

Levy, C. (1992) ARVN as faggots: inverted warfare in Vietnam. In M. Kimmel and M. Messner (eds.), *Men's Lives*, pp. 183–98. New York: Macmillan.

Lorber, J. (1994) *Paradoxes of Gender*. New Haven, Conn.: Yale University Press.

Lovell, J. (1964) The professional socialization of the West Point cadet. In M. Janowitz (ed.), *The New Military*. New York: Russel Sage.

Messerschmidt, J. (1993) *Masculinities and Crime*. Lanham, Maryland: Rowman and Littlefield.

Messner, M. (1992) *Power at Play*. Boston, Mass.: Beacon Press.

Messner, M. and Sabo, D. (eds.). (1990) *Sport, Men, and the Gender Order*. Champaign, Ill.: Human Kinetics Books.

Morgan, D. (1994) Theater of war: combat, the military, and masculinities. In H. Brod and M. Kaufman (eds.), *Theorizing Masculinities*. Thousand Oaks, Calif.: Sage.

Roper, M. and Tosh, J. (eds.). (1991) *Manful Assertions*. London: Routledge.

Rotundo, E. (1993) *American Manhood*. New York: Basic Books.

Sabo, D. (1992) Pigskin, patriarchy and pain. In M. Kimmel and M. Messner (eds.), *Men's Lives*. New York: Macmillan.

Seidler, V. (1989) *Rediscovering Masculinity*. London: Routledge.

Stouffer, S. (1949) *The American Soldier vol. II*. New York: Wiley.

Strange, P. (1983) *It'll Make a Man of You . . . A Feminist View of the Arms Race*. Nottingham, England: Russell Press Ltd.

The Tailhook Report. (1993) New York: Office of the Inspector General.

West, C. and Zimmerman, D. (1987) Doing gender. *Gender and Society*, 1, 125–51.

Whitson, D. (1990) Sport in the social construction of masculinity. In M. Messner and D. Sabo (eds.), *Sport, Men and the Gender Order*, pp. 19–30. Champaign, Ill.: Human Kinetics Books.

Zurcher, L. (1967) The naval recruit training center: a study of role assimilation in a total institution. *Sociological Inquiry*, 37, 85–98.

5

The Belly of the Beast:
Sex as Male Domination?

Lynne Segal

'Man is complicated', Catherine Stimpson announces, introducing one of the early North American texts in 'Men's Studies'.[1] The more we explore the social and historical dimensions of masculinity, the more it is revealed as heterogenous and contradictory, defined through a series of hierarchical relations: rejection and suppression of femininity and homosexual desire, command and control over (often seen as 'protection of') the 'weak' and 'inferior'. But while the notion of masculinity becomes ever more complex, the 'problem of men' becomes ever more pressing. We may come to understand sexual difference in terms of a shifting reality – a multiplicity of meanings rather than simple opposition – but the cultural, social and political domination of men over women persists. The vexing paradox for feminists has been the need to criticise and challenge the social construction of 'woman' as definitively less-than, subordinate to or complemented by, 'man', while at the same time retaining for ourselves those aspects of womanhood which we value but which are disparaged in dominant male-centred discourses and realities. In consequence we may end up defending notions of feminine experience which we need to demolish as *exclusively* 'feminine'. A similar paradox in relation to men lies in the importance of challenging the existence of any fixed essence of 'man', while at the same time insisting upon the continuing practical problem of men. The danger here is that we may end up dismissing the diversity and changing meanings of 'masculinity', some of which we might need to help strengthen as a challenge to the more traditional ones.

In the early 1970s, when the women's liberation movements of the West emerged from the radical movements of the sixties, men were not identified as the central problem. Feminists, with the excitement and confidence of what they saw as the 'boundless possibilities' of a brand new beginning, were busy taking control of their own lives.[2] They were challenging women's subordinate place within radical politics and radical perspectives, while attacking the language and iconography of a form of 'sexual liberation' in which women as 'chicks' remained the passive objects of men's desires, instead of the self-affirming subjects of their own. Above all, they were busy enjoying the pleasures and excitement of their own company. They were, for the first time in their lives, meeting together in small groups simply as women, talking about sex and relationships, organising for nurseries, playgrounds, better jobs and training, and demanding control over their own fertility.[3]

Men were an issue in these early days insofar as feminists knew they must exclude them from the women's liberation movement – in the face of fierce hostility in Britain from a small group of Maoist women who consistently opposed the idea of an autonomous organisation of women.[4] Men, as women then knew from working with them in radical groups, would otherwise dominate and silence women, insisting upon their own political agendas. Only once the women's movement grew stronger and more powerful, drawing in women with different histories, did some women begin to speak about the previously unspeakable, to discuss men's violence and their fears of men. The problem of men intruded itself, often uninvited, upon these passionate feminist beginners, as the prevalence of rape and men's domestic violence against women and children began to enter feminist consciousness. It emerged as women began paying more attention to the pains and burdens of the women around them, and voicing their own inner fears. Contemplating the extent of men's violence against women, their sexual coerciveness, and what, once sensitised to it, soon appeared as a seemingly boundless landscape of cultural misogyny, feminist anger against men rose throughout the seventies.

The universality and tenacity of men's dominance over women began to undermine the earlier optimism that women's conscious rejection of ideologies of female subordination could eventually create a future of gender equality – at least, once it joined up with struggles against social policies, workplace practices, and domestic arrangements which were exploitative of women. The decline of all progressive radical movements and socialist groups and parties from the late seventies, with the successful rise of the political right internationally, also played a large part in this process. More feminists were drawn to a type of feminist analysis which blames individual men for women's oppression, and stresses men's transhistorical primordial drive for power, rather than one which explores how changing social arrangements and their ideological articulations institutionalise men's power.[5]

The sexuality of men

In seeking a single transhistorical basis for male dominance, the most popular and accessible feminist writing from the late 1970s, most of it coming from North America, was focusing on male sexuality. In the early 1980s the US feminist attorney Catherine MacKinnon summarised this new type of radical feminist orthodoxy: 'I think that feminism fundamentally identifies sexuality as the primary social sphere of male power.'[6] Sexuality in and of itself, it was suggested, is at the heart of male dominance. In addition, MacKinnon, Andrea Dworkin, Robin Morgan, Susan Griffin and others were now arguing, male sexual dominance is at the heart of all other power relations in society. As MacKinnon expresses it: 'That male sexual dominance, a social construct, may be centrally involved in the nuclear arms race, imperialism, colonisation, psychoanalysis[!], class exploitation, political torture, fascism, and racism may have been obscured and underestimated, including by women.'[7]

Ironically, the origins of this new radical feminist analysis of the phallic imperative as the literal motor of human history is, we should be clear, neither radical, nor feminist. It is the old conservative common-sense we were raised on, associated, most prominently, up to and including the present, with the thinking of the right rather than the left; with arguments against sexual equality, and against feminism (and, especially with that bastion of male evil – psychoanalysis!). Right-wing ideologues like Roger Scruton have always warned us that women's primary task is to work tirelessly to 'quieten' and 'constrain' the 'unbridled ambition of the phallus'.[8] He claims to see feminist ideology as a perfidious plot hatched by men, in the hope that they could thereby 'rid the sexual impulse [which he sees here as exclusively male] of its debilitating commitment ...and so allow no claims of allegiance to extinguish the claims of power.'[9]

There is no doubt that Dworkin and MacKinnon, on the one hand, and Scruton on the other, are repeating the dominant contemporary cultural discourses and iconographies surrounding sexuality. The new 'scientific' study of sex, with the birth of sexology in the mid-nineteenth century, depicted male sexuality as an overpowering instinct which, as Richard von Krafft-Ebing wrote at the time, 'with all-conquering force and might demands fulfilment'.[10] Today, popular magazines, advertising, hard- and soft-core pornography, are all saturated with the same image of 'masculinity' as some type of insatiable sexual appetite. The Western literary canon has its own dramas and metaphors of phallic power. 'Down, Wanton, Down', Robert Graves expresses men's boastful narcissism, here thinly disguised as self-mockery, when lovingly addressing his penis, and conferring upon it a life of its own.[11] 'He never understands when certain things can be done and when they can't', the fictional hero, Rico, similarly addresses his genital organ, in Alberto Moravia's short story, *The Two of Us*.[12] The standard discourses of the natural sciences contain elements of the same ideology, as they have for the last hundred years and more: 'Males will always strive to control female reproductive behaviour', biologists Randy Thornhill et al. deduce from their study of the behaviour of scorpion flies of the genus, *Panorpa*, in 1986; 'this may result in a conflict of male and female reproductive interests.'[13] More popularly, as Rosalind Coward has pointed out, we are daily bombarded in our living-rooms with the folk wisdom of a Desmond Morris or a Richard Dawkins in nature programmes which illustrate for us the inevitability of male sexual dominance: the male instinct in every living creature propelling its tireless pursuit of the female to disseminate anywhere and everywhere conception may ensue.[14]

The ubiquity of the discourses and imagery of 'conquest/submission', 'activity/passivity', 'masculinity/femininity' constructing heterosexual intercourse as *the* spectacular moment of male domination and female submission, is inescapable: 'The man "mounts" and penetrates; the woman spreads her legs and "submits"; and these postures seem to ratify, again and again, the ancient authority of men over women.'[15] But we must be cautious in assuming an equation between such sado-masochistic discourse and people's lived experience of sexuality. Internal and external meanings are not always identical. Our experiences do not simply mirror social meanings; though they are inevitably filtered through them. We must tread very carefully if we wish to tease out the connections between the nature and significance of many layers of sexual and bodily experience for both women and men. These include the subjective of psychic experience of sex from infancy onwards; the cultural ideas and values surrounding sex; the social contexts allowing or forbidding sexual expression; the medical and other social practices applied to the body – particularly women's bodies – all of them taking place within the wider context of gender hierarchy. The place to begin, I believe, is a recognition of the cultural force of the equation of 'the phallus' with power – solid and unlimited.

It is the phallus which creates the seemingly ineluctable bond between 'male sexuality' and power. Yet this symbol of the phallus as power, grasped by boy and girl child alike, cannot be equated with the lived experience of male sexual domination. Childhood sexuality, those who acknowledge its existence would agree, takes both active and passive forms, with multiple outlets and objects, most of them not congruent with the meanings attached to adult heterosexuality. [...] Psychoanalytic accounts have been used to argue that it is the physical visibility of men's genitals which creates men's swaggering commitment to putting them to use, from boyhood onwards, while women's apparently invisible equipment creates their greater sexual reticence. But, while the anthropological debate over cultural relativism is an intricate and vexed one, the literature overwhelmingly suggests that the meanings attached to anatomical difference are neither fixed nor universal.[16] Even within Western culture, the meanings and significance given to male and female anatomy have shifted over the last hundred years. It seems more plausible to assume that the phallus as symbol condenses the multiple significances of the whole configuration of male dominance, with its diverse social practices at once conferring power and authority on 'men', and giving most actual men some real power over the lives of others – at the very least within domestic life. The whole configuration, I have suggested, includes divisions of labour (with their differing connections to technological expertise and financial reward), institutions of authority (political, juridical, educational, medical) and, finally, family arrangements, tied in with patterns of desire and the expression and control of sexuality. All of these structures and practices work in concert with ideologies of 'femininity' and 'masculinity' to construct women as dependent on men; dependent, at least, on men within their own class and group.

Bolstered by the multifaceted reality of men's power, the phallus, as a symbol, is not, however, available for individual men to possess. It is that which they attempt to possess, or perhaps to reject; or maybe that which they approach with uncertainty and disquiet. We still need to explain how it is – if it is – that men's sexual performance, or their psychic and physical experience of sexuality, becomes a (and on the new radical feminist/old conservative analysis, *the*) source of male dominance. So the question remains: to what extent does the actual reality of men's sexual lives, the deployment of the penis, give men power and control over women? Can we assume that there is something about men's shared experience of the physical presence of the penis which underlies the way men in general relate to their bodies, and gain a sense of 'masculinity' and power? Or are we to assume that there is something else common to men's experience of sexuality which constructs a shared masculinity, and hence 'male dominance'?

There are, of course, the all too familiar rituals of male bonding produced through derisive sexist sniggering, the inexhaustible joking, the suggestive gestures, around 'cunts', 'pricks', 'queers', 'studs', 'shafting' and 'wanking'. Men's workplace culture, particularly it seems in manual jobs, is built around this form of sexual signalling: 'In the machine noise, a gesture suggestive of masturbation, intercourse or homosexuality was enough to raise a conventional smile and re-establish a bond over distances too great for talking.'[17] Collectively, it is clear, calling up images of male sexual performance serves to consolidate and confirm masculinity, and to exclude and belittle women. Sociologists like Gagnon and Simon, or therapists like Ethel Spector Person, convincingly argue that the need to reassert and confirm masculine gender identity lies behind the obsessive force propelling men into sexual engagement, or at the least, into pornographic thoughts of sexual engagement: 'An impotent man always feels that his masculinity, and not just his sexuality, is threatened. In men, gender appears to "lean" on sexuality... In women, gender identity and self-worth can be consolidated by other means."[18] Heterosexual performance may be viewed as the mainstay of masculine identity, but its enactment does not in itself give men power over women. (Even in violent situations, it is the use of muscular force or weapons which gives men the power to sexually abuse other men, women or children.) Most of the men who can talk honestly about their heterosexual experiences, admit to considerable confusion, often feeling it is the woman who has all the power.[19] The tub-thumping white cocksman Norman Mailer, for example, quite rightly describes himself as a 'Prisoner of Sex', a 'Prisoner of Wedlock', for 'he had never been able to live without a woman'. Like many an egotist, Mailer prefers to contemplate the fascinating phenomenon which is himself in the third person: 'Four times beaten at wedlock, his respect for the power of women was so large that the way they would tear through him (in his mind's eye) would be reminiscent of old newsreels of German tanks.'[20] Women lost their respect for men, he concludes, when pregnancy lost its danger. Once, he mourns, a woman had known that her lovers might be the agency of her death: 'Conceive then the lost gravity of the act, and the diminishment of man from a creature equally mysterious to woman (since he could introduce a creation to her that could yet be her doom) down to the fellow who took lessons on how to satisfy his wife from Masters and Johnson and bowed out to the vibrations of his superior, a vibrator.'[21] In Mailer's view, technology, 'by extending man's power over nature, reduced him before women'.[22] Such paranoid bleating, from the brave bull contemplating his own lost power, contains, to my mind, a certain truth. Whatever the meanings attached to 'the act' of sexual intercourse, for many men it confirms a sense of ineptness and failure: the failure to satisfy women. Images of a sexually satisfied woman are culturally relative, and our culture has increasingly impressed upon men the importance of the female orgasm – a man must, as it were, stand firm as the instrument of repeated female orgasm. Yet we also know, from myths and narratives of popular culture, if not from clinical evidence of the castration complex, the force of psychoanalytic observations on men's sheer terror of female genitals and female sexuality.[23]

Unsurprisingly then, for many men it is precisely through sex that they experience their greatest uncertainties, dependence and deference in relation to women – in stark contrast, quite often, with their experience of authority and independence in the public world. And certainly for many men it is precisely through experiencing themselves as powerless and submissive that they experience the greatest sexual pleasure. [...] As Nancy Friday discovered in her survey of three thousand sexual fantasies sent in to her by men, overpowering women against their will seem to be the exception, rather than the rule, of men's fantasy. By a ratio of four to one, men's fantasies were masochistic.[24] (She received only three fantasies of enacting rape from men, whereas being raped or forced were the most popular themes among women respondents.) Her findings accord with the evidence we have from sex workers, who reveal that more of their clients pay to play the victim than the aggressor in sexual encounters. Men are almost as likely as women to select a masochistic role in fantasy, seeing pain as the symbolic price for pleasure, feeling guilty about wanting something they see as 'dirty'.

Eileen McLeod interviewed thirty prostitutes and twenty male clients (all 'normal' and married men, and thus representative of the men who go to prostitutes) for her book on prostitution, and concluded that a 'common feature of men's sexual activity with prostitutes is the opportunity it provides to escape conventional male heterosexual roles with their heavy emphasis on masculine prowess and dominance'.[25] As one prostitute comments of her clients, 'I think they must all have it in their minds somewhere they'd like a woman to take advantage of them'; or another, 'It makes them feel relaxed, they haven't got to put on a performance ... be a big stud or produce multiple orgasms or anything like that.'[26] The clients spoke of liking what they experienced as the 'role shift': 'Here is the woman doing to the man'; 'I go there because I know I can lie down and just leave it to the girls'.[27] The desire for the passive experience of 'domination' and the feminine experience of dressing as women were also identified by both prostitutes and clients as the most consistent of men's desires after straight sex, oral sex or masturbation. (About a quarter of the prostitutes' customers expressed such desires.) North American studies of thousands of prostitutes and their clients have revealed similar findings, with 48 per cent of men classified as desiring to be 'sexually passive' in one study, 74 per cent in another.[28]

Men's fantasies, desires, and experience of sex in actual relationships with women are not, it seems, so very different from women's in terms of images of submission – presumably recalling pre-pubescent fantasies in both sexes. Here is Dave Feintwick's story of his sexual awakening.

If we did not know his sex, we might have assumed it was female. Certainly, his memories are little different from my own erotic history when, as a young girl, my fantasies always focused upon some older woman:

> Going back to when I was five or six, my earliest sexual fantasies included the (conventionally) attractive mother of one of my class-mates. I imagined myself sitting on the wooden swing...and her coming up to me...arms outstretched like a biblical figure, and kissing and stroking me...Later I fantasised about my women teachers both chastising me and being kind to me...[Later again] My fantasies became more complex. They involved most of the females I knew from everyday life and saw in the media. Age and conventional good looks were largely irrelevant as in my mind I dreamt of women who would be nice to me, make love to me and who would enjoy acting out sadomasochistic scenes. To an extent these fantasies still attract me, but have diminished power and impact as I have found completely different involvement and satisfaction in a good physical sexual relationship, something which I thought would never happen...I cannot banish them [the fantasies], but they are slowly being disarmed as I begin to actually like rather than feel neutral, or even arrogantly disdain, other people with whom I have begun to feel myself luxuriously close.[29]

Neither men's masturbatory fantasies, nor men's experience of sex in relationships with women, reduce to the conventional rituals of sex as male dominance. As Nancy Friday's survey shows, men strongly desire to be caregivers just as much as women, though their need to give love can conflict with their rage at past rejections and at being made to feel dirty and guilty.[30] Men dream about intimacy with women, at the same time as they fear it. Similarly in Britain, Wendy Hollway's interviews of men and women's heterosexual experience describes the complex negotiation of power which occurs.[31] Women often fail to perceive men's dependence on them ('That guy – I didn't even know he was so *dependent* on me – I had no *idea*'), while men, in line with Freud's thoughts on castration anxiety, often perceive women as all-powerful ('She was very strong and very emotional...I didn't feel safe I wasn't going to be knocked out and sucked in by her.'[32]) The dominant 'male sexual drive' discourse encourages these misrecognitions – men's denial of need and vulnerability, women's denial of their own power in sexual relationships. Hollway criticises a feminism which reproduces the assumption of men's power through sex as monolithic:

> Heterosexual sex is the site of politics because it is so contradictory, because it is a primary site of women's power and of men's resistance. A part of that politics is the production of alternative – feminist – accounts of

men's sexuality which do not corroborate in sexist assumptions that the power of the penis is incontestable. It is not. The power of the penis is a 'knowledge' produced by sexist discourses; a knowledge which is motivated and thus reproduced by men's vulnerability to women because of the desire for the Other/mother.[33]

The point is that it seems wilfully blind for feminists to buy into the bravado behind many men's repression of their sexual anxieties and insecurities, by endorsing myths of the inevitable link between sexuality and male dominance. It becomes a way of women colluding in men's defensive denial of their own confusion and doubts about sexuality, concealing that which we most need to reveal and understand. Male sexuality is most certainly not any single shared experience for men. It is not any single or simple thing at all – but the site of any number of emotions of weakness and strength, pleasure and pain, anxiety, conflict, tension and struggle, none of them mapped out in such a way as to make the obliteration of the agency of women in heterosexual engagements inevitable. Male sexuality cannot be reduced to the most popular meanings of sex acts, let alone to sex acts themselves. It becomes intelligible only if placed within actual histories of men's intimate relationships with others – or the lack of them.

Carole Vance and Ann Snitow, two North American feminists who have written extensively on the debates on sexuality within feminism, and who reject the new feminist 'common-sense' of the eighties which equates sex and male dominance, consistently highlight the complexity of sexuality – male and female – and criticise the radical feminist reduction which takes ideology to be lived behaviour:

> If patriarchy fuses gender and sexuality, the analytic task of feminism is to take them apart. The political task of feminism is to work for concrete material changes that enable women and men to experience sexuality less attached to and formed by gender. These changes include social and economic equality; the end of compulsory heterosexuality; access to birth control, abortion, and sex education; recognition of children as sexual; a reconsideration of public/private distinctions; and the protection of mothers and children outside of marriage.[34]

What power male sexuality does have in perpetuating male dominance does not simply obtain at the level of symbolism. While certainly facilitating male bonding and mediating some of the most oppressive ways both men and women relate to men's bodies, men's talk of sex has an ambiguous relationship to their experiences of sexual pleasure; male sexual dominance derives from the way in which the general social power of men sustains the symbolism of phallic power through encouraging or controlling how women and men may relate to their bodies. It is not, for instance, that male sexuality is irredeemably violent, coercive or connected with emotions of domination – often it is not – but, that the possibility of men's sexual coerciveness towards women has been socially tolerated, often, indeed, both expected and encouraged. It is not that women's experience of sex is irredeemably linked with danger and sentiments of submission – often it is not – but that men, through such institutions as marriage, medicine and law have managed to exert extraordinary levels of control over it. The level of the symbolic does not operate autonomously. It is sustained or diminished by the impact of social practices upon it. Change in the dominant gendered meanings surrounding sexuality is possible.

Indeed, transforming the meanings attaching to sexuality is a political task which men and women can share. But the recognition of its necessity is still fragile; and the task itself fraught with difficulties. Reflecting on male sexuality in 1979, the editors of the British anti-sexist magazine, *Achilles Heel*, concluded: 'There's a lot wrong with current patterns of heterosexuality – one of the main things that's wrong is that there just aren't very many really positive images of heterosexual relationships.'[35] Why should this be? We all know that many women are not gentle, many men not violent. These universal constructions of sexual difference are challenged in our fantasies, and, at times, in our experiences, of sexual engagement. Yet despite two decades of fierce feminist criticism, ridicule and the use of every available weapon to undermine and transform sexist ideology and practice in the West, male sexuality is still constantly presented to us as predatory and overpowering. Indeed, in these same decades, we have seen the pornography business become the fastest growing industry in most Western countries, and the number of reported sexual attacks and violence against women continue to increase. If pessimism and despair now pervade so much feminist reflection on sex, its focus on rape, pornography and violence against women is hardly surprising. Before we can rest upon those joyful shores where more positive meanings connect to sexuality, we have to wade through the swamp in which men's pornographic fantasy and actual sexual violence suffuse our consciousness of sex.

Should we even embark upon such a journey? We have been warned that it may be pointless. If 'the sexual dynamic of history', as a group of British feminist historians has written, reveals that one of 'the deep structures that serve male domination is heterosexuality',[36] who dares defend sex? If Peter Sutcliffe, the murderer and mutilator of 13 women was, as feminist graffiti in Britain explained in the 1980s, 'Not Mad, Not Bad, But MALE', then maleness is nothing more nor less than murderous insanity. This graffiti encapsulates the conviction of the impossibility of a sexual politics *vis-à-vis* heterosexuality. The thinking behind it has helped reverse the promise of sexual liberation of the sixties, and weakened the more confident feminist sexual politics of the early seventies. The journey, it is clear, will be a rough one.

NOTES

1 Catherine Stimpson, (1987), Foreword to Harry Brod (ed.), *The Making of Masculinities*, p. xl, London, Allen & Unwin.
2 Anon. (circa 1971), *Why Miss World?*, Pamphlet, London (n.d.).
3 See Michelene Wandor, (1972), (ed.), *The Body Politic: Writings from the Women's Liberation Movement in Britain 1969–72*, London, Stage One.
4 See Sheila Rowbotham, (1989), *The Past is Before Us: Feminism in Action Since the 1960s*, p. 64, London, Pandora.
5 See Lynne Segal, (1987), *Is the Future Female? Troubled Thoughts on Contemporary Feminism*, chapter 2, London, Virago Press.
6 Catherine MacKinnon, (1982), 'Feminism, Marxism, Method and the State', in *Signs*, vol. 7, 3, p. 529.
7 Catherine MacKinnon, (1984), Comments in *Signs*, vol. 10, 1, p. 182.
8 Roger Scruton, (1983), *The Observer*, 22 May.
9 Roger Scruton, (1983), *The Times*, 15 February.
10 Quoted in Jeffrey Weeks, (1985), *Sexuality and Its Discontents*, p. 69, London, Routledge & Kegan Paul.
11 Quoted in Peter Schwenger, (1984), *Phallic Critiques*, p. 76, London, Routledge & Kegan Paul.
12 Alberto Moravia, (1972), *The Two of Us*, p. 111, London, Secker & Warburg.
13 Randy Thornhill et al., (1986), 'The Biology of Rape', in Sylvana Tomaselli and Roy Porter (eds), *Rape*, p. 113, Oxford, Basil Blackwell.
14 Rosalind Coward, (1984), 'The Sex Life of Stick Insects', in *Female Desire*, London, Paladin.
15 Barbara Ehrenreich et al., (1986), *Re-Making Love: The Feminization of Sex*, p. 203, New York, Anchor Press.
16 For example, according to studies of New Guinea Highlands societies a person's gender 'does not lie locked in his or her genitals but can flow and change with contact as substances seep into and out of his or her body'. This quotation is cited in Fitz John Porter Poole, 'Transforming "natural" woman' in Sherry Ortner and Harriet Whitehead, (1981), (eds), *Sexual Meanings*, p. 118, Cambridge, Cambridge University Press. See also G. Eichinger Ferro-Luzzi, (1980), 'The Female Lingam', in *Current Anthropology*, vol. 21, 1; Shirley Ardener, (1987), 'A note on gender iconography: the vagina' in Pat Caplan (ed.), *The Cultural Construction of Sexuality*; Olivia Harris, (1981), 'The power of signs: gender, culture and the wild in the Bolivian Andes' in MacCormack and Strathern (eds), *Nature, Culture and*

Gender, Cambridge, Cambridge University Press. For one of the most recent anthropological texts assessing universalist fallacies surrounding Western notions of men, women and 'gender' see Marilyn Strathern, (1989), *The Gender of the Gift: Problems with Women and Problems with Society in Melanesia*, California, University of California Press.

17 Quoted in Andrew Tolson, (1977), *The Limits of Masculinity*, p. 60, London, Tavistock.

18 Ethel Spector Person, (1980), 'Sexuality as the Mainstay of Identity: Psycho-analytic Perspectives', in *Signs*, vol. 5, 4, p. 619.

19 Gad Horowitz and Michael Kaufman, (1987), 'Male Sexuality: Toward A Theory of Liberation' in Michael Kaufman (ed.), *Beyond Patriarchy*, Toronto, Oxford University Press.

20 Norman Mailer, (1972), *The Prisoner of Sex*, p. 12, London, Sphere.

21 Ibid, p. 126.

22 Ibid, p. 127.

23 See, for example, H. R. Hays, (1964), *The Dangerous Sex*, New York, Putnam; Wolfgana Lederer, (1968), *The Fear of Women*, New York, Harcourt Brace; Mervyn Meggitt, (1976), 'A Duplicity of Demons', in *Man and Woman in the New Guinea Highlands*, Special publication, American Anthropological Association, no. 8.

24 Nancy Friday, (1980), *Men in Love: Men's Sexual Fantasies*, p. 471, New York, Arrow Books.

25 Eileen McLeod, (1982), *Women Working: Prostitution Now*, p. 59, London, Croom Helm.

26 Ibid, p. 69.

27 Ibid, p. 70.

28 British and US figures quoted ibid, pp. 70–2.

29 David Feintwick, (1979), 'Men's Lives: extract from an autobiography' in *Achilles Heel*, 2, p. 38.

30 Friday, op. cit.

31 Wendy Hollway, (1984), 'Women's Power in Heterosexual Sex' in *Women's Studies Int. Forum*, vol. 7, 1, pp. 63–8.

32 Ibid, pp. 65–6.

33 Ibid, p. 68.

34 Carole Vance and Ann Snitow, (1984), 'Towards a Conversation about Sex in Feminism', in *Signs*, vol. 10, 1, p. 131.

35 Editorial collective, (1979), 'Notes from the collective' in *Achilles Heel*, 3, p. 5.

36 London Feminist History Group, (1983), *The Sexual Dynamic of History*, p. 4, London, Pluto Press.

6

Power and the Language of Men

Scott Fabius Kiesling

Introduction

Power is usually cited as the most important factor when discussing the ways in which men's identities are constructed.[1] For example, in 'Men, inexpressiveness, and power', Jack Sattel argues that: 'the starting point for understanding masculinity lies, not in its contrast with femininity, but in the asymmetric dominance and prestige which accrues to males in this society' (1983, p. 119). In this chapter, I aim to show how issues of power and dominance as they relate to male identities are more complex than previously suggested. I will provide examples of some of the discursive strategies used by individual men in order to create and demonstrate power, showing how each man adopts a unique and personal approach when doing so. In particular, I will demonstrate how sequentiality and activity type must be taken into account when exploring the construction of men's identities through language.

It cannot be denied that men have more power than women in modern Western society. Men still dominate the upper echelons of government and business, and women continue to perform most of the unpaid labour of housework and child care. In addition, women still frequently earn less than men for comparable work, and professions dominated by women are less valued monetarily than those dominated by men (see Hewlett, 1986). Along with the freedom brought by power, however, comes the expectation (or requirement) that a man will somehow embody this power in his identity. This expectation is by no means as restrictive as those which obtain where women's identities are concerned; when a man constructs a powerful identity, it is usually connected in some way to 'real' power. Thus, the expectation of a 'powerful' identity for men is not symmetrical to the expectation of a 'powerless' identity for women, since a man's powerful identity is *rewarded* (with power), whereas a woman's non-powerless identity may be *punished*.

Following Sattel's suggestion, therefore, I take the power of men as a starting point for investigating how men construct their identities through language; I unpack the concept, describe different kinds of power, and show how these work with specific regard to four individual men.

My analysis is based on data gathered during a continuing ethnographic study of a fraternity in the United States. A fraternity is an all-male social club at a university, in which membership is selective. Typically, the fraternity becomes the central organization around which members structure their college lives, especially socially. It is a 'community of practice' (Eckert and McConnell-Ginet, 1992), defined sharply from the rest of the university through various means – initiation rituals, secret ceremonies and exclusive social events. Cynthia McLemore (1991) has worked on intonation in the female counterpart to the fraternity – the sorority. She showed that this type of community is ideal for studying language and society, especially the language of society's privileged members, because it is an intensely social, well-defined community, and its activities are based primarily on talk (e.g. meetings and parties). In addition, fraternities exhibit processes typical of other social groups more intensely: entrance into the community is carefully guarded, its members change completely every four years, and yet it manages to retain a unique history and ideology. Finally, fraternities are important to study because they prepare their members for the world of work after college. By analysing the strategies that men learn in fraternities, we can therefore gain insights into how men acquire, construct, and reproduce certain social practices in anticipation of dominance over others in later life.

In this chapter, I will explore how the fraternity's ideology and the immediate speech situation work together to constrain the members' identities. I use the term 'constrain', rather than 'affect' or 'determine', because identity construction is, to some extent, a creative endeavour. In theory, the men are free to create any identity they want, but in practice, they are pushed (and push themselves) towards identities which do not challenge the perceived values of the fraternity or of dominant US society. Each man also has different discursive resources (e.g. storytelling ability, joking ability, a powerful structural role, a loud voice, etc.) in order to draw upon disparate types of power. And crucially, each member has his own personal history within the fraternity, which further constrains the kind of identity he can display at any given time. Each time he speaks, then, the man must produce an utterance (and posture, gaze, etc.) that satisfies these constraints as far as possible. At the same time, he must make the utterance coherent within each current speech situation.

Because I am focusing on power, I will begin by outlining the framework of power used in my analysis. I will then discuss the specific ideology of power at work in the fraternity in question, exploring, for example, the kinds of constraints which the community places on a member's presentation of self. Finally, I will analyse excerpts from my corpus in order to illustrate how men draw upon, and construct, different types of power through their use of language.

A framework for power

Before applying a concept to any analysis, it should be well defined. When power is used as an explanation in sociolinguistic analyses, however, it is frequently undefined and unanalysed. Because I am taking power as the starting point for my work, I will briefly sketch the theoretical approach which is to be employed.

Following Foucault (1982), power is action that modifies action. The effect of this action need not be immediate, direct or even real. So, for example, because power takes place in actions, it is exercised to the extent that people *believe* that they should perform an action because of another action. However, power is not something that individuals may suddenly pull out and use. It must be salient to the situation; the people being acted on must believe in it. Thus, illusions can be powerful motivators. People believe that they should act in certain ways with certain people because they feel that not acting in these ways would have serious consequences. The reasons for performing a given action might therefore seem irrational, such as the avoidance of embarrassment, or the appearance of foolishness or 'weakness'. But what constitutes a serious consequence is, in turn, dependent on the community in question and its own particular values. This means that any analysis exploring issues of power must be based on a primary analysis of the local community's values and its ideology.

Whilst this view of power is flexible, it lacks analytical force. At a practical level, therefore, I assume that people have power because they occupy roles – some so enduring as to seem eternal and necessary, some fleeting and unnoticed, and some newly created within specific interactions. People place themselves in roles by using language because different ways of speaking are associated with such roles. A new role may be thrown together out of bits of others, and, in some cases, a single role may dominate a personality. But such roles can only really be discovered by analysing the discourse of community members, and by examining the community's formal and informal structures through ethnographic observation and interviewing.

On the basis of my own study, I have identified seven types of power processes from which local roles may be built: physical (coercive and ability), economic, knowledge, structural, nurturant, demeanour and ideological. I distinguish between two types of physical power: *coercive physical power* is the power of the mugger, while *ability physical power* is an action made possible by physical ability or skill. *Economic power* is the process that rewards one action (e.g. labour) with the possibility of another action (e.g. purchasing goods). *Knowledge power* is the process of gaining knowledge in order to perform an action. *Structural power* is the power of a place within a structure, classically (but not necessarily) a hierarchy. *Nurturant power* is the process of helping another, as in teaching or feeding. *Demeanour power* is the power of solidarity: moral authority, being liked, being 'a good guy'. The process of demeanour is not normally addressed by views of power, because the actions in this type of power act on emotions. Thus a person exhibits demeanour power when others feel happy, entertained, involved, respectful, etc.

But it is the ideological process which is the most important. This is a 'defining process', because individuals evaluate the other types of power processes through the ideological process. This defining process – which I will refer to as *ideological power* – ratifies certain traits as powerful, and determines which of the other processes are available (i.e. identifies the roles in the community). Within each of the other processes, ideological power identifies what is, and what is not, powerful. Thus, ideological power is the process of power whereby ways of thinking about the world are naturalized into a community's behaviour.

Each of the seven types of power outlined is not isolated from the others, but all are closely connected to form what Foucault refers to as: 'a net-like organization [...] something which circulates, or rather (as) something which only functions in the form of a chain' (1980, p. 98). In this way, an ideology such as the competitive, hierarchical, group ideology frequently identified as typical of all-male interaction is likely to affect the way in which men structure their groups, change their demeanour and learn disciplines. Men may be inclined to form hierarchical communities, act in ways that always seem competitive, and see education and work as a competition. The success with which they learn to think and act in these ways will, in turn, affect their ability to use economic, structural, physical, knowledge and demeanour processes of power.

Power is therefore a way of viewing local practices globally: an etic framework filled in by emic values. Power in this view (as a role focused on – or created in – a community-defined structure) is similar to concepts of footing and alignment (see Goffman, 1981). However, by using the framework I have outlined, we can identify the types of roles which are available and created vis-à-vis power. As a consequence, we will not be limited to analyses using broad, universal categories. Moreover, we can approach some comparability across communities by looking at the ways in which different communities deal with similar ideologies of power, and similar communities deal with different ideologies of power.

'Ideology power' in a fraternity

In the light of the framework I have outlined, I need to discuss the ideology of the fraternity in question before analysing how power works in the fraternity's discourse. The way a man presents himself within a fraternity is of ultimate importance because he becomes a member of and gains status in the fraternity by projecting the right kind of identity.

Gaining membership to a fraternity is contingent upon successfully negotiating the process of 'rush', which is not unlike courtship. In this process, current members meet prospective members (known as 'rushes') at organized social functions; they also socialize informally, for example, by talking in dormitory rooms. Prospective members gauge whether they want to be a part of the fraternity, and current members consider whether they want to invite the prospective members to join. The rushes selected by the current members are then offered an invitation for membership, and can accept or reject the 'bid', as the offer is known. Once they have accepted a bid, the rushes become probationary members, or 'pledges'. During the 'pledge period', which lasts for six to eight weeks, pledges learn the fraternity's traditions, and pledge education activities take place in unofficial secret ceremonies, which are similar to military 'boot camps'. Pledges are treated as second-class citizens, subordinating their autonomy and identities to the fraternity as an institution, and to individual older 'brothers', as members are called. Pledges 'earn respect' and the privilege to become members themselves. They also learn the fraternity's customs, traditions and oral history. During this time, a strong bond tends to form between so-called 'pledge brothers', who are members of the same 'pledge class', because of their common adversity as second-class citizens.

The pledge period culminates in initiation, a formal clandestine cere-mony where the secrets, rights and responsibilities of membership are imparted. However, the newly initiated brother – known by the acronym 'nib' – is still inexperienced in the eyes of the fraternity. He lacks know-ledge and past accomplishments in order to prove that he will function well in a fraternity office. In the social sphere, nibs normally follow the older brothers' lead, show respect to them, and defer to their judgement. But nibs still have more latitude here than in the fraternity's 'business' sphere, which will be discussed below. As a brother becomes older, he has a chance to prove himself by performing services for the fraternity. Also, simply by becoming older, he gains the respect of younger 'generations' of members.

In the fraternity I studied for over a year, which I will call Gamma Chi Phi (ΓΧΦ), almost all of the men were Caucasian. Out of fifty-seven members, one was Korean-American, and four were Arab-American. Most were of college age (17–22 years old); three alumni members were in their late twenties. By comparison, the university as a whole is 88 per cent Caucasian, 10 per cent Asian and 6 per cent African-American.

I was able to gain entry into this fraternity because, as an undergradu-ate, I was a member of the same national fraternity. I first contacted the national fraternity to describe my project, attending several meetings of the steering committee, the National Council. Once I had chosen the local chapter, I contacted the president of that chapter (whom I had met previously at the National Council meeting), and described the project to him in detail in a letter. I told him that I was interested in studying interaction among men, and that I would be observing and audio-tape-recording, as well as conducting interviews with members. He then asked the members for permission to allow me to go ahead with my research at a general meeting of the fraternity, and the members approved. I was permitted to attend any function and visit any individual member. I was also allowed to attend secret ritual ceremonies, but not to tape the ceremonial portion of the ritual activities. The names of the fraternity and all members are aliases.

At ΓΧΦ, there is an overt distinction between the formal, governing sphere of the fraternity, on the one hand, and the social sphere, on the other. However, the border between the two is fuzzy; older, office-holding members tend to associate together, and personality plays a large role in deciding who is elected into fraternity offices. Nonetheless, the ideo-logical organization is the same throughout the fraternity, and can best be described as hierarchic.[2]

The hierarchical nature of the fraternity is already evident in the stages of acquiring membership outlined above. First, because only certain men are accepted into membership, the fraternity experience begins by valuing one identity over another. In ΓΧΦ, demeanour and physical power are highly valued. If someone is rich, caring or gets good grades, they are not more likely to be offered membership. The current members value skill at playing sports[3] – so a prospective member who played baseball in high school will be highly respected because he can help the fraternity win at intramural softball. Demeanour power is, however, most important in terms of gaining membership.[4] Members told me in interviews that the main reason they joined was because they thought the fraternity was 'a good group of guys'; similarly, bids are offered because a prospective member seems like 'a good guy'.

But what is 'a good guy'? Members themselves had difficulty defining this characteristic. For them, a good guy would seem to be someone who others enjoy being with, and someone who would appear to exemplify the members' own ideology. Thus, it may be someone who tells funny stories, or who is the subject of funny stories. Because of the hierarchic, competitive ideology of the organization, a man who acts strong, competitive and quick is valued. Friendship and community is shown through what seems like competitive talk filled with insults, boasts, orders, and embarrassing jokes and stories. A 'good guy' is someone who exemplifies powerful, competitive traits in all spheres: he works hard, gets things accomplished, is seen as a leader, and is verbally skilled in the 'competitive cooperative' style through which the men build solidarity. By selecting only men with certain characteristics, the fraternity creates a hierarchy between its members and outsiders (although non-members are also ranked).

Once access to the fraternity has been gained, there is still an implicit hierarchy evident in all stages of membership. The pledges begin their fraternity experience by being treated as unknowledgeable, childlike servants, and even when the pledges become full members, they are still not valued as highly as older members. Usually, only after at least one year of membership does a man have the power to affect, through his own actions, the actions of the fraternity and its members. When attempting to influence the fraternity in this way, ability and demeanour power are highly valued, along with knowledge power. This is especially evident during elections, for example, where members evaluate candidates' work ethic, experience, personality and skills.

Thus, the main constraint that the men place on each other is to present a competitive, successful, confident identity. The fraternity ideology also values hard work, especially work that promotes the good of the group. In this way, members are taught to protect and care for each other.

Data analysis: power and identity in practice

In this section, I will explore how four men employ different discursive means in order to construct powerful identities. The excerpts I analyse come from an election meeting involving the entire fraternity membership. Ordinary meetings are held every Sunday evening in a campus classroom, but elections are held only once a year, usually in the autumn.

Because they are speaking in a meeting, the four men in question have much at stake. Initially, they must show that they have the authority to speak. But because their identities are on public display in the business sphere, the men are more constrained than usual by the competitive, hierarchic ideology of the fraternity. Through the varying employment of mitigation, mood, pronoun use and personal experience, these members orient themselves towards different processes of power. The processes they draw upon are consistent with the identities that they have constructed previously in the fraternity, but are nevertheless specific to the time of speaking.

The excerpts I analyse are taken from a discussion during elections for the office of chapter correspondent, whose job it is to communicate with the national fraternity through letters published in the fraternity's national magazine. The position traditionally goes to a younger member because it requires little experience or knowledge of how the fraternity works. After the four candidates – Kurt, Ritchie, Mullin and Ernie – give their speeches, they leave the room so that other members can discuss the candidates' strengths and weaknesses. The four members I shall focus on are: Darter, Speed, Ram and Mack.

Darter

The first speaker I consider is Darter, a newly initiated brother. He no doubt still feels deferential to those men who, until a few weeks ago, had almost total control over his life. Although he was the president of the pledge class, and is recognized as a possible future leader of the fraternity, he is not in a position to exercise demeanour or structural power because he is a nib, and does not hold a high position. In his comments, the first he has made in the elections, Darter bases his argument on his knowledge of the candidates' abilities. Two of the candidates are his pledge brothers, Ritchie and Ernie. Kim is Korean-American; Speed is an older brother.

Excerpt 1

48	DARTER:	Um *Ri:tchie* may come off like he's really like a dumb ass
49		and everything but uh
50		he's like one of the smartest people
51		I know y'know
52		I went to high school with him
53		and he was like ranked *fifth* in our class.
54		and he can he can write like rea:lly well
55	KIM:	He's A:sian man, what
56		do you expect?
57	SPEED:	(sarcastic) Is he really?
58	DARTER:	I mean he he *types* like unbelievably…quick.
59		um I just think this would be a good position for him
60		to hold because he's a really good writer,
61		I mean I've read a lot of papers of his.

Because he is young and a new brother, Darter does not normally speak in meetings. But in this comment Darter draws from his specialized knowledge – his high school friendship with Ritchie – to assert his right to speak. He begins by acknowledging the identity that Ritchie has in the fraternity (line 48).[5] Darter then contrasts this identity with the identity he remembers from high school (lines 50–4). He then states his position: 'I just think this would be a good position for him to hold.' He mitigates his statement through the use of 'I just think', which suggests his opinion is not very valuable. By using 'I think' and the conditional 'would', he frames his statement as a suggestion, rather than a fact (e.g. 'this is a good position for him'). Instead of simply making this more direct statement, he includes a dependent clause that explicity highlights his reasoning ('because he's a really good writer'), which is implicit from his statements in lines 50–4. (I show below that the older brothers do not need to provide this kind of justification.) Darter then emphasizes once again how he knows that Ritchie is a good writer. He thus explicity justifies his support for Ritchie through his knowledge of the latter's writing abilities. His power is therefore not based on his demeanour or position in the fraternity, but on knowledge, which he is careful to highlight extensively. He presents himself as holding information important to the debate, but as unsure of its worth.

Speed

The next speaker I introduce is Speed, a third-year member. Of the four men I am considering, he speaks next in the meeting. His statement is short and to the point.

Excerpt 2

```
83  MICK:   Speed.
84  SPEED:          Ri:tchie. I like Ritchie 'cause he's smart
85          and he probably writes really good too:
86          so let him do it dude.
```

Speed at first does not justify his statement. He merely states Ritchie's name. Then he notes that Ritchie is smart and (extrapolating from line 84) that Ritchie is capable of doing the job. His short statement indicates that for him the choice, based on Ritchie's ability, is simple. It is just a matter of 'letting him do it'. In addition, by first only uttering Ritchie's name, Speed implies that members should be swayed by the mere fact that he is for Ritchie.

Ram

Ram presents his powerful identity in a different way. An older brother, he has just finished a year as treasurer. He creates a fatherly, 'wise elder' identity through his comment:

Excerpt 3

```
119  RAM:   um I'd like to endorse David here, surprisingly
120         I mean the kid–
121         I don't want to see him fall into another–
122         and I'm not saying that he would
123         Kevin Fierst type thing,
124         I think we need to make him–
125         we need to strongly involve him now
126         I think he's pretty serious about it, y'know
127         and with a little guidance I mean he'll do a fine job.
```

Ram creates a powerful identity by putting himself in the role of a person with age and experience: he refers to David as 'the kid', and he shows off his knowledge of past members of the fraternity (Kevin Fierst was a member who dropped out of school because of substance abuse problems). He further highlights his position through his use of the phrase 'with a little guidance', suggesting that he is qualified to give that guidance. He also shows concern for David ('I don't want to see him fall into another...Kevin Fierst type thing'), which suggests a fatherly position. Thus, he draws on the part of the fraternity ideology that stresses 'looking out for' another brother. Finally, he also uses the device of speaking on behalf of the fraternity ('we need to strongly involve him now'), although he mitigates his statement more than Mack, in the next section, by embedding it in 'I think'.

Mack

Contrast Darter and Speed's comments with those made by Mack, a fourth-year member, who was Darter's pledge educator (in charge of the programme and activities during the pledge period). Mack affects actions through his demeanour, using little mitigation in his statements, and through the imperative mood. Mick is the president, Pencil is the graduate advisor.

Excerpt 4

184	MICK:	Mack.
185	MACK:	*Okay...*
186		This is *it...*
187		Somebody said something about =
188	PENCIL:	=Again, we need to reorganize (?).
189	MACK:	yeah somebody's–
190		we need to look at what we have left here,
191		and there are certain positions
192		that everybody fits into perfectly.
193		Ernie does *not* fit into this: (0.1)
194		I'm not sure where Ernie fits in just yet.
195	?:	historian
196	MACK:	*but* I: a:m afraid that we are going to *waste* uh
197		one of the few brains *left*. in someplace that that
198		uh historian has potentially been a
199		non-existent position. uh I think for a couple
200		semesters yahoo took some pictures,

```
201  PENCIL:  We're talking about chapter correspondent now
202  MACK:    What's that? I know
203  PENCIL:  and he can hold both positions
204  MACK:    I understand that. (0.3)
205           But he won't.
206           (0.5)
207           I see– I see Kurt– I see Kurt– I see Kurt–
208  PENCIL:  Then talk about chapter correspondent.
209           point of order.
210  ?:       we have we have four left.
211  PENCIL:  point of order.
212  MACK:    I see Kurt as chapter correspondent.
213           not Ritchie damn it.
```

Mack begins by serving notice that his word is gospel: 'This is it'. It is unmitigated and imperative. Unlike Darter, Mack does not justify his statement at all. This non-mitigation and non-justification presents a role of someone who can make a proclamation – someone with power. In line 190, he emphasizes this view by instructing the members on how to go about making a decision ('We need to look at what we have left'). He does this by using the first person plural subject without any hedges (or 'I think', as Darter does), and by using 'need' instead of 'should'. Contrast his statement with what might be termed its 'opposite': Mack might have said 'I think we should look at what's left'. By using a bald imperative, then, Mack implicitly puts himself in a role of structural power. However, Mack is not constructing a new place for himself in the fraternity, but continuing in a carefully constructed role: that of the elder, wise, behind-the-scenes manipulator. In an interview, he indicated this manipulator role was the one he seeks for himself. Although he has held few fraternity offices, he goes to other members before elections, and suggests that they run for certain positions, then makes comments in their favour during elections.

Mack was also the pledge educator for the newly initiated brothers, which may affect his comments in two ways. First, he has had a position of supreme authority over the new members until recently – he was their teacher and 'drill sergeant' – so that they perceive him as an authority within the fraternity. Second, he can claim to know the new members better than any other member (except perhaps the new members themselves). Thus, he can claim to be qualified to make these pronouncements. He can use his structural and demeanour power to influence the new members, many of whom will vote in the election, and he can employ his knowledge power to influence older brothers.

Mack also demonstrates his role by where he sits in the classroom in which the meeting is held. Older members sit on the right-hand side of the room, and Mack sits as far to the right as possible. Darter, in contrast, sits on the 'younger' left-hand side, towards the middle (the extreme left-hand side is empty). Mack's cadence is also significant. Though not evident in the transcript, he speaks with a slow, pause-filled cadence that gives the impression of thoughtfulness and wisdom, while Darter speaks very quickly.

Mack continues to use unmitigated, authority-laden devices throughout his comments. In lines 191–4, he sets up a system in which each member has his place, and Mack knows who belongs where. He presents his statements as axiomatic truths by using 'there are' without any indication that he is actually voicing a personal opinion. Had he used modality markers, such as 'may', he would be implying that members can decide the issue for themselves. Instead, he leaves no room for doubt. In line 196, he presents himself as advisor to the fraternity ('I am afraid'). In contrast, instead of using these devices to speak for the collective in a leader-like role, he might have said something like 'I think Ritchie is overqualified for this position'. It is unclear where his argument is going from line 197 forward, because he stops his sentence, and begins to discuss the historian position. It looks as if he planned to highlight his age, by discussing the past worth of the historian position in lines 198–200 ('historian has potentially been a non-existent position'). Pencil then argues with him about discussing one position at a time (lines 201–11), which prompts Mack to finish his statement. Mack ends by simply stating that 'he sees' Kurt as correspondent, again without any justification (in fact, with less justification than at the beginning of his comments). This construction, 'I see', is used by other brothers to create a similar air of authority, as though the speaker were a visionary, who speaks with the wisdom of the ages.

Thus, there is a large difference between the way in which the older brothers and a younger brother present themselves. The older brother has a position of experience and respect that he can implicitly draw upon, while the younger brother, lacking this structural and demeanour power, is explicit about his reasoning to sway votes in his direction. While both are under similar general pressures to present a 'powerful' identity, each has different resources and solves the problem in his own way.

Speed

Now contrast Mack and Ram's remarks with a later comment by Speed. After Mack speaks, other older members have taken up the discussion of finding offices for the newly initiated brothers. Speed responds to this trend, and returns to his utilitarian theme. Speed's comments are given in a hurried, shouting voice, as if he is angry.

Excerpt 5

```
245   SPEED:   All right look.
246            first of all, you guys need to realize we do not
247            ha:ve to ne– necessarily make a:ll the new
248            brothers, put them in positions right away.
249            a lot of the new brothers already have positions.
250            they can get elected next year or next semester.
251            there are some positions that are semesterly.
252            we don't have to make sure that every one of them
253            has a position. they need time to learn and grow–
254            it's better that// they're– that they're =
255   ?:       I need an assistant
256   SPEED:                                   =shut the fuck up.
257            it's better that they're–
258            that they're almost like I was with Tex.
259            I was Tex's like little bitch boy...graduate
260            affairs, and I learned a lot more there,
261            than I would if I got stuck in some leadership
262            role, so fuck 'em,
263            I don't care if any of 'em don't get a position.
264            but I'm telling you right now,
265            I think Ritchie should do it because like Kim
266            said, people are gonna read this shit,
267            Kurt might get ha:mmered and write some shitty..
268            fuckin' letter, Ernie can't write,
269            fuckin' Mullin already has a position,
270            so put Ritchie in there,
271            and stop fuckin' trying to..set everybody up in
272            a position. Christ.
273   MICK:    Alex.
274   SPEED:   I:'d like one
275            (laughter)
```

Speed is an older brother, but he has created an adversarial identity in the fraternity, resisting those in formal offices. He relies on a different presentation of power, one that sets him up in opposition to others. Even though he is a third-year member, he always sits on the 'non-powerful' left-hand side, in the back of the room, thus showing his contempt for the fraternity hierarchy. Speed's argumentative identity is evident in this speech, but he uses some of the same linguistic devices as Mack. Like

Mack, Speed uses the imperative. He begins by saying 'All right look', which is similar in tone to Mack's 'This is it'. In line 246, Speed states that 'you guys need to realize', which is similar to Mack's 'we need to look at what we have left'. Speed then shows his knowledge of the fraternity, continuing in an imperative mood, saying 'we don't have to make sure that every one of them has a position', which contrasts with Mack's 'we need to look at what we have left here'.

Speed then draws on his personal experience (as Ram did) in the fraternity for an example in lines 259–62 (notably in a low position – 'I was Tex's like little bitch boy'). This statement disparages 'leadership positions', and implicitly the organizational structure of the fraternity. Next, he uses an aggravated, bold statement to show his indifference to the brothers' aspirations in lines 262–3 ('*so fuck 'em . . .*'). Speed then again presents a utilitarian argument for voting for Ritchie by pointing out why other candidates are unqualified (lines 264–70). In line 264, he uses a pedagogic tone similar to Mack's ('I'm telling you right now'). Note that this rhetoric is consistent with his argumentative, impatient identity: he sums up each person quickly, with aggravation and profanity. Then, at the very end (line 274), he injects some self-directed humour. Throughout the elections, he has been unable to get elected, and this has become a running joke. When he says 'I'd like one', he adds to his demeanour with a joke making fun of himself. Ending with a joke is a common device used by the members in these comments; it builds de-meanour power by easing the tedium that accompanies the election meetings.

Thus Speed, while staying within the constraints of the hierarchic fraternity ideology, manages to construct an identity that appears to reject the manipulative structural power used by some of the older brothers. He accomplishes his identity by focusing on the value of com-peting against a structure of power; rebellion and independence are consistent with the fraternity's competitive ideology. He also focuses on the need to do what is best for the group by highlighting why Ritchie is best qualified for the position. Thus, Speed, Mack and Ram, while using similar linguistic devices to convince the members and present their identities, nevertheless construct very different identities. Because he is younger, Darter, on the other hand, has different constraints on the identity he presents in the meeting. He does not have a demeanour or structural power process working in his favour, so the problem presented to him – of creating an identity consistent with the fraternity ideology – is much different than the problem presented to Speed, Mack and Ram. Darter must create a means of influencing voting (an action that will affect other actions) without any prior history of being able to do so. He must also construct a role for himself that fits within the constraints of being a nib, but nevertheless convinces people to vote for his favoured candidate. Darter therefore draws on his specialized knowledge of the candidate.

It is important to notice also that Speed was genuinely impatient with the discussion at the time of his second statement, as seen by a comparison of his two utterances. In the first statement, he simply says why Ritchie is qualified for the position. In the second, however, he is arguing *against* other members – especially Mack – as much *for* Ritchie, in addition to arguing about the progress of the debate generally. This place in the discussion (he is nearly the last speaker) sets up a context in which he can position himself as the defender of ability power over structural power for its own sake. In other words, he can make clear his dislike of voting members into structural positions without any clear functional reason for doing so. This secondary argument was not possible in Speed's first comments because none of the older members had suggested considering all the new members, and what offices they should occupy. His identity construction in the second statement therefore shows the situated, sequence-dependent nature of identity.

Speed also exhibited this adversarial identity in an interview, however. The semester before the interview, Speed had been the pledge educator, but was ousted because of what he sees as his 'independence':

Excerpt 6

```
1  SCOTT:  Did you keep it ((the pledge period)) the way
2          you had it?
3  SPEED:  I tried to, man, but they wouldn't let me so:
4          I had to I had to succumb to their rules
5          th th– th– they got all pissed off at me and tried to take my
6          position away from me and all that shit,
7          man. (1.0) Bunch a dicks.
```

Speed's independence shows through in this excerpt when he says 'I had to succumb to their rules'. Speed also sees that he lost his position because he didn't follow the dominant ideology, but evaluates that ideology – or its proponents – negatively ('Bunch a dicks'). Thus, Excerpt 6 provides more evidence for an ideological clash between Speed's alleged independence, and the fraternity's expectation of sacrifice in return for structural power.

All the men discussed create powerful identities, but they each use disparate strategies in order to achieve a different kind of power. Differences can be seen in how the men orient themselves to various features of the fraternity ideology. Most appeal to what will be best for the fraternity. Darter and Speed focus on the ideology of being rewarded for ability. They both argue that Ritchie is simply the most qualified candidate, and voting for him will benefit the fraternity the most. They therefore appeal to the part of the ideology that puts the group before the individual. Ram also appeals to this value, but in another way. He argues that the fraternity will lose Kurt if they don't involve him in it. Mack, however, focuses on the fraternity's hierarchical nature; for him, some jobs are more important than others, and must be 'assigned' to more important members. Thus, he wants Ritchie to have a job other than chapter correspondent. Mack also sees his own role as that of manipulator, and uses his structural position of age to put members in the offices that he 'sees' for them. Finally, Speed fights against this focus on structural power.

The elections are very important to the members. They care deeply about the fraternity and its future. Who they elect very much affects what happens in the fraternity. In addition, the outcomes affect their own power within the fraternity and, even more important perhaps, their ability to affect the actions of others in the future.[6]

Discussion

I have thus shown how four men employ both similar and varied discursive devices in order to construct a particular kind of identity, given certain constraints on that identity. All four manage to present some kind of identity valued by the competitive, hierarchic fraternity ideology. Darter had to justify his statements overtly. Ram created a fatherly image. Mack spoke with a voice of the elder. Speed 'resisted' the dominance of structural power over ability, and the good of the fraternity and its members over trying to control every detail of the fraternity's future. While being men in a fraternity affected their language in similar ways, their individual solutions in time and space were unique. It is worth pointing out, however, that I have only had sufficient space to consider one speech activity here; in fact, the men's identities vary even more when other speech activities are analysed.

Sociolinguists often group people together based on criteria external to the community, and focus on how people of certain groups use language in a similar way. Generalizations about men and women are among the most common. But within these generalizations we find many variations. Within the fraternity community, for example, we can group older members together, because they tend to use less mitigation and justification and, more importantly, because age is one way the members group themselves. Clearly, then, it is essential, when considering the language of men, to explore how gender is mediated by age, status, and so on, in the same way that this has been necessary when analysing the speech of women. But even grouping Speed, Ram and Mack together as elder members of the fraternity ignores their very different individual presentations of self.

Meaningful generalizations are, however, still possible and necessary. We can still say that, in some general sense, many men in the United States construct powerful, competitively oriented identities. Moreover, due to the ideology of difference in US society, the motivation for men to construct these identities is of a different nature than for women, and the outcomes for 'resistance' are different for each of the two sexes. Men who construct the 'preferred' gender identity are rewarded with power, while women are not rewarded in the same sense when they construct the identity that society 'prefers' for their gender. In fact, a 'powerless' identity that many researchers have shown to be the 'preferred' identity for a North American woman could actually be seen as punishing women. Real resistance to the gender order, for instance a 'powerful female' identity or a 'powerless male' identity, may have similar consequences. But many men arguably have little motivation for such resistance. Speed, for example, appears to be resisting 'the establishment', but he is nevertheless using that 'resistance' as an alternative way of constructing a powerful, individualistic identity that is ultimately ratified by the fraternity ideology.

The way in which the fraternity men create different yet powerful identities suggests that particular roles, such as workplace and family roles, may be the specifics that make up what people idealize as 'masculinity' and 'femininity'. The men discussed here adopt elements of archetypal male roles: loyal friend, concerned father, wise elder, pragmatic individualist. In addition, two of the men identify *themselves* as having the identities they present in the election.

As Sattel (1983) points out, many men are expected to take on positions of leadership. But the direction of the indexing of men's identities and leadership is not clear; we might also say that society expects leadership positions to be held by men. Work such as Bonnie McElhinny's (1993) study of female police officers in Pittsburgh similarly highlights the importance of work and family roles in society's view of masculinity and femininity. Further research is needed in this area to learn more about such roles and their relationship to the construction of gender. In my research, I plan to return to the fraternity to test whether new members take on the same kinds of roles as older members who have left. Does Darter become a 'wise elder', a 'concerned father figure', an 'impatient individualist'? Or does he create an entirely new role, or a combination of all?

Conclusion

In this chapter, I have explored the way in which the identities of four fraternity members are constructed through interaction in an election meeting. My findings have, however, a number of implications for work on language and gender in more general terms. For example, I have shown how the four men construct their own identities, drawing upon both the same, and different, types of power processes through the language they use. Thus, although all the men manage to evoke some type of power with their language, it would be extremely difficult to draw specific conclusions on the types of linguistic structures (e.g. tag-questions, hedging etc.) used by men 'as a group' on the basis of my data since their usage is highly contextualized.

TRANSCRIPTION CONVENTIONS

Turn-taking

//	Bounds simultaneous speech.
=	Connects two utterances that were produced with noticeably less transition time between them than usual.
(number)	Silences timed in tenths of seconds.
(.)	Noticeable silence less than 0.2 second.
#	Bounds passage said very quickly.

Sound production

^	Falsetto.
TEXT	Upper-case letters indicate noticeably loud volume.
*	Indicates noticeably low volume, placed around the soft words.
text	Italics indicate emphatic delivery (volume and/or pitch).
–	Indicates that the sound that precedes it is cut off, stopped suddenly and sharply.
:	Indicates that the sound that precedes it is prolonged.
,	Indicates a slight intonational rise.
?	Indicates a sharp intonational rise.

Breathiness, laughter, comments

h	An audible outbreath.
'h	An audible inbreath.
he, ha	Laughter.
(text)	Transcript enclosed in single parentheses indicates uncertain hearing.
((comment))	Double parentheses enclose transcriber's comments.

NOTES

1   I have chosen the term 'men's identities', rather than 'masculinity', for several reasons. First, 'masculinity' is not a neutral term; it connotes a single stereo-type of male identity, for example, John Wayne and Arnold Schwarzenegger in their movie roles. However, the majority of men in Western culture do not present themselves as copies of these movie heroes (Kessler and McKenna, 1978; Segal, 1990). Some men even contradict this view of men's identities. Thus, masculinity, as I use the term, is but one possible (idealized) type of male identity. Similarly, that there is no 'natural', single identity to which men aspire is an important point; hence, I use the plural 'identities'. Men's (and women's) identities are constructed, negotiated and changing, but they are also constrained by social structures that value some types of identities over others. Furthermore, I use the term 'men' rather than 'male' or 'mascu-line' in order to highlight the fact that the identity is a social as opposed to biological construction; it is gender, not sex. 'Identity' is an intersection between a social presentation of self, and a psychological understanding of that self.
2   This hierarchic ideology is similar to Connell's characterization of hegemonic masculinity (1987, 1995).
3   Interest in sports, of course, is also connected to competition; in this case, the desire is to be the best fraternity on campus in intramural sports.
4   The fact that demeanour is of primary importance in the fraternity supports its inclusion as a type of power, and not something other than power.
5   Line numbers match those from a complete transcript.
6   Ritchie won the election.

REFERENCES

Connell, R. W. 1987: *Gender and Power*. Stanford, CA: Stanford University Press.

Connell, R. W. 1995: *Masculinities*. Cambridge: Polity.

Eckert, Penelope and McConnell-Ginet, Sally 1992: Think practically and look locally: language and gender as community-based practice. *Annual Review of Anthropology* 21, 461–90.

Foucault, Michel 1980: *Power/Knowledge: Selected Interviews and Other Writings*. New York: Pantheon Books.

Foucault, Michel 1982: The subject and power. *Critical Inquiry* 8, 777–95.

Goffman, Erving 1981: *Forms of Talk*. Philadelphia: University of Pennsylvania Press.

Hewlett, Sylvia Ann 1986: *A Lesser Life: The Myth of Women's Liberation in America*. New York: Warner Books.

Kessler, S. and McKenna, W. 1978: *Gender: an Ethnomethodological Approach*. New York: John Wiley & Sons.

McElhinny, Bonnie 1993: We all wear the blue: language, gender and police work. Unpublished Ph.D. dissertation. Stanford, CA. Stanford University.

McLemore, Cynthia 1991: The pragmatic interpretation of English intonation: sorority speech. Unpublished Ph.D. dissertation. Austin: University of Texas at Austin.

Sattel, Jack 1983: Men, inexpressiveness and power. In B. Thorne, C. Kramarae and N. Henley (eds), *Language, Gender and Society*. Cambridge, MA: Newbury House, 119–24.

Segal, L. 1990: *Slow Motion: Changing Masculinities, Changing Men*. London: Virago.

7

Violence, Rape, and Sexual Coercion: Everyday Love in a South African Township

Katharine Wood and Rachel Jewkes

In the past decade, sexuality has become an important area of research and development intervention, in response to concerns about reproductive health, notably the spread of HIV/AIDS, and concerns about fertility control and global population growth (Ulin 1992). The predominant focus has been on educating women, through sexual health programmes, to use contraception, and particularly condoms, as ways of controlling their fertility and protecting reproductive health (Dixon-Mueller 1993). However, health promoters frequently discover that although they can generate high levels of awareness and concern among women about contraception and sexually transmitted diseases, including HIV/AIDS, they are much less successful in getting women to change their sexual practices.

In this chapter we present findings of anthropological research in an African township in Cape Town among pregnant teenagers. Although the original scope of inquiry of the study concentrated on contraceptive use, bodily reproductive knowledge, and pregnancy, the emergence of violence as a central issue in informants' narratives led us to focus more on sexual dynamics within adolescent relationships.[1]

All but one of the informants interviewed described assault as a regular feature of their sexual relationships. We discuss the implications of these findings for promoting healthy sexuality. All too frequently, health promotion interventions fail to acknowledge sexual encounters as sites in which unequal power relations between women and men are expressed. It is these power relations which determine women's ability – or inability – to protect themselves against sexually transmitted disease, pregnancy and unwelcome sexual acts. In the context of unequal power, it is invariably men who determine the timing of sexual intercourse and its nature, including whether a woman should try to conceive, and whether or not condoms will be used.

Power relations between men and women take multiple forms, but in South Africa they are commonly manifested as and imposed through sexual violence and assault. An estimated 1.3 million rapes take place each year (*The Times*, 1997). This background of violence as a part of everyday life worsens the problems faced by women in negotiating about sexual activities, as possibilities of resistance are more limited, and the consequences of trying to resist are potentially very serious.

Male control over sexuality

Among the informants interviewed, it was usual for male partners to define the conditions and timing of sex. At the outset of the relationship, the men encouraged their partners to understand teenage love affairs as necessarily involving penetrative intercourse: as one adolescent woman explained, 'he told me that if I accept him as a lover we have to engage in sexual intercourse, and do the things adults do.' If girls accepted male requests to establish a liaison, the agreement 'to love' here, as in other parts of South Africa where we have undertaken research, was equated specifically with having penetrative intercourse and being available sexually. This equation appeared to derive from the men, who were reported to have explained that sex was the 'purpose' of love and that people 'in love' must have sex 'as often as possible'. Relationships were often contractual in nature, with the girl being expected to have penetrative sex when the man wanted it in exchange for presents of money, clothes, school fees, and food.

In most cases, the young women reported that men used violent strategies from the start of the relationship, forcefully initiating partners who often had no awareness about what the sex act involved: 'he forced me to sleep with him in his home, he beat me, made me take off my clothes, then made me lie on the bed and forced himself on top of me. It was very painful.' Many girls reported that they attempted resistance, but had felt forced to submit to the demands when assault was threatened or carried out: 'he told me that if I didn't want to do it, he would force me to. He beat me up and forced my underwear down.' These findings are in line with other recent research in South Africa, which asked girls about the circumstances of first intercourse. This found that 30 per cent reported that they were 'forced' to have sex the first time (Richter 1996, Buga 1996, Jewkes 1997).

Repeatedly, the language of the girls' narratives was of compulsion: 'he made me', 'he just pushed me and overcame me', 'he forced himself onto me', 'he did as he wanted with me', 'what could I do?' Our informants stated that in the absence of sexual knowledge on their part (which could potentially have been provided by female peers but was not), their ignorance was reinforced by the male partners who reportedly refused to explain what was about to occur. For example, one girl had asked her partner what he would do, and had received no answer except 'you'll see'. One teenager who was 11 years old when she first had sex described how, after the event, 'I met a friend of mine who told me to stop crying, and promise not to tell my mother or anyone else, she told me that all the girls my age to do it, that I should go home, clean myself up and keep quiet about what happened.'

Men continued using physical assault to enforce the contract, beating their partners if they refused to have sex, with belts, sticks, and shoes, often until visibly injured: as one teenager said, 'they don't care, they'll hit you anywhere, face and all. You'd think they would at least avoid that, because your parents will see the bruises and the injuries, but they don't care.' Physical assault was so commonplace that women stated that many of their female peers saw it as an expression of love: some of the informants used phrases such as 'he forced me to love him', and 'I fell in love with him because he beat me up', which expressed this contradiction. In some cases, violence was said to be the main reason why the girl continued to have sex; in the words of one informant, 'I continue because he beats me up so badly that I regret I said no in the first place.'

The extent of assault in adolescent relationships has been demonstrated in other research; in a study of 600 pregnant and non-pregnant teenage women in Cape Town, 60 per cent said that they had been beaten by the male partner (Jewkes 1997). The pregnant group, on average, reported having been beaten more than ten times during their average of two years of sexual activity (Jewkes 1997).

Men also controlled the relationships in other ways. Several girls described how their partners had torn up their clinic contraceptive cards in anger that they were using contraceptives; thus for some, even protection against pregnancy in the form of 'invisible' hormonal methods appeared to be non-negotiable.

Informants reported being beaten not only when they tried to refuse to have sex, but also when they were seen talking to another man on the street, when they informed the men that they wished to terminate the relationship, and when they were suspected of sexual infidelity. On this last point, it was normal for men to sustain double standards, taking multiple sex partners for themselves, while disallowing their regular girlfriend from even speaking to other men. Female refusal to submit to sexual demands was interpreted by men as a sign that girls had other sexual partners and were 'worn out'. Some informants reported control over them being enacted and reinforced by brutal means; gang-rape of adolescent girls by the man's friends was reported to happen 'often' in the community, as a way of 'punishing' them for actual or suspected infidelity (a practice which has been widely reported anecdotally elsewhere in South Africa).

Awareness of unequal power

Since violence was perceived to be very common among married and unmarried people alike (and is very likely to have been witnessed in the home context), it was accepted as an inevitable part of relationships. The South African teenagers interviewed were generally aware of the power inequalities and double standards operating within constructions of love and sex, but resistance was complex in the extreme because of male violence, and peer pressure. As one girl explained, 'as a woman you have no rights, you must keep quiet and do as the man wants.'

In Jewkes' study, of the 60 per cent of teenagers who had been beaten, only 22 per cent of pregnant teenagers and 28 per cent of the non-pregnant control group said that they had in the past left a boyfriend because of assault (Jewkes 1997).

Interactive models of sexuality

The degree to which women are able to control various aspects of their sexual lives is clearly a critical question for health promotion. Our research was a fairly small and exploratory study, yet it underlines the need for issues of gender power to be considered in the design and impact assessment of HIV/AIDS and reproductive health interventions.

To date, many of these programmes have promoted the use of the male condom, based on a 'knowledge leads to action' model. The condom is seen as a simple protective device to be introduced into the sexual act at the 'right' moment. This implies that the individual is an independent person who can make decisions regardless of the opinions and behaviour of others, and of the wider social context (Campbell 1995). This ignores the realities of power dynamics, not least of which are the gender inequities which structure heterosexual relations. The fact that the degree of empowerment for women in their sexual lives varies widely according to context points to the need for specific, detailed, situational analysis as part of the development of locally useful interventions. It is strikingly evident from our research, and confirmed by other South African research, that women commonly find themselves wholly unable to negotiate the timing of sex, and the conditions under which it occurs. Many of them feel powerless even to protect themselves against pregnancy. Condom use is far from being a possibility in their sexual lives.

The implications for health promotion are clear: an understanding of difference derived from local analysis, and reinforced by a comparative perspective, is essential for interventions to be useful. As researchers from the AIDS and Reproductive Health Network in Brazil have observed: 'strategies of health promotion for women in especially acute situations of sexual oppression or violence cannot be the same as for women whose cultural or social setting offers them more effective means for the negotiation of sexual and reproductive practices' (1995, 7).

The questions which need to be considered in designing appropriate interventions include:

- How, why and when are decisions made by individuals to have sex, and to engage in specific sexual practices?
- How are gender inequities played out and resisted in the community? For example, how far are practices such as condom use and female sexual refusal negotiable and negotiated between individuals in different settings?
- How is individual control asserted when there is conflict?

Violence: an issue for men

Although gender violence is recognised internationally to be a common feature of women's daily experiences (Beijing Platform of Action 1995), most of the literature discussing health and sexuality completely fails to recognise the implications of violent domestic contexts.

In this South African setting, in which extreme disempowerment of women is portrayed, it is apparent that for development interventions promoting healthy sexuality to focus only on women would be wholly inadequate. The focus should be widened to consider the issue of gender violence, and male behaviour. Male violence against women is a major problem across the world, while South Africa is considered to have one of the highest rates of a country not at war. Although the definition of abuse varies across societies, cross-cultural research does indicate that 'virtually wherever the issues have been researched, a massive, under-recognised burden has been unveiled' (Heise 1994: 1176). Four recent survey-based studies in sub-Saharan Africa, for example, demonstrate that 46 per cent of Ugandan women and 60 per cent of Tanzanian women reported being regularly physically abused; in Kenya and Zambia the figures were 42 per cent and 40 per cent (Heise 1994).

There is a danger of non-governmental organisations (NGOs) neglecting work with men. In fairness, in view of the mismatch between the scale of the problem of domestic violence and the scant resources available for work to promote its eradication, it is not entirely surprising that NGOs working in the field in South Africa have predominantly concentrated on providing crisis support for female victims though counselling, refuges, or help with court interdicts. Many organisations do not work with men either as perpetrators or as victims of rape, because they prefer to allocate their scarce resources to women. However, there is a risk that in so doing, they may be unwittingly promoting the idea that violence is a 'women's issue', and suggesting, even though most NGO workers recognise this to be false, that if a woman can be removed from one violent context, with the necessary empowerment, she will be able to prevent abuse of her body in future.

Our research suggests that there is a need for NGOs to move beyond crisis management to reducing the prevalence of violence by engaging with men as perpetrators or potential perpetrators and recognising the contexts of abuse within sexual partnerships. Not only should gender violence be made a focus of sexuality intervention programmes, but attention should be shifted towards changing the attitudes and practices of men.

Incorporating men into gender programmes

Work on gender issues, both research- and intervention-oriented, has long been equated with work with women, without adequate recognition of the relational and contextual aspects of their lives. Men have been largely ignored. The main consequence of this omission in the work of NGOs and the health services has been a set of assumptions about women's ability to control their bodies and thereby achieve and sustain sexual health: assumptions which have significantly limited the impact of interventions.

Within the South African context we can more confidently identify the (currently neglected) potential of sexuality interventions which could be aimed at men, rather than give examples of current good practice, partly due to our own limited experience in the NGO arena. Our research has provided pointers which we hope will be further developed by both the education sector, and NGOs working with young people. There is clearly a need to work with pre-adolescent children; in terms of developing alternative patterns of interpersonal interaction and reducing levels of violence in the country as a whole, this age group is crucial.

Basic needs for information must be met, including in the areas of reproductive biology, contraception, sexually transmitted diseases including HIV/AIDS, and condom use. Our research has found that adolescents of both sexes lack this information, or alternatively have information which is inaccurate or unbalanced.

Adolescents also need education on the many meanings of love and sexual relationships. Our research has shown that adolescent girls want to be able to have relationships which do not involve sexual intercourse, but are unable to do so because this is the dominant model of male–female interaction. One of the factors associated with violence in adolescent relationships, which affects both sexes, is poor communication skills and a lack of specific vocabulary with which to discuss sexual experience and desires. These skills also need to be developed at an early age, and are vital if verbal communication is to replace physical violence in relationships.

Interventions based on participatory techniques such as workshops, theatre, and games, can enable communities to develop awareness and skills in this area. One example of a training manual for community workshops on HIV/AIDS and communication and relationship skills which uses participatory methods is Alice Welbourne's programme Stepping Stones (1995) which has been used successfully in sub-Saharan Africa in particular.

Another example of a participatory intervention used by community workers in developed countries is Man's World, a small-group game for young men, which focuses on issues of masculinity and sexism and was developed by the B-Team (Resources for Boyswork) in Britain (1993). Development interventions like this which focus on building self-esteem among children of both sexes are valuable, since research repeatedly reveals an association between low self-esteem among men, and physical abuse of women. Similarly, developing attitudes of respect for personal autonomy, particularly of women, is essential.

The challenge is to put these ideas into practice. There is no doubt that if sexual health programmes are to become more effective in bringing about real change, there is an urgent need for them to take the lead from recent research on sexuality and domestic violence, and incorporate men fully into their focus. Unless the spotlight shifts towards men, health promotion initiatives in the field of sexual health will continue to be inadequate.

NOTE

1   In-depth semi-structured interviews were conducted in Xhosa with 24 pregnant adolescent women, recruited and interviewed in the township Midwife Obstetric Unit to which they had come for antenatal care. The age range was 14 to 18, with an average age of 16.4 years, and most had male partners about five years older.

REFERENCES

AIDS and Reproductive Health Network (Brazil) (1995) 'Gender, sexuality and health: building a new agenda for sexuality research in response to AIDS and reproductive health' (Unpublished).

B-team (Resources for Boyswork) (1993) *Man's World*, London: Resources for Boyswork.

Buga G, Amoko D, Ncayiyana D (1996) 'Sexual behaviour, contraceptive practice and reproductive health among schooled adolescents in rural Transkei', *South African Medical Journal* 86(5): 523–527.

Campbell C (1995) 'Male gender roles and sexuality; implications for women's AIDS risk and prevention', *Social Science and Medicine* 41 (2): 197–210.

Dixon-Mueller R. (1993) 'The sexuality connection in reproductive health', *Studies in Family Planning* 24 (5).

Heise L, Raikes A, Watts C, Zwi A (1994) 'Violence against women a neglected public health issue in less developed countries', *Social Science and Medicine* 39 (9): 1165–1179.

Jewkes R, Maforah F, Vundule C (1997) 'A case-control study of factors associated with teenage pregnancy in peri-urban Cape Town' (Data being analysed).

Richter L (1996) 'A survey of reproductive health issues among urban Black youth in South Africa'. Final grant report for Society for Family Health.

The Times, 5 April 1997, London, UK.

Ulin P (1992) 'African women and AIDS: negotiating behavioural change', *Social Science and Medicine* 34 (1).

UNICEF (1995) *Beijing 1995 Platform for Action Report*.

Welbourne A (1995) *Stepping Stones: a training package on HIV/AIDS, communication and relationship skills*, London: Actionaid.

Wood K, Jewkes R, Maforah F (1995) *Sex, violence and constructions of love: adolescent relationships in a Cape Town township*, Medical Research Council technical report.

PART III
Masculinities in the Public Domain

The public sphere has traditionally been held to be that place where males 'become men', and, thus, have their manliness and masculinity validated. Although the public and private can be recognized as a 'false dualism', the myths, discourses, and ideologies that permeate them are powerful, compelling and persistent. In recognizing this, part III explores some key arenas which inform and constitute the public world of men: organization and management; media imagery; education; and sport.

The section opens with David Collinson and Jeff Hearn's comprehensive and detailed examination of masculinities, work, organization and management. The chapter begins by drawing attention to the way in which men and masculinity are taken as given in management literature, yet are rarely the focus of critical examination. It is as if notions of 'leadership', 'organizational control' and 'management' are so imbued with dominant ideas around maleness, that men as gendered subjects and as a gender category are rendered both omnipresent and invisible. In 'Naming Men as Men' in organizations and management, Collinson and Hearn expose the **silence surrounding men in management** which has helped serve the processes of hegemonic masculinity across the public and private spheres. In illuminating a powerful part of the gendered public domain, Collinson and Hearn's work makes a significant contribution to understanding how men's power is performed, protected and privileged in management and organizational life. Their study goes on to examine multiple masculinities in contemporary organizations, in the process highlighting unities, differences, discontinuities, opportunities and tensions within the gender class of men.

'Masculinity and Machismo in Hollywood's War Films' is the title of Ralph Donald's exploration of masculine hegemony in a most influential part of the public domain – the media. Donald argues that one source of heroic idealism upon which masculine hegemony depends in order to perpetuate its ideological power lies in images of men in war films. **Television and cinema are media through which young boys find male heroes,** and many boys, Donald claims, spend more time with these images than with their own fathers. He discusses the portrayal of warriors, the initiation rituals that mark war as an exclusive male preserve, the importance of excluding women, of winning, and of suppressing emotions, especially fear. The image of the six-gun-toting cowboy in Westerns is easily transferred to the portrayal of soldiers in war movies, providing dramatic portrayals of virile men performing courageous deeds, protecting helpless victims from savage aggressors. In these movies, war is often depicted as an initiation into manhood, where recruits learn they must earn manhood by achieving success. Some films, including the classic Howard Hawks movies, emphasize the importance of men excluding women in order to perform their jobs efficiently, and of relegating them to supportive roles – as mothers, chattels to acquire, and whores. In these films, men display quiet dignity, are depicted as emotionless but capable of stoically enduring privations and pain, and able to tolerate stress. Finally, many of these images reinforce the importance of 'winning' which then becomes a central theme in constructing a boy's self-image over much of his life.

The educational setting is increasingly recognized as a key public arena wherein masculinities are performed, power displays enacted, adolescent identities constructed, and cultural capital developed or not. In 'Masculinity, School, and Self in Sweden and the Netherlands', Alan Segal reveals how schools communicate dominant beliefs around masculinity and femininity, and in so doing subject gay and lesbian adolescents to popularist codes and **normalizing discourses of gender and sexuality.** Segal interviews boys and girls in Swedish and Netherlands schools and demonstrates how these two societies both uphold and transgress their reputations as sexually liberated and egalitarian. Although these are two liberal societies that purport to be open and accepting of a variety of gender forms, the author explores the shifting and complex identities that these boys and girls have to negotiate as they attempt to account for their sexual feelings and reconcile them with the gender categories that their respective societies legitimate. Segal demonstrates that these students often struggle as they experiment with a range of identity discourses and discover the advantages and social costs of each. Some pupils alternate between identifying as gay for a certain period, only to experience feelings of disgust as they discover the social costs of such a label and the resources such identity includes and excludes. In seeking to avoid rejection, being one thing or another is often a choice undertaken for the sake of clarity and social acceptance, rather than as an accurate rendering of one's sexual interest in either or both sexes.

Issues of male power, resistance and identity in the public domain are further developed by Richard Majors, whose piece 'Cool Pose: Black Masculinity and Sports' is already a classic in the sociology of masculinity. Within a socio-economic system that restricts economic and political power to minorities, black males often utilize sports as a means of masculine self-expression. 'Cool pose' is an expressive lifestyle behaviour that black male athletes often employ as a response to racist institutions that limit conventional opportunities for self-expression. Black men find themselves in a double bind. As men they are expected to conform to definitions of masculinity embodied in roles that require them to be the breadwinner, to be successful, to be strong and powerful. Yet as minorities, they often live in socio-economic conditions that exclude them from access to those very resources that constitute 'successful masculinity'. This leaves some black males obsessed with proving their manliness. If they cannot utilize the resources of institutional settings, they rely on more interpersonal spheres of life to engage in masculine display. One strategy, according to Majors, is the adoption of **'cool pose', an expressive behaviour intended to display strength, pride, and potency** and which serves as an identity survival strategy for black males.

8

Naming Men as Men: Implications for Work, Organization and Management

David Collinson and Jeff Hearn

Men neglecting men in organizations

A critical analysis of men and masculinities is particularly important in the study of work, organizations and management. Yet an examination of the available literature reveals a recurring paradox. The categories of men and masculinity are frequently central to analyses, yet they remain taken for granted, hidden and unexamined. Men are both talked about and ignored, rendered simultaneously explicit and implicit. They are frequently at the centre of discourse but they are rarely the focus of interrogation. So texts on organizations have appeared which fail to examine masculinity despite explicitly citing men in their title, for example, *Men who Manage* (Dalton 1959), *Organization Man* (Whyte 1956), *Men at the Top* (Elliott 1960) and *Man on the Assembly Line* (Walker and Guest 1952). Alternatively, some writers in industrial relations, industrial sociology and organizational behaviour have talked about 'managers', 'workers', 'shop stewards', 'the working class' and implicitly treated these categories as interchangeable with men (see Collinson 1992; Hearn 1992b). Hence many scholars have seemed extraordinarily unaware of the men in organizations about whom they write.

The study of management is a case in point. Management theory throughout the twentieth century has tended to neglect gender issues (e.g. Lawrence and Lorsch 1967; Mintzberg 1973, 1975, 1983, 1989; Reed 1989). This is to be seen in developments from scientific management to human relations theories, organizational psychology and motivation theories, systems and contingency theory, theories of job design and job enrichment, and so on (Calás et al. 1991). The literature on management tends to treat the managerial function in a peculiarly neutered, asexual way. It has therefore failed to acknowledge that historically and in different societies, leaders generally and managers more specifically have been predominantly men (Hearn and Parkin 1988; Parkin and Hearn 1994). Managerial texts are usually written for or about the 'male manager' even where reference is made to the 'changing aspirations of women' (Rothwell 1983). Thus the function is still often seen to be synonymous with men.

This neglect of gender and implicit conflation of men and masculinity with management and authority is illustrated by the study of leadership in organizations. Within this burgeoning literature a persistent and pervasive domain assumption has been that leadership is synonymous with men and that gender therefore is not an issue worthy of exploration (Hearn and Parkin 1988; Parkin and Hearn, 1994). This is the case in Weber's (1968) work on ideal-typical forms of authority, in Taylor's (1947) 'scientific' approach to management, and in conventional organizational psychology where the major contribution to the prescriptive study of leadership has emerged (e.g. Fiedler 1967; Vroom and Yetton 1973). The same historical neglect of gender in the study of leadership persists in the psychological literature today. For example, a recent influential American review of the literature on 'power and leadership in organizations' (Hollander and Offerman 1990) devotes only two sentences to women in organizations and totally neglects issues of masculinity in relation to power and leadership. Its prescriptions for future research equally ignore gender.

The theme of charismatic leadership has also been a primary influence on the emergence in the 1980s of a highly prescriptive managerial discourse on corporate culture. Psychologists, such as Schein (1985), and management consultants, such as Peters and Waterman (1982), have emphasized corporate leaders' responsibility for 'managing meaning' (Morgan 1986) and establishing strong organizational cultures (Deal and Kennedy 1982). Writers such as Peters and Austin (1985) have presented long taxonomies of prescriptions on how to be a visionary leader who, above all else, can and must manage and manipulate organizational culture. Yet charismatic leadership styles and the establishment of strong corporate cultures often draw upon the gendered imagery of the organization as a family (e.g. Woolsey-Biggart 1989). Such familial imagery is a condition and consequence of management's position as patriarchal 'heads' of the family whose authority is expressed in paternalistic discourses. The inherent masculinity of this discourse is rarely addressed in the literature. Similarly, the way in which particular workplace cultures appeal to highly masculine values of individualism, aggression, competition, sport and drinking is often neglected even by more critical studies of corporate culture (e.g. Alvesson 1988).

Naming men

Feminist studies have been particularly valuable in revealing the way that 'most organizations are saturated with masculine values' (Burton 1991, p. 3). Kanter (1977) has explored the deep-seated masculine cultures of the managerial function and its dependence on the dual support of the 'office wife' and wife at home. Pringle (1989) more recently examined the gendered dynamics of the power relations between men managers and women secretaries. Cockburn (1983) has unpacked the highly masculine culture of shopfloor life in the printing industry as well as the ways that men in various industrial sectors and hierarchical levels resist equal opportunity initiatives (Cockburn 1991). Similarly, Walby (1986) has outlined the labour market strategies of male-dominated trade unions designed to exclude or segregate women job-seekers.

These ethnographic studies have highlighted the embeddedness of masculine values and assumptions in the structure, culture and practices of organization. In critically analysing the centrality of the masculine model of lifetime, full-time, continuous employment and of the family breadwinner for the organization of paid work, these studies have emphasized the importance of the gendered nature of power relations in contemporary organizations. Relatedly, they have revealed the importance of paid work as a central source of masculine identity, status and indeed power. For many men, employment provides the interrelated economic resources and symbolic benefits of wages/salaries, skills and experience, career progress and positions of power, authority and high discretion. Typically, it seems men's gender identities are constructed, compared and evaluated by self and others according to a whole variety of criteria indicating personal 'success' in the workplace. In turn, these measures of success in paid work come to reflect back on men's sense of masculine identity. The foregoing studies also provide extensive and detailed evidence of the ways that these organizational resources of power and status are less accessible to women employees.

In developing these critical studies on men, that focus in particular upon gendered power relations, a number of concepts have been prominent. First and most obviously, there is the concept of 'men'. The distinction of sex from gender has been problematized so that the notion of biological 'male' is no longer the basis of masculine gender. Men are now seen as a social category, whether this applies to particular men, all men, or the very possibility of this category in the first place. Second, the concept of 'masculinity' may be thought of as representing the discourses and practices which indicate that someone is a man, a member of the category of men. Third, and more recently, the concept of multiple masculinities has been developed (Carrigan, Connell and Lee 1985; Brittan 1989) to refer to the diversity of forms of masculinity across time and space. In particular it has been elaborated to convey the way in which specific forms of masculinity are constructed and persist in relation *both* to femininity and to other forms of masculinity. Accordingly, different forms of masculinity are embedded in relations of power, and particular forms may be characterized as 'hegemonic' or 'subordinate' in relation to each other. In turn, these masculinities are not fixed, but continually shifting. They have been shown to be culturally and historically contingent. Reflecting and reinforcing this growing interest in gendered power relations, and in the naming of men as men, has been an increasing recognition of the centrality of patriarchy, sexuality and subjectivity for organizational analysis. Here again, analyses have paralleled this focus on multiplicity and diversity.

A number of feminist and pro-feminist critiques in the late 1970s (e.g. Rowbotham 1979; Atkinson 1979), suggested that the concept of 'patriarchy' was too monolithic, ahistorical, biologically overdetermined, and dismissive of women's resistance and agency. In the light of this, greater attention has been given first to the historicizing and periodizing of 'patriarchy', and second, to the presence of multiple arenas, sites and structures of patriarchy. Walby (1986, 1990) has specified the following sets of patriarchal structures: capitalist work, the family, the state, violence, sexuality, and culture (also see Hearn, 1987, 1992b). Both the historicized and diversified approaches to patriarchy highlight the place of organizations within different historical societal forms and social arenas of patriarchy. The significance of public patriarchy, for example, lies partly in the fact that organization became the prime social unit of men's domination. Indeed, organizations can be seen as mini-patriarchies in the sense that they structure in particularly gendered ways the formation and reproduction of social relations; the growth and development of corporate hierarchies, policies, processes and practices; and the organizational construction of 'persons' (Hearn 1992b).

A similar focus on multiplicity and diversity has also developed in the analysis of sexuality(ies) which in turn has come to be seen as a central feature of men's domination of organizations. This growth of interest comes not only from feminist and gay theory and practice but also from post-structuralist theory and psychoanalytic work. Throughout recent critical studies of sexualities there has been a continuing concern not only with the dominance of men's heterosexuality, and more specifically male (hetero) sexual narratives, but also with the co-existence of homo-sociality and even homosexual/gay subtexts. This latter theme is especially important in cultural studies and approaches to social phenomena informed by cultural perspectives (e.g. Wood 1987). In parallel with these debates has been a further concern with the interrelation of men's sexuality, violence and sexual violence. This is clearest in the enactment of pornography and other sexual violence, but it also applies in the more general analysis of the form of dominant sexuality of men (e.g. Buchbinder 1987).

These debates on men's sexualities have a direct relevance for the understanding of gendered power in organizations. They raise a large number of questions beyond the important recognition of sexual harassment as a form of sexual violence in the workplace. In particular, organizations provide significant social *contexts* and *resources* through which instances of men's sexualities can be enacted (Hearn 1985; Collinson and Collinson 1989). Within these contexts, resources and instances, there are recurring tensions between the domination of heterosexuality and homosociality/homosexuality and between asexuality and sexualization/ the eroticization of dominance and hierarchy.

In the examination of the way that gendered power relations in organizations are reproduced, subjectivity has become a central concern. This increasing focus on subjectivity has also reflected and reinforced a growing interest in multiplicity and diversity. For example, Henriques et al. (1984) have critiqued the unitary and rational subject found in much social science. They conceptualize subjectivity as embedded in prevailing power relations, discourses and practices and as a specific, historical product that is ambiguous, fragmentary, discontinuous, multiple, sometimes fundamentally non-rational and frequently contradictory. This approach is particularly relevant to the analysis of gendered power, men and masculinities, not just in the sense of acknowledging subjectivity variation, for example in the different 'types' of men and masculinities (or women and femininities), but also in the way that these are perceived and experienced and may shift over time and place.

Increasingly research highlights the way that men in organizations often seem preoccupied with the creation and maintenance of various masculine identities and with the expression of gendered power and status in the workplace (Willis 1977; Knights 1990; Collinson 1992). Men's search to construct these identities often draws upon a whole variety of organizational resources, discourses and practices. This 'identity work' (Thompson and McHugh 1990) also appears to be an on-going, never-ending project which is frequently characterized by ambiguity, tension and uncertainty (Brittan 1989). Masculine identities constantly have to be constructed, negotiated and reconstructed in routine social interaction, both in the workplace and elsewhere. These identities also have to be achieved (Kerfoot and Knights 1993). Various studies have highlighted the fragility and precariousness underpinning and surrounding masculine identities that superficially appear strong, authoritative and self-assured. Masculine identities have been shown to be threatened by social and economic forces such as new technology (Cockburn 1983; Baron 1992); unemployment (Walter 1979), feminism/equal opportunity initiatives (Cockburn 1991) and intensified class and status divisions within organizational hierarchies (Sennett and Cobb 1977).

Furthermore, it is not simply these visible events, changes and processes that seem to threaten masculine identities. Attempts by men to secure and hold on to clearly defined and coherent identities may in themselves further reinforce this sense of threat. For, as critical writers on subjectivity have emphasized (Knights 1990; Willmott 1990; Collinson 1992), an irreducible ambiguity characterizes the process by which *all* social identities are constructed and reproduced. The dual experience of 'self' and 'other' as both subject and object is a central and highly ambiguous feature of human subjectivity which is reinforced by the multiple nature of identities (Kondo 1990). In so far as attempts to construct and sustain particular identities frequently seem to be intended to deny this ambiguity and uncertainty, they are likely to be unsuccessful. Given the socially constructed, multiple and shifting character of identities, these attempts may reinforce the very uncertainty and ambiguity they are intended to overcome. However, as the following section elaborates, this emphasis on difference and 'multiple masculinities' in organizations does carry with it a number of inter-related uncertainties and unresolved difficulties which need to be acknowledged.

Multiple masculinities

Although the focus upon multiplicity and diversity has made a valuable contribution to the analysis of men and masculinities in contemporary organizations, it also raises significant analytical problems. The following discussion outlines four main areas of conceptual difficulty that, we believe, need to be examined.

(i) Exclusion

First and foremost, there is the danger of the emphasis upon difference and pluralized masculinities becoming a new, and perhaps more sophisticated means of forgetting women, of losing women from analysis and politics. We must guard against the possibility of these critical studies being sidetracked by a narcissistic preoccupation with talk exclusively about men. The analysis of men and masculinities is likely to be enhanced, we contend, when the relation to women and femininity is acknowledged. This exclusionary tendency is a serious difficulty with the 'men's studies' approach advocated by Bly (1990) for example. A further problematic tendency here is for men to redefine themselves exclusively as *victims* of historical processes, the likely outcome of which is that women are either blamed for men's problems or are rendered invisible and are excluded as participants in and subjects of discourse.

(ii) Differences

Second, a focus on difference can collapse into a descriptive preoccupation with 'types' and objectified categories of men which generates the response 'so what?'. A more sophisticated critique might be that typologies themselves constitute a masculine and/or managerial preoccupation with the control of the world and the meanings in it; a totalizing exercise intended to achieve a kind of closure. Categorization in itself fails to address either men's lived social experience as men, or the fluidity, shifting and changing character of all social relations, identities and practices (Kondo 1990). Static categorization also has difficulty in acknowledging the sheer complexity of the very large number of possible permutations and interrelations of types of men in organizations. The numerical combinations are themselves complicated by the diversity of ways in which interrelation can exist and develop.

An important contribution in this regard has been made by Connell (1985, 1987) who criticizes several strands of feminism for relying upon the two absolute and undifferentiated categories of 'women' and 'men'. 'Categorical theory' (1987, p. 54), as he terms it, neglects the processes and practices by which these categories are constituted. To avoid this problem, we suggest that analyses need to reflect and explore the dynamic, shifting and often contradictory social relations and identities through which men's differences, and their perception of differences, are reproduced and transformed in organizational practices and power asymmeteries. The foregoing analysis of 'identity work' in organizations suggests that men appear to attempt to define themselves and their difference, status and power through the subjective processes of identifying with some men (e.g. with a specified group or with individuals) while simultaneously differentiating themselves from others (e.g. from other men and from women). These processes of identification and differentiation frequently seem to characterize men's routine relations, discourses and practices.

On the shopfloors of male-dominated workplaces, for example, the informal inter-actions between men manual workers are frequently highly aggressive and derogatory, humorous yet insulting, playful yet degrading (Hearn 1985; Collinson 1992). New members are teased and tested to see whether they are 'man enough' to take the insults couched in the humour of 'piss taking'. Those who display a willingness to 'give it and take it' are accepted into the masculine sub-culture, membership of which in turn is then believed to differentiate individuals from other groups such as white-collar employees and managers 'who never have a laugh and a joke' (Collinson 1988).

Hence men manual workers frequently seek to maintain masculine identities and their sense of difference through these simultaneous discourses and practices of identification and differentiation within identity-threatening organizational conditions of persistent job insecurity, low status and tightly controlled jobs. Patriarchal shopfloor discourses and practices, including those related to men's sexuality, appear to be fundamentally shaped by these subjective concerns with defining 'self' and 'other'; i.e. the creation and protection of masculine working class identity in organizational conditions of its erosion. These concerns, however, are not only frequently contradictory, but can also shift and change over time and space (Kondo 1990). Processes of identification and differentiation underpinning identities and subjectivities are by no means static or unambiguous, but are liable to shift, sometimes in unforeseen and contradictory ways. However, identity work and the preoccupation with difference is by no means the exclusive concern of men. This raises questions regarding the meaning of masculinity to which we now turn.

(iii) Meaning

The concept of masculinities remains somewhat vague and imprecise, lacking in definition (indeed this is the case in its singular as well as pluralized form). Does it refer to behaviours, identities, relationships, experiences, appearances, discourses or practices? If it includes all of these, precisely how does it do so? Are masculinities irreducibly related to men or are they discourses in which women can also invest? While a greater understanding of these processes has been developed, the meaning of masculinity/masculinities still remains unclear. In particular, many studies in this area have emphasized the discursive, ideological and symbolic aspects of masculinity thereby rejecting essentialist or deterministic perspectives. A minority have also focused upon the material and economic dimensions of men's power and identity in organizations. Suffice it to say here, that for us any adequate account would examine *both* the material and discursive features of particular masculinities and their interrelationship in specific practices (Collinson 1992; Hearn 1992b).

It could be argued, however, that women in organizations behave in similar ways to men, invest in equivalent discourses and engage in analogous strategies of power and identity. On all-female shopfloors, for example, research suggests that women often swear and participate in aggressive and sexualized forms of behaviour (Pollert 1981; Cavendish 1982; Westwood 1984). Such practices do indeed display similarities with those of men in the all-male shopfloor settings mentioned earlier. Since issues of gender and/or masculinities are by no means exhaustive of the social relations and practices in which they are embedded (Kerfoot and Knights 1993), it seems reasonable to assume that certain commonalities may exist between men's and women's experience of and response to subordination, for example in relation to class and control. This in turn raises the question 'what is specifically masculine about particular masculinities?'.

(iv) Power

The emphasis upon multiple masculinities raises important questions regarding the way that we analyse workplace power relations and the practices through which they are reproduced. Teasing out the relationship between masculinities and other key features of organizations and, in particular, other social divisions and inequalities, requires further attention. Rarely, if ever, is it possible to reduce complex organizational processes and power relations *exclusively* to issues of gender and/or masculinity. Managerial control and labour resistance, for example, might in certain cases be shaped by specific masculinities, but they will not be totally determined by them. Particular masculinities are frequently embedded (but often unacknowledged) in organizational power relations, discourses and practices. To focus upon gender and/or men and masculinity will not provide a complete account of these complex processes, but equally their neglect often renders critical analyses of power relations fundamentally flawed.

In emphasizing multiple masculinities there is a danger of excluding other social divisions and oppressions in organizations and above all the interrelations of these divisions and inequalities. On the one hand, it is important to acknowledge the way in which masculinities can change over time, could be shaped by underlying ambiguities and uncertainties, may differ according to class, age, culture and ethnicity etc. and might also be central to the reproduction of these other social divisions (and vice versa). Yet on the other hand, this emphasis upon multiplicity and difference ought not to degenerate into a diversified pluralism that gives insufficient attention to structured patterns of gendered power, control and inequality. As Cockburn writes, a focus upon multiple masculinities should not 'deflect attention from the consistency in men's domination of women at systemic and organizational levels, from the continuation of materials, structured inequalities and power imbalances between the sexes' (1991, p. 225). She argues that this increasing emphasis on difference, plurality and multiplicity needs to retain a focus upon the structured asymmetrical relations of power between men and women.

Hence, within critical studies on men and masculinities there appears to be an unresolved tention between the analysis, on the one hand, of multiplicity and diversity and on the other, of men's structured domination, their shared economic and symbolic vested interests and sense of unity within patriarchal societies and organizations. We refer to this unresolved and somewhat polarized debate as the unities and differences between men and masculinities (Hearn and Collinson 1993). Here a particularly important question is whether the unities or differences should be attributed analytical primacy? And how are they to be related? We would argue for the need to examine *both* the unities and differences between men and masculinities as well as their interrelations. By examining these processes *simultaneously*, we can develop a deeper understanding of the gendered power relations of organization, the conditions, processes and consequences of their reproduction and how they could be resisted and transformed.

On the one hand, men's power in organizations is maintained through their unification and identification with each other. Men are frequently united, though not necessarily consciously, by dominant sexuality, violence and potential violence, social and economic privilege, political power, shared concerns and interests and culturally based values. Cockburn (1991), for example, reveals how men resist equal opportunity policies in organizations by generating institutional and cultural barriers to women's 'progress'. She concludes that organizations are dominated by a group that has the power to define all other groups as inferior, 'It is a white male heterosexual and largely able-bodied ruling monoculture' (1991, p. 219). One way of understanding such unities or potential unities of men is through the concept of gender class. Just as there may be a gender class of women, so it might be possible to identify a gender class of men, whether seen in terms of biological reproduction (Firestone 1970; O'Brien 1981), sexuality (MacKinnon 1982) or household relations and work (Delphy 1977, 1984). All of these and indeed other social relations could be interpreted as possible social bases of the gender class of men (Hearn 1987, 1992b). Up to now, there has been far more attention given to the implications of gender class analysis for women than for men.

On the other hand, however, the idea of a unity of men is *also* problematic (Brittan 1989). Indeed one of the ways that men's collective power is maintained is through the perpetuation of the assumption of hegemonic forms and of men and masculinities as the most important or sole form. The persistence of the assumption of white heterosexual able-bodied men to the exclusion of other kinds of men remains a major issue for practical politics and theoretical analysis. From this perspective, the notion of a 'monoculture' is difficult to sustain given the hierarchies, 'pecking orders' and stratified differences that exist even between white male heterosexual and largely able-bodied men. Instead of there being just one kind of men, dominant or otherwise, there are many different ways in which particular kinds of men and particular kinds of masculinities are reproduced, often in relation to other social divisions.

We argue that these differences must be examined in connection with the stated unities that co-exist between men in organizations. It is important to take analytical account of both the unities *and* differences between men and masculinities as well as the ways that these overlap and are often interwoven in specific organizational processes and practices. This, we believe, could contribute important insights into the conditions, processes and consequences of gendered power relations in organizations and the ways that these are reproduced, rationalized and/or resisted.

To take just one example, we would suggest that the failure to recognize the embeddedness, flexibility and dominance of these multiple masculinities within conventional power relations in organizations is a major reason for the ineffectiveness of many equality initiatives. The possibility of sabotage by men at various hierarchical levels (and sometimes women too) in the construction of many programmes, has only recently begun to be addressed (see Collinson et al. 1990; Cockburn 1991). Buswell and Jenkins (1993), for example, contend that equal opportunity programmes often become merely a vehicle for men managers 'to talk to other men' and to deny that gender inequalities continue to exist. Such programmes not only unite men, but also individualize and divide women, particularly between 'full-time achievers and the rest' (1993, p. 14).

A parallel debate concerning 'sameness' or 'difference' has been a recurrent concern in feminist theorizing about women and men (Banks 1981). Should women be treated as similar to or as different from men? Some writers have sought to emphasize sameness and deny women's difference (e.g. Kanter 1977; Rosener 1990), while others advocate the celebration of women's difference both from men and between women (e.g. Gilligan 1982; Griffin 1982). Bacchi (1990) criticizes the polarized nature of these debates, arguing that a concern with sameness *or* difference 'places unacceptable boundaries on the possibilities for change' (1990, p. xv) and distracts attention from the pressing need for institutional transformations in gender relations based on specific policy initiatives.

Rejecting the reduction of women to a unitary category, Cockburn (1991) insists that women have 'identities formed in gender processes that vary according to whether they are black or white, whether they are lesbian or heterosexual and whether or not they experience disabilities' (1991, p. 3). Drawing upon Bacchi's work, Cockburn criticizes the polarized character of feminist debates that emphasize the importance of *either* sameness or difference. Favouring an analytical framework incorporating both dimensions, she argues that women can be the same *and* different from each other and from men 'at various times and in various ways' (1991, p. 10). As discussed, a somewhat similar unresolved debate has characterized critical studies on men and masculinities. Drawing upon the arguments of Bacchi and Cockburn, we emphasize a corresponding need to acknowledge these tensions and to consider the unities, differences and their interrelations in developing an analytical framework for critical studies on men and masculinities. Thus in organizations there are tensions between the collective power of men and masculinities, and differentiation amongst men and masculinities. Of especial importance are the differentiations between men and between masculinities that are in part defined by other social and organizational divisions and inequalities such as those between managers and workers.

In sum, the analysis of gendered power relations continues to be characterized by various conceptual difficulties. We suggest that the increasing emphasis on multiplicity and differentiation needs to be combined with a consideration of men's unities and their interrelations. In order to develop the critical analysis of gendered power relations and men and masculinities in contemporary organizations, we also argue that an examination of the relations, discourses and practices of managers

and managements constitutes a potentially illuminating as well as frequently neglected area. A great deal of critical work on gender in employment has explored the experience of subordination, and of being
managed, while comparatively less attention has been paid to the gendered conditions, processes and consequences of those who exercise
considerable hierarchical power in organizations. While much of the
literature on management has neglected gender issues, critical studies
on gender have frequently failed to examine management and managers.
Drawing upon the foregoing theme of unities and differences between
men and masculinities, the following section seeks to highlight some of
the key issues to be addressed in the analysis of organizations and
managements.

Multiple masculinities and managements

So, how are these multiple masculinities historically embedded in organizational practices? What would a simultaneous emphasis upon unities
and differences look like? We now outline several masculinities that seem
to remain pervasive and privileged in organizations broadly and management more specifically, and examine their reproduction through the
subjective search to identify and differentiate self. This account is by no
means intended to be exhaustive, but rather seeks to be suggestive of new
ways of analysing men and masculinities and thus power relations in
contemporary organizations. It is concerned to emphasize not only how
various masculinities frequently shape managerial practices, but also the
ways in which managerial practices can impact on the emergence of
various masculinities in the workplace. In what follows we identify five
discourses and practices of masculinity that appear to remain pervasive
and dominant in organizations: authoritarianism; paternalism; entrepreneurialism; informalism and careerism. These are particularly inter-
related with different managerial styles. Seeking to illustrate the way
that power is routinely exercised in organizations, they are presented in
an ideal-typical and discrete way, whereas in practice they are likely to
overlap and co-exist within specific processes.

Authoritarianism

Authoritarianism is typically but not exclusively related to those in
positions of seniority. It is characterized by an intolerance of dissent or

difference, a rejection of dialogue and debate and a preference for coercive power relations based on dictatorial control and unquestioning obedience. Maddock and Parkin (1993) refer to this as the 'barrack yard culture' highlighting the way in which aggressive masculinity is deeply embedded in such autocratic practices. Based upon bullying and the creation of fear in subordinates, authoritarianism celebrates a brutal and aggressive masculinity; a criterion by which self and others are judged. It is therefore a primary source of identification with and differentiation from others. Hostility is aimed at those who fail to comply with this aggressive masculinity, for example, women, and men as individuals or in groups that possess little institutional power and status. In dismissing these groups as 'weak', those who invest in authoritarianism try to differentiate and elevate their own masculine identity and power. The coercive regime of Harold Geneen at International Telephone and Telegraph is a vivid illustration of an authoritarian, highly masculine style of management (Morgan 1986, pp. 125–6; Pascale and Athos 1982).

Paternalism

By contrast, in paternalism, men eschew coercion and seek to exercise power by emphasizing the moral basis of cooperation, the protective nature of their authority, the importance of personal trust relations and the need for employees both to invest voluntarily in their work task and to identify with the company. Highlighting the interdependent nature of hierarchical relations, paternalism engages in the 'pretence of equality for the purpose of securing instrumental gain' (Kerfoot and Knights 1993, p. 670). It is also a specifically masculine discourse of control that draws on the familial metaphor of the 'rule of the father' who is authoritative, benevolent, self-disciplined and wise. A central self-justifying claim of paternalism is that power is exercised in positive ways which enhance subordinates' self-interests. Such practices are usually represented by their perpetrators as 'benefiting' and 'protecting' their victims (Pollert 1981; Lown 1983; Bradley 1986). 'Power is exercised for the "good" of the recipient' (Kerfoot and Knights 1993, p. 665). Paternalism frequently has the effect of reinforcing employees' compliance and legitimizing managerial prerogative both for those who are excluded (or 'protected') from decision-making and for the decision-makers themselves (Collinson et al. 1990).

Investing in paternalism, managers seek to differentiate themselves from women and identify with other men. Older men in particular are likely to be paternalistic towards their younger male colleagues.

Maddock and Parkin (1993) term this 'The Gentleman's Club': a polite, 'civilized' and exclusive male culture where women (and indeed younger men) are kept firmly in established roles by older male managers who are courteous and humane. So long as women conform to conventional notions of female identity, they will experience little hostility. Within these protective practices, women are treated as too 'delicate' and 'precious' to be involved in the so-called harsh world of business (Collinson and Knights 1986). Such practices can be traced back to a 19th-century middle-class conception of masculinity in which men are expected to behave in accordance with 'gentlemanly principles' and where authority was ascribed on the basis of seniority, social privilege and birthright.

Entrepreneurialism

By contrast, entrepreneurialism articulates a 'hard-nosed' and highly competitive approach to business and organization and is associated with more recent management styles. Prioritizing performance levels, budget targets, 'penetrating new markets and territories' profits, production and costs, entrepreneurialism elevates economic efficiency and managerial control at the expense of all other criteria. Within this discourse, men as managers identify with other men who are as competitive as themselves, willing to work at a similar pace, endure long hours, be geographically mobile and meet tight production deadlines. These requirements tend to exclude some men who are not considered 'man enough' or predatory enough to satisfy them and most women, whose employment, particularly in senior positions, is often seen as incompatible with entrepreneurial concerns.

Differences between men regarding entrepreneurialism are likely to be articulated along the axis of age, often with younger men being more willing to invest in this discourse than their older counterparts, many of whom may be more comfortable with a paternalistic workplace culture. This is illustrated by the selling function of many organizations where men over forty-five (approximately) find it increasingly difficult to compete for business with younger colleagues and thus to perform according to the expectations of their employer. Many older men in sales and middle management have lost their jobs in the retrenchment of the late 1980s and early 1990s. For the younger men who remain, however, their performance is likely to be increasingly monitored, evaluated and stratified. Embroiled in the struggle to be 'constantly productive and achieving, their masculine identities are likely to be precarious and insecure constantly preoccupied with purposive action in the drive to be in control' (Kerfoot and Knights 1993).

Equally, within this discourse of gendered entrepreneurialism, pregnancy and domestic commitments are often treated as taboo because they are perceived to challenge and even undermine everyday business practice and the taken-for-granted masculine discourse of control that separates 'public' and 'private' life (Martin 1990). Returning to our example of selling, research suggests that a deep-seated antagonism to women's conventional domestic commitments frequently pervades this organizational function. Only those women who can comply with the male model of breadwinner employment patterns are likely to be acceptable within this dominant discourse. These women are liable to be divorced with dependent children. Hence, like young salesmen, they are perceived to bring their motivation with them, they are 'needy and greedy' (Collinson and Knights 1986).

Informalism

Research has revealed the way in which men often try to build informal workplace relationships with one another on the basis of shared masculine interests and common values (e.g. Cockburn 1983; Gray 1987; Collinson 1992). Within these informal relationships men are often concerned to identify with other men within the 'in-group', while simultaneously differentiating themselves from other groups of men and from women. Typically, the informal currency between men at various hierarchical levels will concentrate on humour, sport, cars, sex, women and drinking alcohol. In the worst cases, these informal and aggressive dynamics of masculinity in the workplace may also result in sexual harassment, the reduction of women in the organization to sexual objects and, where career successful, the undermining of their competence on the grounds that they must have used their sexuality to secure hierarchical advance.

The conditions, processes and consequences of informal relationships between men are not merely confined to working-class employment settings such as those outlined earlier (Scase and Goffee 1989). Maddock and Parkin (1993) refer to this informalism that tends to exclude and subordinate women as 'the Locker Room Culture'. They argue that 'It is not just junior women who are subjected to Locker Room Culture, women with power but who are isolated as chief executives or directors tell us that they have to listen to endless references to sport and sex in both formal and informal situations' (1993, p. 5). Moreover, these informal relations between men frequently transcend organizational boundaries. Relationships are developed with men working in other organizations, for example through occupational meetings (e.g. regional meetings of the Institute of Personnel Management) and through leisure/ sports groups (e.g. squash, cricket, football, golf clubs).

A particularly familiar example of the influence of informal social relations on employment practices can be found in academic work. Morgan (1981) describes the influence of informal interactions between male academics, particularly those conducted in the faculty club, staff bar or local pub. He argues that such informal dynamics frequently counterbalance the potentially divisive tendencies of 'academic machismo'. Arguing that the pub is still perceived as a male dominated arena, Morgan refers to this tendency of men to feel more at ease in other men's company as 'male homosociability' (1981, p. 102). While the exclusion of women (and some men) from these informal interactions and relationships need not always be deliberately intended or acknowledged, he argues they are likely to have these effects. This can be particularly important, according to Morgan, because social drinking between academics can provide an enormous amount of valuable work-related as well as personal information.

So far, we have discussed four discourses and practices of masculinity that seem to reflect and reinforce a simultaneous sense of unity and differentiation for men in organizations. Indeed these unities and differences appear to be mutually reinforcing. However, they are also quite fragile, precarious and shifting. Accordingly, they do not always establish the mutual trust, cooperation and loyalty that is claimed for them. The depth and extent of these shared unities and masculine identifications between men should therefore not be overstated. One primary reason for the fragility underpinning these unities is the extent to which more individualistic and competitive concerns also simultaneously characterize men and masculine discourses in organizations.

Careerism

Competition between men in organizations can take many symbolic and/ or economic forms. In the case of middle-class masculinities especially, competition is often expressed in the widespread preoccupation with hierarchical advance; careerism. The search to validate masculine identity through upward progress inevitably intensifies competition within organizations. Careerism can become a primary orientation to work characterized by an excessive concern with impression management and the differentiation and elevation of self. Such competitive strategies often reflect the way in which (middle-class) men in organizations routinely define themselves and are defined as the privatized breadwinner whose primary purpose is to 'provide' for their families. Competition for career progress comes to be synonymous with conventional masculinity. Upward mobility can therefore become a key objective in the search to secure a stable masculine identity. A 'successful' career may be an important medium through which middle-class men seek to establish masculine identities in the workplace. Yet careerism is also likely to intensify the threat to such identities in the current conditions of 'delayering', widespread redundancies and extensive career bottlenecks (Cascio 1993).

Committed to upward progress, men in organizations are willing to work longer hours, meet tight deadlines, travel extensively, participate in residential training courses and move house at the behest of the company. These work demands are likely to be incompatible with domestic responsibilities. Seeking to comply with the increasingly unrealistic expectations of corporate cultures and of 'total quality management', for example, men in junior and senior management frequently depend upon the support of wives to manage all domestic and familial matters. Paradoxically, attempts to create a corporate culture in the workplace can therefore distance aspiring men from their own domestic concerns and responsibilities. The search for the 'happy family' in employment may be at the cost of an increasingly unhappy family in the domestic sphere. In consequence, the pressure to conform to corporate demands, combined with individuals' own concern with career progress, creates deep-seated divisions, not only between men employees, but also between their paid work and home life.

These differences, divisions and conflicts between men and multiple masculinities in organizations are particularly acute within the managerial function. Contrary to the views of earlier critical writers on management who tended to emphasize the function's unity, homogeneity and omniscience (e.g. Braverman 1974; Edwards 1979), there are a great variety of real and potential differences, divisions and/or conflicts within and between managerial groups and hierarchies. Managerial differences, for example, may be related to hierarchical position, age, industry and organization, region and country and, in particular, discipline and function. They may also be significantly shaped and reproduced through multiple masculinities. Managerial differences can quickly turn into sources of conflict. For example young managers adhering to an 'entrepreneurial' philosophy may be in conflict with older managers who prefer a more 'paternalistic' style. Similarly, marketing managers may be struggling for power and influence with their managerial counterparts in production or accounting, as Armstrong (1984, 1986) has revealed.

These differences and conflicts between managers may be related to structural struggles for organizational power and influence and/or they may be shaped by the identity preoccupations of individual managers concerned with self-differentiation, self-elevation and the negation of others. In either case, we argue that multiple masculinities may well shape the motives, processes and outcomes of these intra-managerial conflicts for organizational power, status and identity.

Conclusion

This chapter has sought to contribute to the growing interrelated concerns to name men as men and to examine the gendered nature of power relations in contemporary organizations. In particular, it has considered the value, problems and unresolved difficulties of focusing upon multiple masculinities as they emerge in organizational process of control, compliance and resistance. We have outlined several dominant masculinities that seem to remain pervasive, persistent and privileged especially (but not exclusively) within the discourses and practices of managers and management. In addition to identifying these masculinities, we have been concerned to examine the conditions, processes and consequences of their reproduction in routine organization practices.

These masculinities in contemporary organizations have been shown to be characterized by contradictory tensions. On the one hand, men often collaborate, cooperate and identify with one another in ways that display a shared unity and consolidate power between them. Yet on the other hand, these same masculinities can also be characterized simultaneously by conflict, competition and self-differentiation in ways that highlight and intensify the differences and divisions between men. There seem to be deep-seated tensions, ambiguities and contradictions at the heart of these dominant masculinities in the workplace. All the more so when we recognize that men often seek to construct a collective sense of unity and identification with some men, based upon their differentiation from women (and other men). In consequence, these unities between men should not be overstated since they are often precarious, shifting and instrumental.

This is especially the case in the area of management where analyses of gender and masculinity have been particularly neglected both by conventional and radical writers alike. Studies in this area have the potential to develop new forms of analysis of power in organizations. For example, more work could focus upon the conditions, processes and consequences of men's networks in managerial hierarchies. Relatedly, the impact of 'mentoring' between older and younger managers and the transferring of power from one generation of men managers to another could receive much more detailed attention. Research might examine not only the unities, commonalities and mutual identifications between men and between masculinities, but also the various ways in which these are threatened by current developments in organizations. For example, the current tensions in many organizations between different styles of managers and of managing are particularly important to explore. Equal opportunity initiatives, the need to compete with women for particular jobs, career bottlenecks and redundancies all constitute significant challenges to men's conventional gender identities. Widespread organizational downsizing, short-term contracts and work intensification seem to be reinforcing the fear, anxiety and insecurity of middle-range men managers in particular, who are increasingly having to recognize that their working lives are constantly being evaluated and are often outside of their own control. One possible response to these economic and symbolic pressures will be to engage in further practices of impression management.

Furthermore, attention could usefully be paid to the management of paid work and the domestic sphere, of 'public' and 'private' life. All employees are involved in managing themselves and the relationship between paid work and home. A crucial aspect of this management process, as feminist writers have reminded us, is the organization of child care; a responsibility that men and managers have generally avoided and have left to women. Men as managers and managers as men have frequently 'distanced' themselves from children and family responsibilities thereby reinforcing their sense of separation between paid work and domestic life. Within organizations such 'distancing' strategies are often interpreted in a positive light as evidence both of commitment to the company and of strength in the individual displayed in their ability to control 'private life' by keeping it separate from employment. Men often feel compelled to accept organizational requests to be geographically mobile, for example, despite the likely disruptive consequences that will ensue for children, relatives and wives (who may be pursuing their own career). Given the increasingly evaluative nature of organizational practices, men believe that they cannot afford to be seen as 'out of control', as being unable to separate 'work' from 'home'. Hence they invest in displaying a distance from the domestic sphere and thereby reproduce and reinforce the deep-seated 'masculinity' of shopfloor, office, managerial and boardroom cultures.

To conclude, this chapter has been concerned to name men as men and to highlight some of the interrelationships of gendered power and multiple masculinities with a whole variety of organizational roles, relations, processes and practices. These are frequently mutually embedded and mutually constituting. More research studies are needed that critically examine the conditions, processes and consequences through which the power and status of men and masculinities are reproduced within organizational and managerial practices.

NOTE

For more recent analyses of these issues see Hearn 1994; Collinson and Hearn 1996, 2000; Hearn and Collinson 1998.

REFERENCES

Alvesson, M. (1988) *Management, Corporate Culture and Labour Process in a Professional Service Company.* Paper presented at the 6th UMIST-ASTON Organization and Control of the Labour Process Conference, Aston University, Birmingham.

Armstrong, P. (1984) Competition between the organisational professions and the evolution of management control strategies. In K. Thompson (ed.) *Work, Employment and Unemployment* 97–120. Milton Keynes: Open University Press.

Armstrong, P. (1986) Management control strategies and inter-professional competition: the cases of accountancy and personnel management. In D. Knights and H. Willmott (eds.) *Gender and the Labour Process*, 19–43. Aldershot: Gower.

Atkinson, P. (1979) The problem with *patriarchy. Achilles Heel*, 2, 18–22.

Bacchi, C. L. (1990) *Same Difference.* London: Allen and Unwin.

Banks, O. (1981) *Faces of Feminism.* Oxford: Martin Robertson.

Baron, A. (1992) Technology and the crisis of masculinity: the gendering of work and skill in the US printing industry. In A. Sturdy, D. Knights and H. Willmott (eds.) *Skill and Consent*, 67–96. London: Routledge.

Bennis, W. (1989) *On Becoming a Leader.* Wilmington, Mass.: Warren Bennis Inc.

Bly, R. (1990) *Iron John: A Book About Men.* New York: Addison-Wesley.

Bradley, H. (1986) *Men's Work, Women's Work: A Sociological History of the Sexual Division of Labour in Employment.* Cambridge: Polity.

Braverman, H. (1974) *Labour and Monopoly Capital.* New York: Monthly Review Press.

Brittan, A. (1989) *Masculinity and Power.* Oxford: Blackwell.

Brown, C. (1981) Mothers, fathers and children: from private to public patriarchy. In L. Sargent (ed.) *Women and Revolution: The Unhappy Marriage of Marxism and Feminism*, 239–267. New York: Maple; London: Pluto.

Buchbinder, H. (1987) The socialised penis revisited. In H. Buchbinder, V. Burstyn, D. Forbes and M. Steedman (eds.) *Who's on Top? The Politics of Heterosexuality*, 63–82. Toronto: Garamond Press.

Burton, C. (1991) *The Promise and the Price*. Sydney: Allen and Unwin.

Buswell, C. and Jenkins, S. (1993) *Equal Opportunities Policies, Employment and Patriarchy*. Paper presented at the Labour Process Conference, Blackpool, March.

Calás, M., Jacobson, S., Jacques, R. and Smircich, L. (1991) *Is a Woman-Centered Theory of Management Dangerous?* Paper at the National Academy of Management Conference, Women in Management Division, Miami, FL, August. Mimeo. University of Massachusetts, Amherst, MA.

Carrigan, T., Connell, R. W. and Lee, J. (1985) Toward a new sociology of masculinity. *Theory and Society*, 14, 5, 551–604.

Cascio, W. F. (1993) Downsizing: what do we know? What have we learned? *Academy of Management Executive*, 7, 1, 95–104.

Cavendish, R. (1982) *On the Line*. London: Routledge.

Cockburn, C. (1983) *Brothers*. London: Pluto Press.

Cockburn, C. (1991) *In the Way of Women: Men's Resistance to Sex Equality in Organizations*. London: Macmillan.

Collinson, D. L. (1988) Engineering humour: masculinity, joking and conflict in shop floor relations. *Organization Studies*, 9, 2, 181–199.

Collinson, D. L. (1992) *Managing the Shopfloor: Subjectivity, Masculinity and Workplace Culture*. Berlin: Walter de Gruyter.

Collinson, D. L. and Collinson M. (1989) Sexuality in the workplace: the domination of men's sexuality. In J. Hearn et al. (eds.) *The Sexuality of Organization*, 91–109. London: Sage.

Collinson, D. L. and Collinson M. (1990) Review of 'Becoming a Leader' by W. Bennis. *Leadership Quarterly*, 1, 3, 209–213.

Collinson, D. L. and Collinson M. (1992) Mismanaging sexual harassment: protecting the perpetrator and blaming the victim. In *Women in Management Review*, 7, 7, 11–17.

Collinson, D. L. and Hearn, J. (eds.) (1996) *Men as Managers, Managers as Men: Critical Perspectives on Men, Masculinities and Managements*. London: Sage.

Collinson, D. L. and Hearn, J. (2000) Critical perspectives on men, masculinities and management. In M. J. Davidson and R. J. Burke (eds.) *Women in Management: Current Research Issue II*, 263–278. London: Sage.

Collinson, D. L. and Knights, D. (1986) Men only: theories and practices of job segregation in insurance. In D. Knights and H. Willmott (eds.) *Gender and the Labour Process*, 140–178. Aldershot: Gower.

Collinson, D. L., Knights, D. and Collinson, M. (1990) *Managing to Discriminate*. London: Routledge.

Connell, R. W. (1983) *Which Way is Up?* London: Allen and Unwin.

Connell, R. W. (1985) *Theorizing Gender*. Sociology, 19, 2, 260–272.

Connell, R. W. (1987) *Gender and Power*. Cambridge: Polity.

Dalton, M. (1959) *Men Who Manage*. New York: John Wiley and Son.

Deal, T. E. and Kennedy, A. A. (1982) *Corporate Culture: The Rites and Rituals of Corporate Life*. Reading, MA: Addison-Wesley.

Delphy, C. (1977) *The Main Enemy: A Materialist Analysis of Women's Oppression*. London: WRRC.

Delphy, C. (1984) *Close to Home: A Materialist Analysis of Women's Oppression*. London: Hutchinson. First published in French, 1970 onwards.

Edwards, R. (1979) *Contested Terrain: The Transformation of the Workplace in the Twentieth Century*. London: Heinemann.

Elliott, O. (1960) *Men at the Top*. London: Weidenfeld and Nicolson.

Ferguson, K. E. (1993) *The Man Question: Visions of Subjectivity in Feminist Theory*. Berkeley, CA: University of California Press.

Fiedler, F. E. (1967) *A Theory of Leadership Effectiveness*. New York: McGraw.

Firestone, S. (1970) *The Dialectic of Sex*. London: Paladin.

Friedman, S. and Sarah, E. (eds) (1981) *On the Problem of Men*. London: Women's Press.

Gilligan, C. (1982) *In a Different Voice: Psychological Theory and Women's Development*. Cambridge, Mass.: Harvard UP.

Gray, S. (1987) Sharing the shop floor. In M. Kaufman (ed.) *Beyond Patriarchy*, 216–234. Toronto: Oxford University Press.

Griffin, S. (1982) The way of all ideology. In N. O. Keohane, M. Z. Rosaldo and B. C. Gelpi (eds.) *Feminist Theory: A Critique of Ideology*, 273–292. Chicago: University of Chicago Press.

Hanmer, J. (1990) Men, power and the exploitation of women. In J. Hearn and D. H. J. Morgan (eds.) *Men, Masculinities and Social Theory*, 23–42. London and Boston: Unwin Hyman.

Hearn, J. (1985) Men's sexuality at work. In A. Metcalf and M. Humphries (eds.) *The Sexuality of Men*, 110–123. London: Pluto Press.

Hearn, J. (1987) *The Gender of Oppression: Men, Masculinity and the Critique of Marxism*. Brighton: Wheatsheaf; New York: St. Martin's.

Hearn, J. (ed.) (1989) Men, masculinities and leadership: changing patterns of new initiatives. Special Issue. *Equal Opportunities International*, 8, 1.

Hearn, J. (1991) *Men and Gender-Divided Organisations – or Patriarchies, Sexualities, Masculinities and Managements*. Paper at Men and Work Life Seminar, University of Tampere, Finland. Mimeo. University of Bradford, UK. In Conference Proceedings Miehet Työelamass (Men in Working Life), Helsinki: Sosiaali-ja terveysministeriö, 1992.

Hearn, J. (1992a) Changing men and changing managements: a review of issues and actions. *Women in Management Review*, 7, 1, 3–8.

Hearn, J. (1992b) *Men in the Public Eye: The Construction and Deconstruction of Public Men and Public Patriarchies*. New York and London: Unwin Hyman/ Routledge.

Hearn, J. (1994) Changing men and changing managements: social change, social research and social action. In M. J. Davidson and R. J. Burke (eds.) *Women in Management: Current Research Issues*, 192–209. London: Paul Chapman.

Hearn, J. and Collinson, D. (1993) Theorizing unities and differences between men and between masculinities. In H. Brod and M. Kaufman (eds.) *Theorizing Masculinities*. Newbury Park, CA.: Sage.

Hearn, J. and Collinson, D. (1998) Men, masculinities, managements and organizational change. In *Zeitschrift für Personalforschung*, 12, 1, 210–222.

Hearn, J. and Parkin, W. (1988) Women, men and leadership: a critical review of assumptions, practices and change in the industrialized nations. In N. J. Adler and D. Izraeli (eds) *Women in Management Worldwide*, 17–40. New York: M. E. Sharpe.

Hearn, J. and Parkin, W. (1993) Organizations, multiple oppressions and postmodernism. In J. Hassard and M. Parker (eds.) *Postmodernism and Organization Theory*, 148–162. London: Sage.

Helgeson, S. (1990) *The Female Advantage: Women's Ways of Leadership*. New York: Doubleday.

Henriques, J., Hollway, W., Urwin, C., Venn, C. and Walkerdine, V. (1984) *Changing the Subject*. London: Methuen.

Hollander, E. P. and Offerman, L. R. (1990) Power and leadership in organizations. *American Psychologist*, 45, 2, 179–189.

Kanter, R. M. (1977) *Men and Women of the Corporation*. New York: Basic Books.

Kaufman, M. (ed.) (1987) *Beyond Patriarchy*. Toronto: Oxford University Press.

Kerfoot, D. and Knights, D. (1993) Management, masculinity and manipulation: from paternalism to corporate strategy in financial services in Britain. *Journal of Management Studies*, 30, 4, 659–677.

Kimmel, M. S. and Messner, M. A. (eds.) (1989) *Men's Lives*. New York: Macmillan.

Knights, D. (1990) Subjectivity, Power and the labour process. In D. Knights and H. Willmott (eds) *Labour Process Theory*. London: Macmillan.

Kondo, D. K. (1990) *Crafting Selves, Power, Gender and Discourses of Identity in a Japanese Workplace*. Chicago: University of Chicago Press.

Lawrence, P. R. and Lorsch, J. W. (1967) *Organization and Environment*. Cambridge, MA: Harvard University Press.

Lown, J. (1983) Not so much a factory, more a form of patriarchy: gender and class during industrialisation. In E. Gamarnikow, D. H. J. Morgan, J. Purvis and D. E. Taylorson (eds) *Gender, Class and Work*, 28–45. London: Heinemann.

MacKinnon, C. A. (1982) Marxism, feminism, method and the state: an agenda for theory. *Signs*, 7, 3, 515–544.

Maddock, S. and Parkin, D. (1993) Gender cultures. *Women in Management Review*, 8, 2, 3–9.

Martin, J. (1990) Deconstructing organizational taboos: the suppression of gender conflict in organizations. *Organization Science*, 1, 4, 339–359.

Mintzberg, H. (1973) *The Nature of Managerial Work*. New Jersey: Prentice Hall.

Mintzberg, H. (1975) The manager's job: folklore and fact. Harvard Business Review, July/August, 49–61.

Mintzberg, H. (1983) *Power in and Around Organizations*. New Jersey: Prentice Hall.

Mintzberg, H. (1989) *Mintzberg on Management*. New York: Macmillan.

Morgan, D. H. J. (1981) Men, masculinity and the process of sociological enquiry. In H. Roberts (ed.) *Doing Feminist Research*, 83–113. London: Routledge.

Morgan, D. H. J. (1992) *Discovering Men*. London and New York: Unwin Hyman/Routledge.

Morgan, G. (1986) *Images of Organization*. London: Sage.

O'Brien, M. (1981) *The Politics of Reproduction*. London: Routledge and Kegan Paul.

Parkin, W. and Hearn, J. (1994) Frauen, Männer und Führung. In A. Kieser, G. Reber and R. Wunderer (eds.) *Handwörterbuch der Führung*. Stuttgart: C. E. Poeschel.

Pascale, R. T. and Athos, A. G. (1982) *The Art of Japanese Management*. Harmondsworth: Penguin.

Peters, T. J. and Austin, N. (1985) *A Passion for Excellence*. New York: Random House.

Peters, T. J. and Waterman, R. H. (1982) *In Search of Excellence: Lessons from America's Best Run Companies*. New York: Harper and Row.

Plummer, K. (ed.) (1992) *Modern Homosexualities: Fragments of Lesbian and Gay Experience*. London: Routledge.

Pollert, A. (1981) *Girls, Wives, Factory Lives*. London: Macmillan.

Powell, G. N. (1988) *Women and Men in Management*. Newbury, CA: Sage.

Pringle, R. (1989) *Secretaries Talk*. London: Verso.

Reed, M. (1989) *The Sociology of Management*. London: Harvester Wheatsheaf.

Roper, M. (1993) *Masculinity and the British Organization Man, 1945 to the Present*. Milton Keynes: Open University Press.

Roper, M. and Tosh, J. (eds) (1991) *Manful Assertions: Masculinities in Britain since 1800*. London: Routledge.

Rosener, J. (1990) Ways women lead. *Harvard Business Review*, 68, 6, 119–125.

Rothwell, S. (1983) *Is Management a Masculine Role?* Paper presented at the Journal of Management Studies Conference, Manchester Business School.

Rowbotham, S. (1979) The trouble with patriarchy. *New Statesman*, 98, 2344/5, 970–971.

Scase, R. and Goffee, R. (1989) *Reluctant Managers: Their Work and Lifestyles*. London: Unwin Hyman.

Schein, E. (1985) *Organizational Culture and Leadership*. San Francisco: Jossey Bass.

Sennett, R. and Cobb, J. (1977) *The Hidden Injuries of Class*. Cambridge: Cambridge University Press.

Taylor, F. (1947) *Scientific Management*. New York: Harper and Row.

Thompson, P. and McHugh, D. (1990) *Work Organizations*. London: Macmillan.

Vroom, V. H. and Yetton, P. W. (1973) *Leadership and Decision-Making*. Pittsburgh, PA: University of Pittsburgh Press.

Walby, S. (1986) *Patriarchy at Work*. Cambridge: Polity.

Walby, S. (1990) *Theorizing Patriarchy*. Oxford: Basil Blackwell.

Walker, C. R. and Guest, R. H. (1952) The man on the Assembly Line. Harvard University Press.

Walter, J. A. (1979) *A Long Way from Home*. Exeter: Paternoster Press.

Weber, M. (1968) *Economy and Society*. New York: Bedminster Press.

Weeks, J. (1977) *Coming Out: Homosexual Politics in Britain from the Nineteenth Century to the Present*. London: Quartet.

Westwod, S. (1984) *All Day Every Day: Factory, Family, Women's Lives*. London: Pluto Press.

Whyte, W. H. (1956) *The Organization Man*. New York: Simon and Schuster.

Willis, P. (1977) *Learning to Labour*. London: Saxon House.

Willmott, H. (1984) Images and ideals of management work. *Journal of Management Studies*, 21, 3, 349–368.

Willmott, H. (1990) Subjectivity and the dialectics of praxis: opening up the core of labour process analysis. In D. Knights and H. Willmott (eds.) *Labour Process Theory*, 336–378. London: Macmillan.

Wood, R. (1987) Raging Bull: the homosexual subtext in film. In M. Kaufman (ed.) *Beyond Patriarchy*, 266–276. Toronto: Oxford University Press.

Woolsey-Biggart, N. (1989) *Charismatic Capitalism*. Chicago University Press.

9

Masculinity and Machismo in Hollywood's War Films

Ralph R. Donald

In *Sands of Iwo Jima* (1949), John Agar bitterly recalls his Marine colonel father's disapproval of his sensitive, intellectual son, revealing his own jealousy over the colonel's admiration of macho Sergeant Stryker (John Wayne):

> I embarrassed my father. I wasn't tough enough for him – too soft. 'No guts' was the phrase he used. Now Stryker: He's the type of man my father wanted me to be...yeah. I bet [my father and Stryker] got along just fine together. Both of them with ramrods strapped on their backs.

As American boys become socialized, parents, relatives, and peers assail them with hundreds of admonitions describing what they must *not* become. Unfortunately, most of these caveats, delivered by well-meaning relatives and friends, amount to simplistic, anxiety-arousing prohibitions against any behavior deemed vaguely stereotypical of the female or the homosexual male (Hacker, 1957; Hartley, 1976; Sabo & Runfola, 1980). Also, because maleness is a difficult concept to define in positive terms, and because men themselves are often closed-mouthed regarding it, youngsters are mostly left to their own devices to learn manly behaviors.

Increasingly in our television-centered culture, boys find that male heroes in our popular media are among the most accessible, frequently encountered, and publicly approved models for manly socialization. It is a sad but true commentary on our society that often these youngsters spend more time per week with these mediated men than with their own fathers (Barcus, 1983).

There are many kinds of simplistic examples of stereotypical manhood readily available to children and young adults on television: They range from older, basic types, such as the heroes found in Westerns and war pictures, to the newest permutations of the warrior, as found in *G. I. Joe* and the *Teenage Mutant Ninja Turtles*. It is in these portrayals of the warrior that the aggressive qualities of the male of the species are the least inhibited by the moderating influences of civilization.

For males over the age of 35, the cowboy was one of their earliest images: 'the rugged "he-man," strong, resilient, resourceful, capable of coping with overwhelming odds' (Balswick & Peek, 1976). Thus, many of these boys' first male-role-play simulations consisted of imitating this six-gun-toting symbol of understated masculinity. It is no wonder, then, that this first generation of young men to display the results of television's conditioning power (those raised on Hopalong Cassidy and the Lone Ranger) would dream dreams of frontier life similar to Phillip Caputo in his book and TV miniseries, *A Rumor of War* (1978):

> I would dream of that savage, heroic time [the old West] and wish I had lived then, before America became a land of salesmen and shopping centers. This is what I wanted, to find in a commonplace world a chance to live heroically. Having known nothing but security, comfort and peace, I hungered for danger, challenges and violence.

Also consider Komisar's observation (1976):

> Little boys learn the connection between violence and manhood very early in life. Fathers indulge in mock prize fights and wrestling matches with eight-year-olds. Boys play cowboys and Indians with guns and bows and arrows proffered by their elders. They are gangsters or soldiers inter-changeably – the lack of difference between the two is more evident to them than to their parents. They are encouraged to 'fight back,' and bloodied noses and black eyes become trophies of their pint-sized virility.

As both Carpenter (1990) and J. Smith (1975) suggest, in many ways war films are Westerns taking place in locations other than the West. After all, in addition to their many specific similarities, both are essentially melo-dramatic portrayals of men performing virile, courageous deeds designed to protect helpless civilians from some sort of aggressor. Whether these villains are land-hungry cattle barons, rampaging Indians, or rapacious Nazis, Japanese, and Viet Cong, the outcomes (good triumphs over evil) are the same. Thus, regardless of the passage of time and the popularity of genres, sooner or later, most young boys' playacting evolves in sophis-tication into the twentieth-century equivalent, the soldier in modern warfare.

Jeffords (1989), Leed (1989), and others maintain that war itself is a gendering activity, one of the few remaining true male experiences in our society. Even the increasingly androgynous American armed forces' most recent liberalizing of regulations regarding sexual equality stops short of parity in combat assignments. Our paternalistic culture seems always to stop short of ordering women into harm's way. When women do fight in American war pictures, Hollywood usually shows it to be an aberration. For example, in *A Guy Named Joe* (1943), Irene Dunne flies a dangerous bombing mission, but does so without permission, and with guardian angel Spencer Tracy to assist her with the tactical aspects. In *The Edge of Darkness* (1943) and *This Land is Mine* (1943), Ann Sheridan and Maureen O'Hara end up fighting back against the Nazis, but only as civilians attempting to resist an occupying force, not as soldiers. In *Aliens* (1986), Sigourney Weaver finds herself in deadly personal combat with an army of monsters, but only after all of the platoon of Marines sent for that purpose have been killed or wounded.

In short, whenever the powers that rule can help it, combat is reserved exclusively for males, for whom the quality of belligerent performance is also clearly prescribed:

> Be a man. Conceptions of masculinity vary among different American groups, but there is a core which is common to most: courage, endurance and toughness, lack of squeamishness when confronted with shocking or distasteful stimuli, avoidance of display of weakness in general, reticence about emotional or idealistic matters, and sexual competency. (Stouffer, Lumsdaine, Lumsdaine, Williams, Smith, Janis, Star, & Cottrell, 1976)

If one accepts the preceding as both a culturally sanctioned definition of maleness and a blueprint for male role models in war, then the specifics that follow will serve as a more detailed explanation of this socializing influence.

Initiation rites

In most human cultures, there exists some rite of passage from the relatively sexless existence of a child into the adult community of their sex. In this transition, each sex possesses its own set of rituals. In many human cultures, becoming a warrior goes hand in hand with becoming a male adult. In examining the ceremonial rubrics of several native cultures, vanGennep (1960) describes a process that bears close resemblance to the basic training regimen practiced by the American armed forces:

Candidates for male adulthood are first separated from their families, most specifically from the world of women, which has been their childhood milieu. More often than not, initiates are also stripped of the clothing they previously wore, their hair is shaved and/or rearranged in the fashion of adult males. Then they undergo a period of instruction in the behaviors and responsibilities of adult males/warriors. Frayser (1985) notes that in these rituals initiates must passively and submissively obey all orders given them by their male elders, as befits their status as neophytes. Tiger (1970) also points out that this process often includes ordeals and tests of manly endurance. These range from the American Indian practice of hanging a would-be brave by thongs pierced through his pectoral muscles, to 'depilation, head-biting, evulsion of teeth, sprinkling with human blood, drinking human blood, immersion in dust or filth, heavy flogging, scarification, smoking and burning, circumcision and subincision.' Finally, properly reconditioned and educated, the initiates 'graduate' and take their place as full-fledged adult males.

So there is great similarity between this process and armed forces basic training, as portrayed in such films as *Full Metal Jacket* (1987), *Take the High Ground* (1953), and *The D.I.* (1959). Recruits are separated from their families and local subcultures, and removed to training depots that are usually located in some other part of the country. For the majority of their training, they are deprived of all female contact. In *Full Metal Jacket* the drill instructor even insists that the recruits substitute their rifles for their high school sweethearts. To reinforce this point, the men are ordered to sleep with their weapons.

In all three films, the men are deprived of their former hairstyles and are given the standard G.I. butch haircut (the practical equivalent of primitive head-shaving). As well, their clothes are exchanged for uniforms and a set of Marine/Army gear.

Routinely, recruits are not given the status of soldiers at the outset. They are 'boots,' 'trainees,' or 'young people,' but never Marines or soldiers. Sometimes, in these films, recruits are not even allowed the status of males. Often derisively called 'girls' or 'ladies' by their D.I.s, recruits must earn manhood by achieving success in their training. In *The D.I.*, when Jack Webb reports to his company commander that a certain recruit continuously 'fouls up' in his training, the captain offers to assist Webb in 'cutting the lace off his panties.' In *Full Metal Jacket*, when a recruit says that he hails from Texas, the D.I. retorts with this verbal assault:

D.I.: Holy dog shit! Texas! Only steers and queers come from Texas, Private 'Cowboy,' and you don't much look like a steer to me, so that kinda narrows it down. Do you suck dicks?

COWBOY: Sir, no sir!
D.I.:   Are you a peter pumper?
COWBOY: Sir, no sir!
D.I.:   I bet you're the kinda guy who would fuck a person in the ass and not
            even have the goddamn common courtesy to give him a reach-around!
            I'll be watchin' you.

Despite all these indignities, recruits are required to passively submit to all orders, no matter how disgusting, demeaning, or physically taxing they are. For example, also in *Full Metal Jacket*, a feeble-minded recruit whom the D.I. has used as the platoon scapegoat is punished for failure to properly respond to drill commands. He must march behind the others with his thumb in his mouth, his trousers around his ankles, his hat turned backward, and his rifle carried on his shoulder upside down.

But finally, suitably reconditioned and instructed in proper soldierly behavior, the initiates, now full-fledged Marines or soldiers, graduate and are transferred to advanced training.

The men's club

Of all of these initiatory customs and practices, probably the most significant is the physical and symbolic separation of candidates from the world of women. But unlike Tiger's native tribesman, Americans begin to establish this separation long before a boy reaches puberty. Kimmel (1987) states that gender is a relational construct, providing males with the opposite sex as a basis of comparison and a clearly drawn negative role model. Practically from the time an American boy-child is old enough to understand English he hears that 'Big boys don't cry – only girls do,' or 'Don't play with dolls; dolls are for girls,' or 'That scraped knee doesn't really hurt a little man like you, does it?' In various ways, boys are shown multiple examples of the allegedly lesser, more flawed kind of human being they must avoid becoming: a female. By the time most boys reach manhood, many have become firmly convinced that females must be grossly inferior to males – at least with respect to traditionally male activities. And by systematically excluding females from sports teams, clubs, the 'old boy network' in business, from top government positions, and from combat roles in the military through the years, a self-fulfilling set of male role definitions becomes firmly embedded in our history and culture. And needless to say, in Hollywood, a patriarchy if there ever was one, virtually every picture is written and produced from the paternalistic perspective, as if there is no other possible point of view on the planet.

This attitude is most clearly seen in the motion pictures of director/producer Howard Hawks. In virtually all the genre films Hawks made, there is one overriding misogynist theme: The fraternity of men and the jobs men must perform only function efficiently when women are excluded. Plus, many of the problems that inhibit Hawks' heroes from professionally completing their tasks are caused by women. For example, in *Air Force* (1943), the officers of the bomber 'Mary Ann' become momentarily distracted from fighting the Japanese due to a misunderstanding over a woman.

In most war films, men relegate women to three basic roles: mothers to revere and respect, chattel to acquire and use legally in marriage or illegally via rape and pillage, or whores to provide temporary satisfaction while the men are away from home. In each case, women are clearly the 'out-group,' a separate entity men find distracting to the task at hand, but a commodity to think, dream, and make plans about (Komisar, 1976).

Basinger (1986) reminds us that countless combat films contain 'mail call' scenes, in which young soldiers write and receive letters from their revered mothers (p. 62). In *Guadalcanal Diary* (1943), Richard Jaeckel, the 'kid' of the platoon, even attempts to appear more manly by pretending that a letter from his mother is a love note from a sexually submissive girlfriend. In *The War Lover* (1962), pilot Steve McQueen considers co-pilot Robert Wagner's English girlfriend simply a prize to capture and use. In *Platoon* (1987) and *Casualties of War* (1989), soldiers consider young Vietnamese girls the spoils of war and can even rationalize away their rape and murder.

This separation of the 'men's club' from the world of women is seen clearly in *Navy Seals* (1990), described by one reviewer as having the highest testosterone count since *Rambo*. These highly trained super commandos exist in a world in which only three basic things occur: (a) their team goes out on suicidally dangerous missions; (b) they train and plan more suicidally dangerous missions; and (c) they drink, womanize, and carry on like Vikings celebrating the sacking of a town.

In one sequence, 'The Chief,' a member of this tightly knit team, has made what his buddies consider a serious error in judgment: He's getting married in the morning. Too taken aback by this situation to continue the drive to the church where the ceremony is about to begin, one Seal leaps from a moving auto, plunging off a bridge into a river. Later, as the bride walks down the aisle, the Seal team's electronic pagers begin beeping, which means that they have been summoned back to their base for a mission. Without blinking an eye, 'The Chief' leaves his bride at the altar, and he and the other Seals make a run for their cars. 'Saved by the beeper,' one of them remarks. Later, 'The Chief' and his fiancée discuss rescheduling the wedding. But throughout the conversation there is one thing that is virtually implicit: When she marries him, she must accept 'the whole package,' which means that her husband's fraternity of warriors comes first: Before all, he is a Seal, a member of the male fraternity. She must resign herself to the role of 'the little woman,' someone to whom her man will return when naval duties and other unofficial male-bonding rituals (drinking, partying, pranks, and so on) permit.

The quiet man

There are many subtle characteristics to war films' stereotype of the American male warrior. Key among them is that he should be a man of few words but mighty deeds, capable of stoically enduring privations and pain, and be able to pass the stress test that war imposes on these qualities.

Farrell (1976) explains that since showing emotion is considered a feminine characteristic (and therefore should be avoided), men cultivate the image of quiet dignity. The fewer words said, the better. John Wayne typifies the foolish extremes to which this philosophy can be extended in *She Wore A Yellow Ribbon* (1949), when he gives his admonition to young officer Harry Carey, Jr.: 'Never apologize, mister: It's a sign of weakness.'

The ability to watch one's comrades die and yet appear to suffer no emotional trauma is shown to be a valued commodity in most war pictures. In the 1958 film *The Hunters*, fighter group commander Richard Egan proudly calls Robert Mitchum 'the iceman,' because of Mitchum's ability to perform his lethal tasks in an emotionless manner, oblivious to the deaths of his comrades. Showing that wars and warriors adjust to the times while fundamental maleness criteria remain intact, in *Top Gun* (1986), Val Kilmer, the most coolly efficient, emotionless pilot attending the fighter weapons school, also adopts the nickname 'iceman.'

Fear is also an emotion that men in war must hide. Also in *The Hunters*, pilot Lee Philips becomes a drunk because he cannot meet his own expectations of fearlessness. Especially when he compares himself to 'iceman' Robert Mitchum, Philips considers himself a coward – this despite the other pilots' assessment of Philips as the 'bravest man in the squadron.' They consider him brave because despite his fear, despite his mediocre flying ability, and despite the fact that he can turn in his wings to the flight surgeon at any time and take a desk job, Philips still willingly goes in harm's way.

Actually, when a war movie hero does admit fear, it is usually to punctuate the fact that fear is intentionally hidden. For example, in *Sands of Iwo Jima* (1949) and *Destination Tokyo* (1943), young troops about to face death for the first time confess to John Wayne and Cary Grant that they are frightened. Much to the amazement of these young-sters, Wayne and Grant admit to being afraid themselves before a battle, and to steer clear of men who say that they are not. Implicitly, both heroes show by example that one routinely hides any emotions counter-productive to the belligerent objective.

If a warrior gives in to this fear and commits some act of cowardice, the usual war film plot 'conversion convention' calls for him to pay some price for this offense (Donald, 1990). The most common expiative act follows this scenario: After the character decides to reject the coward's role, he attempts some heroic act, during which he is killed or seriously wounded. For example, in *The Fighting 69th*, James Cagney's cowardice causes the death of some of his comrades. He is jailed prior to a court-martial for his sins, but fate intervenes and he escapes. Faced with a choice of flight or a return to the trenches, Cagney chooses the latter, and is killed while fighting bravely. Again the point is made: Even if a soldier is guilty of as grave an offense as 'showing the white feather,' there is a manly option and a formula for redemption.

Although it is acceptable for G.I.s to gripe about the lack of warm food and decent lodging, an almost invisible line is drawn between acceptable and taboo complaints. In *Platoon*, only in his letters to his grandmother does Charlie Sheen admit that the physical and emotional stress of 'humping the boonies' (fighting the jungle war in Vietnam) may be too much for him to bear; to his comrades-in-arms, Sheen just quietly does his job.

Not even painful wounds are an acceptable reason for movie soldiers to resort to emotionalism. Early in *Platoon*, a sergeant confronts a soldier screaming in pain from a gunshot wound: 'Shut up, shut up! – take the pain,' he orders. The compliant soldier obeys. Leed (1989) characterizes this self-destructive self-delusion this way: 'Men become what they are, realizing a masculine character and a strength through what they lose rather than what they gain.' In *The Longest Day* (1962), John Wayne suffers a compound fracture of the lower leg in a parachute drop – but does he complain? No. It does not even slow him up much. Wayne orders the medical corpsman examining his injury to re-lace his combat boot tightly, so he can continue hiking along with his men. In *They Were Expendable* (1945), Wayne becomes extremely indignant when he is ordered to stand down from a mission because of an injury to his arm.

Despite being told that if he does not rest and submit to antibiotic therapy he may lose his arm to gangrene, Wayne tells the doctor to 'slap a little iodine on it and let me get outta here.'

The immortal legion

Shatan (1989) writes that military trainers 'fear that the death of a beloved buddy will render a soldier useless for combat. Instead, training fosters "antigrief" – soldiers are absorbed into the corporate entity of the "immortal legion."' Countless war films reinforce this, showing how unprofessional and unsoldierly it is to unduly fret over the death of a comrade. For example, in *Top Gun*, the death of 'Goose,' Tom Cruise's electronic warfare officer, co-pilot, and best friend, causes him to lose his courage and become unable to engage the enemy. Only when he is willing to 'let Goose go' can Cruise fight again.

In war, succinctly described by ship's captain Richard Crenna in *The Sand Pebbles* (1966) as 'the give and take of death,' there must be some kind of carrot dangled in front of warriors to compensate for the possibility of having to give up one's life. Immortality is the key, allowing the finality of death to be denied and the grief suffered by a deceased warrior's friends to be assuaged. On graduation day in *Full Metal Jacket*, the D.I. explains it this way:

> Today you people are no longer maggots. Today you are Marines. You're part of a brotherhood. From now on until the day you die, wherever you are, every Marine is your brother. Most of you will go to Vietnam; some of you will not come back. But always remember this: Marines die, that's what we're here for. But the Marines Corps lives forever, and that means *you* live forever.

To reinforce this concept in some World War II combat films, a crescendo of patriotic music would rise at the end of the picture, appropriate narration would reinforce the gratitude of a nation for those who gave their lives, and then the smiling faces of the men who died during the film would be superimposed, ghost-like, over the picture on the screen. Thus, as members of the immortal legion, the dead live on in glory.

However, there still must be some manly outlet for emotion over lost buddies. Shatan describes the 'authorized' manly alternative for grief and remorse at the death of a comrade as 'militarized grief and ceremonial vengeance' (pp. 137–138). These behaviors can take the form of either dedicating the next enemy kill to the deceased comrade, or by generally raising the level of mayhem. Examples of both are found in *Destination Tokyo*. An older, much-revered submarine crew member named Mike is stabbed in the back by a downed Japanese pilot whom he was attempting to rescue. His shipmates cease attempting to rescue the pilot and instead repeatedly and redundantly pound him into the water with slugs from a 50-millimeter machine gun. Later the crew paints the dedication, 'For Mike, torpedoman first class, R.I.P.' on the next torpedo the sub fires at a Japanese ship. In the 1940s skillful screen writers routinely sanitized and thereby legitimized such vengeful enthusiasm. However, in recent years, Vietnam war films have provided audiences with more starkly realistic portrayals of soldierly revenge. In films such as *Platoon* and the 1980 television miniseries *A Rumor of War*, soldiers and Marines commit atrocities like that at My Lai as a way of exacting vengeance for the loss of their buddies.

Following the manly credo, Hollywood's contemporary soldiers prefer committing war crimes to sitting down and having a good cry over a lost friend.

Risking one's life daily with buddies on whom one grows to depend for survival often leads to natural feelings of affection and to lifelong friendships. But there is a strict homophobic code to follow in expressing this amity. When the protagonists of both *Platoon* and *Casualties of War* protest the rape of young Vietnamese girls, the would-be rapists accuse these protagonists of being homosexuals. As previously mentioned about *Full Metal Jacket*, the D. I. threatens a recruit with the label of homosexual to achieve dominance. In another basic training film, *Biloxi Blues* (1989), a recruit is discovered to be homosexual. He is immediately arrested, handcuffed, and whisked away from the platoon as if he were a dangerous criminal suffering from leprosy. Under certain circumstances, namely combat, men may partake in activities that would be sexually taboo in civilian life. Mellen (1977) reminds us that in *Wings* (1927) and in *Beau Geste* (1938), what amounts to tender love scenes between two men are allowed to occur. Of course, this overflow of emotion and affection is only permitted because one of the two men is either dying or already dead. Only then is a man allowed to cradle another man in his arms, or to plant a chaste kiss on his forehead. Easthope (1986) puts a near-masochistic spin on this scenario:

> In the dominant versions of men at war, men are permitted to behave towards each other in ways that would not be allowed elsewhere, caressing and holding each other, comforting and weeping together, admitting their love. The pain of war is the price paid for the way it expresses the male bond. War's suffering is a kind of punishment for the release of homosexual desire and male femininity that only war allows.

On other selected occasions, the buddies of less-than-mortally wounded men are allowed similar 'unmanly' liberties. In *Platoon Leader* (1988), a lieutenant tenderly cradles his badly wounded sergeant in his arms. But later, when the sergeant's wounds have healed and the noncom is sent back to the platoon, all he can expect from the lieutenant is a brotherly pat on the back. Once again, friendship verging on love reverts to the manly rules of personal contact that govern relationships between teammates in sports.

Sports metaphors

General George Patton is credited with saying that the problem with wars is that they aren't always there when you need them. Between armed conflicts, American males participate in alternative rites of passage that simulate warlike behavior. In our culture, among the closest substitutes for war are contact sports such as football or boxing. Fiddick (1989) reminds us that 'the use of helmets [as opposed to "caps"] and such terms as "the bomb" and the "blitz" make football ideal as a central metaphor of war.' Hoch's (1980) observations at a football game are similarly enlightening:

> The movements of the cheerleaders are plugged into what amounts to a set of stereotyped military drill routines. Watching the drum majorettes and girls' drill teams prancing about in their mini-skirted mock uniforms, in precision goose steps, it is hard to miss the symbolism of sexuality subordinated to militarism, sexuality used as an advertisement for militarism, and frustrated sexuality used as a spur to militarism and machismo generally.

It will also not come as a surprise that war films also make use of sports metaphors. For example, in *Air Force*, there are countless allusions to baseball, such as Harry Carey's statement that the Japanese mounted their sneak attack on Pearl Harbor 'before Uncle Sam had a chance to come to bat.' Throughout the first portion of the picture, Carey and John Ridgely try to preach sports teamwork to malcontent John Garfield. Finally, Garfield agrees to 'play ball' with the rest of the bomber's crew.

Boxing is also a sport that is frequently alluded to in war films. In *Thirty Seconds Over Tokyo* (1944), the Doolittle raid is described as 'Uncle Sam's first counterpunch in this war.' Countless motion pictures describe their particular war mission as the one that will provide the 'knockout punch' against the enemy.

A conclusion: warning about 'winning'

An integral part of sport in America is the paramount importance of *winning*. Shatan (1989) says, 'In the United States, winning is the central theme in the making of a boy's self-image. Boys learn early that "any boy can win." Corporations love Coach Lombardi's motto, "Winning isn't everything. It's the only thing."' But the male fixation with winning has its dangers: Fear of showing weakness by backing down from a school-yard fight can result in, at worst, a bloody nose. When Presidents Johnson and Nixon refused to back down from the debacle of Vietnam, 57,000 Americans were killed (Fasteau, 1976; Komisar, 1976). Consider Mellen's (1977) statement concerning film heroes she describes as 'indomitable males':

> The stereotype of the self-controlled, invulnerable, stoical hero who justi-
> fies the image of unfeeling masculinity as a means of winning in a world
> that pounces on any sign of weakness.... Male heroes pontificate plati-
> tudes such as that invoked by an elderly John Wayne in *The Shootist*: 'I
> won't be wronged, I won't be insulted, I won't be laid a hand on. I don't do
> these things to others, and I require the same of them.'

Winning has become much too important in our culture. In *Heart-break Ridge* (1986), Clint Eastwood's Marine gunnery sergeant characterized his entire career as if it were a won-lost statistic on the sports page: When the film ended, he was satisfied, and finally ready to retire, now that his war record was evened out at '1 - 1 - 1,' one win (Grenada), one loss (Vietnam), and one tie (Korea).

Perhaps this obsession with winning is the most serious and most potentially dangerous of all the absurd notions that Americans and their war films stuff into the psyches of their male young. But it is the most outmoded and the least helpful value in a contemporary world in which everyone must adapt, change, and compromise. If half-century-old governments and political philosophies can give way, if all the world is changing and adapting, perhaps the macho, uncommunicative, unemotional, pseudo-athletic misogynists America seems intent on turning out should also consider some fundamental alterations.

REFERENCES

Balswick, J. O., & Peek, C. W. (1976). The inexpressive male: A tragedy of American society. In D. S. David & R. Brannon (Eds.), *The forty-nine percent majority: The male sex role* (pp. 55–57). Boston: Addison-Wesley.

Barcus, F. E. (1983). *Images of life on children's television: Sex roles, minorities and families.* New York: Praeger.

Basinger, J. (1986). *The World War II combat film: Anatomy of a genre.* New York: Columbia University Press.

Caputo, P. (1978). *A rumor of war.* New York: Ballantine.

Carpenter, R. H. (1990). America's tragic metaphor: Our twentieth-century combatants as frontiersmen. *Quarterly Journal of Speech, 9,* 1–22.

Donald, R. (1990). Conversion as persuasive convention in American war films. In P. Loukides & L. Fuller (Eds.), *Beyond the stars II: Plot convention in American popular film* (pp. 36–52). Bowling Green, OH: Popular Press.

Easthope, A. (1986). *What a man's gotta do: The masculine myth in popular culture.* London: Paladin/Grafton.

Farrell, W. (1976). The politics of vulnerability. In D. S. David & R. Brannon (Eds.), *The forty-nine percent majority: The male sex role.* Boston: Addison-Wesley.

Fasteau, M. (1976). Vietnam and the cult of toughness in foreign policy. In D. S. David & R. Brannon (Eds.), *The forty-nine percent majority: The male sex role.* Boston: Addison-Wesley.

Fiddick, T. (1989). Beyond the domino theory: Vietnam and metaphors of sport. *Journal of American Culture, 12,* 79–88.

Frayser, S. G. (1985). *Varieties of sexual experience: An anthropological perspective on human sexuality.* New Haven, CT: Human Relations Area Files Press, Inc.

Hacker, H. (1957). The new burdens of masculinity. *Marriage and Family Living, 19,* 231.

Hartley, R. (1976). Sex-role pressures and the socialization of the male child. In D. S. David & R. Brannon (Eds.), *The forty-nine percent majority: The male sex role.* Boston: Addison-Wesley.

Hoch, P. (1980). School for sexism. In D. F. Sabo, Jr., & R. Runfola, (Eds.), *Jock: Sports and male identity.* Englewood Cliffs, NJ: Prentice-Hall.

Jeffords, S. (1989). *The remasculinization of America: Gender and the Vietnam war.* Bloomington: Indiana University Press.

Kimmel, M. (1987). Rethinking 'masculinity': New directions in research. In M. S. Kimmel (Ed.), *Changing men: New directions in research on men and masculinity* (pp. 9–24). Newbury Park, CA: Sage.

Komisar, L. (1976). Violence and the masculine mystique. In D. S. David & R. Brannon (Eds.), *The forty-nine percent majority: The male sex role.* Boston: Addison-Wesley.

Leed, E. (1989). Violence, death and masculinity. *Vietnam Generation, 1,* 168–189.

Mellen, J. (1977). *Big bad wolves: Masculinity in the American film.* New York: Pantheon.

Sabo, D., & Runfola, R. (Eds.). (1980). *Jock: Sports and male identity.* Englewood Cliffs, NJ: Prentice-Hall.

Shatan, C. (1989). Happiness is a warm gun: Militarized mourning and ceremonial vengeance. *Vietnam Generation, 1,* 127–151.

Smith, J. (1975). *Looking away: Hollywood and Vietnam.* New York: Scribner.

Stouffer, S. A., Lumsdaine, A. A., Lumsdaine, M. H., Williams, R. M., Jr., Smith, M. B., Janis, I. L., Star, S. A., & Cottrell, L. S., Jr. (1976). Masculinity and the role of the combat soldier. In D. S. David & R. Brannon (Eds.), *The forty-nine percent majority: The male sex role* (pp. 179–183). Boston: Addison-Wesley.

Tiger, L. (1970). *Men in groups.* New York: Random House.

vanGennep, A. (1960). *The rites of passage.* Chicago: University of Chicago Press.

10

Masculinity, School, and Self in Sweden and the Netherlands

Alan Segal

How we render individual experience requires understanding the processes and details of social emergence. We conceptualize this emergence in different ways, but whether we refer to identity, the self, or to subjectivity, what we are grasping is the construction of, and our placement in, the world. Interviews carried out in the winter of 1998 in Sweden and the Netherlands explored whether and how a group of Europeans hold to a concept of (sexual) identity, and to gender, masculinity, and the school as factors in its construction. I requested a general explanation of identity and self-knowledge and asked if these were merely different labels for the same concept, or were distinguishable from each other. Following this were more specific analyses of sexual identity and school experience – referring to curriculum, other students, the social makeup and environment of the schools, and the behaviour and attitude of school personnel. All participants were between 15 and 23, two are heterosexual, and one is a female-to-male transsexual. Seven people will be discussed; their discussions of normalcy and otherness, and of masculinity as one of the boundaries complicating this relation, partially outline the politics of sexuality and sexual identity in their respective societies.

Michael Bach (1995) writes that our narratives of others and 'other' reflect how our own selves are established. Especially in Sweden, less overtly in the Netherlands, interviews communicated totemic narratives of masculinity. These narratives are the discursive attire of what Bach calls 'the institutionalized masculine' (p. 43). Diana Fuss (1995), focusing on more than masculinity, recommends 'identification' as a more auspicious conceptual mine.

I mention Fuss's work because she offers a psychological explanation for the complicatedness of identity, something noted by the interviewees. Also, Fuss suggests identification brings us closer to understanding the volatility of our expressions of identity, a state of affairs also cited in the interviews. Finally, she indicates that our identity vocabulary is inadequate descriptively and prescriptively. We cannot precisely see ourselves as we are, so we would learn more about ourselves by understanding the psychological foundations of our identifications. The interviews analyzed here are not intended to uphold or nullify Fuss's ideas. But they do indicate a range of identity discourse. On one hand, to be seen as somebody who is constantly changing might invite speculation about one's psychological stability, but to be seen as living an imperative that remains unchanged invites questions about one's capacity to grow. Growth gathers together in some kind of alignment, our epistemological and ontological understandings.

By 'alignment' I do not mean harmony or unity. I have in mind Probyn's (1993) comments on the self, which she describes as 'a mode of holding together the epistemological and the ontological' (p. 4). Self and identity are not synonymous in this view, but they are intimates of each other. One question in my mind as I traveled to Europe was how this holding together played out in daily life, in places supposedly quite unlike Canada.

A tale of two countries

Often we reduce the differences between and within countries to one cultural 'personality.' From a distance, Sweden and the Netherlands appear to many Canadians and Americans to be centres of sexual liberation and enlightenment. They assume a casualness about sex and gender in these places. Neither country in this research comes out looking so idyllic; they differ from the afar-romanticized image of them, and from each other as Swedes and Dutch and discrete nationals.

For example, differences were minimal when talking about schools. Discussing whether schools influence students' perceptions and expressions of identity and gender bewilders us. Doesn't every systematic effort to teach imply outcome? In my research conversations, the assurance softens as the words flow. People know the phenomena of human existence; they just can't be sure that any of it comes from a specific institutional locale. Most end by saying the universe shapes us, or every little institutional bit helps, or we learn from everything. How the school fits into the 'everything' is harder to explain, although interviewees know it's there. Overall, the Swedes and Dutch were convinced that schools do impress students.

Who were these participants? Jamie, 16, identifies himself as bisexual. He recently came to some resolution about his sexual and emotional interests, having found the singularity of hetero or gay sexuality perplexing and problematic. Camilla, 20, declares herself lesbian by choice. Finding no niche for herself as a feminist heterosexual woman, she locates it as a gay woman. Niklas, 18, has been independent for a few years. He is in a relationship with another male and has his family's support. Victoria, 21, gradually realized her lesbianism when she imagined hypothetical sexual relationships with people and saw that she contemplated only women. Bas, 20, is self-respecting and at ease with his sexuality. Maurice, 22, is visceral and physical in his self-description as gay. 'In my fantasies, in my viewing on the street, in my own world, sexual basis, I only like guys. But it's only sexual, emotional it doesn't matter for me if someone is a girl or boy, or no, it's pure sexual that makes me gay.' Jan, 23, began life with female genitals. At 16 he recognized that his birth sex did not match his identification as male.

Masculine Sweden: a discourse of disgust

In his study of gay life in Goteborg, Sweden from the 1940s through the 1960s, Nilsson (1998) identifies masculinity as a central feature of working-class experience. Males, whether interested in men or not, were not considered homosexual if they were masculine. Men with same-sex sexual affinities were presumed to be feminine. These affinities were not usually for other feminine people, but were directed at 'real men' whose self-representations were very masculine. Furthermore, Nilsson states, homosexual activity between masculine males was not condemned. Feminine males associated with each other, but were rarely joined by masculine men in casual public interaction because the latter feared others connecting them with the feminine crowd. While its forms have changed since the period Nilsson writes about, the public aversion and private liaison he describes have a legacy in the attitudes about masculinity expressed by the subjects.

Jamie is one example of the legacy. During the interview he stated he was bisexual, an identification having more to do with his fluctuating feelings about being gay than with feeling strong attractions to women and men. His first impressions of life as a gay person were that it was a joke and disgusting, yet interesting. However, disgust and mirth do not hold hands in this example.

Being gay means being emotionally interested in men, and bisexuality indicates an emotional inclination toward men and women, he says. Recognizing the implications of otherness, Jamie says he is bisexual. This suggests bisexuality is an easier state to live in and to live with than is being gay, begging the question of why disgust obliges acknowledgment of oneself as bisexual, in a supposedly very sexually open country that accepts non-heterosexuality.

In the year prior to the interview, Jamie came out as a gay person and joined a gay youth group, a membership he still holds and values. However, soon after coming out he retracted and said he liked girls and was disgusted that he considered himself a gay person. At one time, he told me, he thought he had to be heterosexual or gay. Now he realizes he can be both. This is not the same thing as saying he is both. In a doubly ironic take on otherness, Jamie moves from exclusive gayness because of a discourse of disgust, to the comfort of bisexuality, something he told me is more difficult to enact than being exclusively gay or heterosexual. In a country like Sweden, where, according to Jamie, homosexuality is normalized through one dominant gay institution, RFSL ('Riksforbundet for Sexuelt Likaberattigande'), and through broad gender expectations, being one thing or another has more clarity than being bisexual. Jamie seeks assurance in a vaguely defined identity.

Jamie's life in, and awareness of, otherness, was not limited to gay experience. He told me what I heard from other Swedes as well – that Sweden is not a country that integrates immigrants easily. Foreigners, certainly immigrants, struggle for good jobs. 'Swedes don't tolerate difference well.' Furthermore, he said, people must look typically Swedish.

And gays are in the same category as immigrants.

I met Jamie at BHUS ('Bi- and Homosexual Youth in Stockholm'), a drop-in centre and meeting place for gay youth in Stockholm. He appreciated the group because it was not RFSL, because it did not have a preconceived idea of what gay youth ought to be like or of what questions and concerns they should have. But Jamie knows from where such assumptions and expectations come.

School, he says, is where we learn about normalcy and not being different. School communicates society, and society traps people emotionally and economically. Hence the ideological and economic marginalization of immigrants. And since gays and lesbians are also different, they too are marginalized, even if in a country that rarely sees violence against them. The subjectivity of the other is established through institutional ascriptions that legitimate or deny people individually and collectively.

To suggest that gays and lesbians are as 'other' as immigrants, though, would alter Jamie's understanding of the politics of daily life. In contrast to Victoria's outlook expressed later, he thinks lesbians are more accepted in a male-dominated society than gays because of pornography. People (by which I think he means mainly heterosexual men) misunderstand lesbianism. They think women need men, and pornography communicates this. Regardless of the sexuality portrayed in pornography, women are objects of (heterosexual) men's desire. Women not desiring men are incomprehensible. Also, males have penises and holes and can do everything. Consequently gay males' behaviour can be a significant social challenge.

Perhaps without full awareness of the implication, Jamie notes an articulation of gay masculinity with heterosexist masculinity. All men inhabit the same gender envelope, but in the hierarchy of masculinity gay men are downgraded. Penises confer status on all males, but gays invoke the paradox described by Brian Pronger (1992). He says paradox unsettles gender myths acted out in daily life. However, important as it is, paradox is one aspect of the rejection of one's *place* in gender, not a rejection of gender itself.

This might explain Jamie's feelings of disgust, in that paradox and its provocation, in any society that emphasizes normalcy, can lead to disgust. Aversion and attraction are two sides of the identity coin. Interest and disgust are fueled in a parallel development of gender and sexuality.

Niklas is both a contrast and a complement to Jamie. He has a powerful sense of sexual selfhood. He decided he was gay when he was 13. At 17, he revealed this to his family and school friends. He expected reasonable treatment and received it from most. However, this was not his general expectation for all sexual identities. In his outlook on transvestites and transsexuals can be seen a subtle hint of the disgust that Jamie felt more openly.

Niklas's outlook is not a conscious condemnation. It is placed in a discourse of reciprocal relations – a practical approach to learning from and teaching, and getting along with, other people. 'It's accepting people for what they are. . . . If you want to get accepted as a person, whether you are homosexual or not, you have to accept other people. And if you're tolerant, you accept other people for what they are, and then they will probably accept you.' However, Niklas qualifies his statement because a society, and individuals, should have limits to what they deem acceptable.

> As long as these people *aren't dangerous to other people . . . dangerous for the society, like Nazis* or something . . . because they . . . are a threat to the democracy and the society. A good example is transvestites. I wouldn't

dress up like a woman but I accept . . . I want them to accept me and I want other people to accept me. (Author's italics)

When I pointed out that he had mentioned Nazis and transvestites, though not completely congruently, and asked him if he though that transvestites were beyond a limit, Niklas answered,

> Yes, for some people it's taboo, not many people are open with being transvestites. . . . It's not taboo in the gay world. . . . But I know some gay people who think it's awful being gay and being feminine. . . . I think it's the society that thinks that's really more unnatural than being gay. . . . I guess they aren't as much as gay and lesbian people are, a part of society. Now I don't mean they aren't a part of society in general, but they're not represented in debates and discussions like gays. And there aren't many that are open with that, they are transvestites. It's still beyond the limit. But maybe in a couple of years it won't be, because in 10 years the situation and the accept [*sic*] of gays and lesbians have improved incredibly fast, and today homosexuality is no longer something taboo, and questions about homosexuals are a common subject in media and in political discussions, and politicians and other people listen to homosexuals and their opinions. Now there is, of course, a big difference between homosexuals and trans-vestites because your homosexuality is a part of your life that you always carry with you, something you never forget. A transvestite change [*sic*] between being man or woman, they don't have the same reasons to fight for equal rights or an improved situation. To explain it further, they have of course the right to have the same security and the same rights as other people, but they have that, if they're heterosexual.

Gender normalization appears to operate together with gender polariza-tion, such that normalization can be compromised by transvestism. Transvestites are not part of an ongoing social debate. They are outside of common gender discourse by 'changing' from male to female. Nor-malization and masculinity are two strands of the same social fibre.

The change mentioned by Niklas represents a rift noticed by society. In a manner similar, perhaps, to what Nilsson outlined, transvestites become a contemporary form of the feminine man. If one can be either a real man or a feminine homosexual, where do people fit who occupy neither position? On the other hand, while looking upon transsexuals and transvestites as other sexual beings, Niklas does say that transvestites are, after all, heterosexual. So, while pointing to them as beyond normal in that they are not part of public debate, Niklas also concedes them normalcy because they are heterosexual.

Ironically, transvestite portrayal is a safe demonstration for the mascu-line man, for he knows that when he sheds the clothes he also sheds a danger of exposure and possible embarrassment. But for those who revel in the sensation of wearing women's clothing, and whose gender bends in sensing it, there can be only a risk of public shame. Niklas professed not to have the same perspective on these matters as other Swedes, in that he believes everyone has a right to self-expression. His desire to create a humane society without persecution is genuine, but it vies with the functionalist necessity of social taboos. And in the hierarchy of masculinities, transvestites are below gay men.

Transvestites and transsexuals solidify this hierarchy that gives gays a sufficiently masculine location, such that they are understandable to heterosexuals. However, according to some research participants, this also means women remain subordinate. So the more serious-looking are transvestite men's portrayals of women, the more seriously challenging they are of traditional gender values. And the more likely they are to arouse disgust in others. The people interviewed by Nilsson in his historical study referred to the disgust they heard and saw around them.

If Niklas's thoughts about being male and female are accurate, Swedish society conceptualizes women subordinately. Which is why greater shame would befall men who were noticeably gender-dissident. Symbolically the dress of transvestites, for instance, reifies a masculine–feminine opposition. And somewhat from this opposition, Niklas develops an epistemology of otherness. At one point he stated he knows himself more deeply than heterosexuals because he is gay.

Masculinity in Sweden develops from heterosexist assumptions. The homoeroticism of Niklas's world is not normalized sufficiently to prevent a heterosexist response. Gay people might be normalized, but not necessarily homoeroticism. Masculine gay men might soften the boundary between masculine and non-masculine behaviour, but not usually enough to make effeminate males acceptable or to eliminate a disgusted reaction.

Niklas was not always at ease about the place of lesbians and gays in Swedish society. Whereas being gay did not bother him, he was watchful of the circumstances of his eventual disclosure of it to friends and family. Swedish newspapers had articles on coming out, and a representative from RFSL once spoke in his class. Niklas remembers his feelings that day.

> I think when you're that young, and before you come out, you really try to hide it. I felt that I wouldn't want to say anything positive about gays because of what people then might think. But I wouldn't want to say anything negative either, because then people might have thought that he can't be gay, and in some way I wanted them to realize that I was a homosexual.

Even in a society like Sweden's, that sees itself as sexually open and culturally liberal, the politics of identity can create difficult currents through which gays and lesbians must make their way. Disgust need not be overt and strident. It can operate in a subdued, yet significant way. Most of those interviewed pondered the consequences of establishing themselves as homosexuals. But in Sweden the open consideration of being masculine was most evident.

How does identity fit into Niklas's broader outlook on masculinity and gender, on otherness and social cohesion, and on Swedish society? Importantly, it is a society in which he can identify himself as a gay man. But Niklas tries to link this to wider ideas about identity.

> I think that identity's everything that you are. Your experiences, memories, ethics, culture, background, and all that you've learned and seen during your life. But it's also national identity, emotional and sexual identity, and political identity.... But maybe it's not the right picture of your identity, it's something false you built up because you don't see ... yourself in the right way that other people maybe see you.

Does any of this understanding of identity and self-knowledge come from school? Not entirely, says Niklas. School is an adjunct to identity, not its essential underpinning.

In Sweden, schools were described as rarely discriminatory or derogatory in atmosphere or curriculum. Niklas said he could remember no incident or negative comment, and he never felt excluded or insulted by anything in the curriculum. Niklas believes his identity comes from a wide net of undertakings, exposures, and realizations. However, schools are focal points of external discourses that take hold in its corridors. In his early teens Niklas spent a lot of time grooming himself, especially his hair. Sometimes a few girls in the school, older than he, would say he was gay because of his self-attentiveness. Later, when Niklas was in the Gymnasium, the final segment of pre-university education, a government official visited the school. Before 300 people Niklas stood up to voice his opinions on homosexuality, and he was happy to hear afterward only support and praise from other students. Niklas felt considerable pride doing something he could not have done before. He had become mainstream and visible to his schoolmates.

School environment was important to this display. Niklas's school experience was not explicitly antagonistic to homosexuality, but nothing was overtly supportive of it either. He described schooling that gradually emphasized rules of order less frequently, and described the Gymnasium, which has students who are 16–19 years old, as a place that gives students a lot of autonomy to do their own work. Along with this autonomy, he said, the school shows respect for students in a wide variety of ways. Niklas offered an example that involved a teacher of his, coincidentally the person who acquainted him with my research.

> ...another thing about my Gymnasium, the teacher who told me about this interview, when he started in the school – I think it was like 15 or 20 years ago – the principal told him that maybe he [the teacher] would quit teaching at this school because there were a lot of rumors about him, because somebody had heard that he was gay. But then he went out in all the classes with the school's welfare officers and I think some teachers, and told everybody that he's gay. So then people stopped talking about him because everybody knew. But the principal said that before, about that he would quit his teaching because——was a very conservative community. But he stayed there and after that the rumours were gone.

Niklas invests a lot in this evidence of response and institutional change. Apart from it showing the responsiveness of a school, it also exemplifies how individual action can defuse rumour and dislodge opinion. That such action was necessary to begin with because of a principal's reaction to a rumour, that personal disclosure was required to uphold or deny the rumour in order to defuse it, is not a matter Niklas pursued. But he can see the effect of seizing an opportunity to make a point and insist on change, as Niklas himself did in the assembly before 300 people.

Niklas was at ease with his sexuality. But in his outlook on taboo and normalcy, on transvestites and transsexuals, there is the basis for the kind of disgust felt by Jamie, and for what was said to Nilsson in the interviews he conducted. Normalcy as an organizing precept of society facilitates abhorrence of abnormality. Disgust is the companion of abhorrence.

Other interviewees agree with Niklas's view that schools are not usually hurtful to lesbians or gays. Then they continue to speak of issues that Mac an Ghaill (1994) might address. He writes of various masculinities organized around characteristics of schooling: of divisions in programs and among students based on gender, gender role, curriculum program, personal ambition, social class background, sexuality, curricular policy set by government and school practice, and race. He indicates how students can be etched by school experience substantially not determined by the students themselves. Lesbians and gays, even in schools that deal with them humanely, but which are devoted to normalizing homosexuality, often find themselves ignored.

However, occasionally students end up in programs with an unusual proportion of people who don't identify themselves as heterosexual. This declares an alternative presence in the social curriculum. Victoria, 21 years old, had such an experience. And both Victoria and Camilla, the only women referred to in this chapter, offer an obverse position to those of the males, on masculinity and gay men. Nevertheless, masculinity discourse entwines them and the males.

Masculinity in Sweden: a discourse of pretense

In the Swedish interviews disgust as a weight of masculine discourse is a male response. The women on the other hand see the contradictions and fragmenting implications of the discourse. Its weight for them is awareness of its pretense and their desire for self-containment.

Contradiction, pretense, and adjustment were vivid in Victoria's account of her school experience. In the Gymnasium she was in a class for acting and dancing students. Victoria says about half the students were bisexual or gay. The school itself was, at best, indifferent to them. Some students displayed hostility, but nothing Victoria couldn't handle. She spoke mostly of the silence constructed around gay people by other students in the school.

> [M]ost pretended that they didn't even know about us, that they didn't understand. I mean, we were practically going around with signs . . . saying we were gay. We were happy about it. . . . They didn't understand. I mean, you could walk around talking to a friend about problems with your girlfriend, boyfriend, whatever, and the people that was standing next to you would six months later come out and say I heard that you had a girlfriend or boyfriend . . . and it was like they didn't hear what we were saying. But there were some programs that were very, very homophobic . . . almost non-theoretical whatsoever. They just work with their hands . . . we thought our intelligence was above them. So what they say was things that we've heard since we were kids, we didn't care. But . . . it was as if the gay part of us didn't exist in school at all. . . . When we did our final productions in acting there were one girl in my group that once sat with me, had a meeting about this production, when a friend of mine . . . sat down at the table and asked me questions about my current girlfriend. And . . . then he talked about his boyfriend . . . I was convinced that the other girl knew already. . . . She didn't say anything so I figured . . . she doesn't care. But she came up to me two or three months later and said 'you know what, I heard rumours that you had a girl friend.' So she hadn't been listening at all to our conversation.

Whether resentment explains Victoria's expression of intellectual superiority or not, Mac an Ghaill's observations have a parallel here.

Resentment follows the contours of division among students, and a divisiveness nurtured and encouraged by schools. Why think that working with one's hands makes someone less intelligent? Why would being theoretical count as a higher form of achievement, one used to differentiate oneself from peers who did not contemplate theory?

Masculinity encloses Victoria in two ways. First, while the gay part of her in one sense did not exist in school, it did in the subtle homophobia she witnessed. Also, considerations of Victoria's comment, alongside Nilsson's analyses of gay life in Goteborg in an earlier period, suggest that for some Swedes contemporary working-class masculinity remains a 'real men' mentality. Manual labour, homophobia, and masculinity are linked. This might be Victoria's deeper view when she dismisses the offensive students as 'almost non-theoretical.' Her pretense is that their comments had no bite.

Perhaps Victoria judged students too harshly. Perhaps people in their middle teens can't easily speak about sex with anyone, so they hear conversation but pretend not to. If Victoria had read Pronger's work, might she see in her school experience a hint of paradox? I think not, because the push of paradox does not come from noticing the differences between oneself and others. Irony, and recognition of the power in society that makes an ironic reaction the necessary choice among the less powerful, arouses awareness of paradox.

I asked Victoria if, when the girl approached her to say 'I heard you were gay,' this could have been the other student's way of acknowledging Victoria as a lesbian without letting on that she had heard the earlier conversation. Because maybe the time to mention it had passed, but that saying it when she did was the time for her to let Victoria know that she knew Victoria was a lesbian. Victoria agreed this was one explanation, but she expressed then a deeper consideration of Swedish society.

> [M]any people are very afraid of their own reaction towards gay sexuality, and so that instead of being confronted with their fear or whatever, it's easier for them to just shut the ears and . . . say, 'Oh, I didn't understand, I didn't listen, I didn't know.' Because then they wouldn't have to answer to whatever their own thoughts would be . . . . In Sweden it's sort of a trend to be as open as you can be, to have absolutely no prejudice about anyone. But I mean, people have prejudice. I have, about many groups of people. But it is such a sin to have them at all that people go around saying 'I'm not a racist but,' and then they come up with a horrible prejudice about blacks, everyone. But it's sort of, you're supposed to be open, and if you feel I can't be . . . as open as everyone thinks I should be, then you just, you turn it off, you don't hear, you don't see, you don't know about anything. Because it's a lot easier, because then you don't have to explain yourself. And it's quite common about regarding everything that isn't normal, so to speak.

This passage is a powerful indictment of education and contemporary society (and not just in Sweden). It indicates how discourse of normality, while supposedly drawing everyone together in wholesome unity, stifles educative encounters that might dispel prejudice. And in this statement otherness is granted, but to the extent that it must not be exposed through one's own prejudice. If homosexuality was once the love that dared not say its name, so is prejudice the awareness of otherness that dare not say itself.

Is there a need for education that goes beyond teaching students to conform? Do normalizing slogans on behalf of anything leave any community deprived of moral perspective and ethical goals? Does a society in which we don't have to explain ourselves to each other become one in which we never explain ourselves to each other? Any society that might leave us feeling secure but without meaningful, passionate connections can bring us no closer to the meeting of minds, emotions, ideas, and mutual enthrallment that I think Victoria seeks. Moreover, while she desires mutuality among lesbians and gay men, she condemns their frequent alienation from each other.

I know gay men that have enormous amounts of prejudice against lesbians. Many gay people have prejudice and...look down at bisexuals. A few lesbians that I've...known or listened to have prejudice about gay men. Many gay people have prejudice about black immigrants....I can't understand why gay men are so prejudiced about lesbians. I know a lot of gay men and I sort of count ourselves to being the same, because we are, when it comes to society, we are included in the same minority. We are, we have mostly the same rights, and we have mostly the same things we can't do, and we are exposed...we're vulnerable in the same way...[but] it's okay for you to be lesbian as long as you don't show it in any way. As long as you're still feminine in the way you dress, if you can still say about a man who walks down the street that he's attractive, if you don't narrow down people that are attracted to being women....If you're a lesbian, then you're strange, you're weird, you're someone that is not quite from this planet...and if you are the least bit masculine...that's a bad thing.... A boy...asked me just a few months ago if it was tough to be a lesbian. And I said well, yeah...it is in many ways. And he said, 'no, no, I don't mean like in society, other people.'...He thinks it's the worst kind of sex you could ever have, must be between two women. He is disgusted when he sees two women kiss each other. So I'm sort of accepted by him, and I'm okay as a person so long as I don't show him that I have a sexuality that is towards other women. And he is like that regarding every lesbian that he ever runs into.

Victoria said 80 percent of the gay men she knows or meets exhibit these attitudes. The strangeness of lesbians is a linchpin of patriarchal masculinity, in that it is preserved by virtue of what women do and are; but, to the gay men Victoria knows, less so by what *they* do or are. Furthermore Victoria recounts that,

> they [gay men] treat lesbians in many ways just the same as heterosexual men treat heterosexual women...it's well, you're okay but we're better than you. And the gay men know that they're often more accepted by heterosexuals than lesbians are, and they tend to take advantage of that in attitudes toward lesbians.

Gay males may violate expected standards of gender and masculinity, but they still count as males, especially if they aren't effeminate. Lesbians, particularly masculine lesbians, violate the standards completely.

When Victoria considered when and how awareness of her lesbianism developed, however, the relationship between construction and identity was not plain. How did she realize she is lesbian?

> It was a number of incidents when a friend of mine and I – she was a bit older than I, very, very sexually active – and of course the subject [of] sex came along, sooner or later, and I remember that she asked me once sort of hypothetically, if I could choose anyone to go to bed with, who would that be? And I couldn't think of any man.... I assumed that, well, it's just, you know, experiment, sort of curiosity. So I didn't reflect on my own answers to her question.

Not reflecting did not mean remaining unperturbed. What Victoria could not do, despite knowing the word 'lesbian,' was say it. She did not use 'lesbian' until she moved to Goteborg and saw gay people holding hands publicly.

Pretense comes with different facades, and Victoria sees several of them. Victoria might indeed have been merely curious about same-sex affinity, but her reluctance to call herself lesbian insinuates a deeper comprehension of the risk of disclosure and the disgust that could follow, including that observed in gay men. Victoria detects a facade in those students who 'suddenly' discovered she is not heterosexual. Another is evident in her hurt and anger when told by gay men who know she is lesbian, that she should feign heterosexual interest in males – yet another pretense.

When our conversation moved to the broader idea of identity, Victoria began with some casual descriptions.

> I think identity is mostly everything about you, because your looks can be part of your identity...you can feel comfortable wearing certain clothes, having your hair done in a certain way...identity is, I think, a lot about

your moral standards, your prejudice is part of your identity too, because that tells a lot about a person.... Identity is what you have left when you're all alone in the world, nobody calling on the phone, nobody being there.... You're sort of isolated, so that you only have yourself to think about, to answer to. So it's sort of not your soul but your, the core of your soul, the little piece deepest inside.

Identity here is not something you give in to, as some in this research have feared, but is a private nurturance and a solitary detection. If we distill from our lives all that is adjustment, accommodation, or resignation; when we face ourselves alone, what is left is who we are. This is more than isolation from the world. What Victoria cannot evade is that the idea of a soul, and its use as a reference for identity, is discursive. And when she continues musing about identity, and goes back into the world in her mind, she sees its epistemological and ontological limits and possibilities.

I think that it's for the best if you don't have a complete identity in your entire life, because I think that we have to sort of process that all the time, and revalue things, rethink about everything, and sort of rebuild ourselves, our ideas, our thoughts, our goals in life, everything, over and over again, all the time, because if we, so if I sort of complete my identity, that would also mean that I don't bring in new ideas, new people, new emotions, new values.... So, I think we have to construct our identity as an ongoing process throughout the entire life. But... I don't think that we can be open to everyone and everything, because then we would sort of lose ourselves.... You have recognized yourself as a certain identity, and having that safety and knowledge and acceptance about yourself makes a foundation that is solid and then won't change.... I've learned that being lesbian makes me an outsider no matter what.... So I tend to be very protective of what I have, what I am, the friends I have, the people I love, my family, everything. Because *I don't want to make myself stand outside of society more than I already do.* I don't want to be more alone than I already will be because of my sexuality, because of the people I will fall in love with or spend my life with. (Author's italics)

Identity, as Victoria explains it, can be a reassuring presence even when it's not fully observable. However, the emphasis on being normal, on not being a masculine woman, disrupts the reassurance. The pretense demanded of her is immediate. She is already the other, both to mainstream Swedish society and to most gay men she knows. She doesn't want to make herself stand out more. She is born into discourse, but her desire to live a self-directed, self-respecting life leads her to place the onus of being something, of effecting identity, on her shoulders. This reflects what many others in this research have said.

Cindy Patton (1993) says that rather than try to fasten identity in our minds, we must appreciate that a chaotic understanding of it accounts more reasonably for the turmoil we undergo as it develops. Unlike Fuss, whom I will mention later, Patton is not troubled by the conceptual or vocabulary deficiencies often seen in articulations of identity. Her question is whether people can feel rooted through identity. She concludes that 'identity is an issue of deontology, not ontology; it is a duty of ethics, not of being' (pp. 147–148). Victoria and Camilla would not agree with Patton.

To them, being and ethics are not irreconcilable. When Victoria says she cannot understand gay men, who live under the same strictures as lesbians; when she refers to forthright prejudice – the better to deal with it openly and constructively, Victoria reaches for the ethics of being. When she claims that gay males and lesbians are in the same minority, she does not realize that she might be numerically right, but conceptually she is mistaken. Masculinity makes gay men in Sweden different. Their minority is not congruent with that of lesbians. What Victoria wants may not be achievable; she wants ethics and being that make all homosexuals incumbent in the establishment of their identities.

Camilla's response to the pretense she sees is quieter, but not less astute than Victoria's. She articulates the contrast between sexual attraction and romantic attachment. Her sexual attractions were to men initially, and her romantic bonds were with women. As Camilla's feminist views became clearer, however, her sexual responsiveness to women developed. She decided she did not want heterosexual relationships.

This suggests an identity in which gender, intellect – especially a feminist one – romance, and sex, fold in on each other. Folding in, however, does not convey harmony, for it is the conflict around each of these that moved Camilla to identify herself as lesbian. This does not mean that Camilla realized her authentic identity, for that is something she denies is possible. When speaking of identity in general and not of sexuality and romantic involvement, Camilla claims multiple sets of identities for all of us. We have many identities, she says, but our main one is what we show or what we know when talking to ourselves. Note the reference to a main identity, not an authentic one.

This 'self-narrativizing' has epistemological and ontological importance, in that Camilla develops identity out of the myriad frames of woman, feminist, lesbian, Swede as citizen, Swede as cultural conveyer, and heterosexual woman, to name only the more explicit among them. Accentuating the significance of this is her belief that we are all part of each other, that all identities are part of us, but that authenticity, which presumably refers to an elemental and unique state, is not in any of us. In such a condition of inauthenticity, by implication we should strive to know our main identity.

Such effort can be futile, however, in a society so tenacious about masculinity and femininity. Camilla's sense of otherness comes partly from her discomfort in a heterosexual realm. Why wouldn't romance have followed the lead of her early sexual attraction to men? Why was it the sexual part of her life that shifted to those with whom she had stronger emotional bonds? In her reach for personal identity, Camilla enters Pronger's state of paradox. Sexuality and romance eventually coincided with a profound emotional and intellectual interest in women. Paradox and pretense were not irrelevant to the coincidence.

On the other hand, paradox becomes noticeable through the distress of living in a gap. When we assume authentic identity, and find ourselves stymied and distorted as we grope for it, we can discover paradox. If we assume authenticity is beyond us, or is perhaps not even desirable, it is more difficult to become troubled by paradox. Camilla sits somewhere between these positions. She chose lesbianism, after all, to counter a rigid culture that 'pushes us into heterosexuality.' Camilla believes we are all born bisexual, but we become 'specialized' as we pass through cultural filters. (This essentialist idea of sexuality was mentioned by almost everyone I interviewed in Sweden.) To be gay or lesbian should mean rejecting narrow constructions of masculinity and femininity.

Normal in/difference: sexuality and gender in the Netherlands

Interviews in the Netherlands – conducted in Amsterdam, Utrecht, and Nijmegen – delineated a social environment not less committed to normalization than Sweden's, but one that complicated its commitment with apparent indifference. This is not to say that anything sexual is acceptable, but that confronting variations is not a Dutch characteristic.

First impressions of the Netherlands from a North American standpoint suggest the reputation of sexual liberalism is justified, especially if the first real exposure to the country is Amsterdam. For people looking for homosexual exploration, the Spartacus Gay Guide lists numerous bars, clubs, social and political organizations, all attuned to a wide array of interests. More generally, prostitution and explicit pornography catering to many sexualities add to the impression. However, this is the surface of a society very cognizant of its adaptations and daily compromises.

As in Sweden, the Netherlands has had a national gay organization, the COC (Dutch Organization for the Integration of Homosexuality). It has existed for more than fifty years, during which there has been occasional conflict over its purpose and philosophy. Some people have accused it of being too eager to melt homosexuals into the Dutch cultural landscape. This conflict was part of a larger tapestry. In the late 1970s, some gay activists condemned cruising and public sexual activity because it contradicted the more desirable image of the homosexual they were trying to establish in the public mind (van Lieshout, 1995). And in his discussion of the murders of gay men by younger males who'd been sexual partners of the victims, van Gemert (1994) notes the reluctance of the older men to have their same-sex interest disclosed, and some of the younger males' contemptuous attitude toward gay men. A society oblivious to sexual variety and its manifestations, and to norms organized around gender, would rarely produce these attitudes.

On the other hand, normalization has achieved integration. Hekma and van der Meer (1992) state that lesbians and gays do not see their social, political, and love lives as the founding principle of their sexual communities. To be gay or lesbian is not synonymous with setting the boundaries of one's existence. To what extent did participants in this work inherit and experience these social currents?

Of the total number of interviews completed in the Netherlands, only one subject said that sex education in schools covered sexuality thoroughly. Interviewees stated that, of whatever attention was offered, the proportion of the curriculum given to gay sexuality was far less than what the topic merited. And frequently it was not mentioned at all.

Having said this, however, the Dutch participants easily expressed their sexuality. Bas, for example, describes himself as being openly gay, always and everywhere. He did hear 'putdowns' directed at him in school, but he was always able to deflect or ignore them with his self-respect and humour.

His sense of self is forthright, as is his statement that 'identity is just how a person is.' Explaining self-knowledge proved more formidable, especially when I inquired if it was another way of speaking to identity.

> That's a tricky one. No, I don't think so. If you have a lot of self-knowledge you know your identity. But I don't think it's the person who you really are. I mean, I know about myself, but I still don't know my complete identity, and I don't know if I'm going to know everything about my identity.

This viewpoint is close to the views expressed by Camilla and Victoria.

Epistemologically and ontologically, Bas claims to have learned rarely from other gay people. When I asked him if gays and lesbians received the same attention and treatment in school from peers as he did, he said he hadn't noticed anything. Occasional razzing, he said, didn't bother him so he didn't detect what other gays might have gone through. On the other hand, when we discussed whether schools influence students, he said yes and gave an example.

> If... you're only in class with people who are against the Turkish people, and they always say... ah, those Turkish people, and they're wrong and bad, and now you would also get those opinions, you always, you will get started sometime by saying Turkish people are bad.

Race was a more noticeable example of how curriculum and social attitudes create difference than was gender or sexuality. Whereas Bas does not identify explicitly with Turks, he does use a discriminatory classroom regime to highlight his point. Awareness of prejudice, difference, and otherness does not come to him through sexuality because he is so ardently and happily gay. But he is not blind to subordination.

Maurice, 22, was not as attuned to this as Bas. He was the one who said that sexuality makes him gay, but that he can have emotional bonds with people of either sex. His school background was in a 'little city' with two schools, one strict, the other a more relaxed Free School. Students in both places were racially and economically alike. Maurice did mention that his school years were lonely because he didn't feel he could participate in discussions about heterosexuality. 'I never felt like I was part of that culture,' he told me.

Thinking about the breadth of identity rather than sexual identity specifically, Maurice said, 'Identity is what you are... what you believe in and how you look at things.... A part of my identity can be how I interact with other people. For example, I find it important that I treat everyone with the same respect.' I speculate that for Maurice, being gay and learning the value of respect go together. Masculinity was not a basis of differentiation as it was in Sweden, but normalization was.

We do not have to melt all sexualities into one before we can speak of similarities in human experience. In a society indifferent to sexual variations, detachment from peers might transpire for other reasons than one's sexuality. Obviously the culture as Maurice experienced it was not indifferent enough, despite him saying he had no idea of the experience of other gay people in his school. If the data from people in the Netherlands is accurate, very little discrimination is evident in Dutch schools. However, this does not mean none exists. Maurice did learn through subtle exclusions the knowledge of difference.

When I asked if self-knowledge in his case had any connection to not feeling part of 'that [school] culture' and to his identity, Maurice said,

> I think self-knowledge is that part of your identity for which you are familiar with, you know about yourself, it's about you think you are that way... and you know that's important to you. But I think your identity is always part hidden agenda, like a hidden agenda you do not know about yourself.

Unlike Camilla, who thinks authentic identity is a myth and thus unachievable, Maurice postulates identity as something personal but not really knowable. We are 'other' to ourselves, in that a part of us is indiscernible. A hidden agenda need not indicate ulterior motives, but given its inscrutability, that is what might be concealed.

Diana Fuss (1995) might draw our attention to another meaning of hidden agendas, available to us through identification. She believes this helps us understand inscrutability. Identity is not irrelevant, but Fuss considers identification a more profitable link to the self.

> Identification inhabits... identity. It operates as a mark of self-difference ...a self that is perpetually other. Identification... does not... stand against identity[,] but structurally aids and abets it.... Identification is a process that... prevents identity from ever approximating the status of an ontological given, even as it makes possible the formation of an illusion of identity as immediate, secure, and totalizable. (p. 2)

Moreover, identification accounts for our evasions and psychological compensations. To whatever degree this may pertain to Maurice, his veiw of identity as something never fully identifiable states its intricacy and vastness. This is the detail most contributors to my research cannot describe. This is the part of identity that fascinates, torments, captivates, eludes, and lures all of them. Even after they move to the brink of it, they rarely look over the edge.

Jan is an exception. He looked over the gender edge and saw himself as a man, not as a woman. Jan knew finally he wanted to be a man when he was around 16, but nothing in his environment forcefully prodded him toward gender self-scrutiny at an earlier age. He sensed a difference in himself, but nothing that he named until later. 'I suppose that maybe my classmates thought I was lesbian, I don't know. Because I always behaved like a boy.' Jan was born female but identifies himself as a gay man. As gender behaviour became more important to his peers, and Jan's discomfort began, his thoughts focused on linkages – of identity, body, gender, and societal values. Even in a relatively open society such as the Netherlands, where I was told changing one's sex is easier to accomplish than in many other places, difference, and the focusing of issues around it, complicate self-realization.

Even when I realized that I was born in the wrong body, then I didn't really want to deal with this, and just try to be like the other kids. . . . I think it's very clear I did feel something first and later on had the vocabulary. I think that's with most people. Um, actually some of my friends I've talked with, straight girls, and after I told them . . . I am transsexual, and funny enough, it made some of them think. Because all of a sudden they thought like, oh well, I was a tomboy when I was younger, well, what makes me do things? . . . It does surprise me that they tried that label on themselves. . . . There are guys as well as women in this. Sometimes they play with gender identity as well. I was always paranoid of people finding this out.

The epistemology of gender identity perplexes as it goads. Jan had an avenue – gender reassignment – but this upheld the dualistic doctrine of gender at the same time as it permitted escape. Nevertheless, Jan's realization that he was in the wrong body still left him unable to declare it openly to himself, and paranoid about others finding it out.

Language carries a disproportionate burden of consequence. Perhaps the people Jan mentions asked if they might be transsexual because they wanted to recreate a foundation of friendship with Jan, that they were worried might change with his disclosure he was going to be a man. Or maybe Jan's example stirred them to seriously analyze gender and sexuality. Regardless of their reasons, their stance was safer than Jan's, which I think explains partly why he was surprised at how easily they were prompted to reassess the connection of label and identity. What did they reappraise? Whether being a tomboy meant they were not the females they thought they were. Jan, on the other hand, wasn't trying out the vocabulary, he was momentously fusing vocabulary and bodily identification. The subjects constituted by language in these two instances are different. To the extent that ontology and epistemology are differentiated based on gender, so to that degree was Jan's life to become infinitely complicated. Are there more powerful triggers of paradox than the dogged contradictions of gender identity?

. . . people will always say 'yeah, I was 3 when I knew.' But I'm not sure how this is . . . maybe because when I was a kid my primary school was traditional and had conventional ideas about gender. Still, until I was about 12 I could always do as I wanted. I could play with girls and boys. *So I never felt myself placed into any kind of gender category.* Also at home, but my father now says if I had been born a boy he would have raised me differently. But, still, the way I perceive it is, he did include me in many of the things that he did. So I don't really see it as a problem. . . . So maybe because I could behave and feel the way I felt, and wanted to feel and behave, until I was 10, that this didn't prompt me to think about it. It took me a while. (Author's italics)

Daily experience crafted Jan's understanding of the external world. Dutch indifference does not extend to being uninterested in what gender children become. However, in his case social experience and personal imperative were not so variant or mutually incoherent that he felt a different gender was trying to claw its way out of him. Being a girl did not, in his earlier years, require behavioural expectations that he was unable to meet. And he did not feel rebuked by his father, who, Jan thinks, had such a close relationship with him anyway that, though his father told him he would have raised Jan differently had he been male, the difference in the rearing Jan did receive as a girl was not noticeable to him. (Jan's mother was not mentioned.) Overt paradox was a later experience.

When he explained his desire to change his sex, Jan spoke of it as a persistent call from within. His family asked,

> 'How do you know this? You aren't a guy, so how do you know you should be a guy?' It's almost impossible. . . . I tried to explain to them that it's a gut feeling, it's something I know. My body just doesn't feel right. . . . My parents asked, 'aren't you just a lesbian?' . . . [But] the first time I came across transsexuality in an article I immediately had this realization of recognition. Although this was about a male-to-female, I immediately felt, oh my god, this does feel familiar.

When Jan related this to me, his tale of disclosure was apolitical. He was, he thought, just telling his family that a daughter/sister was becoming a son/brother. But it was important enough to his family to ask if he were not just a lesbian. Same-sex identity in Dutch society is sufficiently normalized that this was an alternative that could be suggested to Jan.

The gender clinic offering sex changes has particular assumptions about gender and identity. At one time some people in the program who knew they were lesbian or gay hid this from the professionals operating the program because, Jan said, they worried 'this might make the people who were treating them think that they weren't really transsexual.'

Hekma and van der Meer (1992) indicate that gays and lesbians don't base their communal relations on sexual identity. But this does not mean it is found nowhere in Dutch society. Also, while sexual identity might not serve as a foundation for this organizing, gender ethos and practise might. Simple statements about one's gender or sexuality can have political, cultural, and social implications. In the Netherlands I was told that transsexualism is not necessarily considered an identity in its own right. A person is one gender or another. Jan agrees. He is gay, not transsexual.

His decision to undergo a sex change altered also his interpretation of identity.

> ...if somebody says you're transsexual, I will say no, I'm sorry, I'm not. And actually, this is funny, because before I started with this I saw it more often as identity, now I see it more of a phase, I suppose. I assume that once you have self-knowledge, then you can distill from this your gender identity.

Distillation sounds easy, yet not until Jan read about the transsexual experience of another individual did he realize he was transsexual himself.

Dutch society acknowledges transsexualism, but not as a viable alternative in itself. Transsexuals' status in gender discourse is transitional, not definitive. Indeed, the people I spoke with who had been or are in the gender clinic indicated they would not disclose they had once been male or female after all procedures were finished, because they could not be sure that people would treat them well. This suggests a difference between a concept of identification as transsexuals and a concept of identity as males or females, as men or women. Social indifference does not imply that we accept whatever we are indifferent to.

In Jan's life, epistemology and ontology meet in his answer to my question, 'do you lack... life experience that you think others... have?' His answer resounds with awareness.

> Yeah. Very much so. For me, although I know that I'm gay, this is more theoretical knowledge. So if I hadn't been transsexual I'm sure that I would have had sexual experience which now I lack. On the other hand, I do think that, uh, this has given me some sort of experience that other people don't have. You do have to question many things to go through this whole procedure.

In this straightforward summation of self-respect and personal audacity is the succinct tie around the experience of all the people I have discussed. Especially in the last two sentences, we find the incentive to create our identities and the spirit to persist in the face of adversity.

The end of the tale

School experience described in Europe indicates a general lack of antagonism, vicious taunts and intimidation, and of persistent derogatory comments from students and teachers. However, Sweden and the Netherlands also appear as societies preoccupied with normalization.

In an earlier phase of this research conducted in Canada (see Segal, 1995), most participants condemned external emphases on normality, but also wanted to be normalized – in the curriculum, in the social life of the school, and in society at large. Europeans mentioned here say they already live in such societies. There are, however, significant gender differences in how they perceive this, and in their measurement of its limits. Most of them felt their minority situation. In Sweden, the discourse of masculinity permeated the responses.

For all their renowned tolerance and supposed easy attitudes about sex, gender normalcy is a powerful social doctrine in Sweden and the Netherlands. Derogatory terms meaning 'homosexual' are used as epithets. And though participants say the words are generic, that they do not mean something specifically anti-gay, it is a phenomenon I have encountered everywhere I have researched. These terms are precise in their denunciation and ridicule of gays and indicate how a supposedly neutral term has prior and post-usage negative meanings for them and for others of alternative sexualities.

Minority status does not obligatorily become a basis for discrimination, but gender practises that stress masculinity create a premise of otherness. While Foucault (1980) would say we are not simply 'other' or not, Diana Fuss asks '[I]s it possible to separate so completely the imitation from what it imitates? Is it possible for the mimicking subject to inhabit fully a performance of role while still remaining largely outside it?' (p. 151).

From a sociological standpoint, does Jamie's and Niklas's disgust establish them as inhabiters or outsiders of a role? Does Jamie's bisexuality render him more or less a mimicking subject than is Niklas? As Jan moved from self-recognition as a transsexual – an identity he then dismissed as not viable – toward becoming a male, was he repositioning himself, or being repositioned, in male subjectivity? Fuss says that identifying as leads to identifying with; is this what Victoria refers to when she says that most gay men she knows enact masculinity in heterosexist ways, and treat women as heterosexual men treat women? When she says gay men and lesbians are the same minority, Victoria mistakenly thinks that a lesbian's awareness of her adjustments and accommodations to a larger society is what establishes gay men similarly as subjects. However, normalizing discourse in Sweden differentiates gay men from lesbians. They and lesbians are not commensurately a minority.

I disagree with Fuss's reduction of habitation to mimicry, but I value her query about the possibility of remaining outside while incarnating the position. We become the norm even as we may try to repudiate it. And often we do not resist at all.

Elspeth Probyn (1993) gives greater credence to identity than Fuss does. Probyn asks if we can live identity in ways that do not prejudge and preclude others through a 'disjuncture between the articulated and the lived' (p. 22). And Pronger's reference to paradox is a cognate concept of Probyn's disjuncture.

Victoria and Camilla perceived disjuncture, between romance and eroticism, between masculinity and femininity. But Pronger speaks of degrees of rejection of one's place in gender and not a rejection of gender itself. So when Swedish gay men think their lesbian compatriots aren't feminine enough, but that gay guys are masculine men, they become examples of what Pronger is talking about.

This reference does not mean that gendered social relations are unique to Sweden. Connell (1995) observes that

> [M]asculinity is shaped in relation to an overall structure of power (the subordination of women to men), and in relation to a general symbolism of difference (the opposition of femininity and masculinity). Men's counter-sexist politics is dissidence directed towards the former, gender-violation is dissidence directed towards the latter. (p. 223)

Camilla responds to her society by converging eros and romance and identity. Victoria condemns the lack of counter-sexist politics among most gay men she knows, and Niklas's description of transsexuals and transvestites speaks of the discomfort that disjuncture causes Swedes. Nevertheless, for all the discomfort, dissidence is minimized because the politics of being lesbian, gay, transsexual, transgendered, or queer is deflected into normalized gender relations.

Sexuality and gender can crystallize disjuncture and paradox anywhere, but Bas in the Netherlands failed to notice it. And while Maurice did not stipulate any ruptures, he did comment on hidden agendas as an aspect of identity. What is veiled can also be disjunctive.

Where does the school fit in this? Respondents in both the Netherlands and Sweden stated that sex education, while a formal part of the curriculum, was only occasionally included in their schooling. Homosexuality was briefly discussed, if at all, and often teachers, no matter their ages, were uncomfortable teaching anything about sex. Despite moderate or no hostility to them in Swedish and Dutch schools, respondents still felt somewhat outside 'normal' society.

Life experience is the core of what these people strive to understand. This is the domain they want to bring to their classmates. When Niklas said he was proud to have put a question to a speaker at a school assembly on behalf of gay rights, this is partly what he meant. In their desire to communicate themselves to their peers, the subjects view their life experience as the crux of their identities.

Identities are our discursive pennants, and we furl or flaunt them according to possibilities embedded in our cultures. Schools communicate culture by piquing our sensibility and our bigotry; they instill assumptions about the workings and limitations of the universe. Anything in society that is designed to evoke patterns of thought and frameworks of values is part of the technology of developing not only the guideposts of knowledge, but also the understanding of what it means to be knowledgeable. And from this knowledge we gain our placement in the world. European contributors to this work reveal that we complicate it with gender and the ideology of difference.

REFERENCES

Bach, M. (1995). Uncovering the institutionalized masculine: Notes for a sociology of masculinity. In T. Haddad (Ed.), *Men and masculinities* (pp. 37–55). Toronto: Canadian Scholars' Press.

Connell, R. (1995). *Masculinities*. Berkeley: University of California Press.

Foucault, M. (1980). *Power/knowledge*. New York: Pantheon.

Fuss, D. (1995). *Identification papers*. New York: Routledge.

Hekma, G., and van der Meer, T. (1992). Gay and lesbian studies in the Netherlands. *Journal of Homosexuality, 24*(1/2), 125–136.

Mac an Ghaill, M. (1994). *The making of men*. Buckingham: Open University.

Nilsson, A. (1998). Creating their own private and public: The male homosexual life space in a Nordic city during high modernity. In J. Lofstrom (Ed.), *Scandinavian homosexualities. Essays on gay and lesbian studies* (pp. 81–116). Binghamton, New York: The Haworth Press.

Patton, C. (1993). Tremble, hetero swine. In *Fear of a queer planet: Queer politics and social theory* (pp. 143–177). Minneapolis: University of Minnesota.

Probyn, E. (1993). *Sexing the self*. New York: Routledge.

Pronger, B. (1992). *The arena of masculinity*. Toronto: University of Toronto.

Segal, A. (1995). *Schools, identity, and homosexuality*. Unpublished doctoral dissertation, University of British Columbia, Vancouver.

van Gemert, F. (1994). Chicken kills hawk: Gay murders during the eighties in Amsterdam. *Journal of Homosexuality, 26*(4), 149–174.

van Lieshout, M. (1995). Leather nights in the woods: Homosexual encounters in a Dutch highway rest area. *Journal of Homosexuality, 29*(1), 19–39.

11

Cool Pose: Black Masculinity and Sports

Richard Majors

Sport, as a social institution, emerged in the 19th and 20th centuries in response to a shifting constellation of class and gender dynamics. Not only did sport make a crucial contribution to the ideological naturalization of men's superiority over women, popular belief held that working-class men and men of color could not possibly compete successfully with 'gentlemen.' Thus, as a homosocial environment within which white upper- and middle-class males sharpened their competitive skills, sport became an important institution in which the superiority of hegemonic masculinity was supported and reproduced, while women and other (subordinated) men were marginalized (Connell, 1987).

Interestingly, since World War II – and especially in the last 15 years – athletic roles within major organized sports in the United States have come to be dominated by black men. The dynamics of this historic shift – and the extent to which the contemporary dominance of certain sports by black males is more a sign of continued racism than a sign of progress – have been examined elsewhere (H. Edwards, 1973, 1984; Tygiel, 1983). The goal of this chapter is to illustrate how contemporary black males often utilize sports as one means of masculine self-expression within an otherwise limited structure of opportunity. After a brief discussion of contemporary black men and masculinity, this chapter will show how what the author calls 'cool pose' (i.e., a set of expressive lifestyle behaviors) is often developed and used by black men as a response to the limits that institutionalized racism places on their other opportunities for self-expression. This chapter will argue that sport has become a major institutional context for the expression of cool pose, and that although self-expression through athletics does offer a small number of black males an escape from the limits imposed by poverty and racism, for the majority, sport is a form of self-expression that ultimately can lock them into their low-status positions in society.

Black men and masculinity

Despite the recent proliferation of men's studies programs and the resultant publications based on this growing academic interest in masculinity (Brod, 1987; Kimmel, 1987), research on how ethnicity, race, and socioeconomic status affects the development of masculinity remains limited. In particular, black males are either rendered invisible or are viewed as helpless victims of a racist system. With a few exceptions (e.g., Cazenave, 1984; Franklin, 1984; Majors, 1986, 1987), there has been a noteworthy dearth of literature on black men's actual responses (i.e., survival strategies, coping mechanisms, and forms of resistance) to a limited structure of opportunity. The problems facing black males today are so serious, and their consequences so grave, it is tempting to view these men primarily as victims. In fact, Stewart and Scott (1978) have argued that there is a contemporary 'institutional decimation of black males,' which these authors describe as the 'coordinated operation of various institutions in American society which systematically remove black males from the civilian population' (p. 85). Indeed, recent research has shown that young black males are experiencing unprecedented setbacks in their struggles for economic and educational equality in the United States, a nation that holds equal opportunity as one of its founding principles (Gibbs, 1988; Larson, 1988). Black men are among the predominant victims of an entire range of socioeconomic, health, and stress-related problems. These problems include, but are not limited to, higher rates of heart disease, hypertension, infant mortality, mental disorders, psychiatric hospitalization, homicide, unemployment, suspension from school, imprisonment, and morbidity and low life expectancy (Bulhan, 1985; Cordes, 1985; Gite, 1985; Heckler, 1985).

Black males have responded in various ways to this constricted structure of opportunity. What is of interest here is how black males' relationships to dominant definitions of masculinity have figured into their responses to institutionalized racism. Many black males have accepted the definitions, standards, and norms of dominant social definitions of masculinity (being the breadwinner, having strength, and dominating women). However, American society has prevented black males from achieving many aspects of this masculinity by restricting their access to education, jobs, and institutional power. In other words, the dominant goals of hegemonic masculinity have been sold to black males, but access to the legitimate means to achieve those goals has been largely denied black males (Staples, 1982). As a consequence of these conditions, many black males have become *men manqué*; because of the many frustrations resulting from a lack of opportunities in society, many black males have become obsessed with proving manliness to themselves and to others.[1] Lacking legitimate institutional means, black males will often go to great lengths to prove their manhood in interpersonal spheres of life (e.g., fighting, the emotional and physical domination of women, and involvement in risk-taking activities; Majors, 1986; Staples, 1982).

Cool pose as an expression of black masculinity

Institutional racism and a constricted structure of opportunity do not cause all black males to exhibit antisocial behaviors, nor do these problems succeed in erasing black men's expressions of creativity. In fact, black men often cope with their frustration, embitterment, alienation, and social impotence by channeling their creative energies into the construction of unique, expressive, and conspicuous styles of demeanor, speech, gesture, clothing, hairstyle, walk, stance, and handshake. For the black male, these expressive behaviors, which are a particular manifestation of what the author has elsewhere described as cool pose (Majors, 1986, 1987), offset an externally imposed invisibility, and provide a means to show the dominant culture (and the black male's peers) that the black male is strong and proud and can survive, regardless of what may have been done to harm or limit him. In other words, the expressive lifestyle is a 'survival strategy that makes oneself interesting and attractive to others... through [the process of] making oneself an interesting object, through the cultivation of an aura... that elicits rewarding responses from others' (Rainwater, 1966, p. 214).

Although black people have been forced into conciliatory and often demeaning positions in American culture, there is nothing conciliatory about the expressive lifestyle. It is adaptation rather than submission. In that sense, then, cool pose is an attempt to carve out an alternative path to achieve the goals of dominant masculinity. Due to structural limitations, a black man may be impotent in the intellectual, political, and corporate world, but he can nevertheless display a potent personal style from the pulpit, in entertainment, and in athletic competition, with a verve that borders on the spectacular. Through the virtuosity of a performance, he tips the socially imbalanced scales in his favor and sends the subliminal message: 'See me, touch me, hear me, but, white man, you can't copy me!' The expressive lifestyle invigorates the demeaning life of black men in white America. It is a dynamic vitality that transforms the mundane into the sublime and makes the routine spectacular.

Black male expression and sport

Sport has become one of the major stages upon which black males express their creativity. For example, in football, Butch Johnson and Billy 'Whiteshoes' Johnson were two well-known athletes who exhibited expressive lifestyle behaviors on the playing field. Both men were known for their fancy dances and 'spikes' in the end zone after a touchdown. To further accentuate themselves (i.e., to be 'cool'), these athletes wore wristbands and hung towels from their pants. In basketball, Julius 'Dr. J' Erving, Darryl Dawkins, Michael Jordan, and other black players have been known for their expressiveness as well as their considerable skills. Erving may best symbolize the emergence of this expressive style among black basketball players. On the court, Erving was known for his very creative, graceful, and agile performance. His style of play was exemplified by his famous 'ceiling-climbing, high-flying, gravity-defying' dunks, for which he would often start his take-off at the foul line.

Cool pose in sport can sometimes be interpreted as cultural resistance to racism. The fists-raised demonstration on the victory stand in the 1968 Olympics was not the only characteristic of Tommie Smith's and John Carlos's protests against racism in the United States – these athletes also ran while wearing black socks and sunglasses. Similarly, Muhammed Ali's expressive style – his boasting, his poetry, his dancing, his ritualistic 'hair combing' while holding a mirror after his bouts – can be interpreted not simply as personal vanity but as one athlete's defiant expression of resistance to a society that uses black males as its warriors – both as pugilists in the ring and as soldiers in Vietnam. Because black (and hispanic) men showed up disproportionately as drafted combat soldiers, and then as casualities in Vietnam (Staples, 1982), it is not surprising that many U.S. blacks identified with the style and substance of Ali's perform-ances. Meanwhile, many whites in the media, the government, and the public were profoundly threatened by it.

Expressive behaviors are not, of course, restricted merely to profes-sional athletes. College, high school, and playground athletes also mimic, develop, and use expressive styles. As Wolf (1972) has noted of young black males,

> The school yard is the only place they can feel true pride in what they do, where they can move free of inhibitions, and where they can, by being spectacular, rise for the moment against the drabness and anonymity of their lives.... When you jump in the air, fake a shot, all without coming back down, you have proven your worth in incontestable fashion... thus, when a player develops extraordinary 'school yard' moves... [they] become his measure as a man. (p. 170)

Black males' appropriation of sports as an arena of self-expression is an example of human agency operating within structural constraints. Faced with a lack of resources, facilities, services, goods, information, and jobs, black males who live in poor black communities have taken a previously white-dominated activity and constructed it as an arena in which they find accessible recreation, entertainment, stimulation, and opportunities for self-expression and creativity. Sports play an important and – in some limited ways – a positive role in many black males' lives. However, as we shall see, there is a downside to the relationship between black males and sports.

Black males and organized sports

The sports establishment does not operate as an apolitical, asocial enterprise, but as part of the larger society. As such, sports are not an alternative to 'real life,' but a reflection of the racist economic and social system that supports them (W. Morgan, 1983). [...] This reflection is often distorted in such a way that, for the individual, sport often appears to be one of the few arenas that provides true equal opportunity. This distortion of reality draws young black males into athletic careers in disproportionately high numbers, and this distortion ultimately guarantees that the vast majority of black males will find sports to be a professional dead end (H. Edwards, 1984).

Despite its apparent equality and integration, sport remains an extension of the dominant racist economic system, which serves to exploit those who are already professional or college athletes and to mislead those who are merely aspiring athletes. In fact, even the apparent integration at the player level is misleading (H. Edwards, 1982; Yetman and Eitzen, 1972). As evidenced by recent statements made by prominent white men in professional sports concerning how blacks supposedly 'lack the necessities' to be field managers, racism lives on within organized sports. Indeed, black managers, coaches, and front-office personnel are exceedingly rare, with most sports organizations owned, operated, and managed exclusively by whites. Furthermore, there is racial segregation in sport by playing position (Curtis and Loy, 1978; Eitzen and Tessendorf, 1978), as any devotee of football is especially aware after the media attention Doug Williams received for being the first black quarterback to start in the Superbowl. Black males also find themselves represented in disproportionately high numbers as athletes in sports to which they have had access, such as basketball, football, baseball, boxing, and track. Meanwhile, blacks are underrepresented in sports to which they have not had access, such as golf, auto racing, swimming, hockey, and soccer. As H. Edwards (1984) writes,

> Patterns of black opportunities in American sport are consistent with those in society at large, and for the same reason – deeply rooted traditions of racial discrimination. I contend that racial discrimination in both sport and society is responsible for the disproportionately high presence of extremely talented black athletes in certain sports on the one hand and the utter exclusion of blacks from most American sport and from decision-making and authority positions in virtually all sports on the other. (p. 9).

Despite the large number of black males who participate in sports, less than 6% of all the athletic scholarships given in the United States go to blacks. Just as damaging is the fact that an estimated 25 to 35% of high school black athletes do not even qualify for scholarships because of academic deficiencies. Of those black athletes who ultimately do receive athletic scholarships, as many as 65 to 75% may not ever graduate from college (H. Edwards, 1984; Spivey and Jones, 1975; Talbert, 1976). Among the approximately 25 to 35% of the black athletes who do graduate from college, about 75% of them graduate with either physical education degrees or with degrees in majors that are especially created for athletes. As one might suspect, such 'jock degrees' are often not acceptable in the job market, given the growing emphasis on the need for math, science, engineering, and computer training in today's high-tech market. In the final analysis, because such a small percentage of these college athletes will be drafted by a pro team, and those who actually play will find that the average professional career is short, many once-aspiring black athletes will find themselves back out on the streets with academic degrees that may not help them survive – much less succeed – in the 'real world.'

Summary and conclusion

It has been argued here that cool pose (expressive lifestyle behaviors) as expressed by black males in sports may be interpreted as a means of countering social oppression and racism and of expressing creativity. Moreover, the demonstration of cool pose in sports enables black males to accentuate or display themselves (i.e., 'Here I am, world; watch me, see me, hear me, I'm alive'), obtain gratification, release pent-up aggression, gain prestige and recognition, exercise power and control, and express pride, dignity, and respect for themselves and for their race. However, the emphasis on athletics and on cool pose among black males is often self-defeating, because it comes at the expense of educational advancement and other intellectually oriented activities that are integral aspects of the dominant forms of masculine power and success today.

Furthermore, although cool pose is an example of creative agency in response to one form of social domination (institutionalized racism), cool pose also illustrates the limits of an agency that adopts another form of social domination (hegemonic masculinity) as its vehicle. Because hegemonic masculinity is ultimately about men's domination of women (and some men's domination of other men), black men's adoption of cool pose as a response to institutionalized racism is often self-defeating. This response ultimately does not put black males in positions to live and work in more egalitarian ways with women, nor does it directly challenge male hierarchies. Cool pose demonstrates black males' potential to transcend oppressive conditions to express themselves as men. In rejecting the false promise of patriarchal privilege, black males might move from individual transcendence to social transformation. A critical examination of black males' relationship to sports is an important requisite of this movement.

NOTES

I would like to thank Michael Messner and James T. Todd for their invaluable assistance in the development of this chapter. Thanks also to Glenn W. Martin and Emily Collias for their help. This chapter, which is based on the author's doctoral dissertation (Majors, 1987), is dedicated to Uncle Charles Hughes (who was my sport hero) and to my friend Eugene Scott, who together taught me how to use masculinity with sensitivity and grace.
1   For more discussion of what the author has termed 'the problem of selective indiscrimination', see Majors (1987).

REFERENCES

Brod, H. (1987) *The making of masculinities: The new men's studies.* Winchester, MA: Allen & Unwin.

Bulhan, H. (1985) Black Americans and psychopathology: An overview of research and therapy. *Psychotherapy,* 22, 37–378.

Cazenave, N. (1984) Race, socioeconomic status, and age: The social context of American masculinity. *Sex Roles,* 11, 639–657.

Connell, R. W. (1987) *Gender and Power: Society, the person and sexual politics.* Stanford, CA: Stanford University Press.

Cordes, C. (1985, January) Black males at risk in America. *APA Monitor,* 9–10, 27–28.

Curtis, J. and Loy, J. (1978) Positional segregation in professional baseball: Replications, trend data and critical observation. *International Review of Sport Sociology,* 4(13), 5–21.

Edwards, H. (1973) *The sociology of sport.* Homewood, IL: Dorsey.

Edwards, H. (1982) Race in contemporary American sports. *National Forum,* 62, 19–22.

Edwards, H. (1984) The collegiate athletic arms race: Origins and implications of the 'Rule 48' controversy. *Journal of Sport and Social Issues,* 8, 4–22.

Eitzen, D. S. and Tessendorf, I. (1978) Racial segregation by position in sports. *Review of Sport and Society,* 3, 109–128.

Franklin, C. W. (1984) *The changing definition of masculinity.* New York: Plenum.

Gibbs, J. T. (1988) Young black males in America: Endangered, embittered, and embattled. In J. T. Gibbs (Ed.), *Young, black, and male in America: An endangered species* (pp. 1–36). Dover, MA: Auburn House.

Gite, L. (1985, November) Black men and stress. *Essence,* pp. 25–26, 130.

Heckler, M. (1985) *Report of the secretary's task force on black and minority health.* Bethesda, MD: U.S. Department of Health and Human Services.

Kimmel, M. (1987) Men's responses to feminism at the turn of the century. *Gender and Society,* 1(3), 261–283.

Larson, T. E. (1988) Employment and unemployment of young black males. In J. T. Gibbs (Ed.), *Young, black and male in America: An endangered species* (pp. 97–128). Dover, MA: Auburn House.

Majors, R. (1986) Cool pose: the proud signature of black survival. *Changing Men: Issues in Gender, Sex and Politics,* 17, 5–6.

Majors, R. (1987) *Cool Pose: A new approach toward a systemic understanding and study of black male behavior.* Unpublished doctoral dissertation, University of Illinois, Urbana.

Morgan, W. J. (1983) Towards a critical theory of sport. *Journal of Sport and Social Issues,* 7, 24–34.

Rainwater, L. (1966) The crucible of identity: The lower class negro family. *Daedalus,* 95, 172–216.

Spivey, D. and Jones, T. (1975) Intercollegiate athletic servitude: A case study of the Black Illini student-athlete, *Social Science Quarterly*, 55, 937–947.

Staples. R. (1982) *Black masculinity*. San Francisco: Black Scholar Press.

Stewart, J. and Scott, J. (1978) The institutional decimation of Black American males. *Western Journal of Black Studies*, 8, 82–93.

Talbert, T. (1976) *The black athlete in the southwest conference: A study of institutionalized racism*. Unpublished doctoral dissertation, Baylor University, Waco, TX.

Tygiel, J. (1983) *Baseball's great experiment: Jackie Robinson and his legacy*. New York: Oxford University Press.

Wolf, D. (1972) *Foul: The Connie Hawkins story*. New York: Warner Books.

Yetman, N. and Eitzen, S. (1972) Black Americans in sport: Unequal opportunity for equal ability. *Civil Rights Digest*, 5, 20–34.

Part IV
The Private
Lives of Men

The turn of the millennium has seen increasing critical attention given to men's private lives. Whether they are framed around gay and heterosexual identities, relationships, friendships, families, intimacies, emotional labour, or ideologies of sexuality, men's 'inner sense of self' and practices in the private domain are now open to a new and vigorous scrutiny. This section provides an excellent introduction to these new and exciting debates and, in so doing, signals opportunities for further studies and research in the sociology of masculinity.

In 'Family, Gender and Masculinities' David Morgan artfully demonstrates that the notion of 'family' itself is a construct that has evolved as an institution that has both shaped and reflected different notions of masculinity. His analysis reminds us that the notion of the male breadwinner is a fairly recent invention. In 'traditional' societies, families were fluid constructions in which gender was embedded within wider kinship concepts. Contrary to some conceptions, gender relations were subject to variation and there were ranges of masculine identities beyond those subsumed under the notion of patriarchy. Morgan notes that early modern periods marked gendered separations between home and work, private and public – a crucial transition that accompanied the Industrial Revolution and which informed the beginning of an internal division of labour within the family. By contrast, late modernity signifies an increased awareness of women's paid employment opportunities, the distinction between paid and unpaid labour, and a **questioning of men's position as 'head of the household'**. In short, the conventional notion of the nuclear family is now challenged and, with it, the patriarchal values that have long informed the public and private dualism.

Men and emotional intimacy have traditionally been understood as a problematic combination, with men often dismissed as 'emotionally illiterate' and instrumental, thus lacking the 'natural' empathies of women. In 'The Organization of Intimacy' Deborah Kerfoot explores the links between masculinity and emotional intimacy, but does so in the context of an area of social life often understood as unemotional – management and organization. Kerfoot raises some disturbing and provocative questions regarding the 'collusion' between management and masculinity in creating appearances of intimacy in modern business organizations. Under norms of traditional masculinity, subjects seek to maintain control, act instrumentally, and avoid vulnerability; all ways of being that are congruent with the norms of management discourse. However, in contemporary organizational efforts to 'humanize' the workplace, intimacy has **become a way to talk about relationships that are otherwise instrumental**. Kerfoot suggests that there is an increasing call for a language of emotional intimacy and connection, efforts to build up employee commitment and involvement, to increase the potential for social encounters that create a 'customer care' orientation. Employees are encouraged to shape their behaviours to meet customer demand, giving the appearance of momentary intimacy. Kerfoot points out that this way of construing intimacy is at odds with what emotional intimacy means. Emotional intimacy involves authenticity, genuineness, spontaneity, play, letting go of predictable scripts. Emotional intimacy is non-instrumental, is coveted for its own sake rather than to promote some other organizational goal. Thus many men's/managers' performance of intimacy, is, Kerfoot suggests, often little more than a careful masculine performance designed to fit into the 'new' organization culture.

Further developing the theme of masculinity and intimacy, Michael Messner's chapter 'Friendship, Intimacy, and Sexuality' explores the ways in which the competitive activities of **sport provide a setting for men to powerfully bond, without, however, developing intimacy**. Messner's research shows how masculine performances and displays of the self-assured, (hetero) sexually active male, are enacted across US college campuses and in male locker rooms. The subsequent locker-room culture which emerges can be seen to be a hyper-masculine environment where sexually aggressive talk serves to particularly exclude women and gay men. The friendships that arise between men in this arena are used to validate and project a heterosexual and masculine public image, rather than establish a spontaneous emotional intimacy. Messner's research resonates with that of Kerfoot, inasmuch as it signals how intimacies between men, while apparently non-instrumental, are, in fact, shown to often be enacted as a means of achieving an otherwise elusive masculine identity. The hegemonic masculine performance of the sports arena hides a fragile confidence and contingent sense of masculine self. Once again, masculinity reveals itself to be largely mythical and illusory, with, however, very oppressive consequences for those women and men who do not 'fit' into or perform to the prevailing stereotypes.

The importance and centrality of the excluded or feared 'Other' to the formation of men's private selves is further explored by Michael S. Kimmel. He asks the questions: If we take seriously the notion that men's sense of themselves as masculine is not a fixed thing or character trait, then how has it changed and evolved? How is manliness created and maintained? Kimmel traces the history of manhood in America and shows that masculinity has been under continual transformation. From the end of the eighteenth century, men achieved a sense of their masculinity as genteel patriarchs and landowners, as heroic artisans exhibiting physical strength and virtue. But since the mid-nineteenth century, and through to the present day, we see the emergence of a new vision of masculinity, one tied to the capitalist marketplace. In this normative definition of American masculinity, man is now validated through wealth, power and status. Kimmel claims that the story of **how American man became marketplace man** is a tragic tale of men trying to live up to impossible ideals of success. It is a story that plays out in a terrain of power relations and the exclusion of 'others', particularly the exclusion of the feminine. American manhood is a relentless test, embodied in the first rule: 'not being like women'. It also means that masculinity is demonstrated under the surveillance of other men's approval, what Kimmel calls 'homosocial enactment'. Men prove their manhood in the eyes of other men, through demonstration of wealth, accomplishments, and so on. Kimmel argues that the central organizing principle that is behind the drama of masculinity, and thus men's private selves, is homophobia; the fear of other men. Men are afraid of any association with feminine qualities because it could lead to humiliation and shame in the eyes of other men. Thus, the fear of being labelled 'faggot' is more than just a fear of homosexual experience; it is a fear of being accused of not being a real man.

The first four chapters in part IV highlight the problematic dimensions of male intimacies and friendships, with men's emotional literacy and potential for empathy appearing compromised by the ever-present fear of being labelled 'different' or 'non-man'. In short, hegemonic masculinity appears omnipresent and powerful. However, in chapter 16, Peter Nardi offers an example of how friendships between gay men and the subsequent development of networks and neighbourhoods contributes to legitimizing alternative forms of masculinity. Given the dominance of (heterosexual) images of hegemonic masculinity, it is small wonder that gay men have evolved an exclusive set of friendships and communities, mostly within enclaves of urban centres. These friendships have the potential, Nardi claims, to spawn communities, reinforce gay identity, and effect socio-political change on a larger scale. Nardi revisits the history and evolution of gay life, from marginalized and isolated pockets to the emergence of small town bars, to the development of urban neighbourhoods and a 'global civic friendship' devoted to gay issues. What emerges from Nardi's overview is a sense that these communities help members to **find meaning and dignity in a society that attempts to impose hegemonic order.** Thus the private lives of gay men, and their friendships, serve to create 'a vicarious sense of belonging' and thus help sustain a sense of gay 'identity'.

12

Family, Gender and Masculinities

David H. J. Morgan

Introduction

The title of this chapter suggests various inter-changes between gender
and family, focussing specifically around the constructions of masculinities. We need to recognise that the key terms – 'gender', 'family' and
'masculinities' – are all complex and contested terms. Part of the argument of this chapter is that these terms are complex social constructions
and that part of this process of social construction takes place in the
spaces between them. I see terms such as 'gender' and 'family' as primary
colours which we can only see in combination with each other and with
other 'colours'. Thus, I not only argue that family interactions take place
between gendered individuals. I also argue that gender is itself partially
shaped within family contexts and that family relationships are to be
understood and constituted through, to change the metaphor slightly, the
prism of gender.

The specific focus within this chapter will be upon men and masculinities. This is not to claim or reclaim any special privileges on the part of
men. It is partly a reflection of my two main interests, in family and in men
and masculinities, and in an attempt to combine these. It is also a reflection
of the argument that family relationships have often, in the present as well
as in the past, been 'feminised'. There is often an apparent tension between
'men' and 'families' on the other hand (Morgan, 1994). There may also be
a possible tension (one which has previously been explored by sociologists)
between 'the sociology of the family' and 'the sociology of gender'.

The use of the plural term 'masculinities' both reflects widespread
current usages (e.g. Hearn & Morgan, 1990) and represents a clue to

my argument as a whole. Masculinity is not to be understood as a single unified object of study but rather as a plurality. These masculinities, whose number and character will vary over time and between societies, may not of course always be equal and may themselves be arranged in some kind of hierarchy.

In the course of this chapter I shall present a series of models, using the terms 'traditional', 'early modern', 'late modern' and 'post-modern' (see also Cheal, 1991). This may sound like an historical or even an evolutionary account. This is not my intention. They represent a series of sociological models through which historical change is often constructed or understood. Clearly some kind of historical ordering is implied but, even in theoretical terms, there will be considerable overlaps. They should be seen as devices through which one may begin to explore some of the interchanges between 'family' and 'gender'.

Traditional

I am largely using the word 'traditional' here in a Weberian sense, perhaps paying particular attention to his discussions of patriarchalism. In such societies, elsewhere identified as 'pre-industrial' or 'pre-capitalist', the notion of the family would seem to be a somewhat fluid one, merging with wider networks of relationships identified often, if not exclusively, in kinship terms.

Such societies have sometimes been understood as having relatively fixed notions of gender differentiation. However, more detailed comparative research suggests considerable variation both in terms of the degree and nature of gender differentiation and the extent to which these differentiations are manifested in fixed hierarchies and inequalities (Sanday, 1981). Gender here may be both more firmly defined and embedded in wider familial and kinship contexts and more subject to variation. Indeed, these wider familial and kinship identities might be seen as important sources of gender variation. Put another way, while gender differentiation, and other inequalities, may be important themes within such societies, it is rarely simply a matter of gender that is being constructed or reproduced.

In the context of my central concern with men and masculinities, a few brief illustrations may be provided. For example, male initiation rites are to be seen not simply in terms of a transition to and the assumption of adult male identities, rights and duties, but also in terms of identities within a wider nexus of social relationships. Similarly, 'patriarchy', in terms of the older usages of the term, refers not simply to the domination of men over women but to systems based upon interacting combinations of both gender and generation. Further, while 'patriarchy' refers to the 'rule of the father', male positions and masculine identities do not necessarily revolve exclusively around biological or social fatherhood. The concerns of early social anthropologists with the positions of the mother's brother in particular societies may alert us to the possibility of a range of masculine identities which, while they may be located within wider familial and kinship ties, do not necessarily narrow down to social fatherhood.

The main point about this all too brief discussion is to indicate models of societies where gender may be more bound up with familial and kinship identities than would appear to be the case in more modern societies. However, this linkage between gender and familial identities is not necessarily a source of single stranded or fixed gender orders but, on the contrary a source of complexity and variability in gender differentiations and inequalities. There is clearly room for more investigation around such themes.

Early modern

Confusingly, the model that I refer to as 'early modern' is sometimes described by sociologists and others as 'traditional'. However, this model, focussing upon clear gendered separations between home and work and the private and the public, clearly represents an 'invented' tradition. These patterns are more clearly, if not always accurately, identified with the development of a modern industrial society rather than the perpetuation of a timeless tradition.

It is no accident that these models are frequently identified with early and dominant sociological models since, as Cheal has reminded us, sociological accounts arose out of and were concerned to make sense of a transition from a traditional or pre-industrial society to a modern or an industrial society (Cheal, 1991). These models have come to be identified with functionalisms, whether of the Parsonian, Marxist or early feminist variety.

The key elements in this model are well known and do not require detailed amplification. They focus upon a relatively stable set of interchanges between family and gender, mediated through constructed distinctions between the public and the private.

This is a mutually reinforcing system. The family, itself a relatively solid and stable construction, shapes and reproduces gender identities through socialisation and social reproduction and through the internal division of labour. Reciprocally, gender, working through the public/private distinction, shapes ideal family relationships. Indeed, the very definition of the 'family' – centred upon marriage and parenthood – is based upon and reproduces relatively stable notions of gender and, further, (hetero)sexuality.

Within this model, the dominant form of masculinity does not focus exclusively upon the public sphere (although this may provide some of the most dominant and potent images of masculinity) but rather upon the set of interchanges between the private family and the spheres of economy and public life. Male identity revolves around notions of the breadwinner, the assumption of mature adult responsibilities in terms of a wife and children, the settling-down into respectability, duty and security. Conversely, as in the classic Parsonian accounts, the man derives support and strength from the domestic haven in order to participate all the more effectively in the world of paid employment and public life. There may be masculine iden-tities other than that of the male breadwinner, but this is clearly the dominant one and other identities (the young man sowing his wild oats, the bachelor or the retired man for example) derive their meaning in part from their relationship to this central signifier of masculine identity.

It is clear that this model of masculine identity in an early modern context is very much of a middle-class identity (see Davidoff & Hall, 1987 for one historical example). However, the important thing is that the dominance of this male identity rests upon the growing dominance of the middle classes. Moreover, while class becomes a dominant mode of differentiation between men and between masculinities, these class iden-tities are partially maintained and reproduced through families and households even if their origins, theoretically at least, lie elsewhere in the spheres of employment and market relationships. In this early modern model, the man becomes the carrier of class identity; the location of other family members, wife and children, depends upon the class position of the male head of household.

Late modern

I now move to more varied terminology, although all the terms used seek to suggest some change in the relationships between family and the gender order. As well as 'late modern' we might have 'modern', 'modified traditional', 'symmetrical', 'democratic' and so on. The factors that late modern or equivalent models attempt to recognise include:

i The increasing significance of married women's paid employment outside the home;

ii An increasing awareness of a wide variety of paid and unpaid labour, especially within the home;

iii Apparent threats to or departures from the conventional nuclear family model, especially focussing upon divorce and re-marriage and, later, single or lone parenthood.

One theoretical impact of some of these changes was an increasing willingness to talk about the 'household' rather than 'the family' (Pahl, 1984). This usage seemed to reflect a growing awareness of the variety and fluidity of family forms together with a recognition of the economic significance of domestic relationships.

The implication of these changes and their incorporation into family analysis meant that the neat and coherent inter-changes that character-ised early modern models no longer seemed wholly appropriate. At least some modification seemed to be required, if not total abandonment. Gender was understood to be shaped by a multiplicity of factors, many of which were apparently external to the family/household although having a definite and measurable impact upon domestic relationships (see Walby, 1990). The degree and kind of impact is still a matter of considerable debate but there can be little doubt that a nexus linking changes in the experiences and aspirations of women, women's employment outside the home and increasing divorce rates indicated a major site for change in the links between gender and family. Also part of this shift was the impact of feminism and the growing critique of family relation-ships from a feminist perspective. One important example of this was in the area of domestic violence.

Within such a developing framework, one largely influenced by femi-nism, the family and the household (and indeed the very use of the term 'family') came increasingly to be seen as providing brakes on or limita-tions to wider changes in the gender order. One often-cited illustration of this was the apparent resistance of patterns of division of labour between women and men within the home to wider pressures for change. How-ever, it is also possible to argue that family and domestic practices might be a source of some measure of change, or at least innovation, within gender relationships. The understanding that domestic life represented the private sphere, while clearly having its negative features as far as women were concerned, meant that there was a degree of leeway or relative autonomy in the re-ordering of gender relationships in ways which were less possible in organisations outside the home. Thus there has been talk of attempts to develop non- or less sexist modes of child-rearing just as there have been attempts at more substantial re-orderings of domestic divisions of labour. In theoretical terms the increasing use of terms such as 'negotiation' or 'strategies' (Finch & Mason, 1993; Wallace, 1993) (including 'gender strategies') may be seen as representing some recognition of the possibilities for innovation within routine domestic patterns, innovations which might also have some impact on gender relationships outside the home. Thus, there might be increasing pressures for parental leave, maternal and paternal.

In the case of men and masculinities, the late modern framework would seem to include increasing talk of 'crisis' (Morgan, 1992). This was reflected in a growing interest in specific studies of men and their problems. While not all commentators agree with the idea of crisis or with the extent and nature of its supposed impact on male perceptions and practices, the main themes would seem to include the relative loss of a stable patriarchal authority within family relationships coupled with wider challenges to masculine dominance in many spheres of public life. Increasing rates of unemployment and the increasing participation of women in all kinds and levels of employment represent some of the more tangible features of these challenges. The supposed responses on the part of men have, however, been extremely variable including despair and suicide, the search for a new authentic male identity, a backlash against women and feminism or various critical examinations of masculine practices.

Centrally, it seems to be argued that the mutually reinforcing circle of family position and public identity has been lost. One aspect of this might be seen in the attempt to seek masculine identities outside domestic life altogether. This so-called 'flight from commitment' (Ehrenreich, 1983) has been the subject of critical examination on both sides of the Atlantic. Some recent discussion suggests that it has two, opposite, dimensions. On the one hand there is a flight from the breadwinner role or from any kind of domestic commitments on the part of men. On the other hand there is a move away from the commitment to work or a career to a more whole-hearted embracing of domestic identities. The point here is that these retreats or departures are seen as not being confined to bachelors or young unmarried men but as having a wider significance.

At the same time, considerable publicity has been given to the idea of the 'new man', the man who appears to have engaged in a re-negotiation of domestic involvements and who actively and publicly engages in childcare and child responsibilities. While much of the publicity surrounding the 'new man' (at least in Britain) has been less than adequately supported by evidence of real change, it would be wrong to discount the significance of such changes altogether. Perhaps one limitation would seem to be that it appears to be a relatively slender basis upon which to build new models of masculinity. The main, or most publicised, model of the 'new man' appears to be that of the father with a small child or children. Few other family based identities appear to be available for the re-negotiation of masculine gender identities.

Late modern models of the interconnections between gender and family would seem to focus, to varying degrees, on growing contradictions or lack of fit between the two key elements. In particular, the family, apparently standing in the way of wider changes in the gender order comes under criticism both as a theoretical object and as a social institution. At the same time, changes in the constructions of gender, of feminine and masculine identities, are an increasing focus of interest and are seen as necessitating changes in family relationships and practices. The relatively stable nexus of interconnections identified in the modern or functionalist models is found wanting although there seems to be some uncertainty as to whether to modify this model (through introducing more dynamic concepts of negotiation, strategy or life course, for example) or whether to abandon it altogether.

Post-modern

The term 'post-modern' continues to be a contested and controversial one with a range of, often imprecise, usages. In some cases the term would overlap with what I have described as 'late modern' and what others might describe as 'high modernity' (Giddens, 1991). In part, the debate revolves around whether we are to speak of an intensification of or an extrapolation from existing trends or whether we need to conceive of a more radical break with the past, whether that past be described as modern or traditional.

In most of its usages, the idea of post-modernity involves a challenge to all hitherto existing narratives. This would include the ones suggested up to this point, especially in so far as they might be read as constituting an historical sequencing. More profoundly, the very key terms of the narrative – 'family' and 'gender' – would also be subjected to further challenge. The stories of family and gender would seem to be, like all good stories, capable of infinite variation and re-telling, reflecting as much upon the narrator and the circumstances of narration, as on the supposed entities themselves.

This implies an increasing emphasis upon fluidity and diversity, both in relation to these key terms and the supposed interconnections between them. The idea of 'family' as a complex cultural and ideological construction representing a set of processes rather than a thing is not a new understanding and has already been presented in these terms in the context of feminist, and other, critiques. Perhaps less familiar is the critique of the idea of gender itself. Within a post-modern framework – one can scarcely continue to speak of 'models' – the very notion of gender becomes problematic. One significant linguistic shift here is in the increasing use of the words 'gendering' and 'gendered' rather than, simply, 'gender'.

If the key elements of family and gender become more fluid and ambiguous the same must also be true of the supposed relationships between them. Gender identities, in all their plurality and fluidity, are no longer firmly anchored in family relationships or anywhere else for that matter. Family relationships are less obviously organised around gender; there is talk of 'partners' rather than 'spouses' and of 'parents' rather than of mothers and fathers. In so far as family relationships are organised around gendered identities, a plurality of possibilities becomes possible including, presumably, the willing adoption of a more traditional or early modern model.

A further aspect of this post-modernity is to do with increased reflexivity. Thus change is not something that happens to family relationships and the gender order. Further, there is an increasing reflexive monitoring of familial and gender identities and processes. This monitoring is conducted both by specialised experts and institutions (professionals and therapists of various kinds) but also by the social actors themselves. In part this is in relation to perceived or imagined risks – risks of divorce, risks to children and so on (Beck, 1992) – but also in terms of attempts to measure up one's performance as a family member or as a man or a woman in relation to certain supposed standards or measures. One element of this, perhaps particularly relevant in relation to gender, is a kind of ironicisation, a knowing and conscious adoption of certain ways of being or not being a man or a woman. Much of the extensive writing about Madonna focuses on this process of ironicisation.

The implications of the development of a post-modern framework for masculinities may be briefly suggested:

i   As has already been suggested, the pluralisation of masculinities becomes a necessary move in post-modern gender analysis. Further, it is argued, these masculinities are not simply passively available but are open for further elaboration and creation.

ii Implied here is the idea of a more self-conscious search for models of masculinities. Previously these were simply either given or so dominant as to allow for few feasible alternatives.

iii Masculinities located, if not anchored, in family relationships, may provide one mode of 'doing masculinity'. Or, alternatively, the increasingly fluid contexts of family life might provide the basis for increasing questioning of the oppositions between men and women, masculine and feminine.

iv Yet again, masculine identities, consciously sought after and created, may be seen in contrast to and opposition to family commitments and obligations.

Conclusion

I want to stress in conclusion that the models or frameworks that I have presented are theoretical constructions or, perhaps more accurately, constructions of theories. They represent some possible ways in which the complex relationships between family and gender, and the associated specialised areas of study, may be conceptualised and understood.

The focus has been upon the interchanges that might be understood to take place between two theoretical constructions, 'family' and 'gender', interchanges that may in some cases have implications for the very nature of the constructed entities themselves. The relationship may, as in the functional models of early modernity, be seen as mutually reinforcing through a series of feedback loops. Or they may be more fluid and open-ended, leaving room for some more ambiguous, conflictual or contradictory relationships. These conceptualised relationships may not necessarily be mutually exclusive but may be more or less appropriate for the different societies or different stratas at different times.

There are two points that I should wish to emphasise. The first is that the study of masculinities should not be confined to the identities of fathers and the practices of fathering. Certainly, when people talk of 'men in families' this is the image that most frequently comes to mind although a more comparative analysis should remind us of a much wider range of family based identities which could still be of relevance in modern societies. The second is, more generally, that the study of the family and of family relationships is important in the study of gender just as it has been highly apparent in recent years that the study of gender has been crucial for the study of family relationships. This is not to say that family and gender are always of equal importance to each other; their relative importance and the chief direction of the relationship will vary according to our overall theoretical perspective but perhaps also according to historical period or society. It is, however, to argue that each has its own particular concerns and histories; the study of family relationships is not solely a study of gender relationships just as the study of gender relationships cannot be wholly subsumed under the study of the family. Put another way, family relationships are gendered without being simply or solely about gender. If we see gender as a process rather than a thing, then family relationships represent an important site where people do gender.

REFERENCES

Beck, U. (1992), *Risk Society*. London: Sage.
Cheal, D. (1991), *Family and the State of Theory*. Brighton: Harvester/Wheat-sheaf.
Davidoff, L. & C. Hall (1987), *Family Fortunes*. London: Hutchinson.
Ehrenreich, B. (1983), *The Hearts of Men*. London: Pluto Press.
Finch, J. & J. Mason (1993), *Negotiating Family Responsibilities*. London: Routledge.
Giddens, A. (1991), *Modernity and Self Identity*. Cambridge: Polity.
Hearn, J. & D. Morgan, eds. (1990), *Men, Masculinities and Social Theory*. London: Unwin Hyman.
Morgan, D. (1992), *Discovering Men*. London: Routledge.
Morgan, D. (1994), 'The Family Man: A Contradiction in Terms?' Jacqueline Burgoyne Memorial Lecture, Sheffield Hallam University.
Pahl, R. (1984), *Divisions of Labour*. Oxford: Blackwell.
Sanday, P. R. (1981), *Female Power and Male Dominance*. Cambridge: Cambridge University Press.
Walby, S. (1990), *Theorizing Patriarchy*. Oxford: Blackwell.
Wallace, C. (1993), 'Reflections on the Concept of "Strategy"'. In: D. Morgan & L. Stanley, eds. *Debates in Sociology*. Manchester: Manchester University Press.

13

The Organization of Intimacy: Managerialism, Masculinity and the Masculine Subject

Deborah Kerfoot

Introduction

The purpose of this chapter is to explore the linkages between masculinity, the activities of management and intimacy. Intimacy is here discussed as emotional connection with another: expressed otherwise as the 'play' form of human interaction. My concern is with the 'feel' or embodied experience of oneself in relation to another. This is distinguished from, for example, such intimacies as might be experienced – no less real for those involved – as physical or as sexualized forms of intimacy. In drawing this distinction between intimacies, my concern is not to chart a typology of intimacy, or to delineate a hierarchical order of 'rank' within which one might classify such experiences. Nor is the question one that overlooks the oppressive aspects of those forms of sexualized intimacy, organizational or otherwise, now discussed under the umbrella debates surrounding sexual harassment (for a summary and discussion, see Brewis and Grey 1994). The issue is rather one of illuminating, and thence problematizing, what I regard as a form of intimacy that much contemporary management practice would seek to bring about. Instrumental in its desire to capture the subtleties and nuances of social relations for organizational ends, this intimacy is constitutive of a mode of expressing human interaction in given settings. Simultaneously, it provides the means by which other alternative possibilities of intimacy are discounted, displaced or marginalized. My concern here is to shed light on certain of these aspects of intimacy; the alternative possibilities for intimacy which are largely absent in business and management practice.

The site for the discussion is contemporary organizational life, and more particularly the practices of management now in ascendancy in many settings, both public and private sector alike. Drawing on Bologh (1990), I discuss intimacy not as a fixed, essential property of individuals and their interactions, or of organizations, but as a range of possibilities produced in and facilitated by social encounters. Likewise, following Connell (1993), masculinity is held to be 'an aspect of institutions and is produced in institutional life' (1993: 602). Connell's contention on masculinity forces us to recognize the organizational location of masculinity, as a part of what has elsewhere been referred to as the 'public sphere' and its constitution in everyday settings. Alluding to debates on the separation of the public and private sphere, writers elsewhere have sought to discuss masculinity in ways that force a critical engagement with the categories of public and private (e.g. Hearn 1992) and question the seemingly unproblematic existence of a dualism that at once both creates a separation of spheres, and reinscribes precisely the self-same behaviours and practices that it purports to explore (for discussion, see Kerfoot and Knights 1994). In this regard, the intention here in this chapter is further to underline the problematic nature of this dualism in aligning with those writers who would 'transcend the opposition be-tween these spheres by reformulating the relationship between them' (Benjamin 1986: 78). My own attraction to the critical analysis of masculinity in part resonates with a number of writers, male and female, whose experience of 'being managed' by others in the widest sense; of observing management; and of researching, teaching and engaging with managers over a period of many years, is one that has aroused a personal and academic curiosity as to masculinity and the nature of managerial work and organization. Of particular interest is the frenetic and seem-ingly highly labour-intensive character of much activity with which the behaviours and practices of masculinity are 'acted out', so to speak.

In the desire for order, security of identity and stability, those for whom masculinity resonates most loudly appear to be so preoccupied with 'fixing' the world around them and others in it as to detract from the possibilities of other forms of engagement. As a result, in its concern to achieve a fixity in social relations and quash the 'uncontrollable' elements of everyday existence, masculinity expends considerable energy in the drive for success, and overlooks the possibilities for other forms of interaction. Yet even this success in conquering the insecurity that is itself both a condition and consequence of 'the social' and of masculinity, can only ever be so momentary and superficial, such that its achievement requires constant validation. The puzzle then, is one of uncovering – and thence unravelling – an account of the attractions (often but not exclusively to many men in particular, at different times, places and spaces in their lives) of masculine forms of engagement, and why its 'achievement' should be so valued and so highly prized.

More than this, however, the chapter holds masculinity to be an aspect of identity, always fluid and always in process, in that masculinity is an element of human subjectivity and identity. For the discussion that surrounds masculinity is no mere casual excursion around the question of 'why bother?' This is to recognize the political dimension to debates on masculinity and acknowledge the relations of hierarchy and social and economic inequality that can be both an outcome of masculine practices in given contexts and the conditions of possibility for the maintenance of gender inequality in particular. In this regard, and by way of recognizing the problematic and contested nature of even the very term 'masculinity', I develop work begun elsewhere on the concept of the *masculine subject* (Kerfoot and Whitehead 1998). Such discussion is largely underpinned by the work of Foucault (1977, 1988) and other writers, whose theoretical insights on subjectivity and identity have furthered the discussion of the dynamic relationships between discourse and subject, and the interconnections between power and resistance.

Masculinity and the masculine subject

Although not specifically directed to a discussion of the gendered aspects of human interaction or of gender subjectivity, Foucault's understanding of subjectivity and identity, as the ongoing process within which subjects strive to gain security of identity, presents the possibility of advancing the theoretical discussion of masculinity and of intimacy. From such a perspective, men and women as organizational (and other) subjects are active in and embedded within relations of power and resistance: such relations themselves are at once both a condition and a consequence of the multiplicity of discourses and subject positions made available by discourse.

Plainly, the organizational locale is but one site for construction and reconstruction of masculinity amongst many; the home and domestic relationships, for example. Rather than see masculinity as a 'fixed' outcome of biological or other configurations, this is to understand masculinity as actively produced in given settings and in specific moments. The purpose of the chapter, then, is to illuminate one such setting – one such configuration of moments – in the constitution of masculinity and its productive possibilities in terms of intimacy. Moreover, the term 'masculine subject' enables us to avoid the dualism of masculinity and femininity into which much of the discussion of gender differences has been collapsed (for development, see Kerfoot and Knights 1994). The concept of the masculine subject recognizes that both men and women can be masculine, although masculinity, in whatever manifestation, can be conventionally conceived as elevated and privileged as a range of behaviours for many men. Masculinity exists merely as a way of being, most often but not exclusively for men, in which men express what it is 'to be a man' at any one time and in whatever location.

In their (frequently unfulfilled) desire for emotional intimacy with the opposite sex, many women sustain an alternative formulation of the possibilities for intimacy as other than concerned with purposive ends (also Gilligan 1982). Concerned first and foremost to merely 'be' in the moment, these encounters are grounded in a conception of human interaction as serendipitous and immediate in the largest sense, without obvious purpose other than the experience of the shared connection so generated. Part of the frustration experienced by these women stems from the contrast between this desire of experience and connectedness for its own sake, and that preoccupied with specific ends, such as is offered most frequently by the men in and around their lives. This can result in tensions and anxieties, for women and men, born of often competing and seemingly unbreachable perspectives on intimacy and its possibilities; an outcome of which is that non-instrumental formulations of intimacy collapse in the face of an unwilling or unknowing partner, and emotional intimacy recedes ever further.

In whichever manifestation, masculinity or, more particularly, what is here referred to as the masculine subject, can be seen to be concerned – first and foremost – to control the possibilities within which human interaction might take shape. Even in everyday conversation, for example, it is often 'revealed' by many women of their male partners that such men are unforthcoming in terms of being comfortable with the connections between people and events in daily life, and similarly disquieted by the possibilities for emotional intimacy that these encounters might offer. Unconcerned with the narratives of social intercourse for other than purely purposive ends, such men are stereotypically characterized by their womenfolk as 'wooden', or so distanced from their partners and those around them that no spontaneous interaction can take place (see also Duncombe and Marsden 1995). Spontaneity is significant in that, not least for many women, what 'counts' in relations is described as the ability to connect with others in terms of 'the feel' or immediate shared emotional experience of any situation. At one and the same time as these women are disconnected from their male partners, they connect with one another if only in their discomfort and dissatis-faction with the men around them. They forge linkages born of shared experience in a form of tie that binds one to another, if only for the momentary common experience of frustration or dissatisfaction as to their lot.

For masculine subjects, the experience of spontaneity is as threatening as it is precarious and destabilizing. For spontaneity, by definition, comes without a pre-ordered 'script' which might otherwise govern and direct the encounter: while the notion of an unscripted encounter is self-evidently threatening to those subjects whose very *raison d'être* is the control of uncertainty and of the uncertainty generated by their own inability to respond in situations. In managing the uncertainty and un-predictability that is inherent in encounters with others, many men stereotypically have recourse to conventionally masculine behaviours as a means of evading or avoiding social interaction that is evidently un-comfortable. It is uncomfortable in that, because of the emotional intim-acy so desired by many women, such intimacy, by its very nature, requires that the men respond authentically. For in order for the moment to be experienced as genuine, and thereby unscripted, emotional intimacy requires merely responding to the other, rather than drawing on a know-ledge of *how to* respond. To script the encounter in order to provide the means by which it might be managed is at one and the same time to 'lose the moment' and for emotional intimacy to evaporate. Masculinity thus gives the appearance of providing masculine subjects with the knowledge of how to respond, and of how to manage – rather than experience – intimate situations. In consequence, emotional intimacy remains ever on the horizon for masculine subjects, who are ever guarding against its possibility.

In seeking to control the uncertainty that might be generated by emotional intimacy, many men – consciously or otherwise – reach for conventional practices and behaviours or stereotypical masculine behav-iours: masculinity thereby becomes a means of rendering social relations manageable, thus avoiding the emotional intimacy that is so threatening. Emotional intimacy is threatening in that it necessitates 'letting go' of the script that fashions the responses of masculine subjects, and requires that they reveal aspects of themselves as vulnerable; vulnerable since the reactions of others can never be totally predicted or controlled. Ever concerned with their own and others' judgements of themselves as to their competence at being 'on top of' situations, masculine subjects must at all times labour at being masculine and to conceal or downplay personal fears and weaknesses that stimulate a questioning of this com-petence (Kerfoot and Knights 1996). Moreover, since emotional intimacy occurs 'in the moment', its experiences as transient as they are unique, such intimacies are further uncomfortable for masculine subjects (also Seidler 1989, 1992). Since they can never be fully replicated, emotional intimacies necessitate responses that are neither amenable to instrumental control nor capable of being 'learned' in advance. Emotional intimacy is thus doubly precarious for masculine subjects, leaving them bereft of the means to initiate non-instrumental forms of engagement, and unable fully to experience or comprehend the intimacy offered by others. Regarded with suspicion, doubt or outright hostility, emotional intimacy acquires the status of a 'no-man's land' for masculine subjects who are unwilling or unable to let go of the barriers that protect them from the threat of their own vulnerability and its consequences.

Similarly, in the organizational arena, many women, and those men who are less than successful at replicating its behaviours and central tenets, are marginalized by masculine-dominated management practices. For such management practices are concerned, at all times, to control the unpredictability of social interaction and render it 'safe' within the confines of a pre-designated script such as is offered by 'modern' management practice. Partly as a result, many women and some men find a discontinuity between the ideals of a shared and mutually supportive working environment coupled with meaningful work, and the harsh reality of organizations and managements that are increasingly dominated by bottom-line accounting principles. In the shifting cultures of many work organizations, public and private sector alike, they find they are no longer able to risk revealing aspects of themselves as otherwise frail human beings for fear of being interpreted as uncommitted, unproductive, inactive or 'weak'. For such subjects, the experience of managerial and other work is one of dislocation, and a continual sense of being at odds with their environment and the working practices that surround them.

Whether male or female, many managers now find themselves faced with organizational cultures that are dominated by regimes of management practice that are, likewise, increasingly instrumental in their search for success. This form of management and of masculinity is intensely goal-driven, often in the pursuit of abstract targets and objectives, and is purposive-rational in its orientation towards others (for elaboration, see Kerfoot and Knights 1993). All social intercourse and interaction is subjected to a yardstick of its degree of utility to the larger goals of the organization and to the designs of senior management. Thus, contemporary management practice appears to have a 'natural home' and an immediate resonance for masculinity, and for those masculine subjects who are drawn into its discourses and behavioural displays. Moreover, in so doing, masculine subjects at once both reconfirm themselves as masculine in such activities at one and the same time as reconstituting the very discourse with which they engage.

In this regard, masculinity exists merely as a way of being, yet one that is privileged in organizational (as other) sites. A masculine mode of engaging with the organizational world is one in which all encounters and events become potential arenas for instrumental control. Characterized by the pursuit of control of all social relations, this masculinity is elevated in the discourses and practices of management as *the* way of relating to the world and to other persons. Moreover, the dominance of this mode of being in the activities of managing and organizing is such that all persons, regardless of their sex, must 'become' masculine, if only in order to succeed as a manager or to achieve any seniority or credibility (for elaboration, see Kerfoot and Knights 1998). In 'becoming' masculine in this way, managers must adopt those behaviours and practices required of them in order to be masculine, or at very least give the appearance of so doing.

This masculine mode of engaging with the world and with the activities of management is further attractive in that it suggests a way of 'handling' the precarious and uncertain nature of many areas of management work as well as 'managing' – in a very immediate corporeal sense – some of the more distasteful activities involved in contemporary management, often disguised under the euphemisms of 'managing change', 'downsizing', 'restructuring' and 'outplacing'. An additional point here relates to the anxiety and insecurity of managerial work and of identity. For the discourses of masculinity and of management suggest a solution to the experience of insecurity and anxiety, and of the precarious nature of identity. Masculinity and management are thereby further seductive in their possibility for reconciling the tensions of being a man and a manager. Accepting that masculinity is always precarious, contingent and multiple, the argument here is that masculine subjects are active participants in the conditions of the reproduction of masculinity. They breathe life into the discourses and practices of masculinity and of management such that, for many managers, 'being a manager' and 'being masculine' are near synonymous. The following section explores further the argument on management and intimacy.

Managerial discourses and intimacy

The effects of 'marketization' on management practice and the shift of emphasis towards greater and more productive interaction between consumers and organizational members in both the public and private sectors is now clearly documented (for a summary, see Davies and Kirkpatrick 1995; see also Fuller and Smith 1991, du Gay 1996). Buttressed by the discourse of 'the market', the past 10–15 years have seen managerial practices in many public-sector sites turning to the potential of management and staff to 'add value' in social encounters (Keat et al. 1994), most notably with clients, customers or end-users, but also with fellow organizational employees of all persuasions. In referring to the emergence of the narratives of entrepeneurialism and the 'enterprise culture', a number of commentators have noted the ways in which the language and practices of the market have formed a managerial paradigm governing all internal as well as external social relationships. Du Gay and Salaman (1992: 624) refer to it thus: 'In this sense enterprise refers to a series of techniques for restructuring the internal world of the organization along market lines in order to anticipate and satisfy the needs of the enterprising sovereign consumer, and thus ensure business success.'

As an aspect of the attempt to garner commitment to what has been referred to as the 'cult[ure] of the consumer' (du Gay and Salaman 1992), many organizations are increasingly concerned to focus attention on the delivery of service quality to their client base, and with the larger programmes of management that might facilitate improved commitment, both to organization goals in general and to the specificities of the required behaviours thought to bring them about (for discussion, see Wilkinson and Willmott 1995). In the case of managerial discourses such as human resource management (HRM) for example, the expectation on the part of those practitioners, gurus and advocates who might further its advance, HRM is often presented as a means of similarly 'releasing untapped reserves of labour-resourcefulness by facilitating employee responsibility commitment and involvement' (Keenoy 1990: 4). More than this, HRM, whatever its incarnation (for a discussion and a critique, see Keenoy 1997), centres on capturing the creative and productive potential of social encounters for the ends of the organization. Even in those arenas that are previously unaccustomed to its languages and techniques, the public sector in particular, the drive to 'hammer home' the messages of customer orientation and focus on the client as consumer of goods and services has left few aspects of organizational life untouched (Ogbonna 1992, Willmott 1993). For those subordinates subjected to its dictates, HRM requires that social encounters be henceforth transformed – albeit not unproblematically – in such a fashion as to better facilitate the link between the organization and its client base.

Similarly, with a focus on 'customer service' and 'quality', the phenomenon of total quality management (TQM) in service and other industries seeks to rein in the productive potential of sales and service encounters in such a manner as to suggest that 'the customer is king' (Tuckmann 1994). The links between TQM and HRM as both forms of managerial rhetoric and organizational practice have been fully explored by many critical and other writers (for a reprise, see Wilkinson and Willmott 1995). In brief, such linkages commonly centre on ceding a degree of responsibility and accountability to workforces that have hitherto been unaccustomed to these practices. More than this, and in the search for such responsibility and 'quality' of service, staffs are required routinely to nuance their behaviours according to the supposed dictates of the client. In aiming to align embodied behavioural displays with the requirements of each customer, organizational members must tailor their presentation of self so as to create at least the appearance of a momentary intimacy between themselves and the client (Fuller and Smith 1991). For a period, however brief, the employee is called upon to metamorphose him- or herself into whatever is required, in a succession of transient encounters across what is often a wide-ranging client base. In order for the service to be perceived as 'real' by the client, staffs must draw upon a range of social skills and embodied behaviours, often tacitly held (for discussion, see Sturdy 1998). For in giving at least the appearance of effortlessly shifting between modes of display, an objective is to harness the larger knowledge base of the employee as a human being in the call to make embodied social skill a productive element of such organizationally 'efficient' – and thus profitable – social encounters (Ogbonna and Wilkinson 1990).

Plainly, whether clients experience this element of the transaction as genuine depends on an unacknowledged and unspoken 'feel' on the part of employees for the situation at hand. The difference between success and failure in the transaction can rest precisely on employees' ability to create at least the illusion of intimacy from which – in, for example, the case of sales or service encounters – trust might be generated. At one level, however much staff are exposed to the idea(l)s of immersing and rearticulating those very intimate (*sic*) aspects of self within the everyday practices of the organization, they are clearly capable of resisting and reinterpreting managerial designs to re-engineer their interactions with others (Sturdy 1998). Indeed, the core of the debate for commentators concerned with organizational resistance has turned precisely on such matters as the ambivalence and scepticism of employees in resisting managerial designs at cultural control (for a reprise, see Thompson and Ackroyd 1995). Yet, as du Gay and Salaman (1992: 630) express it: 'even if people do not take enterprise seriously, even if they keep a certain cynical distance from its claims, they are still reproducing it through their involvement in everyday practices through which enterprise is reinscribed.' Enterprise arguably revolves not merely on the culture of the consumer but the means by which employees, in the private and public sectors alike, are to deliver the goods that would facilitate its achievement. As I have discussed above, such mechanisms involve the 'capture' for purposive ends of the social skills and potentiality for intimacy that such skills entail.

Regardless of the degree of success or otherwise of this project to 'govern the soul' (with due respect to Rose 1989) of organizational members and in the debates that surround it, the 'synthetic sociability' at the heart of new managerial discourses is at once both panacea and problem for managements. It is panacea in that discourses such as quality management and HRM appear, on the surface at least, to proffer solutions to the uncertainty generated by contemporary managerial work and, in particular, the organizational ills of flagging profit margins, increased competition and the high fixed costs of labour in both private- and public-sector organizations. The notion that staffs themselves might hold 'the key' to greater efficiency and profitability is clearly a seductive proposition to senior managements that are long accustomed to regarding their workforce as little more than a 'necessary evil', in spite of the invocations of their own personnel departments. It is a problem in that, at one and the same time as organizational subordinates are required to 'discover' the potential for the organization of their embodied social skills, managements must, likewise, become acquainted with and accustomed to displaying the very same embodied human behaviours that they require of their employees. The burgeoning demand for social skills and 'emotional awareness' training packages for managers and for the larger feminization of management (for discussion and evaluation, see Calás and Smircich 1993) can be seen as exemplifying this trend for modern managers to 'get in touch with' the skills and abilities long buried by the day-to-day practice of hierarchical management and the unquestioning autonomy exemplified in maxims such as management's 'right to manage'.

That managers might explore their own contribution to the process of humanizing organizational life creates the conditions for the furtherance of their own uncertainty (for development, see Kerfoot and Knights 1996): uncertainty since, while calling for the emotional awareness of staff in the execution of their duties, management are, at one and the same time, forced to recognize their own role in revealing aspects of themselves as otherwise frail human beings. Calls to humanize managerial work arguably rest on the desire to create at least the appearance of intimacy in the relationships between managerial and other staff, if only in so far as such intimacy might itself be amenable to instrumental control (Kerfoot and Knights 1993, 1996). In another context, Peters and Waterman (1982) speculate upon the conditions within which such narratives of organizational intimacy might take hold. In their oft-quoted text on so-called 'excellent' companies in America, they refer to the phenomenon – albeit uncritically and merely as an aside – in one large corporation, discussing the conditions for its resonance with staffs as follows:

> Companies like 3M have become a sort of community centre for employees, as opposed to a place of work. We have employee clubs, intramural sports, travel clubs and a choral group. This has happened because the community in which people live has become so mobile, it is no longer an outlet for the individual. The schools are no longer the social centre for the family. The churches have lost their drawing power as social family centers. With the breakdown of these traditional structures, certain companies have filled the void. They have become sort of mother institutions. (Peters and Waterman 1982: 261)

Although the authors overemphasize the degree to which corporations can substitute for other structures and exaggerate the extent to which social ties have been eroded – as opposed to reconfigured – elsewhere in society, Peters and Waterman nonetheless allude to the conditions of possibility for organizations to be reinscribed as arenas for intimate relations. This point is no mere broad-brush argument such that one steady state is unproblematically supplanted by another; organizations have, like as not, always been arenas for the constitution of intimacy of all persuasions (Burrell 1984). Rather, the point at issue in this chapter surrounds the degree to which intimacy, or more particularly its constitution as a means of instrumentality in organizational relationships, has achieved such significance in contemporary managerial practices.

Flowing from this discussion of the ontology of intimacy in organization and its connections with masculinity and the masculine subject, the larger question concerns the alternative possibilities for intimacy that are displaced within masculine-dominated management practices. Accepting that this displacement is never total, absolute nor achieved, since other intimacies of a non-instrumental nature continually 'seep out' in the interstices of organizational life despite managerial efforts to contain them, the question can be expressed as follows. What other possibilities are there for intimacy and for an intimacy that is non-instrumental in its orientation? Having outlined the argument that surrounds the masculine subject, its link with purposive-rational masculinity and of the form of intimacy that is its expression, the following section explores Bologh's conception of erotic love in developing the discussion of emotional intimacy as one alternative possibility.

On intimacy

Bologh (1990) charts the emergence of a narrative of intimacy in the work of Weber and in his elaboration of the notion of 'sociability'. In producing a scholarly critique of his work, her purpose is to develop a discussion of the concept that she refers to as 'erotic love' as a form of sociability. Bologh holds this (feminist) alternative to be in parallel with Weber's patriarchal understanding. Briefly, it is argued that Weber's discussion of sociability is grounded in a conception of social relations as fundamentally coercive in their character. Here, sociability is defined as:

> ...a relationship in which the presence of one makes a pleasurable difference to, *affects*, the other [...] Sociable relationships may be more or less pleasurable, more or less affecting, more or less stimulating. As such all sociable relationships are erotic relationships. I mean this not necessarily in the narrow sense relating to sexual intercourse but in the broad sense of social intercourse that includes all kinds of mutual pleasuring, mutual stimulation and mutual empowering. (Bologh 1990: 213; emphasis in original)

Recognizing that all cultures, societies and groupings need some means of balancing the coercive nature of individual self-expression with the need for human contact and social involvement, sociability is said to provide the mechanism by which a reconciliation of this fundamental paradox might be achieved. Since individual self-expression requires, to varying degrees, imposing oneself upon the other as recipient of this expression, a willingness on the part of the other person is required in order to facilitate the encounter. The encounter becomes successful only in so far as each respects the rules of social interaction, such that both parties comprehend the manner by which the interaction can take shape, so to speak. At the same time as imposing him/herself upon another, sociability requires that he/she *takes care* for the reaction and feelings of the recipient; hence the aspect of mutuality bound up with sociability. Introducing notions of 'caring' for the other and their feelings separates *caring about* someone in the larger sense of a disembodied or detached manner (similar to the way in which many readers of the quality press in developed Western nations could be said 'to care about' the disenfranchized poor they read of in so-called Third World countries) from *caring for* them. This takes the discussion beyond the level of its most simple human concern for the general good of another. For in 'caring for' the other in social encounters, Bologh's conception of sociability requires that the parties concerned should care for the other as *an embodied human subject*.

Thus, care and caring for a person force us to consider a practical dimension to sociable behaviour and to erotic love as sociability more directly. This practical dimension is no mere matter of 'good form' (Simmel 1950), or simply deploying a kind of etiquette or tact in order to facilitate the encounter by means of certain rules. It calls upon persons to recognize, value and acknowledge the subjectivity of the other, however problematic this may be, even within the terms of the encounter itself. It requires that participants 'take the trouble' to care, with all that this entails, rather than feigning the appearance of care, however well-intentioned such feignings. For in feigning care and the appearance of care, often expressed commonsensically as 'going through the motions', the instrumental orientation of the relationship becomes immediately evident, even within the boundaries and behaviours described by good form.

Furthermore, it is argued that Weber sets up a polarized view of the possibilities for human interaction by virtue of the very means by which sociability is conceived in Weberian theorizing. Thus a dualism is created wherein:

> ...all self-expression which involves imposition is one side of sociable action; concern for and receptiveness to the other's response is the other side. Weber sees this two-sided nature of sociable action in dualistic terms: one either expresses, struggles or opposes or one submits, complies, appeases. [...] [Weber] seems to recognise only interests and conflicts of interest. (Bologh 1990: 216)

In the context of management and organizational practices, one can easily discern the modern trend to 'befriend' the client, patient, student or customer as instances of simulating care in numerous management programmes. From corporate practices such as the ubiquitous name badges, worn by staffs across innumerable public and private organizations for example, through 'personalized service' in hospitals, transport, taxation, education, policing, finance and services, staffs are required routinely to reproduce the manner and demeanour that is suggestive of caring for the client to hand. Similarly, when senior managements 'take the trouble' to display their commitment to staffs, it is often a parody – couched in and accompanied by a kind of 'we' language that renders the exercise so self-evidently synthetic to lower-hierarchy staffs and at odds with their daily experience of life in often fraught and insecure working environments. This intimacy, born of instrumentality, and enforced by management, finds clear resonances for masculinity and for masculine subjects. But for management and masculine subjects, 'taking the trouble' is both 'troublesome' in that it requires investments of time, energy and resources for an unknown – that is, unquantifiable – return, and 'troubling' in terms of their very subjectivity and identity.

As such, the distinction between instrumental intimacy and emotional intimacy lies at the heart of Bologh's conception of erotic love as sociability. For erotic love as sociability rests on each party recognizing the subjectivity of the other as embodied being; subjectivity not as a fixed property of persons, but varying and variable within the context of time, place and discursive constitution. Erotic love as sociability requires then, that each is 'attuned' to, and in tune with, the embodied subjectivity of the other – always shifting and in motion – doubly reinforcing its link with the practical aspects of care and underscoring the effort that is required to engage in emotionally intimate encounters. Furthermore, this is to introduce the concept of play and playfulness in subject positions, to overturn conventional relations grounded in hierarchy and inequality, such as that between layers of management and between managements and staffs or between spouses in (unequal) patriarchal relationships, and to challenge the instrumental intimacy that is their condition and consequence.

In contrast to Weber, whom she regards as sustaining instrumentality in his account of social life, Bologh offers the possibility of a form of relationship defined not by fixed or pre-ordered relations of who is 'in charge', whether patriarchially defined or otherwise. The conditions for emotional intimacy rest primarily on each party being neither subject nor object in the relationship. Emotional intimacy describes:

> ...a relationship of subject–object to subject–object, sometimes stressing the subjectivity of self or other and at other times the objectivity of self or other. [...] each relates to the uniqueness of the other as spirited body, embodied spirit. The particularity of the other does *matter*, does make a difference. (ibid.: 226; emphasis in original)

Emotional intimacy exists only in so far as each party respects and recognizes the other to the point of moving between these subject/object positions according to the demands of the relationship, however fleeting, in any one moment or location. This is to conceive of social relationships and of emotional intimacy as fluid and always in process. Where one party, either by 'accident' or design of managerial or patriarchal relation, requires command of the relationship or calls upon the formalities of a fixed hierarchy in order to script the encounter, then the possibilities for emotional intimacy dissolve.

Clearly paralleling developments in the arena of workplace practices, where the emphasis on social encounters and their productive potential is plainly to the fore, relationships of erotic sociability are likewise said to: 'stimulate creativity; or, as Weber himself relates, [...] erotic interest is "valuable as a creative power"' (ibid.: 213).

In the call for intimacy amongst organizational members, and between employees and consumers in the front line of business, management is at one and the same time faced with the paradox that is an outcome of its own practices. In requiring subordinates to 'be intimate' with others in an authentic way, management at once seeks to generate the conditions within which employees might 'tap' the creative and productive power thought to improve service levels and commitment. At the same time as requiring this authenticity in subordinates, however, management is concerned to shield itself from the revelations of discovery, such as might be uncovered were they themselves to be 'authentic', in whatever form. For, in so doing, managerial practices provide masculine subjects with an opportunity to 'hide behind' hierarchy and formal relations, not only reducing the possibilities for the emotional intimacy that is so threatening, but also further concealing their own instrumentality. Since the activities and practices of both management and masculinity are grounded in hierarchy, not least in terms of symbolic, material and social rewards, this provides masculine subjects with a near-impenetrable barrier that their formal positions offer. The activities of management thus acquire significance as a series of designs and mechanisms for distancing oneself from others and for avoiding and evading such intimacies as may be otherwise 'unleashed'. As Bologh contends:

> ...the more that formalities predominate, the less that personal self-disclosure occurs and the more superficial the relationship remains. [...] Because intimacy breaks down the barriers that formality provides, intimacy promotes vulnerability. Intimacy can be dangerous; one's trust can be betrayed, one's weaknesses exploited, and one's esteem or desire unreciprocated. In other words, one can be hurt and humiliated. On the other hand, intimacy can be protective and intensely pleasurable. Trust can be met with care, vulnerability and tenderness, exposure with recognition and affirmation, esteem and desire reciprocated. In other words, one can be nurtured affirmed and exalted. Because erotic love involves more or less intense desire as well as exposure and disclosure, erotic love involves the greatest personal risk but also the greatest possibility of communion. Hence erotic love can produce the most intense agony and ecstasy. (ibid.: 217)

In this regard, management and masculinity appear as a form of deception: deception in that, most notably in capitalist market environments and organizations, the activities of management serve to conceal the 'real' (unequal) nature of employment relationships, where the primary benefits accrue to employers rather than employees. While giving the appearance of care for employees and lower-hierarchy managers, most notably in paternalistic styles of managing, senior managements deny or downplay the expression of any alternative reality in their subordinates, other than that which is officially sanctioned, controlled or 'protected' by managements themselves, such as employee newsletters, team briefings, quality circles and the like. But, above all else, management and masculinity provide masculine subjects with the ultimate in self-deception. For in their attempts to control their environment, to distance themselves from others and control the perceptions of those around them, masculine subjects live out the belief in a mode of engaging with the social world as grounded in instrumentality and control. But this narrative of self as self-deception can only ever be contradictory; for it denies the linkages with others that are its very condition. In other words, not only are the discourses of management and masculinity internally contradictory in their attempts to refuse and refute the links between persons, but the lived experience of masculine subjects is frequently one of tension, anxiety and daily contradiction in the struggle, however 'well managed' or internalized, to sustain what it is to be 'successful' as a manager and as masculine.

Concerned to maintain and reinforce their protective barriers for fear of the disclosure that might be humiliating or exploitative, masculine subjects further deny the possibility of removing such barriers, since to do so would be regarded as immediately giving a power advantage to the other. In refusing their own vulnerability, to others and themselves, masculine subjects thereby live out the consequences of a narrow and otherwise foreshortened range of possibilities for human interaction. Their impoverishment is twofold: in the concern to maintain control, masculine subjects disavow the possibility of relationships and forms of intimacy that are non-instrumental, relationships 'that are desired *because they are pleasurable and valuable in themselves*' (ibid.: 216, emphasis added). Masculine subjects are further impoverished by the fear of 'letting go' in their engagements with others. Masculine subjects can find confirmation of themselves only in the control that they exercise over events, situations and over others, however unfulfilling its experience:

> ...the more a person needs and desires recognition and response from another without being able to recognise and respond to the needs and desires of the other, the more susceptible the person is to flattery and manipulation of indiscriminate others and the less able to find satisfaction and enhanced pleasure. Consequently, the more the person will need to

engage continually in external exploits and turn to external rewards as a source of pleasure and recognition in an unending search for pleasures and satisfactions that ultimately fail to please and satisfy. (ibid.: 229)

Conclusion

This chapter has sought to explore the links between masculinity, management and intimacy. In particular, I have elaborated certain of the conditions within which intimacy is constituted and expressed in contemporary organizations. Referring to these conditions, I have examined two forms of intimacy, defined here as instrumental and emotional intimacy. My contention is that both masculinity and management deny the ambiguity, fluidity and alternative possibilities of human interaction other than that which is grounded in instrumental intimacy. In this regard, masculine subjects, in seeking to deny the subjectivity of the other, thereby fix and limit human possibilities in such a fashion as to offer the greatest propensity for instrumental control. But this control can never be fully achieved, nor ever fully realized; hence the precarious nature of masculine subjectivity. Moreover, this instrumentality that is a condition and consequence of management and masculine subjectivity *requires*, for its continuance, the repression of the other in social relations. Masculine subjects thereby deny the possibility for 'play' within social relations – of shifting between subject positions – for masculinity and management necessitate that the other is subordinated to self. Masculine subjectivity is equally unreflexive and unreflective in its unwillingness, or sheer inability, to challenge the conditions of its own perpetuation, however self-destructive or impoverishing the consequence.

The notion of play and playfulness corresponds to Irigaray's (1980) notion of 'jouissance', defined as the multiplicity of corporeal, sexual and bodily pleasures, and the pleasure in its largest sense of embodied engagement with others. Here, social relationships are valued for the possibilities that they offer for connection and play and for moving between subject/object positions. My own experience of organizational life in paid work, almost universally based in masculine-orientated and numerically male-dominated public-sector working environments over a period of 20 years, similarly corresponds to and resonates with the notion of play in subject positions. As a woman in a predominantly male and predominantly masculine field of work, I am intrigued and engaged by the possibilities for playfulness in organizations and by the subversive potential of play in organizations. This is not some argument in support of organizational or managerial anarchy but, rather, it is a challenge to the conventional ordering of social relations that would stimulate the conditions for alternative possibilities to emerge; for example, a form of management and organization that is non-hierarchical – one that is other than repressive in its expression and consequences.

Much in the manner of a child's skipping game, emotional intimacy presents a range of possibilities for subject/object positions: social encounters are thus characterized by movement – the to and fro – as participants in the social encounter move within and between subject/object positioning in playful fashion. This playful attitude to relationships stands in contrast to the discourses and practices of masculinity. In their representation of intimacy as amenable to instrumental control, such discourses are founded upon a denial of the very conditions that could make such alternative subjectivities possible. Unable to 'give of themselves', masculine subjects and masculine subjectivity at one and the same time attempt to retain control of the organizational sites wherein such masculinity is reproduced and remain unreflective of the conditions of their own masculinity and its constitution.

Recognizing that contemporary organizations increasingly seek to 'conjure up' intimate moments, in an albeit synthetic manner, for the larger purposes of the organization, I have argued that managerial and masculine practices displace and deny alternative non-instrumental expressions of intimacy and their possibilities for organizational subjects. Outlining Bologh's conception of erotic love as sociability, I have argued that her analysis enables the elaboration of one such alternative expression, that of emotional intimacy.

REFERENCES

Benjamin, J. (1986) 'A desire of one's own', in de Lauretis, T. (ed.) *Feminist Studies/Critical Studies*. Bloomington: Indiana University Press.

Bologh, R. W. (1990) *Love or Greatness: Max Weber and Masculine Thinking – a Feminist Inquiry*. London: Unwin Hyman.

Brewis, J. and Grey, C. (1994) 'Re-eroticizing the organization: an exegesis and critique', *Journal of Gender, Work and Organization*, 1, 2, pp. 67–82.

Burrell, G. (1984) 'Sex and organization analysis', *Organizational Studies*, 5, 2, pp. 97–118.

Calás, M. and Smircich, L. (1993). 'Dangerous liaisons: the "feminine-in-management" meets "globalization"', *Business Horizons* March/April, pp. 71–81.

Connell, R. W. (1993) 'The big picture: masculinities in recent world history', *Theory and Society*, 22, pp. 597–623.

Davies, A. and Kirkpatrick, I. (1995) 'Face to face with the "sovereign consumer"', *Sociological Review*, 43, 4, pp. 782–808.

du Gay, P. (1996) *Consumption and Identity at Work*. London: Sage.

du Gay, P. and Salaman, G. (1992) 'The cult(ure) of the consumer', *Journal of Management Studies*, 29, 5, pp. 615–33.

Duncombe, J. and Marsden, D. (1995) '"Workaholics" and "whinging women": theorising intimacy and emotion work – the last frontier of gender inequality', *Sociological Review*, 43, pp. 150–69.

Foucault, M. (1977) *Discipline and Punish: The Birth of the Prison*. Trans. A. Sheridan. London: Tavistock

Foucault, M. (1988) 'Power and sex', in Gordon, C. (ed.) *Power/Knowledge: Selected Interviews and Other Writing 1972–1977 by Michel Foucault*. London: Harvester Wheatsheaf

Fuller, L. and Smith, V. (1991) 'Consumers' reports: management by customers in a changing economy', *Work, Employment and Society*, 5, 1, pp. 1–16.

Gilligan, C. (1982) *In a Different Voice*. Cambridge, Mass.: Harvard University Press.

Hearn, J. (1992) *Men in the Public Eye: The Construction and Deconstruction of Private Men and Public Patriarchies*. London: Routledge.

Irigaray, L. (1980) 'When our lips speak together', *Signs*, 6, 1, pp. 69–79.

Keat, R., Abercrombie, N. and Whiteley, N. (eds) (1994) *The Authority of the Consumer*. London: Routledge.

Keenoy, T. (1990) 'HRM and work values in Britain', paper presented to the International Society for the Study of Work and Organizational Values, 19–22 August, Prague.

Keenoy, T. (1997) 'Review article: HRMism and the languages of re-presentation', *Journal of Management Studies*, 34, 5, pp. 825–41.

Kerfoot, D. and Knights, D. (1993) 'Management, masculinity and manipulation: from paternalism to corporate strategy in financial services in Britain', *Journal of Management Studies*, 30, 4, pp. 659–79.

Kerfoot, D. and Knights, D. (1994) 'Into the realm of the fearful: power, identity and the gender problematic', in Radtke, L. and Stam, H. (eds) *Power/Gender*. New York: Sage.

Kerfoot, D. and Knights, D. (1996) 'The best is yet to come: the quest for embodiment in managerial work', in Collinson, D. and Hearn, J. (eds) *Men as Managers, Managers as Men*. London: Sage.

Kerfoot, D. and Knights, D. (1998) 'Managing masculinity in contemporary organizational life: a "man" agerial project', *Organization*, 5, 1, pp. 7–26.

Kerfoot, D. and Whitehead, S. (1998) '"Boys own" stuff: masculinity and the management of further education', *Sociological Review*, 46, 3, 436–57.

Ogbonna, E. (1992) 'Organizational culture and HRM: dilemmas and contradictions', in Blyton, P. and Turnbull, P. (eds) *Reassessing Human Resource Management*. London: Sage.

Ogbonna, E. and Wilkinson, B. (1990) 'Corporate strategy and corporate culture: the view from the checkout', *Personnel Review*, 19, 4, pp. 9–15.

Peters, T. and Waterman, R. (1982) *In Search of Excellence*. New York: Harper & Row.

Rose, N. (1989) *Governing the Soul: The Social Shaping of the Private Self*. London: Routledge.

Seidler, V. (1989) *Rediscovering Masculinity: Reason, Language and Sexuality*. London: Routledge.

Seidler, V. (1992) 'Rejection, vulnerability and friendship', in Nardi, P. (ed.) *Men's Friendships*. Newbury Park, Calif.: Sage.

Simmel, G. (1950) *The Sociology of Georg Simmel*, ed. K. H. Wolff. New York: The Free Press.

Sturdy, A. (1998) 'Customer care in a consumer society', *Organization*, 5, 1, pp. 27–53.

Thompson, P. and Ackroyd, S. (1995) 'All quiet on the workplace front', *Sociology*, 29, 4, pp. 615–33.

Tuckmann, A. (1994) 'The yellow brick road: TQM and the restructuring of organizational culture', *Organizational Studies*, 15, 5, pp. 727–51.

Wilkinson, A. and Willmott, H. (eds) (1995) *Making Quality Critical*. London: Routledge.

Willmott, H. (1993) 'Strength is ignorance; slavery is freedom: managing culture in modern organizations', *Journal of Management Studies*, 30, 4, pp. 515–52.

14

Friendship, Intimacy, and Sexuality

Michael A. Messner

Masculine identities and men's friendships

An interesting consensus has emerged among those who have studied gender and friendship in the United States: Women have deep, intimate, meaningful, and lasting friendships, while men have a number of shallow, superficial, and unsatisfying 'acquaintances.' Several commentators have concluded that men's relationships are shallow because men have been taught to be highly homophobic, emotionally inexpressive, and competitive 'success objects.'[1] Lillian Rubin, employing a psychoanalytic perspective, has argued that men tend to place a high value on 'spending time' with other men, but their early developmental experiences have left them with a deep fear of intimacy (which she defines as the ability and willingness to share one's inner life with another person). As a result, Rubin says, men tend to distance themselves from each other by organizing their time together around an activity that is 'external' to themselves.

This chapter draws on the accounts of male athletes, interviewed between 1983 and 1985. In all, I conducted interviews with thirty male athletes, most of whom had at some time in their lives based their identities largely on their roles as athletes and could therefore be said to have had 'athletic careers.' Twelve had played organized sport through high school, eleven through college, and seven had been professional athletes. At the time of the interviews, most had been retired from playing organized sport for at least five years. Their ages ranged from 21 to 48, the median age being 33. In collecting what amounted to life histories of these men, my purpose was to discover how masculine gender identities develop and change as boys and men interact with the socially constructed world of gender.

As Jim P. stated, 'Sports provide that': Here men can enjoy the company of other men – even become 'close' – without having to become intimate in ways that may threaten their 'firm ego boundaries,' and thus their fragile masculine identities. As a result, men's friendships with each other are, according to Rubin, 'emotionally impoverished.'[2]

Within this theoretical framework, we can begin to make sense of former professional basketball player Bill Bradley's seemingly paradoxical description of his relationships with his teammates as 'warm and real, but never intimate.'[3] Bradley seems comfortable with the simultaneous existence of a certain kind of closeness and a clear sense of boundaries and distance. This is understandable when considered in light of the affinity between masculine gender identity and the gendered structure of sport as a social institution: The hierarchical and rule-bound pattern of athletic careers, and especially of 'antagonistic cooperation' on the team, dovetails with men's ambivalent need to develop 'closeness without intimacy' with other men. In short, competitive activities such as sport mediate men's relationships with each other in ways that allow them to develop a powerful bond while at the same time preventing the development of intimacy.

But to simply leave it that men's friendships constitute 'bonding without intimacy' belies the depth of affection that so many of these men expressed for each other. Sociologist Scott Swain has suggested that negative views of 'male bonding' are distorted and unfair. Drawing on Francesca Cancian's observation that since the industrial revolution, social conceptions of love and intimacy have become 'feminized,' Swain argues that Lillian Rubin and others have been guilty of judging men's friendships against the standard of the type of intimate relationships that women tend to develop.[4] Women tend to place a very high value on talk – and indeed, for a relationship between women to be 'intimate,' there must be a willingness and ability to mutually share their inner lives. In this light, since men friends tend to 'do things' with each other, rather than spending their time talking about their inner lives, they are judged to be engaged in 'bonding without intimacy.' Swain asserts that if we instead examine men's friendships from the point of view of men, rather than through a 'feminine model,' we see that men's friendships are in fact characterized by a 'covert style of intimacy.' Men, Swain asserts, already have an 'active style of intimacy' and should not be forced to learn 'feminine-typed skills to foster intimacy in their relationships.'[5] In short, women and men experience and define intimate friendship in different ways, and neither should be judged by the standard of the other.

When I asked Gene H. whether or not he and his closest teammate/ friend shared their thoughts and feelings, he replied, 'We didn't *have* to talk about everything; We just *knew* we were on the same page.' These kinds of statements are consistent with Swain's contention that men share a covert intimacy, and that 'men and women have different styles of intimacy that reflect the often-separate realms in which they express it.'[6] But there is a danger in viewing men's and women's friendships as 'separate but equal.' For example, Swain discusses a man who told him that 'a couple of girls picked [him and his friend] up and we got laid and everything. . . . After, [he and his friend] went out and had a few beers and compared notes.' Swain concludes that 'though this sort of quote might imply sexual exploitation, . . . the commonality gained from a shared life experience did provide meaningful interaction among the men.'[7] Clearly, this talk among men is 'meaningful interaction' when viewed from the point of view of the men. But whatever this implies about the operation of male friendships, it is also crucial to examine the ways that sexual talk among men about women might contribute to certain kinds of attitudes toward and relationships with women. In other words, I am suggesting that we move away from examining men's friendships with each other from a 'feminine' standpoint (Rubin) or from a 'masculine' standpoint (Swain), and instead ask femin*ist* questions: How are male athletes' friendships with each other affected by – and in turn how do they affect – their attitudes toward and relationships with women?

Sexuality and sexual identity

'Big Man on Campus.' 'Sexual Athlete.' For many, these terms conjure up the dominant cultural image of the athlete on campus: He is extremely popular, self-assured, and (hetero)sexually active. Other boys and young men are envious of the ease with which he can 'get women.' My interviews at times revealed a grain of truth to this popular stereotype of the athlete. Chris H. said that even as a second-string professional basketball player, it was 'just the good life.' He laughed, 'I mean, you could wave at one way up in the fifteenth row, and after the game, she's standing right there by the locker room . . . that's what makes it fun, you know.' Similarly, when asked how he related to others when in school, Thomas M. said, 'I liked to be the big man on campus, and sports was a highlight because it gave me that opportunity. *Everybody* knew who I was. Big Tom. *Everybody* knew who I was.'

On the surface, these two statements affirm the stereotype of the athlete as a confident young man at ease with himself and with his sexuality among his peers. Interestingly though, when asked about their specific relationships with girls and women, a very different picture emerged. 'Big Tom,' for instance, stated that 'girls, in high school, were really not prime in [his] life.' He laughingly continued, 'When I was in high school, I thought I was an ugly guy. You know, being under a lot of pressure, and being so much bigger than everybody, and everybody's always looking at you. In high school, you don't know what looks *mean* – it could be good, it could be bad. At one time I felt I was a freak, so I was more or less into myself. I don't think I had one girlfriend.' This youthful awkwardness and insecurity with respect to girls seemed almost universal among the men I interviewed. David P.'s shyness was compounded by his family's difficult economic situation, so for him, sport became an escape from dealing with girls: 'No doubt I was shy, and I think it had to do with the fact that if I did make a date with a girl, how was I goint to go? What was I going to spend? Because I had none of it. So I just used sports as an escape.' Clarence T., who had no trouble paying for dates, nevertheless had similar problems with girls:

> In my senior year [of high school], I remember dating all these girls. It was real bizarre: I had this list I kept of all the girls I wanted to go out with, and it was like twenty-five people, and I went out with twenty of them. I was just going out with people. I wasn't sexually active – I hadn't had inter-course – I might have done a little petting, but never any genital stuff. I think I was popular, and was seen as an attractive boy, but I didn't have a sense of it. I just thought I was absolutely ugly as hell.

Several of the men I interviewed recalled hoping that being an athlete would give them the confidence to overcome their 'lameness' with girls. Jon P. said that he had hoped that being on the basketball team would help him overcome his shyness 'and make it easier to talk with girls. It didn't.' But several of these men reported that they did eventually de-velop ways to talk to girls, despite their shyness. Eldon C., for instance:

> [In high school], I was lame, as they called it. So I didn't know how to do women so well. My stepmother threw a sixteenth birthday party for me and invited a lot of friends, and I remember that day, trying on a lot of the roles that I saw guys playing, and it kind of shocked me because the women took it seriously, you know. That was a big turning point for me. I didn't particularly like – some of the black modes of relating to women, I thought were *stupid*. Like: 'you know, sugar, you know' – just *nonsense* – sweet nothings seemed silly to me. [But] anyway, I tried it, my version of it, and to my surprise some woman took it seriously. That meant it was possible [laughs].

Calvin H. describes a similar transformation from tortured shyness with girls in high school to a smooth 'rap' with women in college:

I was just scared, and bashful and shy. I did not know what to say or what to do. It was very uncomfortable. One of the things that were the rewards of being a good athlete, and you didn't really want it – I mean, you wanted it, but you didn't want it – you know, like, a girl likes you, but then, clamming up and not being able to communicate very effectively. This was a very bad time, because you're always around a lot of girls at parties. [I was] very uncomfortable in groups and with individuals. Finally [I went] off to college and went to the extreme of trying to attract a lot of girls, [and was] semisuccessful. You knew you had to have a date on Fridays, and knew you had to have one on Saturdays, and so you just walked through the student union, and you'd just have this rap you'd thought of, and you'd just put it on. It was peer pressure. I'm naturally a shy person. But somehow in college I was able to somehow fall into the right kinds of things to do and say.

We can see from these stories that developing a 'rap' with women becomes an almost ritualized way that a young man helps himself over-come an otherwise paralyzing shyness, a sense of 'lameness' when trying to relate to young women. This sort of verbal game involves a certain dramaturgy, a conscious self-manipulation ('you'd just put it on'), and one result is that girls and women become the objects of men's verbal manipulation. This kind of manipulation of women does not spring naturally or magically from men's shyness. Rather, it is socially learned through the male peer group. Notice that Eldon C. learned to 'do women' by watching his friends. Calvin H., though somewhat mystified as to how he was able to overcome his shyness and 'fall into the right things to say,' also cites 'peer pressure' as a motivating force. Clearly, an analysis of the development of men's sexual relationships with women must take into account the ways that male peer groups influence attitudes and feelings about sexuality and emotional commitment to women.

Peter Lyman, in his study of college fraternities, argues that there is an erotic basis to the fraternal bond in male groups.[8] In the past, the key to maintaining the male bond was the denial of the erotic. Organized sport, as it arose in the late nineteenth and early twentieth centuries, was based in part on a Victorian antisexual ethic. First, it was believed that homo-social institutions such as sport would masculinize young males in an otherwise feminized culture, thus preventing homosexuality.[9] Second, the popular (and 'scientific') belief in the 'spermatic economy' held that 'the human male possessed a limited quantity of sperm, which could be invested in various enterprises, ranging from business through sport to copulation and procreation. In this context, the careful regulation of the body was the only path to the conservation of energy.'[10] As sociologist Todd Crosset has pointed out, in a society in which it was held that young men's precious energies would be drained off should they expend too much sperm, sport was elevated as the key 'to regenerate the male body and thus make efficient use of male energy.'[11]

Some of the older men in my study went through adolescence and early adulthood when remnants of the ideology of the 'spermatic economy' were still alive. Eldon C. reports that as a young runner, from the late 1940s through the mid-1950s, he had been 'a bit cautious about sex, because [he] still had some old-fashioned notions about sexual energy [being] competitive with athletic stuff.' Most of these men, though, came of age during the sexual revolution of the 1960s and early 1970s, when the dominant credo became, 'if it feels good, do it.'[12] As a result, the male peer group, within the athletic context, became a place where sexual activity and talk of sexual activity (real or imagined) was a key component of the status system.

But if the bond among men is erotic, and the culture is increasingly telling them, 'if it feels good, do it,' what is to prevent the development of sexual relations among young men who are playing, showering, dressing, and living in such close quarters? The answer is that the erotic bond between men is neutralized through overt homophobia and through the displacement of the erotic toward women as objects of sexual talk and practice. In boyhood, adolescent, and young adult male peer groups, 'fag,' 'girl,' and 'woman' are insults that are used almost interchangeably. In this way, heterosexual masculinity is collectively constructed through the denigration of homosexuality and femininity as 'not-male.' Bill S. described nicely how his high school peer group helped to build his own public presentation of his sexuality: 'I was shy [with girls] – I hung out more with guys. I never dated. I never was real intimate with anyone. It was just kind of scary because I thought I'd get teased by my peers.' When I asked him whether he'd be teased for not being involved with women, he replied,

> For *being* involved! But *you've got to* be involved to the point where you get'em into bed, you know, you *fuck'em*, or something like that, yeah, that's real important [laughs] – but as far as being intimate, or close, I wasn't. And that wasn't real important. Just so I could prove my hetero-sexuality it was real important. But I always wanted to look good to females – because I didn't have the personality [laughs] – *to get 'em into bed!* So I wanted to be able to have the *body*, and the sort of friends around who admired me in some sort of way, to have that pull.

This sort of use of women as objects of sexual conquest is important for gaining status in the male peer group, but it also impoverishes young males' relationships with females. As Bob G. put it, in high school, he and his friends would 'tell a lot of stories about girls. I guess it was a way to show our masculinity. [But] I never got emotionally involved with any of the girls I went our with. I never got close to any of them.' The link between young males' tendency to 'tell [sexual] stories about girls' and their lack of intimacy with girls is an important one. As Peter Lyman points out, young males commonly use sexually aggressive stories and jokes as a means of 'negotiating' the 'latent tension and aggression they feel toward each other.' They also are using this joking relationship to 'negotiate the tension they [feel] between sexual interest in the girls and fear of commitment to them. [They use] hostile joking to negotiate their fear of the "loss of control" implied by intimacy.'[13] While talk of sex with females, then, bonds the males together, the specific forms of sexual talk (sexual objectification and conquest of women) helps them deal with their terror of intimacy with women (described, by many, as 'shyness' or 'lameness' etc.). Again, in the words of Lyman, 'In dealing with women, the group separate[s] intimacy from sex, defining the male bond as intimate but not sexual (homosocial), and relationships with women as sexual but not intimate (heterosexual).'[14] In a very real sense, these young males' relationships with females – whether sexual or not – were constructed through (indeed, were often distorted by and subordinated to) their relationships with their male teammates. One logical result is the kind of attitude toward women that former pro football star Jim Brown describes in his book, *Out of Bounds*. When he played football for the Cleveland Browns, he explains, his male 'partners started calling [him] the Hawk' because he was so successful in 'chasing women.' Now at age fifty-three, Brown continues to view women primarily as young, sexual bodies and as objects of consumption: 'My lady right now is nineteen.... When I eat a peach, I don't want it overripe. I want that peach when it's peaking.'[15] Clearly, this attitude tends to preclude Brown's developing a long-term intimate relationship with one woman. After all, every woman eventually ages, her body changes, and she can be discarded and replaced by what Brown sees as an endless supply of younger, firmer bodies.

Unlike Brown, many male athletes do yearn for, and manage to develop, more or less exclusive relationships with one woman. But this happens despite the fact that the male peer group tends to police its own members in terms of intimacy with females. Male peers might taunt boys and young men who start to spend too much time with a girlfriend, who are becoming too attached, telling them that they are 'pussywhipped.' Don Sabo, in writing about his own football career told this tale: 'Once when I was a high school junior, the gang in the weight room accused me of being wrapped around my girlfriend's finger. Nothing could be further from the truth, I assured them, and in order to prove it, I broke up with her. I felt miserable about this at the time and I still feel bad about it.'[16]

Sociologist Timothy Curry found in his participant-observation study of two college male locker rooms that sexually aggressive talk about women usually takes the form of a loud public performance.[17] Curry also observed that any serious discussions between two men about actual relationships with girlfriends usually takes place in hushed tones, often at the edges of the locker room. If this sort of talk is discovered by the group, the speakers are often ridiculed and taunted to reveal details about the woman's body and whether or not the she is sexually 'putting out.' The result of this locker room culture, according to Sabo, is that many men end up suffering a kind of '"sexual schizophrenia." Their minds lead them toward eroticism while their hearts pull them toward emotional intimacy.'[18] Some young men deal with this split by keeping their emotional attachments with women a secret, while continuing to participate in locker room discussions about sexuality with their male peers. Bob G. had one such relationship in high school: 'We started sneaking around and going out late at night and no one else knew. I didn't tell any of my friends. We got along great, sexually and emotionally, though she said I didn't express my feelings enough.'

At times, the male peer group's policing of its members' relationships with females took on a racial angle. Larry W., for instance, said that when he was in college 'the biggest conflict we had was black males dating white girls. The white males would call up the white females and call them whores, bitches, and prostitutes – you know, insulting language, like "If you ball him, you'll ball anybody, so come over here and ball me too."' In this case, the peer group was not only policing intimacy with women, but also imposing controls on interracial sexuality.

The need to prove one's manhood through sexual conquests of women was experienced as a burden by many young heterosexual males, and was sometimes complicated by racial tensions, but it was especially oppressive for gay men. Mike T. threw himself into sport, rather than into dancing, largely because he was terrified that people might find out that he was gay. Sport allowed him to project a masculine public image. But this meant that he also had to project a heterosexual image:

> I hated high school. I mean, I just didn't know who I was. I think I had quite a bit of negative self-esteem at that time, because I really felt different. I mean, I didn't drink, I didn't like to screw around, and this was what all my friends did, so I felt compelled to go along with this stuff, and all the time hating it. I dated some women, some that I loved because they were just really fine people – [but] physically, there was not a great deal of passion. *For males*, there was a passion. [But] homophobia was rampant, especially in athletics. You see, I think a lot of athletes go into athletics for

the same reason I did. They need to prove their maleness. And I did, I readily admit it. I felt I've got to hide this thing – because I know what they were thinking: If I were gay, they would see me as less than a man, or *not a man*. So I'm going to *be a man*, because *that's what I am.*

Though his secret knowledge of his own homosexuality made this process a much more conscious one for Mike, ('I was *clearly* aware of what I was doing'), his public construction of manhood-as-heterosexual was not all that different from what his nongay teammates were doing. Whether gay or heterosexual, the denial and denigration of gayness and femininity (in oneself and in others) were important to these young men's construction of masculine identities and status in their male peer group.[19] As Mike T. said,

> Go into any locker room and watch and listen, and you'll hear the same kind of garbage – I call it garbage now, and I thought it was garbage then, but I felt compelled to go along with it, because I wanted that image. And I know others who did, too. I know a lot of athletes are gay. And I think a lot of athletes are attracted to athletics because they're fighting feelings of tenderness – not necessarily gay – but they're fighting feminine qualities. I know a lot of football players who very quietly and very secretly like to paint, or play piano, and they do it quietly because this to them is threatening if it's known by others.

The pressure to be seen by one's peers as 'a man' – indeed, the pressure to see oneself as 'a man' – kept most young males in conformity (at least on the surface) with this homophobic and sexist locker room 'garbage.' Conformity with locker room culture was a way for both gay and heterosexual men to construct their public masculinity. But gay men were far more likely to see this process as a strategy than were heterosexual men. As Arthur Brittan explains, 'Gender identity... is a set of reflexive strategies which are brought into play whenever gender is put on the line. In everyday life most heterosexuals do not have to do too much identity work because they tend to function in contexts in which heterosexuality is taken for granted.'[20] In the locker room, gay athletes must constantly engage in 'identity work.' Nearly every gay athlete that social scientist Brian Pronger interviewed agreed that being around all of those naked male bodies in the locker room 'feed[s] the homoerotic imagination and provide[s] homoerotic contact.' One gay athlete told Pronger, '[There is] a surprising amount of sexual cruising and activity in the university locker rooms and shower. I've certainly had sex there.'[21] But since homosexual behavior – or even more subtle expressions of desire – violate the kind of masculinity that is common in the locker room, most gay men develop a strategy of identity construction that is 'ironic': On the surface, they conform to the heterosexist masculine culture, while underneath, they view the locker room through their hidden knowledge of its highly charged eroticism.

Even for a few heterosexual men, the 'garbage' of the locker room led them to question – even reject – the jock culture and the specific form of masculinity and sexuality that predominated there. Brent F., for instance, says that toward the end of high school, he 'really got turned off to the way the guys were relating to the girls':

> It was really ugly in certain ways, like just treating them like objects, totally judging them by their surface appearances, talking amongst themselves in really abusive language about girls, how they're going to do this or that to them. I thought it was wrong. I thought that people shouldn't be treated that way. I started to realize that the way I related to women was not the way these guys were relating to them, and therefore I didn't want to relate with them on that level. So I started to distance myself from the same activities, and started to feel really alienated from my buddies.

This rejection of the sexist treatment of women was a rare exception to the rule. It is significant that this realization was made by a young athlete who several years earlier had decided that he was not a 'career athlete.' That he had already begun to disengage from his athletic career meant that he had less invested in the athletic male peer group. For young men who were fully committed to athletic careers, this sort of rejection of one of the key bonds of the group might have amounted to career suicide. So whether they liked it or not, most went along with it. Furthermore, when the 'garbage' went beyond verbal sparring and to sexual behavior, peer group values encouraged these young men to treat females as objects of conquest. Eric M. described a night on the town with his male peers. He was in high school, a virgin, and terrified at his own lack of sexual experience. But when they hit the town, he said, 'We were like wolves hunting down prey. Dave told me, "If a girl doesn't give it up in sixty seconds, drop her!"'

It is this dynamic that is at the heart of what feminists have called 'the rape culture.'[22] One study of date rape revealed that college men who have experienced pressure from their current male friends to engage in sexual activity are more likely to commit acquaintance rape.[23] Similarly, a 1988 national study found that 'involvement in peer groups that reinforce highly sexualized views of women' is an important predictor of 'sexually aggressive behavior' by college males.[24] Robin Warshaw concluded from her research on date and acquaintance rape that 'athletic teams are breeding grounds for rape [because they] are often populated by men who are steeped in sexist, rape-supportive beliefs.'[25] Indeed, sportswriter Rich Hoffman reported in a story in the *Philadelphia Daily News* that between 1983 and 1986, a U.S. college athlete was reported for sexual assault an average of once every eighteen days.[26]

The sexual objectification of women among male athletes is probably, in most cases, a 'rhetorical performance' that rarely translates into actual aggression against women.[27] But there is considerable evidence that men pay a price for these performances. As sociologist Miriam Johnson has argued,

> That the peer group's pressure to be heterosexual occurs in a context in which women are sex-objectified may well have the consequence of making it difficult for males to become sexually aroused in a relationship in which they do not feel dominant over the female. If one learns about sexuality in the context of being rewarded by other males for 'scoring,' for 'getting pussy' or just 'getting it,' then this does not augur well for egalitarian sex.[28]

Though this socially structured denigration of women truly does hurt young males, in terms of making the development of true intimacy with women more difficult to develop, ultimately, it is women – the 'prey' – who pay the price for young men's fear of intimacy with each other.

NOTES

1 For mid 1970s discussions of the shallowness of men's friendships with other men, see W. Farrell, *The Liberated Man* (New York: Bantam Books, 1975); M.-F. Fasteau, *The Male Machine* (New York: McGraw-Hill, 1974); S. F. Morin and E. M. Garfinkel, 'Male Homophobia,' *Journal of Social Issues* 34 (1978): 29–47. J. H. Pleck and J. Sawyer, eds., *Men and Masculinity* (Englewood Cliffs, N. J.: Prentice-Hall, 1974).

2 L. B. Rubin, *Intimate Strangers: Men and Women Together* (New York: Harper and Row, 1983), p. 135. Rubin's definition of 'intimacy,' while helpful in constructing her typology of gender differences in friendship patterns, is clearly class biased. Her emphasis on verbalization of one's 'inner life' is based on a very upper-middle class, therapeutic definition of intimacy, which might ignore or devalue other, nonverbal, forms of expression more common in social groups that are not so immersed in the professional/therapeutic culture. Rubin develops a more complete analysis of gender and friendship in *Just Friends: The Role of Friendship in Our Lives* (New York: Harper and Row, 1985).

3 B. Bradley, *Life on the Run* (New York: Bantam Books, 1977).

4 See F. M. Cancian, *Love in America: Gender and Self-Development* (Cambridge: Cambridge University Press, 1987); and S. Swain, 'Covert Intimacy: Closeness in Men's Friendships,' in B. J. Risman and P. Schwartz, eds., *Gender in Intimate Relationships: A Microstructural Approach* (Belmont, Cal.: Wadsworth, 1989), pp. 71–86.

5 Swain, 'Covert Intimacy,' pp. 71, 85.

6 Ibid., p. 78.

7 Ibid., p. 77.

8 P. Lyman, 'The Fraternal Bond as a Joking Relationship: A Case Study of Sexist Jokes in Male Group Bonding,' in M. S. Kimmel, ed., *Changing Men: New Directions in Research on Men and Masculinity.* (Newbury Park: Sage, 1987), pp. 148–63.

9 Here are some of the roots of the still popular misconception that male homosexuality is connected to some essential 'femininity,' a confusion of sexual identity with gender identity. This confusion is clearly a cultural manifestation. See W. L. Williams, *The Spirit and the Flesh: Sexual Diversity in American Indian Culture* (Boston: Beacon Press, 1986).

10 D. J. Mrozek, *Sport and the American Mentality, 1880–1910* (Knoxville: University of Tennessee Press, 1983), p. 20.

11 T. Crosset, 'Masculinity, Sexuality, and the Development of Early Modern Sport,' in M. A. Messner and D. F. Sabo, eds., *Sport, Men, and the Gender Order: Critical Feminist Perspectives* (Champaign, Ill.: Human Kinetics Publishers, 1990), pp. 45–54.

12 I recall, though, that despite the fact that scientific 'sexology' had long since discredited the notion of the spermatic economy, and despite the fact that Joe Namath had exploded the myth in professional football by showing up for big games, even the Super Bowl, and making thinly veiled statements about whom he had slept with the previous night, I had a community college coach in 1971 who would routinely warn us before every weekened to 'save [our] energies for the games...stay away from the split-tails' (which of course meant women).

13 Lyman, 'The Fraternal Bond as a Joking Relationship,' p. 151.

14 Ibid., p. 156.

15 J. Brown, *Out of Bounds* (New York: Kensington, 1989), pp. 183–84, 190.

16 D. F. Sabo, 'The Myth of the Sexual Athlete,' in *Changing Men: Issues in Gender, Sex, and Politics* 20 (1989): 38–39.

17 T. J. Curry, 'Fraternal Bonding in the Locker Room: A Profeminist Analysis of Talk about Competition and Women' *Sociology of Sport Journal* 8 (1991): 119–135.

18 Sabo, 'The Myth of the Sexual Athlete,' p. 39.

19 Christine Williams points out in her study of the construction of gender in the Marine Corps and in the nursing profession that homophobia and misogyny are a common part of basic training for male Marines. See C. L. Williams, *Gender Differences at Work: Women and Men in Nontraditional Occupations.* (Berkeley: University of California Press, 1989).

20   A. Brittan, *Masculinity and Power* (Oxford: Basil Blackwell, 1989), p. 41.

21   B. Pronger, *The Arena of Masculinity: Sports, Homosexuality, and the Meaning of Sex* (New York: St. Martin's Press, 1990), pp. 195, 199.

22   See, for instance, D. Herman, 'The Rape Culture,' in J. Freeman, ed., *Women: A Feminist Perspective*, 3d ed. (Mountain View, Cal.: Mayfield, 1984), pp. 20–38; T. Beneke, *Men on Rape* (New York: St. Martin's Press, 1982).

23   E. J. Kanin, 'Date Rape: Differential Sexual Socialization and Relative Deprivation,' *Victimology* 9 (1984): 95–108.

24   M. P. Koss, and T. E. Dinero, 'Predictors of Sexual Aggression among a National Sample of Male College Students,' in R. A. Prentky and V. Quinsey, eds., *Human Sexual Aggression: Current Perspectives, Annals of the New York Academy of Sciences* 528 (1988): 133–46. For a similar argument on how young male homosocial groups can promote rape, see P. Y. Martin and R. A. Hummer, 'Fraternities and Rape on Campus,' *Gender and Society* 3 (1989): 457–73.

25   Warshaw, R., *I Never Called it Rape* (New York: Harper and Row, 1988), p. 112.

26   Cited ibid., p. 113.

27   An ethnographic study of a Texas high school football team revealed a lot of what anthropologist Douglas Foley called 'rhetorical performance' about sex in the locker room. See D. E. Foley, 'The Great American Football Ritual: Reproducing Race, Class, and Gender Inequality,' *Sociology of Sport Journal* 7 (1990): 111–35.

28   M. M. Johnson, *Strong Mothers, Weak Wives* (Berkeley: University of California Press, 1988).

15

Masculinity as Homophobia: Fear, Shame, and Silence in the Construction of Gender Identity

Michael S. Kimmel

> 'Funny thing,' [Curley's wife] said. 'If I catch any one man, and he's alone, I get along fine with him. But just let two of the guys get together an' you won't talk. Jus' nothin' but mad.' She dropped her fingers and put her hands on her hips. 'You're all scared of each other, that's what. Ever' one of you's scared the rest is goin' to get something on you.'
>
> John Steinbeck, *Of Mice and Men* (1937)

We think of manhood as eternal, a timeless essence that resides deep in the heart of every man. We think of manhood as a thing, a quality that one either has or doesn't have. We think of manhood as innate, residing in the particular biological composition of the human male, the result of androgens or the possession of a penis. We think of manhood as a transcendent tangible property that each man must manifest in the world, the reward presented with great ceremony to a young novice by his elders for having successfully completed an arduous initiation ritual. In the words of poet Robert Bly (1990), 'the structure at the bottom of the male psyche is still as firm as it was twenty thousand years ago' (p. 230).

In this chapter, I view masculinity as a constantly changing collection of meanings that we construct through our relationships with ourselves, with each other, and with our world. Manhood is neither static nor timeless; it is historical. Manhood is not the manifestation of an inner essence; it is socially constructed. Manhood does not bubble up to consciousness from our biological makeup; it is created in culture. Manhood means different things at different times to different people. We come to know what it means to be a man in our culture by setting our definitions in opposition to a set of 'others' – racial minorities, sexual minorities, and, above all, women.

Our definitions of manhood are constantly changing, being played out on the political and social terrain on which the relationships between women and men are played out. In fact, the search for a transcendent, timeless definition of manhood is itself a sociological phenomenon – we tend to search for the timeless and eternal during moments of crisis, those points of transition when old definitions no longer work and new definitions are yet to be firmly established.

This idea that manhood is socially constructed and historically shifting should not be understood as a loss, that something is being taken away from men. In fact, it gives us something extraordinarily valuable – agency, the capacity to act. It gives us a sense of historical possibilities to replace the despondent resignation that invariably attends timeless, ahistorical essentialisms. Our behaviors are not simply 'just human nature,' because 'boys will be boys.' From the materials we find around us in our culture – other people, ideas, objects – we actively create our worlds, our identities. Men, both individually and collectively, can change.

In this chapter, I explore this social and historical construction of both hegemonic masculinity and alternate masculinities, with an eye toward offering a new theoretical model of American manhood.[1] To accomplish this I first uncover some of the hidden gender meanings in classical statements of social and political philosophy, so that I can anchor the emergence of contemporary manhood in specific historical and social contexts. I then spell out the ways in which this version of masculinity emerged in the United States, by tracing both psychoanalytic developmental sequences and a historical trajectory in the development of marketplace relationships.

Classical social theory as a hidden meditation of manhood

Begin this inquiry by looking at four passages from that set of texts commonly called classical social and political theory. You will, no doubt, recognize them, but I invite you to recall the way they were discussed in your undergraduate or graduate courses in theory:

The bourgeoisie cannot exist without constantly revolutionizing the instruments of production, and thereby the relations of production, and with them the whole relations of society. Conservation of the old modes of production in unaltered form, was, on the contrary, the first condition of existence for all earlier industrial classes. Constant revolutionizing of production, uninterrupted disturbance of all social conditions, everlasting uncertainty and agitation distinguish the bourgeois epoch from all earlier ones. All fixed, fast-frozen relations, with their train of ancient and venerable prejudices and opinions are swept away, all new-formed ones become antiquated before they can ossify. All that is solid melts into air, all that is holy is profaned, and man is at last compelled to face with sober senses, his real conditions of life, and his relation with his kind. (Marx & Engels, 1848/1964)

An American will build a house in which to pass his old age and sell it before the roof is on; he will plant a garden and rent it just as the trees are coming into bearing; he will clear a field and leave others to reap the harvest; he will take up a profession and leave it, settle in one place and soon go off elsewhere with his changing desires.... At first sight there is something astonishing in this spectacle of so many lucky men restless in the midst of abundance. But it is a spectacle as old as the world; all that is new is to see a whole people performing in it. (Tocqueville, 1835/1967)

Where the fulfillment of the calling cannot directly be related to the highest spiritual and cultural values, or when, on the other hand, it need not be felt simply as economic compulsion, the individual generally abandons the attempt to justify it at all. In the field of its highest development, in the United States, the pursuit of wealth, stripped of its religious and ethical meaning, tends to become associated with purely mundane passions, which often actually give it the character of sport. (Weber, 1905/1966)

We are warned by a proverb against serving two masters at the same time. The poor ego has things even worse: it serves three severe masters and does what it can to bring their claims and demands into harmony with one another. These claims are always divergent and often seem incompatible. No wonder that the ego so often fails in its task. Its three tyrannical masters are the external world, the super ego and the id.... It feels hemmed in on three sides, threatened by three kinds of danger, to which, if it is hard pressed, it reacts by generating anxiety.... Thus the ego, driven by the id, confined by the super ego, repulsed by reality, struggles to master its economic task of bringing about harmony among the forces and influences working in and upon it; and we can understand how it is that so often we cannot suppress a cry: 'Life is not easy!' (Freud, 'The Dissection of the Psychical Personality,' 1933/1966)

If your social science training was anything like mine, these were offered as descriptions of the bourgeoisie under capitalism, of individuals in democratic societies, of the fate of the Protestant work ethic under the ever rationalizing spirit of capitalism, or of the arduous task of the autonomous ego in psychological development. Did anyone ever mention that in all four cases the theorists were describing men? Not just 'man' as in generic mankind, but a particular type of masculinity, a definition of manhood that derives its identity from participation in the marketplace, from interaction with other men in that marketplace – in short, a model of masculinity for whom identity is based on homosocial competition? Three years before Tocqueville found Americans 'restless in the midst of abundance,' Senator Henry Clay had called the United States 'a nation of self-made men.'

What does it mean to be 'self-made'? What are the consequences of self-making for the individual man, for other men, for women? It is this notion of manhood – rooted in the sphere of production, the public arena, a masculinity grounded not in landownership or in artisanal republican virtue but in successful participation in marketplace competition – this has been the defining notion of American manhood. Masculinity must be proved, and no sooner is it proved that it is again questioned and must be proved again – constant, relentless, unachievable, and ultimately the quest for proof becomes so meaningless than it takes on the characteristics, as Weber said, of a sport. He who has the most toys when he dies wins.

Where does this version of masculinity come from? How does it work? What are the consequences of this version of masculinity for women, for other men, and for individual men themselves? These are the questions I address in this chapter.

Masculinity as history and the history of masculinity

The idea of masculinity expressed in the previous extracts is the product of historical shifts in the grounds on which men rooted their sense of themselves as men. To argue that cultural definitions of gender identity are historically specific goes only so far; we have to specify exactly what those models were. In my historical inquiry into the development of these models of manhood[2] I chart the fate of two models for manhood at the turn of the 19th century and the emergence of a third in the first few decades of that century.

In the late 18th and early 19th centuries, two models of manhood prevailed. The *Genteel Patriarch* derived his identity from landownership. Supervising his estate, he was refined, elegant, and given to casual sensuousness. He was a doting and devoted father, who spent much of his time supervising the estate and with his family. Think of George Washington or Thomas Jefferson as examples. By contrast, the *Heroic Artisan* embodied the physical strength and republican virtue that Jefferson observed in the yeoman farmer, independent urban craftsman, or shopkeeper. Also a devoted father, the Heroic Artisan taught his son his craft, bringing him through ritual apprenticeship to status as master craftsman. Economically autonomous, the Heroic Artisan also cherished his democratic community, delighting in the participatory democracy of the town meeting. Think of Paul Revere at his pewter shop, shirtsleeves rolled up, a leather apron – a man who took pride in his work.

Heroic Artisans and Genteel Patriarchs lived in casual accord, in part because their gender ideals were complementary (both supported participatory democracy and individual autonomy, although patriarchs tended to support more powerful state machineries and also supported slavery) and because they rarely saw one another: Artisans were decidedly urban and the Genteel Patriarchs ruled their rural estates. By the 1830s, though, this casual symbiosis was shattered by the emergence of a new vision of masculinity, *Marketplace Manhood*.

Marketplace Man derived his identity entirely from his success in the capitalist marketplace, as he accumulated wealth, power, status. He was the urban entrepreneur, the businessman. Restless, agitated, and anxious, Marketplace Man was an absentee landlord at home and an absent father with his children, devoting himself to his work in an increasingly homosocial environment – a male-only world in which he pits himself against other men. His efforts at self-making transform the political and economic spheres, casting aside the Genteel Patriarch as an anachronistic feminized dandy – sweet, but ineffective and outmoded, and transforming the Heroic Artisan into a dispossessed proletarian, a wage slave.

As Tocqueville would have seen it, the coexistence of the Genteel Patriarch and the Heroic Artisan embodied the fusion of liberty and equality. Genteel Patriarchy was the manhood of the traditional aristocracy, the class that embodied the virtue of liberty. The Heroic Artisan embodied democratic community, the solidarity of the urban shopkeeper or craftsman. Liberty and democracy, the patriarch and the artisan, could, and did, coexist. But Marketplace Man is capitalist man, and he makes both freedom and equality problematic, eliminating the freedom of the aristocracy and proletarianizing the equality of the artisan. In one sense, American history has been an effort to restore, retrieve, or reconstitute the virtues of Genteel Patriarchy and Heroic Artisanate as they were being transformed in the capitalist marketplace.

Marketplace Manhood was a manhood that required proof, and that required the acquisition of tangible goods as evidence of success. It reconstituted itself by the exclusion of 'others' – women, nonwhite men, nonnative-born men, homosexual men – and by terrified flight into a pristine mythic homosocial Eden where men could, at last, be real men among other men. The story of the ways in which Marketplace Man becomes American Everyman is a tragic tale, a tale of striving to live up to impossible ideals of success leading to chronic terrors of emasculation, emotional emptiness, and a gendered rage that leaves a wide swath of destruction in its wake.

Masculinities as power relations

Marketplace Masculinity describes the normative definition of American masculinity. It describes his characteristics – aggression, competition, anxiety – and the arena in which those characteristics are deployed – the public sphere, the marketplace. If the marketplace is the arena in which manhood is tested and proved, it is a gendered arena, in which tensions between women and men and tensions among different groups of men are weighted with meaning. These tensions suggest that cultural definitions of gender are played out in a contested terrain and are themselves power relations.

All masculinities are not created equal; or rather, we are all *created equal*, but any hypothetical equality evaporates quickly because our definitions of masculinity are not equally valued in our society. One definition of manhood continues to remain the standard against which other forms of manhood are measured and evaluated. Within the dominant culture, the masculinity that defines white, middle-class, early middle-aged, heterosexual men is the masculinity that sets the standards for other men, against which other men are measured and, more often than not, found wanting. Sociologist Erving Goffman (1963) wrote that in America, there is only 'one complete, unblushing male':

> a young, married, white, urban, northern heterosexual, Protestant father of college education, fully employed, of good complexion, weight and height, and a recent record in sports. Every American male tends to look out upon the world from this perspective.... Any male who fails to qualify in any one of these ways is likely to view himself ... as unworthy, incomplete, and inferior. (p. 128)

This is the definition that we will call 'hegemonic' masculinity, the image of masculinity of those men who hold power, which has become the standard in psychological evaluations, sociological research, and self-help and advice literature for teaching young men to become 'real men' (Connell, 1987). The hegemonic definition of manhood is a man *in* power, a man *with* power, and a man *of* power. We equate manhood with being strong, successful, capable, reliable, in control. The very definitions of manhood we have developed in our culture maintain the power that some men have over other men and that men have over women.

Our culture's definition of masculinity is thus several stories at once. It is about the individual man's quest to accumulate those cultural symbols that denote manhood, signs that he has in fact achieved it. It is about those standards being used against women to prevent their inclusion in public life and their consignment to a devalued private sphere. It is about the differential access that different types of men have to those cultural resources that confer manhood and about how each of these groups then develop their own modifications to preserve and claim their manhood. It is about the power of these definitions themselves to serve to maintain the real-life power that men have over women and that some men have over other men.

This definition of manhood has been summarized cleverly by psychologist Robert Brannon (1976) into four succinct phrases:

1 'No Sissy Stuff!' One may never do anything that even remotely suggests femininity. Masculinity is the relentless repudiation of the feminine.
2 'Be a Big Wheel.' Masculinity is measured by power, success, wealth, and status. As the current saying goes, 'He who has the most toys when he dies wins.'
3 'Be a Sturdy Oak.' Masculinity depends on remaining calm and reliable in a crisis, holding emotions in check. In fact, proving you're a man depends on never showing your emotions at all. Boys don't cry.
4 'Give 'em Hell.' Exude an aura of manly daring and aggression. Go for it. Take risks.

These rules contain the elements of the definition against which virtually all American men are measured. Failure to embody these rules, to affirm the power of the rules and one's achievement of them is a source of men's confusion and pain. Such a model is, of course, unrealizable for any man. But we keep trying, valiantly and vainly, to measure up. American masculinity is a relentless test.[3] The chief test is contained in the first rule. Whatever the variations by race, class, age, ethnicity, or sexual orientation, being a man means 'not being like women.' This notion of anti-femininity lies at the heart of contemporary and historical conceptions of manhood, so that masculinity is defined more by what one is not rather than who one is.

Masculinity as the flight from the feminine

Historically and developmentally, masculinity has been defined as the flight from women, the repudiation of femininity. Since Freud, we have come to understand that developmentally the central task that every little boy must confront is to develop a secure identity for himself as a man. As Freud had it, the oedipal project is a process of the boy's renouncing his identification with and deep emotional attachment to his mother and then replacing her with the father as the object of identification. Notice that he reidentifies but never reattaches. This entire process, Freud argued, is set in motion by the boy's sexual desire for his mother. But the father stands in the son's path and will not yield his sexual property to his puny son. The boy's first emotional experience, then, the one that inevitably follows his experience of desire, is fear – fear of the bigger, stronger, more sexually powerful father. It is this fear, experienced symbolically as the fear of castration, Freud argues, that forces the young boy to renounce his identification with mother and seek to identify with the being who is the actual source of his fear, his father. In so doing, the boy is now symbolically capable of sexual union with a motherlike substitute, that is, a woman. The boy becomes gendered (masculine) and heterosexual at the same time.

Masculinity, in this model, is irrevocably tied to sexuality. The boy's sexuality will now come to resemble the sexuality of his father (or at least the way he imagines his father) – menacing, predatory, possessive, and possibly punitive. The boy has come to identify with his oppressor; now he can become the oppressor himself. But a terror remains, the terror that the young man will be unmasked as a fraud, as a man who has not completely and irrevocably separated from mother. It will be other men who will do the unmasking. Failure will de-sex the man, make him appear as not fully a man. He will be seen as a wimp, a Mama's boy, a sissy.

After pulling away from his mother, the boy comes to see her not as a source of nurturance and love, but as an insatiably infantalizing creature, capable of humiliating him in front of his peers. She makes him dress up in uncomfortable and itchy clothing, her kisses smear his cheeks with lipstick, staining his boyish innocence with the mark of feminine dependency. No wonder so many boys cringe from their mothers' embraces with groans of 'Aw, Mom! Quit it!' Mothers represent the humiliation of infancy, helplessness, dependency. 'Men act as though they were being guided by (or rebelling against) rules and prohibitions enunciated by a moral mother,' writes psychohistorian Geoffrey Gorer (1964). As a result, 'all the niceties of masculine behavior – modesty, politeness, neatness, cleanliness – come to be regarded as concessions to feminine demands, and not good in themselves as part of the behavior of a proper man' (pp. 56, 57).

The flight from femininity is angry and frightened, because mother can so easily emasculate the young boy by her power to render him dependent, or at least to remind him of dependency. It is relentless; manhood becomes a lifelong quest to demonstrate its achievement, as if to prove the unprovable to others, because we feel so unsure of it ourselves. Women don't often feel compelled to 'prove their womanhood' – the phrase itself sounds ridiculous. Women have different kinds of gender identity crises; their anger and frustration, and their own symptoms of depression, come more from being excluded than from questioning whether they are feminine enough.[4]

The drive to repudiate the mother as the indication of the acquisition of masculine gender identity has three consequences for the young boy. First, he pushes away his real mother, and with her the traits of nurturance, compassion, and tenderness she may have embodied. Second, he suppresses those traits in himself, because they will reveal his incomplete separation from mother. His life becomes a lifelong project to demonstrate that he possesses none of his mother's traits. Masculine identity is born in the renunciation of the feminine, not in the direct affirmation of the masculine, which leaves masculine gender identity tenuous and fragile.

Third, as if to demonstrate the accomplishment of these first two tasks, the boy also learns to devalue all women in his society, as the living embodiments of those traits in himself he has learned to despise. Whether or not he was aware of it, Freud also described the origins of sexism – the systematic devaluation of women – in the desperate efforts of the boy to separate from mother. We may *want* 'a girl just like the girl that married dear old Dad,' as the popular song had it, but we certainly don't want to *be like* her.

This chronic uncertainty about gender identity helps us understand several obsessive behaviors. Take, for example, the continuing problem of the school-yard bully. Parents remind us that the bully is the *least* secure about his manhood, and so he is constantly trying to prove it. But he 'proves' it by choosing opponents he is absolutely certain he can defeat; thus the standard taunt to a bully is to 'pick on someone your own size.' He can't, though, and after defeating a smaller and weaker opponent, which he was sure would prove his manhood, he is left with the empty gnawing feeling that he has not proved it after all, and he must find another opponent, again one smaller and weaker, that he can again defeat to prove it to himself.[5]

One of the more graphic illustrations of this lifelong quest to prove one's manhood occurred at the Academy Awards presentation in 1992. As aging, tough guy actor Jack Palance accepted the award for Best Supporting Actor for his role in the cowboy comedy *City Slickers*, he commented that people, especially film producers, think that because he is 71 years old, he's all washed up, that he's no longer competent. 'Can we take a risk on this guy?' he quoted them as saying, before he dropped to the floor to do a set of one-armed push-ups. It was pathetic to see such an accomplished actor still having to prove that he is virile enough to work and, as he also commented at the podium, to have sex.

When does it end? Never. To admit weakness, to admit frailty or fragility, is to be seen as a wimp, a sissy, not a real man. But seen by whom?

Masculinity as a homosocial enactment

Other men: We are under the constant careful scrutiny of other men. Other men watch us, rank us, grant our acceptance into the realm of manhood. Manhood is demonstrated for other men's approval. It is other men who evaluate the performance. Literary critic David Leverenz (1991) argues that 'ideologies of manhood have functioned primarily in relation to the gaze of male peers and male authority' (p. 769). Think of how men boast to one another of their accomplishments – from their latest sexual conquest to the size of the fish they caught – and how we constantly parade the markers of manhood – wealth, power, status, sexy women – in front of other men, desperate for their approval.

That men prove their manhood in the eyes of other men is both a consequence of sexism and one of its chief props. 'Women have, in men's minds, such a low place on the social ladder of this country that it's useless to define yourself in terms of a woman,' noted playwright David Mamet. 'What men need is men's approval.' Women become a kind of currency that men use to improve their ranking on the masculine social scale. (Even those moments of heroic conquest of women carry, I believe, a current of homosocial evaluation.) Masculinity is a *homosocial* enactment. We test ourselves, perform heroic feats, take enormous risks, all because we want other men to grant us our manhood.

Masculinity as a homosocial enactment is fraught with danger, with the risk of failure, and with intense relentless competition. 'Every man you meet has a rating or an estimate of himself which he never loses or forgets,' wrote Kenneth Wayne (1912) in his popular turn-of-the-century advice book. 'A man has his own rating, and instantly he lays it alongside of the other man' (p. 18). Almost a century later, another man remarked to psychologist Sam Osherson (1992) that '[b]y the time you're an adult, it's easy to think you're always in competition with men, for the attention of women, in sports, at work' (p. 291).

Masculinity as homophobia

If masculinity is a homosocial enactment, its overriding emotion is fear. In the Freudian model, the fear of the father's power terrifies the young boy to renounce his desire for his mother and identify with his father. This model links gender identity with sexual orientation: The little boy's identification with father (becoming masculine) allows him to now engage in sexual relations with women (he becomes heterosexual). This is the origin of how we can 'read' one's sexual orientation through the successful performance of gender identity. Second, the fear that the little boy feels does not send him scurrying into the arms of his mother to protect him from his father. Rather, he believes he will overcome his fear by identifying with its source. We become masculine by identifying with our oppressor.

But there is a piece of the puzzle missing, a piece that Freud, himself, implied but did not follow up.[6] If the pre-oedipal boy identifies with mother, he *sees the world through mother's eyes*. Thus, when he confronts father during his great oedipal crisis, he experiences a split vision: He sees his father as his mother sees his father, with a combination of awe, wonder, terror, *and desire*. He simultaneously sees the father as he, the boy, would like to see him – as the object not of desire but of emulation. Repudiating mother and identifying with father only partially answers his dilemma. What is he to do with that homoerotic desire, the desire he felt because he saw father the way that his mother saw father?

He must suppress it. Homoerotic desire is cast as feminine desire, desire for other men. Homophobia is the effort to suppress that desire, to purify all relationships with other men, with women, with children of its taint, and to ensure that no one could possibly ever mistake one for a homosexual. Homophobic flight from intimacy with other men is the repudiation of the homosexual within – never completely successful and hence constantly reenacted in every homosocial relationship. 'The lives of most American men are bounded, and their interests daily curtailed by the constant necessity to prove to their fellows, and to themselves, that they are not sissies, not homosexuals,' writes psychoanalytic historian Geoffrey Gorer (1964). 'Any interest or pursuit which is identified as a feminine interest or pursuit becomes deeply suspect for men' (p. 129).

Even if we do not subscribe to Freudian psychoanalytic ideas, we can still observe how, in less sexualized terms, the father is the first man who evaluates the boy's masculine performance, the first pair of male eyes before whom he tries to prove himself. Those eyes will follow him for the rest of his life. Other men's eyes will join them – the eyes of role models such as teachers, coaches, bosses, or media heroes; the eyes of his peers, his friends, his workmates; and the eyes of millions of other men, living and dead, from whose constant scrutiny of his performance he will never be free. 'The tradition of all the dead generations weighs like a nightmare on the brain of the living,' was how Karl Marx put it over a century ago (1848/1964, p. 11). 'The birthright of every American male is a chronic sense of personal inadequacy,' is how two psychologists describe it today (Woolfolk & Richardson, 1978, p. 57).

That nightmare from which we never seem to awaken is that those other men will see that sense of inadequacy, they will see that in our own eyes we are not who we are pretending to be. What we call masculinity is often a hedge against being revealed as a fraud, an exaggerated set of activities that keep others from seeing through us, and a frenzied effort to keep at bay those fears within ourselves. Our real fear 'is not fear of women but of being ashamed or humiliated in front of other men, or being dominated by stronger men' (Leverenz, 1986, p. 451).

This, then, is the great secret of American manhood: *We are afraid of other men.* Homophobia is a central organizing principle of our cultural definition of manhood. Homophobia is more than the irrational fear of gay men, more than the fear that we might be perceived as gay. 'The word "faggot" has nothing to do with homosexual experience or even with fears of homosexuals,' writes David Leverenz (1986). 'It comes out of the depths of manhood: a label of ultimate contempt for anyone who seems sissy, untough, uncool' (p. 455). Homophobia is the fear that other men will unmask us, emasculate us, reveal to us and the world that we do not measure up, that we are not real men. We are afraid to let other men see that fear. Fear makes us ashamed, because the recognition of fear in ourselves is proof to ourselves that we are not as manly as we pretend, that we are, like the young man in a poem by Yeats, 'one that ruffles in a manly pose for all his timid heart.' Our fear is the fear of humiliation. We are ashamed to be afraid.

Shame leads to silence – the silences that keep other people believing that we actually approve of the things that are done to women, to minorities, to gays and lesbians in our culture. The frightened silence as we scurry past a woman being hassled by men on the street. That furtive silence when men make sexist or racist jokes in a bar. That clammy-handed silence when guys in the office make gay-bashing jokes. Our fears are the sources of our silences, and men's silence is what keeps the system running. This might help to explain why women often complain that their male friends or partners are often so understanding when they are alone and yet laugh at sexist jokes or even make those jokes themselves when they are out with a group.

The fear of being seen as a sissy dominates the cultural definitions of manhood. It starts so early. 'Boys among boys are ashamed to be un-manly,' wrote one educator in 1871 (cited in Rotundo, 1993, p. 264). I have a standing bet with a friend that I can walk onto any playground in America where 6-year-old boys are happily playing and by asking one question, I can provoke a fight. That question is simple: 'Who's a sissy around here?' Once posed, the challenge is made. One of two things is likely to happen. One boy will accuse another of being a sissy, to which that boy will respond that he is not a sissy, that the first boy is. They may have to fight it out to see who's lying. Or a whole group of boys will surround one boy and all shout 'He is! He is!' That boy will either burst into tears and run home crying, disgraced, or he will have to take on several boys at once, to prove that he's not a sissy. (And what will his father or older brothers tell him if he chooses to run home crying?) It will be some time before he regains any sense of self-respect.

Violence is often the single most evident marker of manhood. Rather it is the willingness to fight, the desire to fight. The origin of our expression that one has a chip on one's shoulder lies in the practice of an adolescent boy in the country or small town at the turn of the century, who would literally walk around with a chip of wood balanced on his shoulder – a signal of his readiness to fight with anyone who would take the initiative of knocking the chip off (see Gorer, 1964, p. 38; Mead, 1965).

As adolescents, we learn that our peers are a kind of gender police, constantly threatening to unmask us as feminine, as sissies. One of the favorite tricks when I was an adolescent was to ask a boy to look at his fingernails. If he held his palm toward his face and curled his fingers back to see them, he passed the test. He'd looked at his nails 'like a man.' But if he held the back of his hand away from his face, and looked at his fingernails with arm outstretched, he was immediately ridiculed as a sissy.

As young men we are constantly riding those gender boundaries, checking the fences we have constructed on the perimeter, making sure that nothing even remotely feminine might show through. The possibil-

ities of being unmasked are everywhere. Even the most seemingly insig-
nificant thing can pose a threat or activate that haunting terror. On the
day the students in my course 'Sociology of Men and Masculinities' were
scheduled to discuss homophobia and male–male friendships, one student provided a touching illustration. Noting that it was a beautiful day,
the first day of spring after a brutal northeast winter, he decided to wear
shorts to class. 'I had this really nice pair of new Madras shorts,' he
commented. 'But then I thought to myself, these shorts have lavender and
pink in them. Today's class topic is homophobia. Maybe today is not the
best day to wear these shorts.'

Our efforts to maintain a manly front cover everything we do. What
we wear. How we talk. How we walk. What we eat. Every mannerism,
every movement contains a coded gender language. Think, for example,
of how you would answer the question: How do you 'know' if a man is
homosexual? When I ask this question in classes or workshops, respondents invariably provide a pretty standard list of stereotypically effeminate behaviors. He walks a certain way, talks a certain way, acts a certain
way. He's very emotional; he shows his feelings. One woman commented
that she 'knows' a man is gay if he really cares about her; another said she
knows he's gay if he shows no interest in her, if he leaves her alone.

Now alter the question and imagine what heterosexual men do to
make sure no one could possibly get the 'wrong idea' about them.
Responses typically refer to the original stereotypes, this time as a set
of negative rules about behavior. Never dress that way. Never talk or
walk that way. Never show your feelings or get emotional. Always be
prepared to demonstrate sexual interest in women that you meet, so it is
impossible for any woman to get the wrong idea about you. In this sense,
homophobia, the fear of being perceived as gay, as not a real man, keeps
men exaggerating all the traditional rules of masculinity, including sexual
predation with women. Homophobia and sexism go hand in hand.

The stakes of perceived sissydom are enormous – sometimes matters of
life and death. We take enormous risks to prove our manhood, exposing
ourselves disproportionately to health risks, workplace hazards, and
stress-related illnesses. Men commit suicide three times as often as
women. Psychiatrist Willard Gaylin (1992) explains that it is 'invariably
because of perceived social humiliation,' most often tied to failure in
business:

Men become depressed because of loss of status and power in the world of
men. It is not the loss of money, or the material advantages that money
could buy, which produces the despair that leads to self-destruction. It is
the 'shame,' the 'humiliation,' the sense of personal 'failure.' . . . A man
despairs when he has ceased being a man among men. (p. 32)

In one survey, women and men were asked what they were most afraid of. Women responded that they were most afraid of being raped and murdered. Men responded that they were most afraid of being laughed at (Noble, 1992, pp. 105–106).

Homophobia as a cause of sexism, heterosexism, and racism

Homophobia is intimately interwoven with both sexism and racism. The fear – sometimes conscious, sometimes not – that others might perceive us as homosexual propels men to enact all manner of exaggerated masculine behaviors and attitudes to make sure that no one could possibly get the wrong idea about us. One of the centerpieces of that exaggerated masculinity is putting women down, both by excluding them from the public sphere and by the quotidian put-downs in speech and behaviors that organize the daily life of the American man. Women and gay men become the 'other' against which heterosexual men project their identities, against whom they stack the decks so as to compete in a situation in which they will always win, so that by suppressing them, men can stake a claim for their own manhood. Women threaten emasculation by representing the home, workplace, and familial responsibility, the negation of fun. Gay men have historically played the role of the consummate sissy in the American popular mind because homosexuality is seen as an inversion of normal gender development. There have been other 'others.' Through American history, various groups have represented the sissy, the non-men against whom American men played out their definitions of manhood, often with vicious results. In fact, these changing groups provide an interesting lesson in American historical development.

At the turn of the 19th century, it was Europeans and children who provided the contrast for American men. The 'true American was vigorous, manly, and direct, not effete and corrupt like the supposed Europeans,' writes Rupert Wilkinson (1986). 'He was plain rather than ornamented, rugged rather than luxury seeking, a liberty loving common man or natural gentleman rather than an aristocratic oppressor or servile minion' (p. 96). The 'real man' of the early 19th century was neither noble nor serf. By the middle of the century, black slaves had replaced the effete nobleman. Slaves were seen as dependent, helpless men, incapable of defending their women and children, and therefore less than manly. Native Americans were cast as foolish and naive children, so they could be infantalized as the 'Red Children of the Great White Father' and therefore excluded from full manhood.

By the end of the century, new European immigrants were also added to the list of the unreal men, especially the Irish and Italians, who were seen as too passionate and emotionally volatile to remain controlled sturdy oaks, and Jews, who were seen as too bookishly effete and too physically puny to truly measure up. In the mid-20th century, it was also Asians – first the Japanese during the Second World War, and more recently, the Vietnamese during the Vietnam War – who have served as unmanly templates against which American men have hurled their gendered rage. Asian men were seen as small, soft, and effeminate – hardly men at all.

Such a list of 'hyphenated' Americans – Italian-, Jewish-, Irish-, African-, Native-, Asian-, gay – composes the majority of American men. So manhood is only possible for a distinct minority, and the definition has been constructed to prevent the others from achieving it. Interestingly, this emasculation of one's enemies has a flip side – and one that is equally gendered. These very groups that have historically been cast as less than manly were also, often simultaneously, cast as hypermasculine, as sexually aggressive, violent rapacious beasts, against whom 'civilized' men must take a decisive stand and thereby rescue civilization. Thus black men were depicted as rampaging sexual beasts, women as carnivorously carnal, gay men as sexually insatiable, southern European men as sexually predatory and voracious, and Asian men as vicious and cruel torturers who were immorally disinterested in life itself, willing to sacrifice their entire people for their whims. But whether one saw these groups as effeminate sissies or as brutal uncivilized savages, the terms with which they were perceived were gendered. These groups become the 'others,' the screens against which traditional conceptions of manhood were developed.

Being seen as unmanly is a fear that propels American men to deny manhood to others, as a way of proving the unprovable – that one is fully manly. Masculinity becomes a defense against the perceived threat of humiliation in the eyes of other men, enacted through a 'sequence of postures' – things we might say, or do, or even think, that, if we thought carefully about them, would make us ashamed of ourselves (Savran, 1992, p. 16). After all, how many of us have made homophobic or sexist remarks, or told racist jokes, or made lewd comments to women on the street? How many of us have translated those ideas and those words into actions, by physically attacking gay men, or forcing or cajoling a woman to have sex even though she didn't really want to because it was important to score?

Power and powerlessness in the lives of men

I have argued that homophobia, men's fear of other men, is the animating condition of the dominant definition of masculinity in America, that the reigning definition of masculinity is a defensive effort to prevent being emasculated. In our efforts to suppress or overcome those fears, the dominant culture exacts a tremendous price from those deemed less than fully manly: women, gay men, non-native-born men, men of color. This perspective may help clarify a paradox in men's lives, a paradox in which men have virtually all the power and yet do not feel powerful (see Kaufman, 1993).

Manhood is equated with power – over women, over other men. Everywhere we look, we see the institutional expression of that power – in state and national legislatures, on the boards of directors of every major U.S. corporation or law firm, and in every school and hospital administration. Women have long understood this, and feminist women have spent the past three decades challenging both the public and the private expressions of men's power and acknowledging their fear of men. Feminism as a set of theories both explains women's fear of men and empowers women to confront it both publicly and privately. Feminist women have theorized that masculinity is about the drive for domination, the drive for power, for conquest.

This feminist definition of masculinity as the drive for power is theorized from women's point of view. It is how women experience masculinity. But it assumes a symmetry between the public and the private that does not conform to men's experiences. Feminists observe that women, as a group, do not hold power in our society. They also observe that individually, they, as women, do not feel powerful. They feel afraid, vulnerable. Their observation of the social reality and their individual experiences are therefore symmetrical. Feminism also observes that men, as a group, *are* in power. Thus, with the same symmetry, feminism has tended to assume that individually men must feel powerful.

This is why the feminist critique of masculinity often falls on deaf ears with men. When confronted with the analysis that men have all the power, many men react incredulously. 'What do you mean, men have all the power?' they ask. 'What are you talking about? My wife bosses me around. My kids boss me around. My boss bosses me around. I have no power at all! I'm completely powerless!'

Men's feelings are not the feelings of the powerful, but of those who see themselves as powerless. These are the feelings that come inevitably from the discontinuity between the social and the psychological, between the aggregate analysis that reveals how men are in power as a group and the psychological fact that they do not feel powerful as individuals. They are the feelings of men who were raised to believe themselves entitled to feel that power, but do not feel it. No wonder many men are frustrated and angry.

This may explain the recent popularity of those workshops and re-treats designed to help men to claim their 'inner' power, their 'deep manhood,' or their 'warrior within.' Authors such as Bly (1990), Moore and Gillette (1991, 1992, 1993a, 1993b), Farrell (1986, 1993), and Keen (1991) honor and respect men's feelings of powerlessness and acknowledge those feelings to be both true and real. 'They gave white men the semblance of power,' notes John Lee, one of the leaders of these retreats (quoted in *Newsweek*, p. 41). 'We'll let you run the country, but in the meantime, stop feeling, stop talking, and continue swallowing your pain and your hurt.' (We are not told who 'they' are.)

Often the purveyors of the mythopoetic men's movement, that broad umbrella that encompasses all the groups helping men to retrieve this mythic deep manhood, use the image of the chauffeur to describe modern man's position. The chauffeur appears to have the power – he's wearing the uniform, he's in the driver's seat, and he knows where he's going. So, to the observer, the chauffeur looks as though he is in command. But to the chauffeur himself, they note, he is merely taking orders. He is not at all in charge.[7]

Despite the reality that everyone knows chauffeurs do not have the power, this image remains appealing to the men who hear it at these weekend workshops. But there is a missing piece to the image, a piece concealed by the framing of the image in terms of the individual man's experience. That missing piece is that the person who is giving the orders is also a man. Now we have a relationship *between* men – between men giving orders and other men taking those orders. The man who identifies with the chauffeur is entitled to be the man giving the orders, but he is not. ('They,' it turns out, are other men.)

The dimension of power is now reinserted into men's experience not only as the product of individual experience but also as the product of relations with other men. In this sense, men's experience of powerlessness is *real* – the men actually feel it and certainly act on it – but it is not *true*, that is, it does not accurately describe their condition. In contrast to women's lives, men's lives are structured around relationships of power and men's differential access to power, as well as the differential access to that power of men as a group. Our imperfect analysis of our own situation leads us to believe that we men need *more* power, rather than leading us to support feminists' efforts to rearrange power relationships along more equitable lines.

Philosopher Hannah Arendt (1970) fully understood this contradict-ory experience of social and individual power:

> Power corresponds to the human ability not just to act but to act in concert. Power is never the property of an individual; it belongs to a group and remains in existence only so long as the group keeps together. When we say of somebody that he is 'in power' we actually refer to his being empowered by a certain number of people to act in their name. The moment the group, from which the power originated to begin with...disappears, 'his power' also vanishes. (p. 44)

Why, then, do American men feel so powerless? Part of the answer is because we've constructed the rules of manhood so that only the tiniest fraction of men come to believe that they are the biggest of wheels, the sturdiest of oaks, the most virulent repudiators of femininity, the most daring and aggressive. We've managed to disempower the overwhelming majority of American men by other means – such as discriminating on the basis of race, class, ethnicity, age, or sexual prefer-ence.

Masculinist retreats to retrieve deep, wounded, masculinity are but one of the ways in which American men currently struggle with their fears and their shame. Unfortunately, at the very moment that they work to break down the isolation that governs men's lives, as they enable men to express those fears and that shame, they ignore the social power that men continue to exert over women and the privileges from which they (as the middle-aged, middle-class white men who largely make up these retreats) continue to benefit – regardless of their experiences as wounded victims of oppressive male socialization.[8]

Others still rehearse the politics of exclusion, as if by clearing away the playing field of secure gender identity of any that we deem less than manly – women, gay men, nonnative-born men, men of color – middle-class, straight, white men can reground their sense of themselves without those haunting fears and that deep shame that they are unmanly and will be exposed by other men. This is the manhood of racism, of sexism, of homophobia. It is the manhood that is so chronically insecure that it trembles at the idea of lifting the ban on gays in the military, that is so threatened by women in the workplace that women become the targets of sexual harassment, that is so deeply frightened of equality that it must ensure that the playing field of male competition remains stacked against all newcomers to the game.

Exclusion and escape have been the dominant methods American men have used to keep their fears of humiliation at bay. The fear of emascula-tion by other men, of being humiliated, of being seen as a sissy, is the leitmotif in my reading of the history of American manhood. Masculinity has become a relentless test by which we prove to other men, to women, and ultimately to ourselves, that we have successfully mastered the part. The restlessness that men feel today is nothing new in American history; we have been anxious and restless for almost two centuries. Neither exclusion nor escape has ever brought us the relief we've sought, and there is no reason to think that either will solve our problems now. Peace of mind, relief from gender struggle, will come only from a politics of inclusion, not exclusion, from standing up for equality and justice, and not by running away.

NOTES

Author's Note: This chapter represents a preliminary working out of a theoretical chapter in my forthcoming book, *Manhood: The American Quest* (in press). I am grateful to Tim Beneke, Harry Brod, Michael Kaufman, Iona Mara-Drita, and Lillian Rubin for comments on earlier versions of the chapter.

1 Of course, the phrase 'American manhood' contains several simultaneous fictions. There is no single manhood that defines all American men; 'America' is meant to refer to the United States proper, and there are significant ways in which this 'American manhood' is the outcome of forces that transcend both gender and nation, that is, the global economic development of industrial capitalism. I use it, therefore, to describe the specific hegemonic version of masculinity in the United States, that normative constellation of attitudes, traits, and behaviors that became the standard against which all other masculinities are measured and against which individual men measure the success of their gender accomplishments.

2 Much of this work is elaborated in *Manhood: The American Quest* (in press).

3 Although I am here discussing only American masculinity, I am aware that others have located this chronic instability and efforts to prove manhood in the particular cultural and economic arrangements of Western society. Calvin, after all, inveighed against the disgrace 'for men to become effeminate,' and countless other theorists have described the mechanics of manly proof. (See, for example, Seidler, 1994.)

4 I do not mean to argue that women do not have anxieties about whether they are feminine enough. Ask any woman how she feels about being called aggressive; it sends a chill into her heart because her femininity is suspect. (I believe that the reason for the enormous recent popularity of sexy lingerie among women is that it enables women to remember they are still feminine underneath their corporate business suit – a suit that apes masculine styles.) But I think the stakes are not as great for women and that women have greater latitude in defining their identities around these questions than men do. Such

are the ironies of sexism: The powerful have a narrower range of options than the powerless, because the powerless can *also* imitate the powerful and get away with it. It may even enhance status, if done with charm and grace – that is, is not threatening. For the powerful, any hint of behaving like the powerless is a fall from grace.

5 Such observations also led journalist Heywood Broun to argue that most of the attacks against feminism came from men who were shorter than 5 ft. 7 in. 'The man who, whatever his physical size, feels secure in his own masculinity and in his own relation to life is rarely resentful of the opposite sex' (cited in Symes, 1930, p. 139).

6 Some of Freud's followers, such as Anna Freud and Alfred Adler, did follow up on these suggestions. (See especially, Adler, 1980.) I am grateful to Terry Kupers for his help in thinking through Adler's ideas.

7 The image is from Warren Farrell, who spoke at a workshop I attended at the First International Men's Conference, Austin, Texas, October 1991.

8 For a critique of these mythopoetic retreats, see Kimmel and Kaufman, 1994: ch. 14.

REFERENCES

Adler, A. (1980). *Cooperation between the sexes: Writings on women, love and marriage, sexuality and its disorders* (H. Ansbacher & R. Ansbacher, Eds. & Trans.). New York: Jason Aronson.

Arendt, H. (1970). *On revolution*. New York: Viking.

Bly, R. (1990). *Iron John: A book about men*. Reading, MA: Addison-Wesley.

Brannon, R. (1976). The male sex role – and what it's done for us lately. In R. Brannon & D. David (Eds.), *The forty-nine percent majority* (pp. 1–40). Reading, MA: Addison-Wesley.

Connell, R. W. (1987). *Gender and power*. Cambridge: Polity, and Stanford, CA: Stanford University Press.

Farrell, W. (1986). *Why men are the way they are*. New York: McGraw-Hill.

Farrell, W. (1993). *The myth of male power: Why men are the disposable sex*. New York: Simon & Schuster.

Freud, S. (1933/1966). *New introductory lectures on psychoanalysis* (L. Strachey, Ed.). New York: Norton.

Gaylin, W. (1992). *The male ego*. New York: Viking.

Goffman, E. (1963). *Stigma*. Englewood Cliffs, NJ: Prentice Hall.

Gorer, G. (1964). *The American people: A study in national character*. New York: Norton.

Kaufman, M. (1993). *Cracking the armour: Power and pain in the lives of men*. Toronto: Viking Canada.

Keen, S. (1991). *Fire in the belly*. New York: Bantam.

Kimmel, M. S. (in press). *Manhood: The American quest*. New York: Harper Collins.

Kimmel, M. S., & Kaufman, M. (1994). Weekend warriors: The new men's movement. In H. Brod and M. Kaufman (Eds.), *Theorizing Masculinities*. Thousand Oaks: Sage.

Leverenz, D. (1986). Manhood, humiliation and public life: Some stories. *Southwest Review, 71*, Fall.

Leverenz, D. (1991). The last real man in America: From Natty Bumppo to Batman. *American Literary Review, 3*.

Marx, K., & F. Engels. (1848/1964). The communist manifesto. In R. Tucker (Ed.), *The Marx-Engels reader*. New York: Norton.

Mead, M. (1965). *And keep your powder dry*. New York: William Morrow.

Moore, R., & Gillette, D. (1991). *King, warrior, magician lover*. New York: HarperCollins.

Moore, R., & Gillette, D. (1992). *The King within: Accessing the king in the male psyche*. New York: William Morrow.

Moore, R., & Gillette, D. (1993a). *The warrior within: Accessing the warrior in the male psyche*. New York: William Morrow.

Moore, R., & Gillette, D. (1993b). *The magician within: Accessing the magician in the male psyche*. New York: William Morrow.

Noble, V. (1992). A helping hand from the guys. In K. L. Hagan (Ed.), *Women respond to the men's movement*. San Francisco: HarperCollins.

Osherson, S. (1992). *Wrestling with love: How men struggle with intimacy, with women, children, parents, and each other*. New York: Fawcett.

Rotundo, E. A. (1993). *American manhood: Transformations in masculinity from the revolution to the modern era*. New York: Basic Books.

Savran, D. (1992). *Communists, cowboys and queers: The politics of masculinity in the work of Arthur Miller and Tennessee Williams*. Minneapolis: University of Minnesota Press.

Seidler, V. J. (1994). *Unreasonable men: Masculinity and social theory*. New York: Routledge.

Symes, L. (1930). The new masculinism. *Harper's Monthly, 161*, January.

Tocqueville, A. de. (1835/1967). *Democracy in America*. New York: Anchor.

Wayne, K. (1912). *Building the young man*. Chicago: A. C. McClurg.

Weber, M. (1905/1966). *The Protestant ethic and the spirit of capitalism*. New York: Charles Scribner's.

What men need is men's approval. (1993, January 3). *The New York Times*, p. C-11.

Wilkinson, R. (1986). *American tough: The tough-guy tradition and American character*. New York: Harper & Row.

Woolfolk, R. L., & Richardson, F. (1978). *Sanity, stress and survival*. New York: Signet.

16

'A Vicarious Sense of Belonging': The Politics of Friendship and Gay Social Movements, Communities, and Neighborhoods

Peter M. Nardi

> [F]riendship and its virtues are not merely private: they are public, even political, for a civic order, a 'city,' is above all a network of friends. Without civic friendship, a city will degenerate into a struggle of contending interest groups unmediated by any public solidarity.
>
> Robert Bellah et al., *Habits of the Heart*

Friendship provides more than psychological well-being and social support. It also contains an element of community building, mobilizing, and effecting social change. There is what Hannah Arendt calls, 'the political relevance of friendship.'[1] Dan said that 'most of my friends are those who will show up at the next [political rally]. This is not a deeply thought-out choice; I'm just more interested in those who are active.'

Friendship has the potential to develop and maintain unconventional values and styles of behavior through shared choice and to transform social and political life.[2] How gay people develop an identity by building communities of choice, organize a political presence and transform social life, and structure space (residential, commercial, sexual, global) is related, in part, to friendship networks. The personal can become the political. There are, in other words, social and political consequences to the formation of friendships in gay men's lives, not the least of which is the idea of civil society, as Aristotle explained when he wrote that 'friendship consists in community' and that 'friendship also seems to hold states together.'[3]

For Aristotle, political friendships are connected to familial and personal relationships. Michael Pakaluk interprets Aristotle's idea of 'community friendships' as dependent on household friendships, which are then extended to mediating institutions, such as a tribe or fraternal association, and finally to the state: 'It is in a family that one can acquire love for oneself as someone whose nature is to be in relation to others, and it is this sort of self-love which is extended to the political communities.'[4] From the micro to the macro, from interpersonal relationships that begin in families of choice to gay neighborhoods and organizations, friendships are a powerful social force.

There is little to suggest that the political power of friendships is on the wane in modern societies. Contrary to prevailing notions about market society and personal relations conflicting with each other, sociologist Allan Silver proposes that commercial society promotes friendship patterns that 'connect, not some who are allied in struggle against others, but potentially all, through forms of association that cumulatively contribute to a moralized civil society.'[5] Such eighteenth-century Scottish Enlightenment writers as Adam Smith and David Hume understood friendship in precommercial society as an instrumental, calculated, competitive, and necessary relationship, the purpose of which was to 'help friends and hurt enemies' (as is evidenced in the classical heroic forms of friendship).

In commercial society, however, as Silver puts it, by 'limiting instrumental exchange to the newly distinct domain of the market,' a voluntary, 'morally superior form of friendship' can be founded on sympathy and affection. Such a friendship is 'unconstrained by necessity,' which enhances the 'moral quality of personal relationships,' integrating 'individuals into the larger society, linking them to successively more inclusive groupings,' and resulting in a 'civil society free of exclusivistic relationships hostile or suspicious toward others.'[6] This overly romanticized view of capitalism, however, may understate the competitive individualism that often emerges among men. Solidary networks do occur where traditional ties break down, suggesting a dialectical rather than a causal process between commerce and friendship.[7]

In a civil society that sets up relationships of hostility, especially based on sexual orientation, linking gay men into exclusive groupings is a necessity. Hence, contemporary gay men's friendships have a potential sociopolitical impact in the ways they can challenge the heteronormativity of the dominant culture, not only through mobilization of social movements but also in the possible subversion of hegemonic definitions of masculinity. For example, Robert Martin writes that 'For Whitman such a love [male love] has consequences for the organization of society; it challenges the very order of male power... [I]t was a reordering of affective arrangements that could no longer be contained. Taking its origin in the discourses of male power, it nonetheless sought to explode them.'[8]

R. W. Connell argues that gay men's sexual and friendship relationships have a political potential when he says that the relative equality in gay men's sexuality and their formation of more friendly interpersonal relationships, especially with women, disrupt the social relations of gender: 'A more reciprocal sexuality and pacific everyday interactions are necessary if relations between men and women are to move beyond the current state of inequality, violence, and misogyny.'[9] I want to consider this idea of subverting the hegemonic order by looking at gay men's friendships' potential for facilitating the formation of communities of identity and the development of neighborhoods and spaces that, in turn, can contribute to a civil society and to the mobilization of new social movements – all of which become politicized as they challenge, yet sometimes reproduce, the societal arrangements of male power.

Identity communities and friendships

Fred said that his friendships give him 'a vicarious sense of belonging to a gay movement or community, in the larger sense.' According to Aristotle's philosophy, communities constitute friendships.[10] And for contemporary gay people, according to Kath Weston, 'the historical development of friendship ties among persons whose shared "sexual" identity was initially defined solely through their sexuality turned out to be merely an introductory episode in a more lengthy tale of community formation.'[11] Community concepts (which were especially dominant in the 1970s and the 1980s) have to be understood as cultural constructs that signify ideas of togetherness, solidarity, and face-to-face relationships, in opposition to the larger culture's emphasis on individuality. Because gays and lesbians tend to grow up outside of and sometimes fearing the very identity group they later become part of, they must create their own communities of belongingness, communities that are unlike those of race and ethnicity, in which family provides the images and identities.

Friendship networks, thus, become the primary site where the daily lives of gay men and lesbians are carried out and shaped. Jeffrey Weeks calls the relationship, whether marital or nonmarital, 'the defining element of the sphere of the intimate that provides the framework for everyday life...[I]t is the focus of personal identity, in which the personal narrative is constructed and reconstructed to provide the provisional sense of unity of the self that is necessary in the world of postmodernity.'[12] From there, the potential for identity-based cultural communities to develop emerges. Networks of friendships, often reconceptualized as kinships of choice, become the source for developing communities of identity and equality. Unlike being born into a community of kin, an individual can choose a community of identity that provides norms and relationships that 'stimulate and develop her identity and self-understanding more adequately than her unchosen community of origin, her original community of place.'[13]

However, as became evident, a politics of difference emerged, and concepts of community as a single, homogeneous, and egalitarian category collapsed, especially since sexual orientation is distributed through a variety of class, racial, and gender groups: 'Gay community can best be understood not as a unified subculture, but rather as a category implicated in the ways lesbians and gay men have developed collective identities, organized urban space, and conceptualized their significant relationships.'[14] Differentiation within the gay male community, for example, emphasized class and racial identities and a rejection of belonging to 'the' gay community. Perhaps this led in part to the shift from a discourse centered around a 'family of friends' that was meant to be inclusive of all gays and lesbians, to a language of family/marriage focused on dyadic, interpersonal relationships that often did not include networks of friends. Conceptualizing gay relationships more in kinship terms and less in community language may be one result of the postmodernization of identity and is perhaps nothing more than a relabeling of structures and interactions that did not significantly change.

Yet friendships continue to be the nexus between personal identity and membership into a larger community, whether that be 'the' gay community for some, or a specialized subcultural one for others. This is amply illustrated by John D'Emilio's account of Harry Hay, who cofounded the Mattachine Society in the early 1950s: 'He discovered gay male friendship circles in San Francisco among the city's actors, musicians, artists, and writers. When Hay returned to Los Angeles, friends from San Francisco provided introductions that gave him entree to homosexual networks in southern California.'[15] As philosopher Marilyn Friedman writes, there is 'the additional need for communities of choice to counter oppressive and abusive relational structures in those nonvoluntary communities by providing models of alternative social relationships and standpoints for critical reflection on self and community.'[16]

Linking personal tastes, politics, and sexual styles to subgroups of others who share these dimensions is a process of becoming a member in a community. Claude Fischer makes clear in his work on urban networks that homophily – the sharing of similar values, characteristics, and opinions – is promoted by the complexities and differentiations brought on by the heterogeneity of urban living.[17] Despite the notion that the diversity of cities will result in networks of people who reflect that diversity, the facts point to the importance of both personal preference and structural constraints in the development of subcultures of shared interests and characteristics.

Modernization, Fischer argues, has brought with it an increase in the number of age-graded institutions, resulting in people – especially younger single people – coming together in critical masses in urban areas with others of the same age. Fischer found that the average difference in age between friends was six years and that in more than half the cases it was five years or less. Also important, according to his study, is marital status: married people are much more likely to name other married people as friends, and never-marrieds to name never-marrieds. But these processes of homophily in urban residences vary selectively; for members of majority groups, the possibility of meeting more heterogeneous people is greater, but minority members have fewer choices and are more likely to select fellow minority members as friends. Fischer concludes, 'Thus urbanism can have an asymmetric effect – increasing heterogeneity with respect to those characteristics an individual shares with many people and increasing homogeneity with respect to those he or she shares with few.'[18][...]

In short, urbanism promotes the emergence of communities or subcultures 'formed of people who are minorities in the wider society' and who 'are at least as involved in their social worlds as small-town residents are in theirs, but ... their worlds are more specialized and uncommon.'[19] Of course, not all networks of friends become communities. These subcultures or communities develop as a result of selective migration, accumulation of a critical mass, and intergroup friction. Urban centers attract people from a wide range of places who then form specific social, political, and economic institutions to meet the demands brought on by increasing numbers of differentiated people, and develop an in-group identity in contrast to other groups that conflict with them ideologically and/or compete with them for space, power, and other resources.[20]

The emergence of gay communities and subcultures in the large urban centers of North America during the 1970s verifies that these processes occur. Stephen Murray writes of the institutional completeness of a Toronto gay community in comparison to ethnic communities and argues that the former met the criteria set by sociologists for the definition of a community. Furthermore, he later made a convincing argument that gay people are more than the 'lifestyle enclaves' described by Robert Bellah et al. in *Habits of the Heart*; gay men and lesbians do indeed constitute a community that has a collective history and memory, that can reproduce the complexities of institutional society, and that gets involved in public life beyond its own private interests. He concludes, 'The gay community is at least as much one as any other urban community.'[21]

But what constitutes membership in a gay community: gay identity, same-sex sexual behavior, gay friendship networks, and/or living in a gay neighborhood? Having a gay identity is almost sufficient, according to the overwhelming majority of Murray's white respondents (Asian Americans felt that same-sex sexual behavior and gay identity were necessary in order for someone to be considered a member, and about half of the Latino and African American gay men said either would do). Having gay friends in the absence of a gay identity or a gay neighborhood was not enough to make someone part of a gay community.[22] In short, a network of gay friends does not constitute community unless one also has a gay identity.

But how likely is someone to have a gay identity without having gay friends? Murray states that 'Acceptance of being gay is not just the most important criterion for establishing membership in the category *gay community*...but is the central moral imperative within it,' and it takes place in the company of other gay men.[23] For Ken Plummer, telling coming-out stories – which highlight how a 'sense of identity or self is achieved as gay or lesbian, along with a sense of community' – implies that communities of people exist to hear the narratives and that communities have a set of stories that 'weave together their history, their identity, their politics.'[24] Participation in the gay communities' institutions (bars, baths, restaurants, book stores, media, political and social organizations, etc.) contributes to gay identity achievement, and gay identity leads to the creation and maintenance of gay communities which, in an ongoing dialectic, provide a context for reproducing identity in a newer generation of people searching for meaning and friendship. These gay networks of friends and acquaintances, manifested through the institutions and organizations, assist people in making the transition to gay identity, into gay neighborhoods, and into gay political and social communities. As Aaron, one of my respondents, said about getting to know one of his close friends, whom he met at a meeting of gay professional men, 'I was new in town....He made a real effort to get me into his network of friends, and I remain grateful for that.'

This is not just a recent phenomenon, as George Chauncey makes clear in his study of early twentieth-century New York. He describes how migration of single men to the city from small towns in the 1920s 'was encouraged and facilitated by gay friends who had gone before them, who sent them word about the gay life to be found there, and who assisted them in making the move by providing them initial accommodations and, in some cases, contacts that might lead to employment.'[25] Once in the cities, many of these men developed extensive gay social networks 'and created a distinctive culture that enabled them to resist, on an everyday basis, their social marginalization.'[26] Through these communal ties newcomers were integrated into gay worlds and were given the space and skills to enact their gay identities, which were only one of many identities they managed in their lives.

Older gay men served as mentors to the younger ones, providing them with not only sexual encounters and romance, but also with the skills and information valued by the gay world. Furthermore, 'Perhaps most important, mentors introduced men new to the gay world to their circle of friends,' and soon the 'small circle of new acquaintances came and brought their friends, who brought their friends.'[27] Private parties in people's apartments and houses in the 1930s and 1940s were often the most important venue for gay men to meet others and to become incorporated into a circle of gay friends. And the drag balls of the 1920s and 1930s, which often attracted hundreds and thousands of gay men and connected different gay friendship circles with each other, 'simply could not have been organized without the existence of the elaborate social networks that constituted the gay subculture.'[28]

Social movements and friendships

But it's important to remember that not all gay men participate in gay culture, communities, institutions, and movements: 'Communities are *potential bases* for collective action. . . . Actual participation is characteristic of only a minority of any class, ethnic group, or community.'[29] Aaron spoke about the way friendships could be political, but only at certain points in one's development:

> My experience is that there is a lot of potential for gay friendships to have a political undercurrent when they involve people who are just coming out and/or people who are politically active around a particular issue or set of issues. Being about a dozen years removed from my principal coming-out experiences, and perhaps ten years removed from my most ardent political activism, I don't see as much potential for my gay friendships to be political. . . . Most of my friendships now do not have much of a political bent.

Yet the rise of gay and lesbian movements that mobilized to effect changes in the larger cultural climate is one of the dramatic stories of the 1970s and 1980s, and one that is interconnected with the emergence of gay identities, communities, and friendship networks. Fred argued this perspective when he said there 'is a kind of dialectical process between gay friendships and gay social action. Each promotes and begets the other.' He likes to have friends with a 'moderate degree of activism.'

Friedman states that friendship has 'disruptive possibilities' because it can create 'shared perspectives that generate disloyalties to existing social institutions,' which can lead to 'beneficial social change.'[30] The development of new collective movements characterized by open, decentralized, and participatory organizational structures and focused on postmaterial ideologies and values is well documented.[31] Many of these theorists argue that earlier explanations of social movements – such as the relative deprivation model, rational choice perspectives, or resource mobilization theory – have been supplanted by newer ones that emphasize movements based on cultural politics and quality-of-life issues, depend more on middle-class constituents, and challenge the larger economic and political structures of a society.[32]

The questions of how these new social movement theories apply to the gay and lesbian movement has, however, been subject to some debate. Barry Adam says that 'New social movements theory offers only partial applicability to gay and lesbian mobilization,' since gay and lesbian organizations represent more than a middle-class movement, take on various structural forms in different societies, do more than protect existing living arrangements by innovating newer ones in a much wider range of arenas (such as those of the workplace, housing, religion, media, and health services), and engage with the state more to modify moral regulations.[33]

Changes in the way gay people saw themselves, migrated to large urban centers, and formed residential and commercial areas with greater concentrations of gays contributed to the emergence of collective identity and social movements. Shared gay identity and collective consciousness have been facilitated by the development of residential concentrations of homosexuals which, in turn, has depended on 'the impersonal (bureaucratic) provision of economic opportunity and security.'[34]

Geographic mobility, a critical mass of people in delimited urban spaces, the mobilization of symbolic resources such as the media, voluntary relationships less dependent on family of origin, and evidence that social change is possible are other factors involved in the development of a politics of gay identity and a potential social movement.[35] In fact, for new social movements to become mobilized and continue, personal networks of communication, mass media, and 'high interpersonal interaction density' among members of a value community must play central roles.[36] Political scientist Dennis Chong concludes that 'Preexisting social networks play a central role in the emergence of collective action.'[37] His words lend credence to Larry Kramer's 1985 call to organize and do something about AIDS: 'And who among us does not have friends? Friends to join our first small organization?'[38]

This interpersonal interaction in networks of people with 'culturally derived identities,' and the 'emotional warmth that derives from the network element of the movement' make social movements attractive to individuals.[39] Friedman writes that 'Friendship among women has been the cement . . . of the various historical waves of the feminist movement'; it has also been so for many communities of unconventional women, as is documented by Janice Raymond in *A Passion for Friends*.[40] We know that some of the earliest demonstrations against police raids occurred among patrons of gay bars, the kinds of spots that served as the community gathering place for friends.[41] Political organizations, from the earliest 1950s Mattachine Society to the liberation organizations that dramatically increased in number following the Stonewall rebellion, were often born in someone's living room, where a group of friends had gathered.[42] Mobilizing others to join depended on friends calling friends, a method identical to the snowball sampling techniques used by survey researchers when attempting to reach hard-to-find samples.

A decision-theoretic model of social movements proposes that invisible groups (such as gays) cannot depend on support from nonmembers if they are to organize politically. Rather, they must rely on generating commitment from individuals who first have to identify with the group.[43] The story of the founding of the Mattachine Society illustrates this point: Harry Hay's 'professional heterosexual acquaintances . . . convinced him that a campaign on behalf of homosexuals would have to be initiated by the oppressed themselves.'[44] From that set of people who identify with the invisible group, some, but not most, will contribute to the collective political effort.

Political theorists have developed a variety of models to explain collective action and why people would participate in such action when the public good that accrues from it would benefit even 'free riders' who do not contribute to the movement.[45] Often some sort of material 'selective incentive' must be offered – inducements that can only be enjoyed by those who participate. However, 'direct tangible selective benefits' are rarely available for 'public-spirited collective action'; most people participate in political activities 'out of a sense of obligation to their families, friends, and associates; they go along to get along,' that is, for social and psychological incentives.[46]

Chong argues that by caring for the interests of others, self-interest and genuine sympathy for others results; therefore collective actions need to be understood less for their material incentives and more for the social psychological benefits they offer. Ongoing social relationships and encounters with other members of a community create pressures to cooperate: 'The desires to gain or sustain friendships, to maintain one's social standing, and to avoid ridicule and ostracism are all social goals that constitute selective incentives for individuals to participate in collective action' or to 'inhibit people from participating in a cause that is considered unpopular in their community.'[47]

While these pressures are stronger in smaller groups, large communities can make use of preexisting interpersonal relationships in mobilizing commitments to collective actions by working through networks of smaller organizational units in which 'friendship and familial, religious, and professional relationships create an array of *ongoing* exchanges, obligations, and expectations that individual members have considerable incentive to uphold.'[48] Again, the story of the founding of the Mattachine Society in 1950 demonstrates the role of friendship networks and identity development:

> Early on, [the founders] had recognized the value of their private meetings as a means of cementing relations among themselves and discarding many conventional attitudes about homosexuality. Consequently, even before they had formalized their structure or their goals, they began inviting selected gay friends and acquaintances to a biweekly discussion group on homosexuality.[49]

Although few returned for other meetings in the beginning, the gatherings became semipublic and eventually took off. And out of these meetings, 'friendships formed, and the meetings took on the character of intimate gatherings.'[50] For many of those who get involved in collective actions, gay identity acceptance and friendships precede mobilization; for others gay identity and friendship networks are developed, reproduced, and maintained through participation in the institutions of a gay community, including organizations, bars, and social movements.[...] Clubs and organizations and, to a lesser degree, bars are a major source of friendships in this more middle-class sample.

Friendship networks continue to play an important role as a medium of communications, especially in attempts to mobilize groups of people. Witness the increasing use of E-mail distribution lists to solicit support for a petition, boycott, or other action. Several years ago, when California Governor Pete Wilson vetoed Assembly Bill 101, which would have prohibited discrimination in the workplace and housing based on sexual orientation, people in and around Los Angeles hurriedly organized a march and rally by calling one another on the telephone with information about the time and place. I received a call and was asked to contact at least two or three other friends and spread the word. I was part of an organized phone tree, although many of the people I called were not. In any case, the appearance of several hundred people later that evening was mostly due to friends calling on friends to show up. And for nearly ten unprecedented days, marches throughout the streets continued thanks to word of mouth among friendship networks and to growing media attention.

In order for things as diverse as street rallies and grassroots organizing and formal fund-raising events and benefits to take place, networks of friends and acquaintances who can contact each other is essential. Many gay and lesbian organizations depend on people (usually middle- or upper-class people, with money to donate) to sponsor tables at a fund-raising event and to call nine other people they know to ask them to purchase a ticket at their table for the benefit. People are much more likely to donate money or time if a friend phones; such informal solicitations are much more effective than is attempting to generate financial or volunteer time commitment through ads or mailings initiated by some unknown person or group. Participation in social actions and movements, from checkbook activism to grassroots mobilizing, has depended on the links people have in their interpersonal networks of friends.

Friendship and space

Dan told me how he found his house in a gay neighborhood thanks to a friend: 'Best move I ever made. Nice to be in a place where you're presumed gay, where no one pays notice you're reading the gay magazines waiting in the checkout line.' But Fred had 'somewhat mixed feelings about living in a predominantly gay community. Somehow I dislike the "enclave," barrio, ghetto aspect of it. On the other hand...there is a liberating aspect of being part of [a gay neighborhood].'

Letty Cottin Pogrebin points out that 'Sexual orientation also can affect where people choose to live and, hence, their friendship patterns.'[51] Gay people's friends, and especially their casual acquaintances, are often the fellow gay residents of the district in which they live.[52] There are many gay public spaces, particularly in large urban areas, that provide gay men opportunities to form social circles, cliques, and new friendships. In general men control public space; gay men – and especially white middle-class gay men with their relative economic and political power – have been at the forefront in controlling gay public space.

The arrangement of space within a neighborhood increases the likelihood of getting to know and becoming friends with one's neighbors, simply through the process of passive social contact: 'Those with whom one has the greatest amount of contact are most likely to become one's friends.'[53] And these casual interactions in shared social space contribute to a sense of community and identity, as Henning Bech argues: 'In order for a homosexual neighbourhood to actualize, the individuals will in any case have to leave their dwellings and enter the city or other people's places. But living close to others also has a significance for one's awareness of the potentialities of community and opportunity.'[54]

[...] Gay men seeking refuge with others like themselves were evident in the late nineteenth and early twentieth centuries, when single men migrated from small towns in America and from Europe to New York, and to particular neighborhoods that provided housing and commercial services oriented toward single men. And since many of these single men were homosexuals, Chauncey argues, the beginnings of a gay community were set in motion: 'The existence of an urban bachelor subculture facilitated the development of a gay world.... Rooming houses and cafeterias served as meeting grounds for gay men, facilitating the constant interaction that made possible the development of a distinctive subculture.'[55]

In the first half of the century in New York, gay worlds developed in many of the hotels, apartments houses, restaurants, and speakeasies as the gay men sought security and understanding from like-minded others. Chauncey describes how an apartment building slowly became more and more gay as flats opened up and one of the gay residents 'invited other friends to move in. Several friends did, and some of the newcomers encouraged their own friends to join them.'[56] In addition, various YMCAs developed gay reputations, and many newcomers to the city built 'a network of gay friends' through contacts there.[57]

Throughout the early part of the twentieth century, gay men would occupy other public spaces and convert them into havens for their socializing. And in many of these spaces gay social networks played key roles, contributing to the Harlem Literary Renaissance and to the development of Greenwich Village as a gay enclave. Besides the rooming houses and apartment buildings, gay men 'turned many restaurants into places where they could gather with gay friends, gossip, ridicule the dominant culture that ridiculed them, and construct an alternative culture.'[58] Like the political organizations, these commercial institutions served the needs of both those already part of the gay world and those just entering it:

> Particular restaurants served as the locus of particular gay social networks; overlapping groups of friends would meet regularly for dinner and camaraderie. The role of restaurants as social centers meant they often functioned as a crucial point of entry into the gay world for men just beginning to identify themselves as gay; for men already deeply involved in the gay world, they were a vital source of information about the gay scene, police activity, cultural events, and the like.[59]

Similar spaces provide sources of sexual, romantic, and friendship relationships for gay men today. Although urban centers are much more likely to have developed neighborhoods with economic, residential, and social support resources, even in small towns there are ways for people to meet one another.[60] However, gays and lesbians in rural areas tend to 'rely on social networks with people they have little in common with but their sexual preferences,' often leading to loneliness and isolation and sometimes the formation of incompatible romantic relationships.[61] But the power of friendships and networks of gay men to contribute to the development of a sense of self and a sense of community is evident in all these various guises, from early-twentieth-century restaurants to gay political organizations in contemporary urban centers to small-town bars. And the Internet, with its numerous World Wide Web bulletin boards and lists devoted to gay issues, has become the modern public space that links thousands, if not millions, to a larger community of people who become political friends – a global civic friendship – mobilizing in the struggle to find meaning and dignity in societies that continue to impose a hegemonic order that constrains and limits choices.

The meaning of friendship in gay men's lives

In friendship, people can depart from the routine and display a portion of the self not affected by social control. That is, friendship allows people to go beyond the basic structures of their cultural institutions into an involuntary and uncontrollable disclosure of self – to violate the rules of public propriety, as Gerald Suttles phrases it.[62] Friendship is an escape from the dictates and pieties of social life. It's about identity: who one is rather than one's roles and statuses. And the idealism of friendship 'lies in its detachment from these [roles and statuses], its creative and spiritual transcendence, its fundamental skepticism as a platform from which to survey the givens of society and culture.'[63] For gay men these words illustrate the political potential friendship can have in their lives.

Through friends, gay men get to question the heteronormativity of the roles given to them by the culture. The heterosexual, nuclear family – or at least the ideology of the family – has been the dominant model structuring much of the legal, political, and social norms governing interpersonal relationships. But as the family becomes transformed into other arrangements, so too do the political and social institutions of the society that were originally organized to reproduce the normative structures. For example, the concept of 'domestic partner' challenges insurance companies, public and private workplaces, religious institutions, and the legal system. But not all challenges are necessarily met with revolutionary alterations in the social system; many argue that the attempts to construct same-sex marriage rights and ceremonies merely replicate the dominant and oppressive structures of heterosexual society – something that would not occur if friendships were included in a model of domestic partner and family rather than being excluded from those concepts, which are usually limited to romantic dyadic relationships.

Friendship, perhaps in and of itself, may have the kinds of transforming power necessary to effect real, political changes. This may be even more the case for gay men's friendships, which challenge the social construction of heterosexual masculinity in the way it gets enacted, legitimated, and reproduced by gay people. Aaron stated it succinctly: 'To the extent that being openly gay is political, then the friendships that I have with openly gay men are political.' Michel Foucault said in a 1981 interview that gay culture can invent really new forms and values of relating between individuals and, if this is possible, then 'gay culture will be not only a choice of homosexuals for homosexuals – it would create relations that are, at certain points, transferable to heterosexuals. . . . By proposing a new relational right, we will see that nonhomosexual people can enrich their lives by changing their own schema of relations.'[64] In the myriad ways gay men deal with the contradictions of gay masculinity and hegemonic masculinity, friendship offers one model of successful liberation from the limits of dominant social life and its typically heterosexist institutions – a model that has the power not only to transform interpersonal relationships and psychological well-being, but also to create significant changes in the larger social system. As Graham Little writes:

> The larger formations of social life – kinship, the law, the economy – must be different where there is, in addition to solidarity and dutiful role-performance, a willingness and capacity for friendship's surprising one-to-one relations, and this difference may be enough to transform social and political life. . . . Perhaps, finally, it is true that progress in democracy

depends on a new generation that will increasingly locate itself in identity-shaping, social, yet personally liberating friendships.[65]

Gay men's friendships might someday lead all men to a new, more modern, form of the heroic friendships of the past – one in which valor, bravery, and devotion are inextricably linked to intimacy, sharing, personal disclosure, vulnerability, and emotional support. To alter the dynamics of how gender gets enacted in everyday life would be a powerful and political outcome of gay men's friendships in today's globalized and interconnected world. For it is through friends that gay men 'do' identity and community work. Through friends, a bridge between the micro and the macro aspects of quotidian life is constructed. Networks of friends and acquaintances become the interface between personal identity and membership in cultural and political communities.

And it is here in this network, especially for gay men, where issues of sexuality, masculinity, and social space get reified. Indeed, gay men's friendships may someday become the cornerstone of a new structure of social and personal relationships that has the power to transform everyone's lives and to create a new invincible community and culture of dignity and equality.

As Walt Whitman so eloquently stated in 1860,

> I Dream'd in a dream, I saw a city invincible to the
> attacks of the whole of the rest of the earth;
> I dream'd that was the new City of Friends...

NOTES

The individuals named and quoted in this chapter contributed to a larger study which examined key research on friendship (in historical documents and in contemporary social sciences), summaries of the ways friendships are depicted in books and articles written about and by gay men and lesbians, and results from a questionnaire survey of 161 gay men and from interviews with thirty other gay men. Although data were collected from 122 lesbians, I have chosen to focus on gay men in order to raise specific questions about the ways masculinity is organized in today's society. Throughout the chapter I interweave data from the questionnaire, excerpts from the interview narratives, findings from academic research studies, and quotations from popular writings. I hope that, as a result of my doing this, the reader will get a fairly full picture of the meanings of friendship in the lives of some gay men today.

1   Arendt 1968.

2 Friedman 1993; Little 1989; Jerome 1984.
3 Aristotle 1159b33, 1155a22.
4 Pakaluk 1994, 209.
5 Silver 1990, 1494.
6 Silver 1990, 1481, 1494, 1484.
7 Thanks to Barry Adam (personal communication, January 1998) for these ideas and words.
8 Martin 1989, 182.
9 Connell 1992, 749.
10 Pakaluk 1994.
11 Weston 1991, 122.
12 Weeks 1995, 37.
13 Friedman 1993, 252.
14 Weston 1991, 124.
15 D'Emilio 1983, 58.
16 Friedman 1993, 245.
17 Fischer 1982.
18 Fischer 1982, 190.
19 Fischer 1982, 194.
20 Fischer 1982.
21 Murray 1996, 195.
22 Murray 1996.
23 Murray 1996, 218–19.
24 Plummer 1995, 82, 87.
25 Chauncey 1994, 271.
26 Chauncey 1994, 272.
27 Chauncey 1994, 278.
28 Chauncey 1994, 298.
29 Murray 1979, 171.
30 Friedman 1993, 219.
31 See Melucci 1989; Morris and Mueller 1992.
32 Adam 1995.
33 Adam 1995, 178.
34 Murray 1992, 36.
35 Murray 1996.
36 Kaase 1990, 98.
37 Chong 1991, 35.
38 From 'We Can Be Together: How to Organize the Gay Community,' originally published in the July 17, 1985, issue of *Long Island Connection* and reprinted in Kramer (1989, 91).
39 Kaase 1990, 98.
40 Friedman 1993, 248; Raymond 1986.
41 Achilles 1967.
42 D'Emilio 1983.
43 Gartner and Segura 1997.
44 D'Emilio 1983, 60.

45 Chong 1991.
46 Chong 1991, 232.
47 Chong 1991, 34–35.
48 Chong 1991, 35.
49 D'Emilio 1983, 66.
50 D'Emilio 1983, 67.
51 Pogrebin 1987, 134.
52 It has been shown that the neighborhood is a much better place to meet casual friends than it is to meet close or best friends. See also Levine 1998.
53 Fleming and Baum 1986.
54 Bech 1997, 116.
55 Chauncey 1994, 136.
56 Chauncey 1994, 151.
57 Chauncey 1994, 156.
58 Chauncey 1994, 163.
59 Chauncey 1994, 163–64.
60 Levine 1979. See Schneider (1997), Smith (1997), and Miller (1989) regarding small towns and gay and lesbian lives.
61 Kramer 1995, 211.
62 Suttles 1970.
63 Little 1989, 145.
64 From 'The Social Triumph of the Sexual Will,' an interview conducted in October 1981, originally published in the May 1982 issue of *Christopher Street* and reprinted in Foucault (1997, 160).
65 Little 1989, 154–55.

REFERENCES

Achilles, Nancy. 1967. The development of the homosexual bar as an institution. In *Sexual Deviance*, edited by John Gagnon and William Simon, 228–44. New York: Harper & Row.

Adam, Barry D. 1995. *The Rise of a Gay and Lesbian Movement*. Rev. ed. New York: Twayne.

Arendt, Hannah. 1968. *Men in Dark Times*. New York: Harcourt, Brace.

Aristotle. 1962. *Nicomachean Ethics*. Translated by Martin Ostwald. Indianapolis, IN: Bobbs-Merrill.

Bech, Henning. 1997. *When Men Meet: Homosexuality and Modernity*. Cambridge: Polity, and Chicago: University of Chicago Press.

Bellah, Robert N., Richard Madsen, William M. Sullian, Ann Swidler, and Steven T. Tipton. 1985. *Habits of the Heart*. Berkeley: University of California Press.

Chauncey, George. 1994. *Gay New York*. New York: Basic Books.

Chong, Dennis. 1991. *Collective Action and the Civil Rights Movement*. Chicago: University of Chicago Press.

Connell, R. W. 1992. A very straight gay: Masculinity, homosexual experience, and the dynamics of gender. *American Sociological Review* 57: 735–51.
—— 1995. *Masculinities*. Berkeley: University of California Press.
D'Emilio, John. 1983. *Sexual Politics, Sexual Communities*. Chicago: University of Chicago Press.
Fischer, Claude S. 1982. *To Dwell Among Friends: Personal Networks in Town and City*. Chicago: University of Chicago Press.
Foucault, Michel. 1997. *Ethics: Subjectivity and Truth. The Essential Works of Michel Foucault*, Vol. 1, edited by Paul Rabinow. New York: New Press.
Friedman, Marilyn. 1993. *What Are Friends For? Feminist Perspectives on Personal Relationships and Moral Theory*. Ithaca, NY: Cornell University Press.
Gartner, Scott Sigmund, and Gary M. Segura. 1997. Appearances can be deceptive: Self-selection, social group identification, and political mobilization. *Rationality and Society* 9(2): 131–61.
Jerome, Dorothy. 1984. Good company: The sociological implications of friendship. *Sociological Review* 32(4): 696–718.
Kaase, Max. 1990. Social movements and political innovation. In *Challenging the Political Order: New Social and Political Movements in Western Democracies*, edited by Russell J. Dalton and Manfred Kuechler, 84–101. New York: Oxford University Press.
Kramer, Jerry Lee. 1995. Bachelor farmers and spinsters: Gay and lesbian identities and communities in rural North Dakota. In *Mapping Desire: Geographies of Sexualities*, edited by David Bell and Gill Valentine, 200–13. London: Routledge.
Kramer, Larry. 1989. *Reports from the Holocaust: The Making of an AIDS Activist*. New York: Penguin.
Levine, Martin P. 1979. Gay ghetto. In *Gay Men: The Sociology of Male Homosexuality*, edited by Martin P. Levine, 182–204. New York: Harper & Row.
—— 1998. *Gay Macho: The Life and Death of the Homosexual Clone*. New York: New York University Press.
Little, Graham. 1989. Freud, friendship, and politics. In *The Dialectics of Friendship*, edited by Roy Porter and Sylvana Tomaselli, 143–158. London: Routledge.
Martin, Robert K. 1989. Knights-errant and gothic seducers: The representation of male friendship in mid-nineteenth-century America. In *Hidden From History: Reclaiming the Gay and Lesbian Past*, edited by Martin Duberman, Martha Vicinus, and George Chauncey, 169–82. New York: Meridian.
Melucci, Alberto. 1989. *Nomads of the Present*. Philadelphia: Temple University Press.
Miller, Neil. 1989. *In Search of Gay America*. New York: Harper & Row.
Morris, Aldon, and Carol McClurg Mueller, eds. 1992. *Frontiers in Social Movement Theory*. New Haven, CT: Yale University Press.
Murray, Stephen O. 1979. Institutional elaboration of a quasi-ethnic community. *International Review of Modern Sociology* 9: 165–77.
—— 1992. Components of gay community in San Francisco. In *Gay Culture in America*, edited by Gilbert Herdt, 107–46. Boston: Beacon.

—— 1996. *American Gay*. Chicago: University of Chicago Press.

Pakaluk, Michael. 1994. Political friendship. In *The Changing Face of Friendship*, edited by Leroy S. Rouner, 197–213. Notre Dame, IN: University of Notre Dame Press.

Plummer, Ken. 1995. *Telling Sexual Stories: Power, Change and Social Worlds*. London: Routledge.

Pogrebin, Letty Cottin. 1987. *Among Friends*. New York: McGraw-Hill.

Raymond, Janice. 1986. *A Passion for Friends*. Boston: Beacon.

Schneider, Beth E. 1987. Coming out at work. *Work and Occupations* 13: 463–87.

—— 1997. Owning an epidemic: The impact of AIDS on small-city lesbian and gay communities. In *In Changing Times: Gay Men and Lesbians Encounter HIV/AIDS*, edited by Martin P. Levine, Peter M. Nardi, and John H. Gagnon, 145–69. Chicago: University of Chicago Press.

Silver, Allan. 1990. Friendship in commercial society: Eighteenth-century social theory and modern sociology. *American Journal of Sociology* 95(6): 1474–1504.

Smith, James Donald. 1997. Working with larger systems: Rural lesbians and gays. *Journal of Gay & Lesbian Social Services* 7(3): 13–21.

Suttles, Gerald. 1970. Friendship as a social institution. In *Social Relationships*, edited by George McCall, Michael McCall, Norman Denzin, Gerald Suttles, and Suzanne Kurth, 95–135. Chicago: Aldine.

Weeks, Jeffrey. 1995. *Invented Moralities: Sexual Values in an Age of Uncertainty*. Cambridge: Polity, and New York: Columbia University Press.

Weston, Kath. 1991. *Families We Choose: Lesbians, Gays, Kinship*. New York: Columbia University Press.

Part V
Endings and Beginnings: The Practices and Politics of Changing Men

Like its primary source, feminism, the sociology of masculinity is ultimately concerned with the possibilities and potentials of men to change
and, hopefully, dismantle what Connell refers to as the 'gender order'.
The chapters in this final part consider these personal/political dimensions of men and masculinity, and the endings and beginnings now
signalled by challenges to the gender order and men's social, cultural
and political dominance.

In 'The Crisis of Masculinity and the Politics of Identity', John
MacInnes makes a dramatic claim: that the innovations of late modernity
have undermined the sexual division of labour and the dominant beliefs
which have served to substantiate notions of masculinity. The legacies of
patriarchy and the rationalization of male privilege have reached an
impasse and we are witnessing, according to MacInnes, **the end of
masculinity as a gender identity**. From modern contract theory that
claims that all men (and women) are born free, to the constant revolution
of modernity and capitalism, market forces, advances in technology, and
even bureaucracy now encourage men and women to treat each other as
equals, even if they prefer not to. MacInnes recognizes that male backlashes continue to seek to restore male privilege. However, the trajectory
of change is undeniable. These changes, most of which have occurred in
the last century, are unarguably dramatic: he cites women's involvement

in the labour market, changes in women's legal standing, changes in the domestic division of labour, and the gradual death of the male breadwinner ideology.

MacInnes claims that against this unprecedented background we face an opportunity, as sociologists, to reflect on how we theorize gender. Efforts to theorize hegemonic masculinity, male identity, and male subjectivity have been miscast: they over-psychologize and give the impression that masculinity is something that individuals empirically possess. This misleads us into overemphasizing biology, undestimating the role of social structures that constrain how men and women act, and forgetting that our current notions of masculinity and femininity are tied to modernity and capitalism. With the end of masculinity, it is time, MacInnes claims, to shift our attention away from the self and the politics of identity and focus our attention on another topic: universal human rights.

Men and masculinities are inevitably caught up in diverse social tensions, so any examination of men changing must recognize cultural differences and cross-currents. In a brief but interesting exploration of the possibilities of changes to men's practices and subjectivities in the Caribbean, Niels Sampath turns attention to the construction of masculinity on the multi-ethnic island of Trinidad. He documents a subtle but powerful process by which masculinity is attained and contested in a way that implicates ethnicity and class as well as gender. This drama unfolds against the background of two sometimes incompatible norms – respectability and reputation. Respectability indicates a genteel form of good behaviour typified by upper-class morality. Going to church, for example, gains one a sense of respectability. Working-class culture, however, projects a more competitive and class-based morality. Thus when working-class individuals posture to achieve respectability, they are seen as crabs trying to climb out of the bucket, walking over others, dragging them down. Men and women also seek reputation within and between gender groups. Reputation, unlike respectability, is often achieved through some form of extroverted display. Men, for example, achieve reputation by demonstrating bravado and using sexual banter. Women achieve reputation through displays of fashion. In short, reputation-enhancing behaviour is often the opposite of respectability. Sampath, however, envisions a **potential for change in male Afro-Caribbean culture**. As women become more economically independent, they find ways of escaping from subservience without the burden of 'dragging others down'. Also, he sees women escaping the burden of having to seek respectability. As men consider ways that women enjoy success outside of the competitive syndrome, Sampath's research suggests potential changes for male identity in a complex multi-ethnic environment.

A further contribution to the possibilities of change in black, Afro-Caribbean and Latino male cultures is made by Alfredo Mirandé. He issues an important critique of the new men's studies and challenges the absence of men of colour in these writings. Mirandé explores the implications of an international and multicultural dimension to the sociology of masculinity. In particular, he calls for a **Chicano/Latino pro-feminist men's studies** that could have implications for understanding the dynamics of men changing within non-white cultural settings. Mirandé's study indicates that one consequence of a more considered study of Latino men's lives would be appreciation of the tremendous variation in the concept of machismo. Mirandé demonstrates that machismo is not an uncontested working-class ideology any more than it is viewed as a desirable, positive trait across all categories of Latino men. Indeed, many Latino men see machismo as negative, self-centred egoism. Also, Mirandé claims that we need to widen our perspective to see that women of colour suffer a different type of oppression than white women, partly because men of colour cannot use the same economic mechanisms to subordinate women. Chicanas' subordination and oppression are reinforced by control of sexuality and the threat of exclusion/rejection. In addition, lesbian women of colour suffer an added layer of oppression. Finally, Mirandé makes the point that the meaning of homosexual activity in Latino culture is not equivalent to that in white mainstream culture. In the Latino sexual system, the category of homosexual is an attribute of power, not one based on the choice of same-sex behaviour.

In the penultimate chapter, Stephen Whitehead examines the possibilities for men engaging critically and reflectively with their gendered identity, and, in the process, coming to understand better how dominant discourses of masculinity inform and shape their lives and potentialities. Based on research undertaken in the UK, the chapter reveals the absence of a male reflective self in the subjectivities of a particular group of men – education managers. Whitehead contrasts this **invisible gendered subject** with the narratives and epistemologies of women education managers and concludes that, for these men at least, self-knowledge as gendered subjects is still noticeably absent. By contrast, Whitehead's study shows that women managers have available to them, through their experiences as women in male-dominated sites, an appreciation of how their gender informs the political economy of management and organizations. Whitehead concludes that until men come to recognize that they have a gender, equal opportunities in organizations, and indeed gender equity across the social web, remain only distant possibilities.

In 'Masculinity Politics on a World Scale', R. W. Connell concludes this volume by calling for a refocusing of the research agenda on masculinities. Connell issues a challenge to move beyond seeing gender as the attribute of an individual to considering gender on the large scale of global society. This research agenda calls for appreciating the historical evolution of definitions of gender, including the connection between patterns of trade, investment, and communications that have given rise to patterns of masculinity on a world scale. These influences have given rise to a **transnational business masculinity**, a calculative technical rationality often reflected in business literature and management practices. Contrary to media images, globalization is not a monolithic, homogenizing process sweeping the globe, in which all have equal access to global markets. The world gender order is produced as a complex structure of relationships that interconnect the gender regimes of institutions on a world scale. This gives rise to provocative questions: what is the shape of the global gender structure, how are the structures interconnected, what are the historical conditions that have given rise to this structure, and what is its trajectory into the future? In presenting these questions, Connell suggests that, in this unique historical moment, we must look at the social dynamics in the global arena that give rise to masculinity politics, the local challenges to hegemonic forces, and the emerging forms of gender instability that threaten to disrupt dominant forms of masculinity.

17

The Crisis of Masculinity and the Politics of Identity

John MacInnes

> Man, that plausible creature whose wagging tongue so often hides the despair and darkness in his heart.
>
> (Wrong 1961: 131)

Masculinity can be seen as an ideology produced by men as a result of the threat posed to the survival of the patriarchal sexual division of labour by the rise of modernity. Their monopoly of power, resources and status which they had previously been able to claim directly by virtue of their sex, they now had to assert was due to their socially constructed gender identity which expressed some undefined natural difference. Since this invention of masculinity was essentially a holding operation, however, it has been in crisis ever since, for three reasons. First, by definition, the essence of masculinity can never be grasped or defined. If it comprises essentially social characteristics or capacities, we have to explain on what grounds women have been incapable of, or prevented from, acquiring them. Masculinity is something for the girls as much as the boys, and over time, it must surely come to have no special connection to either biological sex. If, conversely, it comprises something beyond the social, we are back to arguments about maleness and biology, and traditional premodern arguments about nature determining society and males being innately superior to females.

Second, exactly those concepts of masculinity, femininity and gender originally devised to rationalize male privilege could equally be used to attack it, and have been so used ever since. Although it started out as a conservative concept – an attempt to reconcile a patriarchal reality with claims that both men and women participate in history, as it were – the argument could just as easily be reversed and run the other way. If sexual difference was socially expressed or constructed, then it could be changed. Masculinity and femininity could be made differently, or the social mechanisms imagined to produce them could be challenged. The attempt to defend the legacy of patriarchy in the language of contract, by a neat irony of history, provided the conceptual basis for feminism and the challenge that women made to men from the dawn of modernity onwards on the basis of contract theory itself that if all men were born free then so too must all women be. If masculinity, rather than maleness, explained men's privilege, men could be challenged to reform or abolish their masculinity in the name of equal rights, in a way that they could not be asked to change or abolish their sex. The truth of the next three centuries has been ably summed up by Mann (1994: 186–7):

> from about the time of Locke, there was greater interest in tracing political rights and duties to the qualities of abstract individuals...most of the doctrines, when elaborated, made clear that the person and the nation were not universal: servants, almost always, and usually labourers and those without property, were not to be an active part of the political community... Women got similar treatment... Nevertheless, from the 1680s to the 1980s the same liberal rhetoric has been used by radicals to achieve legal and political equality for all men and even for all women. Feminism, like socialism, built on top of the rhetoric... Liberalism... could erect no powerful ideological defences against enfranchising either subordinate classes or women.

Third, the constant revolutionizing and innovation of modernity, the material side of the forces of universalism enshrined in the institutions of the market and bureaucracy, increasingly undermined established aspects of the sexual division of labour and encouraged men and women to treat each other as formal equals. This is not because of any attempt on the part of men or women to change men's personal gender identities – either collectively or individually – but as a result of material forces unleashed by the transition to a modern, market based, technological society. The material pressures of the logic of rationalization and development of the impersonal market encourages individuals to treat each other without regard to their sex, even in situations where they would otherwise prefer to do so. The demographic transition and declining fertility and infant mortality rates shrank the proportion of time that adult females spent in pregnancy or lactation. Technological innovation rendered the secondary physical characteristics of possession of a male or female body less relevant.

The ability of men to sustain a coherent public ideology of what masculinity comprises is constantly being undermined by the material progress of modernity (at a personal level a 'coherent' masculine identity has never been sustainable). In this sense we are witnessing the end of masculinity. Given that we have not reached the end of ideology, let alone the end of history, and given the popularity of ill-proven fin de siècle portents of the finality of this, that and the other, let me make it clear that I do not think that the end of masculinity as such is upon us or that an androgynous Utopia is near. The sexed character of human bodies must have social consequences in any imaginable society. In this limited sense there will never be an end of masculinity, but it would under these conditions be just as sensible to talk of maleness. But we are living through the final period, or at least the beginning of the final period, of belief in masculinity as a gender identity specific to men which accounts for their privileged command of power, resources and status. I suspect that in years to come historians will look back upon the last two centuries as those in which whole societies, as opposed to individual philosophers, started to realize that there was no difference between men and women (aside from their complimentary places in biological reproduction and the anatomical and secondary physical characteristics flowing from that) and to work through the fundamentally revolutionary consequences of that realization. In both the real world, and our analysis of it, it is time for the end of masculinity.

A bad time to be a man?

> Men are now discriminated against in most aspects of life.
> (United Kingdom Men's Movement 1995: v)

It has become something of a cliché to argue that it is now 'a bad time to be a man'. Men's material privileges in the law, economy and politics are under increasing scrutiny and attack. Fifty years ago there were still many institutions that were male bastions where women were either legally barred or totally absent. Although men still monopolize public power, hardly any such institutions survive today, aside from gentlemen's clubs and the Catholic priesthood. Significantly neither has a good reputation. Today's boys cannot assume the privileges their fathers could take for granted or assume to be natural. The public evaluation of masculinity has also undergone a profound shift. What were once claimed to be manly virtues (heroism, independence, courage, strength, rationality, will, backbone, virility) have become masculine vices (abuse, destructive aggression, coldness, emotional inarticulacy, detachment, isolation, an inability to be flexible, to communicate, to empathize, to be soft, supportive or life affirming). A study of the treatment of men as fathers or carers in British newspapers for the month of June 1994 reported the largest single category of stories concerned 'men as monsters', who had bullied, abused or killed their children (Lloyd 1994). In the cinema, television and advertising imagery, the hegemony of the 'male gaze' has been broken. Not only have we seen the rise of the 'female gaze', but the rise of increasingly heterogeneous representations of men, many of which set out explicitly to subvert older images of masculinity. While it is ludicrous to imagine, as some militant men's groups have done, that this attack has brought about anything even approaching substantive equality, let alone a reversal of the balance of power, women have made substantial progress in achieving greater juridical, political and economic equality, especially over the last half century.

It is possible to see such arguments as part of a backlash by men against the impact of feminism: a determination to fight even the smallest gains which women have been able to achieve, in order to preserve male superiority. It is true that there is now a small but vociferous men's movement ready to argue that men are now the oppressed sex (e.g. United Kingdom Men's Movement 1995). It is also true that if it is a bad time to be a man, it is still, in almost every area of life, a worse time to be a woman. What has to be understood, however, alongside the scope of men's continuing privilege, is how far and how fast that privilege has been undermined by the development of modern industrial capitalist society generally, and in particular by its transformations over the last half century.

All premodern societies display a dramatic sexual division of labour. Only a little over three centuries ago we lived in a world where men had always ruled the public sphere and enjoyed virtually arbitrary power in the private sphere, and did so through the universal belief that they were naturally quite different to and superior to women. Mann (1994: 180) is right when he argues that:

> We could write a history of power relations almost up to the eighteenth century and confine it to men, as long as we add the defensive proviso, 'Oh, and by the way, remember that this is a story of the relations between male patriarchs. Underneath them all the time were women (and junior men, and children).'

Fathers could choose husbands for their daughters, who henceforth enjoyed virtually total power over them, including their mutilation or murder.[1] Women's public role, the work they did, or relations they could form, were largely determined by men. There may have been many versions of patriarchy, and many societies where the social division of labour between the sexes was more equal than that found, say, in Britain in the Middle Ages, but we have no evidence of any society where men took primary responsibility for the nurturance of infant children, or women enjoyed any preponderance of public political power over men, or where tasks and social roles were not sex-typed.

The material and ideological legacy of millennia of patriarchy remains in the dramatic material inequality between men and women, the continued dominance of men in the public sphere, especially in politics, in the systematic misogyny of all kinds of mental representations of the sexes and in the ubiquitous physical violence that characterizes sexual relations. In 1996 there were around 350 dollar billionaires in the world; all were men (*The Guardian*, 22 July 1996). Joshi recently estimated that women in the UK lost around half their lifetime earnings potential, compared to men, because of their continued primary responsibility for looking after infants in the home (Davis and Joshi 1990). In a survey conducted in 1994 in Britain less than a fifth of mothers were working full time when they were parents of preschool-age children. The equivalent figure for fathers was more than four-fifths.[2] The same survey in Sweden, a country normally thought of as pioneering advances in sexual equality, produced similar results. Eighty per cent of respondents in Britain who lived as a couple said that it was usually or always the woman's job to do the laundry; a mere 5 per cent reported that it was her job to do 'small repairs'. Again Sweden produced similar responses of 81 per cent and 2 per cent! (ISSP 1994). In the 1990s it was possible for John Major to announce his first cabinet without a single woman member; even 20 years before Edward Heath had felt obliged to include a 'token' woman: Margaret Thatcher. At the 1992 General Election in Britain, Scotland managed to return five women MPs out of 72 – about the same proportion as in the first elections after women secured the vote.[3] In Britain today, less than 3 per cent of men report to supervisors or managers at work who are women.

The 'male gaze' is still strong; 'page 3' pictures of nude women are used to sell newspapers and there is a thriving pornography industry adapting itself to new forms of technology. Jokes about mothers-in-law and women drivers are still common. Cultural associations between women and inferiority, weakness or pollution still abound. A sexual double standard continues to operate. Judges can continue to assume that women wearing 'provocative' clothing in public solicit any sexual violence of which they become victims. Sexual and physical violence by men on women, often their partners or children, is endemic. Scottish police records suggest that wife assault is the second most common violent crime, while estimates of the incidence of rape or sexual abuse range up to one-third or two-fifths of all women in western countries; girls are much more likely to be abused than boys.[4]

Yet there are also strong material and ideological pressures in modern western societies which appear to work against patriarchy. They are forcing or encouraging men to become more involved in childcare and domestic labour and to accept a steadily greater role for women in the public sphere. They are continually undermining traditional ideas about what is 'natural' or appropriate for men and women to do. The force of the constant revolutionizing of the relations of production and the drive towards rationalization is now blowing hard against sexual difference. The solidity of sex is melting into the air, along with other 'fast-frozen relations with their train of ancient and venerable prejudices' (Engels 1968: 38). This does not mean that women have gained equality, or anything like it, or that these processes are inexorable or irreversible, but it is to argue that change in social relations between the sexes has been dramatic, particularly within a longer historical time scale, and the dynamics behind this change needs to be analysed. There is also some evidence that these processes are speeding up and have become stronger over the last half century.

For example, just over a century ago in Britain, husbands married wives who henceforth had virtually no separate legal existence and whose rights were entirely subordinated to them. A husband not only held his wife's property but could rape, beat and virtually imprison her (within certain limits) without legal sanction. She had no right of divorce but he could and sometimes did *sell* her (Pateman 1988). Women were not quite commodities traded by fathers to husbands, but their status was not far removed from that. It is only just over half a century ago that men conceded the franchise to women on equal terms in Britain. It is not much more than a quarter century ago that proscriptions on the employment of women in certain jobs or on the basis of their marital status were made illegal. The marriage bar in the post office was abolished as recently as 1962. Men in the Federal Republic of Germany only lost the legal right to forbid their wives to take paid employment in 1977 (Ostner 1993); men in Spain did so a year later (Threlfall 1996).

In the last 50 years women's employment has continually expanded in all western industrial capitalist countries. Since the start of the 1970s, when the UK was last thought to enjoy 'full employment', the number of jobs held by women has increased by over two and half million, as Table 17.1 shows. The number of jobs today is almost exactly the same as it was 25 years ago, because roughly the same number of men have left the employed workforce so that its sexual composition has changed

Table 17.1 UK employees in employment, seasonally adjusted, in thousands

	All males and females	Males			Females		
		All	Full time	Part time	All	Full time	Part time
June 1971	22,131	13,735	13,133	602	8,396	5,603	2,793
Proportion of all employees (per cent)	100.0	62.1	59.3	2.7	37.9	25.3	12.6
June 1996	22,205	11,227	9,908	1,319	10,978	5,950	5,028
Proportion of all employees (per cent)	100.0	50.6	44.6	5.9	49.4	26.8	22.6
Absolute change 1971–96	74	−2,508	−3,225	717	2,582	347	2,235
Relative change 1971–96 (per cent)	0.3	−18.3	−24.6	119.1	30.8	6.2	80.0

Source: Employment Gazette and Labour Market Trends (various issues).

dramatically.[5] This has been accompanied by a change in the proportion of full and part time jobs; there are now three million more part time jobs than in 1971. Women's full time employment has risen by one third of a million over the period, while men have lost over three million full time jobs – equivalent to one in every four that existed in 1971.[6] As a result of these changes the proportion of all employment held by men declined from 62 per cent in 1971 to just over half by 1996. If this rate of change continues men will soon have fewer jobs in the UK than women.

The dynamics behind this employment change are complex, but four factors stand out. One is the shift away from production industries and from occupations that used skills traditionally associated with men and masculinity such as muscle power. A second factor is the shift towards part time working, but it is far from clear how much this is caused by an increase in employers' *demand* for part time jobs as such, and how far this is caused by the *supply* of female labour, which is relatively cheaper because its access to the labour market is restricted by commitments imposed by the unequal sexual division of labour in the household, combined with low levels of public provision of childcare or subsidies to it. Third is the rise in formal, juridical sexual equality. Men have lost the power to formally exclude women from jobs or education and training simply on the basis of their sex or marital status. A final factor which is often overlooked in these figures is the increase in class inequality that they conceal. The number of households with two adults working has increased, as has the number of single person households. Since the level of employment has not changed, the losers have been the large number of households where there are two adults unemployed. Thus in 1973, both partners were at work in 43 per cent of households comprising couples with dependent children. By 1992 this figure had risen to 60 per cent. In the same year, neither partner was working in 10 per cent of such couples (Condy 1994; General Household Survey 1994).

This feminization of employment (Jensen et al. 1988; Yeandle 1995), which is linked to so many other social changes, is not only occurring in the UK. 'Participation rates' measure the proportion of men or women of working age who are in the labour force. As Table 17.2 shows, male participation rates have been falling and female rates rising across all the countries in the Organisation for Economic Cooperation and Development (OECD). The last line of the table shows how much of the change that would be necessary to equalize participation rates between men and women was actually achieved in the quarter century between the mid-1960s and the end of the 1980s. Across the OECD as a whole something over two-fifths of such change occurred; some countries, such as Sweden, achieved double this amount.[7]

Table 17.2 Working age males and females in the labour force 1960–1990

	All OECD	UK	US	Germany	Sweden
Males					
Labour force as per cent of population aged 15–64 yrs					
Average 1960–67	92.1	97.5	88.2	94.4	93.4
Average 1988–90	83.5	86.9	85.2	81.5	84.9
Change over period	–8.6	–10.6	–3.0	–12.9	–8.5
Females					
Labour force as per cent of population aged 15–64 yrs					
Average 1960–67	45.8	48.1	43.9	48.9	53.5
Average 1988–90	58.7	64.5	67.6	55.9	80.6
Change over period	12.9	16.4	23.7	7.0	27.1
Per cent ratio of female rate to male rate: 1960s	49.7	49.3	49.8	51.8	57.3
Per cent ratio of female rate to male rate: 1988–90	70.3	74.2	79.3	68.6	94.9
Per cent increase in ratio from 1960s to 1988–90	20.6	24.9	29.6	16.8	37.7
Increase in ratio as per cent of increase needed to reach equality in male and female rates	40.9	49.1	58.9	34.8	88.1

Note: Single years have been averaged to remove cyclical effects.

Source: Organisation for Economic Cooperation and Development (OECD) 1996.

While debate over the nature of the 'glass ceiling' remains, women's entry to what were previously male-dominated professions has risen substantially. This has also been supported by state moves to remove some of the formal systems of discrimination in employment. For example in one five-year period, 1978–1983, 62 countries introduced equal pay legislation. Formally equal rights is not the same thing as substantive material equality of opportunity, but it is an important component of the battle to achieve it. These changes have had significant effects in education where the aspirations of young women have moved closer to those of young men, and their performance has come to be better, on average, than that of young men across most subjects at most ages in the UK. This has given rise to concern about the performance of boys which the 'underperformance' of girls rarely produced, an example of ideologies of gender in operation.

There is also clear evidence that such change in women's employment status has had an effect on the domestic division of labour as well. Gershuny et al. (1994: 173), in a recent review of time budget evidence from a range of western industrial countries, concluded that the proportion of unpaid domestic labour undertaken by men had risen from around a quarter in the 1960s to around two-fifths a quarter century later. Thus the same survey which I quoted earlier to provide evidence of areas of highly sex-segregated domestic labour in the household found around one half of both male and female respondents in couples claiming to share such tasks as shopping for groceries (ISSP 1994). Again this does not mean that we are approaching an era of equality in the domestic division of labour, or that more than significant but small minorities of men take equal or principal responsibility for childcare. We have not yet reached a situation where there is public concern, for example, about fathers of young children going out to work. On the contrary, a major obstacle to men's greater involvement in childcare in Britain is the *increases* in average working hours of fathers of young children in a context where 10 per cent of men commit 68 hours or more per week to paid work (Marsh 1991). But in the historical context of men's ability, for millennia, to define childcare and domestic labour exclusively as a woman's job, the changes over the last 50 years are surely significant.

The fundamental material social change of expanding women's employment is linked to many others; a decisive one is the gradual death of male breadwinner ideology. Attitudes to women working vary far more according to generation than by sex. Older men and women still subscribe to the ideology of the male breadwinner and the female homemaker but younger men and women do not (Scott et al. 1996). There is also a clear relationship to female employment trends, both over time and across countries. In countries where women form a substantial part

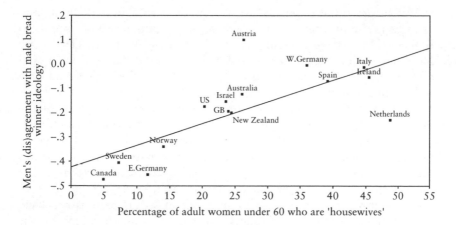

Figure 17.1 Women's employment and male breadwinner ideology

Note: Respondents were asked whether they (strongly) agreed or disagreed with the statement: 'A husband's job is to earn money: a wife's job is to look after the home and family.' A score of −1 was given to respondents who disagreed strongly, −0.5 to those who disagreed, 0 to those who neither agreed nor disagreed, or expressed no opinion, +0.5 to those who agreed and +1 to those who agreed strongly with this statement. Mean scores were then calculated for *male* respondents in each country. For example, a country where all the men agreed strongly with the statement would produce a score of +1. The figure shows these mean scores plotted against the percentage of adult *female* respondents of working age who were neither in the labour force or in training or education in each country. There is a clear relationship, for these industrial capitalist countries, between men's lack of belief in breadwinner ideology, and women's participation in the public sphere.

Source: author's analysis of ISSP 1994.

of the labour force, male breadwinner ideology has all but collapsed in terms of popular support for its core idea, as Figure 17.1 shows. It plots the scale of women's involvement in employment, training or education in several western industrial capitalist countries against the degree of agreement or disagreement reported by men in these countries with the statement, 'A husband's job is to earn money; a wife's job is to look after the home and family'. A clear relationship stands out between the level of *women's* labour market involvement and *men's* loss of faith in breadwinner ideology. There has also been, alongside the survival of what we might call routine popular misogyny, evidence of the partial reversal of the traditional evaluation of stereotypical masculine and feminine traits, which I mentioned above. This is not evidence of the arrival of sexual equality in material or ideological terms, but it is evidence of dramatic change, especially over the period since the Second World War.

This suggests that popular discussion of the 'crisis' in masculinity and changes in the prospects that face men, or the popularity of appeals to rediscover 'the deep masculine' proffered by Robert Bly (1991) are more than an anti-feminist backlash. They are evidence of the material and ideological weakening and collapse of patriarchy. It *is* a bad time to be a man, compared to the supremacy men have enjoyed in the past – and this is a thoroughly good thing. This raises the question of the dynamic behind such change. The answer is that modern capitalism, and the liberal political philosophy which is central to it, is not only not patriarchal; it systematically undermines patriarchy and creates the conditions for feminist struggle in much the same way as it has created the conditions for class struggle. Men may still monopolize the powerful offices in such a society, but in so far as it is a society characterized by 'the rule of offices, not men' it is one in which for the first time these self-same men come under pressure, despite their own desires, to disregard the sex of the people with whom they deal, treat women as their formal equals and limit their sexual solidarity with their brothers.

The politics of identity and the sociology of masculinity

One result of the erosion of patriarchy by modernity has been a reversal in the popular evaluation of what masculinity is imagined to comprise. What were once male virtues are often now viewed as masculine vices – part of the 'crisis' of masculinity. It is now often argued that a major contribution to further progress in equality between men and women would be for men to consciously reform their misogynist and oppressive gender identities. This message can be found in both popular journalism and the more abstract and philosophical reaches of academic discourse. For example it is possible to read Bob Connell's excellent study *Masculinities* (1995) as an analysis of the relationship between forms of masculine gender identity, especially 'hegemonic masculinity', and social institutions and processes that exploit or oppress women and maintain the power of men as a sex over women. This has a strong intuitive appeal. Many powerful men are obnoxious, homophobic and misogynist, and these qualities appear to be vital to maintaining and reproducing a social order which maintains the subordination and oppression of women.

At a more general level male 'instrumentalism' is increasingly seen as central to the dynamics of modern society, and contrasted with the virtues of feminine expressiveness. It is common to encounter the argument that because of their detachment from (what we imagine ought to be) their true feelings, men are a danger to others, the planet and ultimately to themselves. There is an astonishingly broad contemporary consensus which urges men to abandon what is imagined to be traditional masculinity in order to get in touch with their feelings and develop their emotional articulacy, for they have nothing to lose but their inhibitions, loneliness, and alienation from intimacy and the source of their humanity. It is argued that this will benefit men themselves, their intimate associates and wider society. It lies behind the rationale both for progressive men's consciousness-raising groups, and for work with violent male offenders – who are argued to dislike a confrontation with their feelings far more intensely than any varieties of 'short sharp shock' treatment, which from this perspective reinforces rather than reforms their aggression. It lies behind all those approaches that view masculinity as some kind of exchange of 'outer' social public and political power for 'inner' personal sacrifice and pain, such as that of Kaufman (1994). It is a commonplace of men's and women's lifestyle magazines, the ubiquitous counselling or therapy columns in newspapers and the raw material of television documentary, sitcom, soap and drama as well as most Hollywood films.

These ideas are reflected in many aspects of sociology: the expansion of interest in the 'sociology of emotions', in issues of identity, the self and intimate relations, calls for integration of psychology and sociology (Adorno 1968; Connell 1987) and the whole drive towards 'theorizing subjectivity'. This politics of identity approach to masculinity appears in a radical and theoretically explicit way in academic arguments that masculinity is a form of identity that prioritizes instrumental aggressive and politically or ecologically aggressive relationships with other human beings and with nature over expressive nurturance of emotional intimacy. It haunts Giddens's arguments in *The Transformation of Intimacy* (1992), although he ably criticizes its more simplistic variants. For example he argues that women have been the 'emotional revolutionaries' of modernity and characterizes dispassionate instrumentalism as male. For some writers, for example Dinnerstein (1987), such emotional inarticulacy is virtually constitutional of masculine identity, or tied into a longstanding division of labour in childrearing which exists across different cultures and would be difficult to undo. For others, such as Seidler (1989, 1990) or Pahl (1995), the development is tied up with the development of modernity and in particular the divisions of labour that emerged in the industrial revolution. Other observers have been less restrained. Duncombe and Marsden (1993, 1995) have asked if male emotional inarticulacy is 'the last frontier of gender inequality'. Connell explicitly tries to go beyond a politics of equal public rights to an analysis of how 'hegemonic masculinity' reproduces patriarchy in modern societies (1995: 231). From this he invites men to embrace 'gender vertigo' in order to undermine patriarchy, although he concedes that, for example, the green pro-feminist activists he considers, who could be taken as living examples of this political strategy, do not themselves believe that by changing their masculinity they are doing much to change the world. Connell agrees with them.

I think that this approach to masculinity is misleading for four reasons. First, it smuggles in the assumption that it is only men who possess masculinity, by collapsing ideology into identity on the basis of biology. The only common feature of the diverse masculinities studied is that it is biological men who possess these gender identities. There are ultimately as many varieties of masculinity as there are men, however, and this is an unhelpful way to theorize gender identity. If we accept that women too can be masculine (as we must do if we take gender to be socially constructed) it becomes difficult to prevent masculinity becoming a general term for anything we don't like. I have suggested that this is because the fetishism of sexual difference simply reflects back to us as masculinity aspects of our inexorably contradictory personal identities. Thus in much of the literature aspects of modernity which have no intrinsic connection to sex (such as the logic of instrumentalism or the monopolization of the means of violence by the state) come to appear as a product of masculinity. It is not masculinity that creates modernity, however. On the contrary, it is modernity that has created our fetishistic image of masculinity.

Second it has an unbalanced view of the relationship between the personal and the political. The politics of identity retreats from classical sociology's concern with material social structures and forces to applied psychology.[8] By this I do not mean the concern with feelings and emotion rather than norms or ideologies. I mean the understanding of social structures and processes in terms of the individual behaviour or attitudes of people they comprise. It is unhelpful to see organizations or societies that men control as ultimately an expression of their identities (Young 1984). It is not clear that changing the personal identities of individual powerful men would have much impact on social change. This may be an important part of the truth, but sociology also aims to understand both the unanticipated consequences of individuals' actions and the way in which social structures, once created, constrain individuals to act in certain ways regardless of their personalities or predispositions. Modernity is the era of bureaucratization, rationalization, 'the rule of offices, not men'. While Weber may have underestimated the autonomy that more powerful men enjoy, explaining patriarchy in terms of personal misogyny is akin to explaining capitalism in terms of greed. It underestimates the importance of social structures which force men and women to act in certain ways which they might not otherwise choose.[9]

Connell (1987: 57–8), for example, is clear that we cannot posit a 'masculine' predisposition to use physical violence as an explanation of all the social relations of modern violence, including the state and military technology, because these also have other sources and require at least some analysis of how social institutions make use of such a propensity towards violence in a certain way; how it ends up as nuclear confrontation between states for example rather than interpersonal fisticuffs. Segal (1990: Ch. 9) makes a similar point. If this is the case, however, why theorize patriarchy in terms of a psychological 'hegemonic masculinity'?

In an age of bureaucratization and rationalization it is rarely possible to translate personal values directly into routine public action. Office holders have to maintain the personality associated with their office. This is one way modernity undermines patriarchy. Office holders are required in principle not to discriminate between sexes and genders – to some extent to keep their misogyny, ethnocentrism or homophobia private. It is also possible, so long as they fulfil the duties of the office, to maintain an identity widely at variance with the hegemonic pattern. Here is the positive side of what Baumann has called the 'moral invisibility' of bureaucracy. It need be no concern of employers (although they may try to make it so) whether I am gay, or a transvestite, a passionate feminist or hopeless misogynist. All sorts of powerful men, from politicians to business leaders, live out lives distant from the hegemonic 'ideal', fantasizing, for example, about what Connell (1995: 219) calls 'the receptive pleasures of the anus' (Friday 1980). A vital part of any adequate sociology is thus a sense of the distance between the individual and social structure which modernity makes possible and which provides the material basis for feminism and sex equality in the first place.

The third reason is that it ignores the sexual genesis of human beings, and because of that, falls into the trap of imagining that the personal is purely political, which the confusion of sexual genesis and sexual difference produces, giving us the false choice between the politicization of personal identity and its maintenance in a patriarchal form. The danger is that attempts to 'reform' the self, in the pursuit of greater sexual equality, may only reinforce a social process whereby all 'selves', whether male or female, become increasingly subordinated to the demands of the universal market and the associated abstract systems and bureaucracies of modernity. This danger is all the greater both because these same social forces have been responsible for undermining patriarchy in the public sphere – and therefore appear progressive, and because this increasing subordination and weakening of the self is always imagined to be its opposite – the development of a liberated and ever more powerful self, a self capable, for example, of a 'pure relationship' or of 'democratizing' its personal life. Meanwhile, little advance in sexual equality may be achieved; indeed the reverse may occur.

Finally, and most fundamental of all, I think such analyses of masculinity confuse the symptom and the cause. Instead of attempting to discover, for example, what sociological and psychological socialization mechanisms within childrearing produce masculinities, as Chodorow (1978), Dinnerstein (1987) and Benjamin (1990) have all attempted and which follows a tradition going back to Parsons and Freud, instead of using such analyses to speculate on how reform of such socialization might produce androgynous gender identities, or how 'gender vertigo' might be encouraged, we could instead ask: what has made people, including sociologists, psychoanalysts and popular journalists, imagine that individuals possess gender? How have they come to see the connection between sex, self and society in this way? The answer to this question takes us towards the analysis of the changing social relations of the sexual division of labour and the changing ideology of gender this throws up in modernity, and towards the ability to see the arena of the private sphere and the personal as something that lies beyond gender, contrary to the socialization theories that are themselves a product of that ideology.

I think that we can best understand the contemporary appeal of this politics of identity, and the other three changes I have outlined, in terms of changing relations between the sexes, which in turn are based upon a fundamental change working itself out in contemporary modernity of the status of the individual in society, perhaps best summed up in the idea of universal human rights. The essence of this change is a world historical shift in the significance of sex difference brought about by the defeat of patriarchy (the rule of men by virtue of their sex) by the four interconnected revolutions of modernity: capitalism, liberalism, rationalization and the demographic transition. This discussion is therefore about the social relations which characterize the fag-end of patriarchy, about the material and symbolic legacy of millennia of rule by men, about the processes responsible for the collapse of patriarchy, and about the ideologies of gender, masculinity and femininity which women and men use to make sense of the transitional period through which they are now living. Masculinity can be seen as the last ideological defence of male supremacy in a world that has already conceded that men and women are equal. Invented in order to argue that men's power is socially rather than naturally derived, the concept suffers from the patent flaw (from the point of view of defending men's privilege) that what is socially rather than naturally constructed can be socially challenged and changed. I think that we have reached the point where masculinity as a concept obscures the analysis of social relations between the sexes, especially when it is imagined to be something that empirically existing individuals possess, which they might reform.

I would thus like to see the end of masculinity in the sense of turning the focus of the struggle for greater gender equality away from how masculinity is to be abolished or reformed and towards a more thorough pursuit of a politics of equal rights. Such a politics foregrounds questions of which social mechanisms continue to defend men's ability to wield power by virtue of their sex against the corrosive effects of universalism, while also allowing us to resist those aspects of universalism which corrode the independent self rather than patriarchal privilege. Focusing on masculinity has the danger that it leads us into an apparently radical but in practice individualized and conservative cul-de-sac which re-inforces the contemporary preoccupation with the self at the expense of its social context. In contrast to the politics of identity I suggest that pursuing a politics of justice and equal rights to its logical conclusion is a more radical option, once we have solved the problems caused by the confusion of sexual genesis and sexual difference.

NOTES

1 MacFarlane (1986) and others have suggested that fathers' power to do so in Britain was less than elsewhere in Europe.
2 This and other statistics are taken from the author's analyses of the 1994 International Social Survey Program's 1994 survey module *Family and Changing Gender Roles* administered to some 33,000 respondents in 18 countries by national survey research organizations, deposited in the ESRC Data Archive, University of Essex. Those who carried out the original collection and analysis of the data bear no responsibility for the interpretation I have placed on it here. References to this source are referred to below as 'ISSP 1994'.
3 The 1997 General Election changed the position significantly, thanks to the combined effects of the Labour Party's women-only shortlists policy, and the scale of its victory, so that many women were elected in seats which the party might not normally have expected to win. But while the Labour Party had over 100 women MPs in the new parliament, the Conservative Party managed just six.
4 All figures in this paragraph are from Jukes (1993: xv).
5 By 'jobs' I mean employees in employment. The number of self-employed has risen in this period by around 700,000; here too, women's employment has

expanded faster than men's but from a smaller base. I have excluded self-employment from the discussion because a breakdown by sex and status was not readily available for June 1996.

6 Of course, this shorthand expression conceals a rather more complex reality. Since employment is really a flow rather than a stock, the actual jobs (and people occupying them) being counted by these levels of employment will have been continually changing across this period.

7 Of course, equal participation rates do not mean labour market equality; it is possible to be in the labour force, but still have a part time, poorly paid, sex-typed job, or indeed, no job at all.

8 Craib (1989) points out that this was essentially Freud's view of the discipline.

9 For a useful critique along these lines see Young (1984).

REFERENCES

Adorno, T. (1968) Sociology and Psychology. *New Left Review* 47: 79–97.

Benjamin, J. (1990) *The Bonds of Love*. London: Virago.

Bly, R. (1991) *Iron John: A Book About Men*. Shaftesbury, Dorset: Element Books.

Chodorow, N. J. (1978) *The Reproduction of Mothering*. Berkeley, CA: University of California Press.

Condy, A. (1994) *Families and Work. International Year of the Family Factsheet 3*. London: IYF UK Office.

Connell, R. W. (1987) *Gender and Power*. Cambridge: Polity.

Connell, R. W. (1995) *Masculinities*. Cambridge: Polity.

Craib, I. (1989) *Psychoanalysis and Social Theory: The Limits of Sociology*. London: Harvester Wheatsheaf.

Davis, H. and Joshi, H. (1990) *The Foregone Earnings of Europe's Mothers*. Discussion Papers in Economics no. 24. London: Birkbeck College.

Dinnerstein, D. (1987) *The Rocking of the Cradle and the Ruling of the World*. London: Women's Press. Previously published in 1976 as *The Mermaid and the Minotaur*. New York: Harper and Row.

Duncombe, J. and Marsden, D. (1993) Love and intimacy: The gender division of emotion and 'emotion work'. *Sociology*, 27: 221–41.

Duncombe, J. and Marsden, D. (1995) 'Workaholics' and 'whingeing women': Theorizing intimacy and emotion work – the last frontier of gender inequality? *Sociological Review*, 43: 150–69.

Engels, F. (1968) The origin of the family, private property and the state. In *Marx and Engels: Selected Works in One Volume*. London: Lawrence and Wishart.

Friday, N. (1980) *Men in Love: Men's Sexual Fantasies*. New York: Arrow Books.

General Household Survey (1994) London: HMSO.

Gershuny, J., Godwin, M. and Jones, S. (1994) The domestic labour revolution: A process of lagged adaption. In M. Anderson, F. Bechhofer and J. Gershuny (eds) *The Social and Political Economy of the Household*. Oxford: Oxford University Press.

Giddens, A. (1992) *The Transformation of Intimacy: Love, Sexuality and Eroticism in Modern Societies*. Cambridge: Polity.

Jensen, J., Hagen, E. and Reddy, C. (eds) (1988) *Feminisation of the Labour Force: Paradoxes and Promises*. Cambridge: Polity.

Jukes, A. (1993) *Why Men Hate Women*. London: Free Association Books.

Kaufman, M. (1994) Men, feminism, and men's contradictory experiences of power. In H. Brod and M. Kaufman (eds) *Theorising Masculinities*. London: Sage.

Lloyd, T. (1994) *Analysis of Newspaper Coverage of Fathers and Men as Carers* (carried out in June 1994), mimeo.

MacFarlane, A. (1986) *Marriage and Love in England: Modes of Reproduction 1300–1840*. Oxford: Basil Blackwell.

Mann, M. (1994) Persons, households, families, lineages, genders, classes and nations. In *The Polity Reader in Gender Studies*. Cambridge: Polity.

Marsh, C. (1991) *Hours of Work of Women and Men in Britain*, Research Series, Equal Opportunities Commission. London: HMSO.

Ostner, I. (1993) Slow motion: Women, work and the family in Germany. In J. C. Lewis (ed.) *Women and Social Policies in Europe*. Aldershot: Edward Elgar.

Pahl, R. E. (1995) *After Success*. Cambridge: Polity.

Scott, J., Alwin, D. F. and Braun, M. (1996) Changing sex-role attitudes. *Sociology*, 30, 471–92.

Segal, L. (1990) *Slow Motion: Changing Masculinities, Changing Men*. London: Virago.

Seidler, V. J. (1989) *Rediscovering Masculinity: Reason, Language and Sexuality*. London: Routledge.

Seidler, V. J. (1990) Men, feminism and power. In J. Hearn and D. Morgan (eds) *Men, Masculinities and Social Theory*. London: Unwin Hyman.

Threlfall, M. (1996) Feminist politics and social change in Spain. In M. Threlfall (ed.) *Mapping the Women's Movement*. London: Verso.

United Kingdom Men's Movement (1995) *Discrimination Against Men in the UK*. Cheltenham: The United Kingdom Men's Movement.

Wrong, D. (1961) The oversocialized conception of man in modern sociology. *American Sociological Review*, 26: 183–93.

Yeandle, S. (1995) 'Change in the gender composition of the workforce: Recent analyses and their significance for social theory'. Conference paper. European Sociological Association conference, Budapest, 2 September.

Young, I. M. (1984) Is male gender identity the cause of male domination? In J. Trebilcot (ed.) *Mothering*. NJ: Rowman and Allenheld (Littelfield Adams and Co.).

18

'Crabs in a Bucket': Reforming Male Identities in Trinidad

Niels Sampath

The Concise Oxford Dictionary defines 'masculine' as 'characteristic of men ... manly, vigorous ... having qualities considered appropriate to a man'. This definition does not allow for conceptions of masculinity differing according to context. Instead, through suggesting that there is a single, logical, and unquestionable idea of what is 'masculine', the definition reflects the dominance of the Western concept of masculinity.

[...] The notion of 'masculinity' is currently asserting a presence in the analysis of societies and their progression in the world. When dealing with both gender and development issues, one cannot, as has often been done, simply take masculinity and its apparently problematical patriarchal values for granted (Gilmore 1990). As one investigates different cultures and communities, each of which is continually changing over time, one begins to realise that men's voices, often reflecting different identities, are far from homogeneous. While some men may claim to be superior to women, they may also provide evidence of a real fear of, or actual experience of, domination by women (Spiro 1993).

Both masculinity and femininity are cultural constructs and not universal human 'essentials'. Both are formed from 'bits and pieces of biological, psychological, and social experiences' (Levant and Pollack 1995, following Pleck 1981). This fact is accepted for femininity. Few, if any, books or journals are titled '*Femininity and* [insert topic of choice]'. Even as a plural, 'femininities' seems unpopular. Instead, women's changing or changeable *identities* are stressed, usually in a positive sense. By contrast, the stereotypes associated with the Western idea of 'masculinity' seem to have marked it down as the underlying reason for much that is wrong with the world.

Attempts at promoting 'new' male identities (for example, the Western 'New Man' in all his permutations) are often ridiculed or derided. While some women may say 'I am not a feminist, but...', some men will utter a similar phrase: 'I am not a male chauvinist, but...' (Morgan 1992: 11). And for every committed feminist, there are many women who, implicitly or explicitly and in both major and minor ways, support the general male domination ideology, or *masculinism* as Brittan (1989) has termed it, and will reject men and women who do not subscribe to it.

The conclusion to be drawn is that many men, as well as women, feel a sense of entrapment within perceived stereotypes, whether the stereotype's alleged agenda is 'good' or 'bad'. In reality, people tend to 'mix and match' and, to use a Caribbean term, 'creolise' definitions and concepts to suit their own personal circumstances even if they are unable to articulate or effectively react against any social discomfort they feel.[1]

Although gender analysis is almost unavoidably set within a framework of largely Western-developed sociological gender theory, there is every reason to suppose that the same discomfort with, and occasional resistance to, stereotypes also occurs across semi-industrialised societies and those undergoing Westernisation or modernisation (Berreman 1973: 23).

Masculinity with or without patriarchy?

What is meant by 'masculinity'? Gender issues are primarily issues of personal identity, set within the contexts of cultural and social definitions of sexual role. Whenever the term 'gender' is used, it is important to remember that one is not dealing with just a bi-polar concept of male *or* female identities. Within a culture or society, an individual can be faced with different desired, expected or fulfilled roles within a life-time. The level of pressure to conform to these gender roles is not entirely uniform over a life-time for anyone. Gender identities held by women and men can be submissive, complementary, or dominant to each other, depending on factors such as age and status. In this sense, gender identity can often seem, to the individual and community concerned, almost independent of the other sex.

Until recently, masculine identity has tended to be subsumed into studies of 'patriarchy' and its effect on society and women in particular, rather than studied for its own sake. This model is often quite far removed from non-Western or non-academic thinking about gender and sex which people in most developing communities assume and value. It also ignores the social importance of critical but subtle variations within 'masculinity', many of which work against men. I would argue that this makes it less likely that constructive patterns of change will occur through development interventions.

Caribbean men's 'reputation' and 'respectability'

Trinidad is an island in the Caribbean that, although best known for African-Caribbean culture, is in fact quite multi-ethnic. South Asians, or East Indians as they are known, form the largest ethnic group. In addition, the economy is based on oil, and this industry has undergone dramatic boom/bust cycles in the last quarter-century since independence. As one can imagine, these conditions have produced a high degree of social and economic change. In particular, race and gender relations have been challenged by changes in the labour market and increased opportunities for women. With these changes have come strains on what had been considered to be 'traditional' gender relations and masculine identities. (In the following description I have italicised local expressions and they should be read as such.)

Women-centred studies and development programmes have paid attention to the common double standards facing the emancipation of women (sexual and otherwise). African-Caribbean masculine identity, although often reinforcing that double standard, faces a duality of its own in terms of man-to-man interaction. Wilson (1969; 1973) originally outlined West Indian *reputation* and *respectability* characteristics that are key aspects of male identity.

Respectability involves those moral decisions and actions that are seen as positively influenced by European colonialism and the local pyramidal social structure based on class and colour. *Respectability* is a concept reflected by the norms of local genteel femininity: church-going and being 'well-behaved'.

Reputation is a working-class, live-for-today enjoyment of the kind of hedonism that is deemed as *worthless* by the respectable sections of local society. It is a male reaction to *respectability* (Littlewood 1993), and also acts as a control upon men and women who aspire to be respectable when they are locally deemed to be nothing of the kind (Wilson 1969). Honour is given. Honour is taken away.

The local analogy is made to crabs in a bucket: before any one individual can escape and because of the posturing going on within the bucket, that individual is dragged down by the others. Individuals in the 'bucket' of poverty and subservience in colonial or post-colonial society struggle to achieve the *respectability* that is assumed to exist outside their strata of society. As suggested above, going to church on Sunday is one way of beginning this process. However, in the meantime they have to survive within the crowded and extroverted community.

Members of each gender nominally involve *reputation* as their stratagem. For men, this usually takes the form of overt sexual banter and bravado. Women delve deeply into the nuances of party-going and local concepts of fashion. The tactics of both sexes stress individual consumerism and extroverted display.

In line with this, both men and women, but especially men, superficially tout the idea that it is a free society: free for the individual to do as he or she pleases. A strong *reputation* which emphasises personal 'freedom' is deemed important in the post-slavery, post-plantation, post-colonial environment. Having been the perceived perks of the colonial elite, heightened consumerism and fashion are recognised as socially-constructed patterns of attainment of freedom. And freedom is seen to be necessary to ensure success on a day-to-day basis, since it allows one to *move well*, as is said locally. One is unshackled from perceived social constraints and one can conduct social business on a wider scale, not subservient to any other individual. However, even with the possible exception of some sports heroes and heroines, it is rare for men, as well as women, ever to reach a serene level of *respectability* by simply enhancing their *reputation* in this way.

Behaviour that enhances *reputation* is the anti-thesis of *respectability*. If people are seen to aspire to leave the 'bucket' they are branded as *too bright*, or *too high*. For example, in an urban Trinidad factory setting described by Yelvington (1995), the two characteristics define 'idioms of masculine control over women'. Men do not pass up an opportunity to test and verbally probe women's attempts at virtuous *respectability*. For in doing so, and almost no matter what the outcome, men enhance their own *reputation* among other men. According to Yelvington (op. cit.) *reputation* has a 'symbolic violence' which follows a continuum from gentle flirting called *sweet talk* through to less acceptable but more aggressive methods of power enforcement such as spreading malicious rumours or *mauvais langue*.

In such a traditional urban work situation women are left in a no-win situation balanced between either submitting at some point to male advances or engaging in deflective banter, usually in the form of returning the teases and taunts. In the first instance, they have plainly submitted, and in the second instance, they deny themselves *respectability* by re-inforcing *worthless* male *reputation*. While some women may succeed for a while in taking a third course of action, i.e. ignoring male advances, the reality is that many women choose not to put themselves in the situation at all by avoiding the workplace altogether. In this way, the 'symbolic violence' of men trying to achieve a *reputation* effectively keeps women in the 'bucket' of social subservience. Again, it should be noted that the values encompassed by *reputation* and *respectability* can be endorsed, explicitly and implicitly, by both men and women, to themselves, as well as to each other. The 'crabs in the bucket' analogy appears to apply to both genders at all levels.

Yet, at this point it must be stated that the above qualities have supporters, detractors, and 'conscientious objectors' amongst local people of both sexes (as do femininity, feminism, male chauvinism, and the New Man syndrome elsewhere). It is among this plurality of experience and opinion that opportunities for reform and development may be found. A more rural and youthful example further illustrates the point.

In my own fieldwork study in a rural Hindu East Indian village in Trinidad, for every professional flirt such as could be found in the urban factory, there was a hopeless romantic who was socially paralysed by a self-imposed boycott to avoid 'trying to *sweet-talk* women into this and that'.

Tabanka pertains especially to young village men: the word describes social belittlement, and sexual and moral shame. It is usually applied to male African-Trinidadians when a woman's affections are lost to another man (Littlewood 1985). Indian adolescents (and here one must include all unmarried men as well as teenagers) have few opportunities to engage in active heterosexual relationships. So the term *tabanka* has been extended by them to include the common state of unrequited love. Here a *macho reputation* has, for one reason or another, been prevented, rather than lost. In this respect, the effect of the mocking which customarily accompanies their predicament is different.

A 24-year-old individual known as Pastor, who was once an enthusiastic Christian convert who had mocked Hindu idolatry, found himself longing for, though not speaking to, a young woman hairdresser in the village who was rumoured to have broken off with a boy from elsewhere. Pastor gave up *liming* (hanging out) with his *pardners* so that he could walk back and forth in front of her house, hoping for something spontaneous to occur. His *pardners* in turn intensified his *tabanka*: by belittling his situation (and the woman) and telling him to 'make a move on the chick man, she's an old cat'.

Instead, Pastor sought solace in watching Indian films on videos where, for example, after years of separation, the hero and heroine might actu-

ally speak to each other before a painful death. He began re-attending
Hindu prayer meetings. If he went shopping for his family, people would
ask him if he was going to buy *gramazone*, a defoliant commonly used as
a suicide potion.

While Pastor's ex-*pardners* made light of his situation, Pastor attempted to console himself with the relative security of more traditional
'Indian culture'. Lack of 'modern' masculine success and not *moving
well* can be indicated by a reversion to fatalism and a relative over-
concentration on traditional sources (the domestic sphere, dominated
by women, is seen as the haven of traditional culture). To quote one of
Pastor's *pardners*:

> *Poor Pastor. He does want to make a move on the girl but he ain't gettin
> nowhere. He used to mock them star-boys in Indian films and now he
> suffering just like they. Well, that is what does happen. Once you does lose
> courage to take action, bang, tabanka does take hold and you back sitting
> and scratching, doing nothing.*

Pastor, it seems, could not be blamed for being attracted to the girl, but
he could not successfully broker the dominating cultural values involved.
According to his *pardners*, had he not mocked traditional Indian values
in the first place and partly retained their security he might have had the
courage he sought to establish a successful 'masculine identity'.

Based on the Trinidadian urban and rural examples, the problem, it
seems, is that 'masculinity' is based on local perceptions of 'success'. Just
as women are socially valued as 'sex objects', so men are valued as
'success objects' in a context of *reputation*. The two values appear to
complement each other within a patriarchal paradigm. The question then
becomes, how does one begin to escape that paradigm?

Re-forming male identities

While it may appear as if gender relations are trapped in a static web,
there are possible ways forward. Because the local criteria of value as sex
or success objects for both sexes are quite narrow, they tend to produce
many variations of excluded or compromised values and individuals,
which then quietly incorporate themselves within the creolised environment of, for example, multi-ethnic Trinidad. The unfortunate key word
there is 'quietly'. As in our own society, 'alternative' culture is often used
as a defining contrast for that which is largely hidden from the main
stream. By and large, there is still a paucity of acceptable varieties of

expression of masculinity in day-to-day activity within most national cultures. But often the potential for change is already well in place.

In Trinidad and the Caribbean, one has the process of *creolisation*: a mixing within the accepted values of the dominant constituents. This takes place not just between attributes of race, religion, or ethnicity, but between any opposing or corresponding social characteristics on all levels, gender included.

Miller (1994) points to a more positive analytical future partly because he effectively discusses Trinidadian gender issues without making them his absolute focus. He refers to a less gender-laden duo of social characteristics he calls the 'transient' and 'transcendent'. In some ways these still reflect *reputation* and *respectability*. But Miller's analytical terms apparently sort through the rest of society and return to the gender puzzle without being trapped within masculinism's terms of reference. He makes a useful contrast between carnival and Christmas.

Trinidad carnival is a hedonistic free-for-all that tests the boundaries and allows for creative expression that is both male and female. The action is on the street and non-domestic. The past has passed and the future is tomorrow, and for a few days neither matters. In that sense, the carnival is an event which emphasises transience.

By contrast, Trinidad Christmas is, quite apart from Christian religious aspects, a national cultural marker where various influences are appropriated for future recall through family and long-term relationships. In its *respectability* and location in the domestic female domain, Christmas transcends day-to-day life. Yet, neither Christmas nor carnival would be quite the same without the other; and each ensures the other's survival.

What is interesting is that there has been a perception in Trinidad that 'women are [gradually] taking over carnival'. The first indication of this was noted in the 1950s by Powrie (1988[1956]), but since then it has accelerated. Some carnival bands have a ratio of ten women for every man. There are several reasons for this.

To begin with, women in Trinidad, while hardly emancipated to their own satisfaction, have nevertheless made some strides in that direction. But their near predominance in Trinidad carnival is due to more than a simple trend. Carnival acts as an escape valve, a time when notions of traditional *respectability* do not apply. The difference between everyday life and carnival is greater for women than for men.

Indeed, some women say: 'men in Trinidad, they think every day is carnival. But women must think of work.' And so, women are more enthusiastic about carnival. Ironically, many women can maintain 'traditional' concerns about clothes and make-up, and domestic gossip through carnival, but now it can be done extra-domestically and with a greater cultural purpose that they feel legitimises these activities to the masculinist, paternalistic society in general.

There are also economic reasons for women 'taking over' carnival. Men have traditionally been employed in plantation and heavy and manufacturing industry. These activities are in decline. The service sector, including those economic activities maintaining carnival itself, is the growth area, and here women predominate, and are making significant progress into middle-management. Thus, women are increasingly likely to be the steady income earners and are invariably in charge of domestic finances. As a result, women can set money aside specifically for carnival bands and fêting, whereas many men, who feel obliged to try to 'party' (or *lime* as their get-togethers are known) on a constant basis, are invariably short of the required cash.[2] As women have involved themselves with carnival, they have injected it with a transcendent quality to the point where it is now a year-round preparatory industry.

In the rural East Indian village where I did my fieldwork, a similar shift has occurred whereby what was once somewhat *transient* – the existence of increasingly independent women – has become more *transcendent*. Within the space of a few years, families were no longer looking for semi-arranged marriages for their young men to girls who could simply be mothers and 'didn't want to work'.[3] Instead, a good education and a steady job have become something that young girls actively seek out. While young men drop out of school and complain that there are no jobs to study for, young women seem to be less pessimistic (or perhaps less socially able to do anything outside the home other than study or 'take courses').

The economic circumstances affecting urban life have also affected the life of the village. Traditional sugar plantation work has declined dramatically as has higher-paid work in the oil industry. At the same time local (non-plantation) agriculture and related sales and distribution, in which women have always had significant involvement, are part of the new growth in the service industries. While 'service' has connotations of subservience, unlike traditional industry where physical labour was important, a *reputation*, as sought by men, is of little value any more.

In both urban carnival and rural community life, it could be said that women have had less motivational investment in the 'crab in the bucket' analogy. That has always been a primarily male concern. Indeed, academic criticism of Wilson's theories stresses that the notion of the relegation of women from the public sphere, so that they can uphold a 'colonial respectability', is itself both Eurocentric in its framework and ignorant of several areas of women's public interaction (Besson 1993; Douglass 1992).

Women have, perhaps, found other means of escaping from the 'bucket' than dragging others down. They have utilised the transient (carnival) and immediate economic necessity (things that men might use for themselves to enhance their *reputation*) to develop more permanent ways of escape from subservience.

Men have had to adjust their identities accordingly and at least try to delete that component of male success which insists that women cannot also enjoy 'success' in relation to their own. This may not always go smoothly and might initially seem impossible. But in every sphere of life in the Caribbean, the diaspora population, both African and Indian, male and female, has *always* had to make changes to 'tradition'. Changes to male identity would not be a new experience.

Development and male identity

Research into the effects of patriarchy on women has been relatively thorough, but this may have deflected attention away from the fact that men are dominated by other men, and are denied alternative expressions that could be more benign to women. It is only with a recognition of the potential for a range of identities that *the effect by men on men as well as women* can be appreciated. Recruitment to progressive changes should then be easier. It is less socially divisive if men and women are dedicated to the same project.

As I have illustrated using the example of Trinidad, different feminine and masculine identities can exist despite an apparently monolithic stereotype. Unlike the exclusivity of power and status which is suggested by the traditional notion of patriarchy, an inclusive tendency can be fostered given certain conditions. Inclusivity, or 'non-crab-in-a-bucket' behaviour, appears to be intrinsic in those areas where women have contributed to development.

However, with regards to men, constructive and inclusive conditions may be missed or not considered if the initial focus is purely on interactions between women and men, rather than on intrinsic masculine/feminine identities. By examining men's identities more closely, development decisions could promote the positive aspects of masculine identities, assisting *both* women and supportive men in the creation of less patriarchal societies. The 'problem' with masculinity is not masculinity itself, but how it is focused.

NOTES

1 The *Concise Oxford Dictionary* defines 'creolise' as 'make [the] (language of [the] dominant group, in [a] modified form) into [the] sole language of the dominated group.'
2 See also Rodman (1971: 172–173).
3 In Trinidad, the dowry system did not survive the migration from India.

REFERENCES

Berreman, G. D. (1973) 'Self, situation, and escape from stigmatized ethnic identity', in Brogger (ed).
Besson, J. (1993) 'Reputation and respectability reconsidered: a new perspective on Afro-Caribbean peasant women', in Momsen (ed).
Brittan, A. (1989) *Masculinity and Power*, Oxford: Basil Blackwell
Brogger, J. (ed) (1973) *Management of Minority Status*, Oslo: Universitetsforlaget.
Douglass, L. (1992) *The Power of Sentiment: Love, Hierarchy, and the Jamaican Family Elite*, Oxford: Westview Press.
Gilmore, D. D. (1990) *Manhood in the Making: Cultural Concepts of Masculinity*, London: Yale University Press.
Hearn, J. and D. Morgan (eds) (1990) *Men, Masculinity, and Social Theory*, London: Routledge.
Johnson, K. (ed) (1988) *Trinidad Carnival*. Republication of special Carnival edn. of *Caribbean Quarterly*, **4**, 3–4 (1956). Trinidad: Paria Press.
Levant, R. F. and W. S. Pollack (eds) (1995) *A New Psychology of Men*, New York, NY: Basic Books.
Levant, R. F. and W. S. Pollack (1995) 'Introduction', in Levant and Pollack (eds).
Littlewood, R. (1985) 'An indigenous conceptualization of reactive depression in Trinidad', *Psychological Medicine* **15**, 278–281.
Littlewood, R. (1993) *Pathology and Identity: The Work of Mother Earth in Trinidad*, Cambridge: Cambridge University Press.
Miller, B. D. (ed) (1993) *Sex and Gender Hierarchies*. Cambridge: Cambridge University Press.
Miller, D. (1994) *Modernity: An Ethnographic Approach: Dualism and Mass Consumption in Trinidad*, London: Berg.
Momsen, J. H. (ed) (1993) *Women and Change in the Caribbean: A Pan-Caribbean Perspective*, London: James Currey.
Morgan, D. H. J. (1992) *Discovering Men*, London: Routledge.
Pleck, J. R. (1981) *The Myth of Masculinity*, Cambridge, MA: MIT Press.
Powrie, B. E. (1988) [1956] 'The changing attitude of the coloured middle class towards carnival', in Johnson (ed) (1988).

Rodman, H. (1971) *Lower-Class Families: The Culture of Poverty in Negro Trinidad*. New York: Oxford University Press.

Spiro, M. (1993) 'Gender hierarchy in Burma' in Miller (ed) (1993).

Wilson, P. J. (1969) 'Reputation and respectability: a suggestion for Caribbean ethnography', *Man* (NS) **4**, 70–84.

Wilson, P. J. (1973) *Crab Antics*, New Haven: Yale University Press.

Yelvington, K. A. (1995) *Producing Power: Ethnicity, Gender, and Class in a Caribbean Workplace*, Philadelphia PA: Temple University Press.

19

'And Ar'n't I a Man?': Toward a Chicano/Latino Men's Studies

Alfredo Mirandé

In the past twenty years or so a rich body of feminist research and scholarship has emerged. Because this scholarship all too often mirrored the values, orientation, and concerns of upper-middle-class white women, parallel movements have developed among Chicanas/Latinas and other women of color. More recently 'The New Men's Studies' has emerged, focusing on men not as apologists for the status quo but as feminist men in solidarity with feminist scholarship.

Despite increased interest in men's studies, the topic of Chicano/Latino masculinity remains neglected and virtually unexplored both within the so-called new men's studies and feminist scholarship. No less surprising, I think, is the fact that the study of Latino men and masculinity has been equally neglected within Chicana/Chicano scholarship. During the past two decades or so there has been a heightened awareness of Latino women and Chicanas, evident in the publication of several significant works on the topic (see Mora and del Castillo 1980; Sánchez and Martínez Cruz 1977; Melville 1980; Mirandé and Enríquez 1981). Though there has been a proliferation of writing by and about Chicanas and other Latinas (Córdova et al. 1984; Garcia 1989; de la Torre and Pesquera 1993; Acosta-Belén and Bose 1993; and Bose and Acosta-Belén 1995) addressing patriarchy, male oppression, and other important issues, there has been little effort to examine Chicano/Latino men as men or to assess the range and variety of Latino masculinities. Cherríe Moraga (1993), for example, contemplates the idea of a 'Queer Aztlán' or a 'queer nation,' incorporating Mexican nationalism and grounded in our Indian heritage, without directly addressing the issue of masculinity.

Ironically, the Chicano movement and Chicano/Latino scholarship have been gender stratified and have emphasized men as the dominant figures, but there have been few serious attempts to examine either masculinity and machismo or the extent to which Chicano/Latino scholarship reflects particular masculinities.

In this chapter I propose the development of a new Chicano/Latino men's studies and begin with an overview and critique of The New Men's Studies Scholarship (TNMS). Although the call for a separate and autonomous field of Chicano/Latino men's studies may be premature at this point, it is time that we begin to address the extent to which Chicano/Latino men and the varieties of masculinities among them have been ignored by the new men's studies and Chicano(a)/Latino(a) scholarship.

The "good ol' boys" and Latino masculinity

Much of the early research on men was based on a static and stereotypical view of men and served to perpetuate traditional conceptions of masculinity and gender (Pleck 1981, 1). According to Joseph Pleck, the problem with this early research and with the term 'sex role' is not only that there is arguably no such thing as a uniform, unvarying sex role but also that such terminology 'tends to mask questions of power and inequality' (Lopata and Thorne 1978, 719). The new men's studies rejects the tendency of this early research to normalize and justify gender inequality by focusing on men in a way ostensibly designed to augment and support feminist scholarship.

Although TNMS has filled an important void, it has had some serious shortcomings. I propose that the new men's studies is not really new at all. Upon closer analysis it is clear that TNMS is not the study of men qua men but the study of white men. It would thus be more accurate to term it the new white men's studies.[1] When TNMS scholars discuss 'men of color,' the discussion is usually limited to African-American men. These authors apparently have no conception of race beyond the traditional black/white dichotomy. In *The Myth of Masculinity*, a pioneering work in the field, Joseph Pleck, for example, gave only token attention to African-American men and said nothing at all about Latino men. Thus, when Pleck mentioned 'our culture,' he was clearly not referring to Mexicans or Latinos.

After surveying the main currents of recent social science research on masculinity, R. W. Connell, one of the leading figures in the new men's studies, concluded that a coherent science of masculinity has not yet been produced (1995, 67). Connell identified three main projects, or theoretical attempts, to develop a science of masculinity (1995, 7). The first effort was derived from clinical knowledge obtained by therapists and was based on Freudian theory. The second, which Pleck termed the Sex Role Identity Paradigm, was a heavily social psychological approach and was based on the popular notion that there were distinct female and male sex roles. The third has been termed 'the new social science,' or new men's studies, and was stimulated by men's liberation and by sex role psychology but extended well beyond traditional role theory, incorporating recent research in anthropology, sociology, and history (1995, 27).

Connell characterized Pleck's comprehensive evaluation of the male role literature, or the Male Sex Role Identity paradigm, as essentially a critique of functionalist sex role theory (1995, 25). Because the functionalist sex role theory was static and failed to engender a distinct 'politics of masculinity,' it inhibited social change by 'normalizing' male and female sex roles and making them normative (1995, 27). Although Connell presented an insightful critique of the conservative class bias in sex role theory, at the same time he failed to consider the possibility of racial bias within the new men's studies. Like other TNMS scholars, he gives only token attention to Black masculinity under the rubric of 'marginalization' (1995, 80) and ignores Chicano/Latino masculinity altogether.[2]

In an exhaustive work entitled *Manhood in America*, Michael Kimmel attempted to present a cultural history of men, noting that American men have no history of themselves as men (1996, 1–2). Kimmel traced the history of American manhood from 1776 to the present and chronicled the emergence of the 'self-made' man between 1776 and 1865, the unmaking of the self-made man from 1900 to 1920, the 'new man' of the twentieth century, and the contemporary crises of masculinity. Although this is an important book, and a cultural history of American manhood is important and long overdue, Chicano/Latino men are conspicuously absent from this history, leading one to conclude either that we are invisible and have no history or that we are somehow not part of American manhood.

"Reservoir dogs": overview and critique of the new men's studies

Because most academic research and theory has been the work of men and reflects male concerns, orientations, values, and worldviews, many critics fail to understand the need for a new men's studies. Critics of the new men's studies have noted that the existing scientific and academic world could be characterized as 'The Old Men's Studies' (TOMS). Proponents of TNMS such as Connell, Brod, and Kimmel counter that most research and writing has been carried out by men but that there has been an absence of critical, reflective analyses not only of manhood but also of how masculinity affects the conduct of scientific inquiry. According to Carrigan, Connell, and Lee (1985, 551), 'Though most social science is indeed about men, good-quality research that brings masculinity into focus is rare.' Moreover, with the exception of work on the history of homosexual masculinity, most recent studies are below the standard set by early researchers in the 1950s (Carrigan, Connell, and Lee 1985, 551). Harry Brod observed that 'while seemingly about men, traditional scholarship's treatment of generic man as the human norm in fact systematically excludes from consideration what is unique to men qua men' (Brod 1987, 2). Ironically, generalizing from the male to the genetic human experience 'precludes the study of masculinity as a specific male experience' (1987, 2). According to Brod,

> The most general definition of men's studies is that it is the study of masculinities and male experiences as specific and varying social-historical-cultural formations. Such studies situate masculinities as objects of study on a par with femininities, instead of elevating them to universal norms. (1987, 2)

Despite the growing literature on men and masculinity, men's studies has proved to be controversial and problematic. Clyde W. Franklin II (1988, 15–19) identified several important controversies within the field. First, what perspectives should characterize TNMS? There have been two opposing ideological perspectives within the men's movement: profeminist and nonfeminist. While the former recognizes that men have gained privilege from patriarchy and the oppression of women, the latter contends that women benefit from the institutionalization of traditional gender roles and that such roles place men at a disadvantage relative to women. Although most advocates of men's studies have assumed a profeminist stance, a substantial antifeminist strand exists within the larger so-called men's movement. This antifeminist ideology appears to be especially prevalent within the 'men's rights' branch of the men's movement.

The second and perhaps most serious and recurrent controversy has centered around the assertion that TNMS and the call for more generic gender studies programs are simply insidious tactics designed to weaken and co-opt feminist studies. After a turbulent conference on 'Men, Masculinity, and Social Theory' held under the auspices of the Sociological

Theory Group of the British Sociological Association, two feminist critics of TNMS, Joyce E. Canaan and Christine Griffin, admitted they were reluctant to participate in the conference. They also declined to contribute to the ensuing conference volume, *Men, Masculinities, and Social Theory*, edited by Hearn and Morgan (1990), because there were fundamental problems and limitations with TNMS (1990, 2060). One problem they identified is what Connell has termed a 'crisis in hegemonic masculinity,' which has emerged partly as a response to the gains of the women's movement and feminism. According to Canaan and Griffin,

> The problem with the name, 'men's studies,' is that it suggests that studies of men are complementary with those of women. As we know very well, so-called complementary all too often results in power being wrested from the less powerful and the powerless. We recognize that 'men's studies' can literally take women's jobs in teaching and research at a time of financial cutbacks. (Canaan and Griffin 1990, 211)

A third controversy surrounds sexual preference. Critics of men's studies have argued that the field has reflected the needs and concerns of heterosexual men and neglected those of homosexual men. The parent organization for men's studies, the National Organization for Changing Men (NOCM), now the National Organization for Men Against Sexism (NOMAS), however, has taken a strong gay affirmative and anti-homophobic stance. This pro-gay position is said to have led some heterosexual men to question their allegiance to the organization and even to drop out (Franklin 1988, 17). The final controversy revolves around the issue of race. Like its feminist counterpart, the new men's studies has been almost exclusively an elite white men's movement. As has already been noted, Chicanos and Latinos, whether gay or straight, have been conspicuously absent from both the old and the new men's studies.

[...]

The Latino gay voice and the cult of masculinity

Perhaps the most glaring omission in research and writing on gender and masculinities is the absence either of research and writing on Latino gay men or of attempts to articulate a Latino male gay voice. The absence of a Latino gay voice is paradoxical given the persistence of male dominance and the cult of masculinity in Latino culture. Some Chicano writers have hinted at or strongly implied the existence of a same-sex preference, but male Latino writers have remained largely in the academic closet.[3] There simply is no male counterpart to the powerful and moving portrayals of such gay Chicana writers as Cherríe Moraga, Gloria Anzaldúa, and Ana Castillo.[4]

One of the few Latinos who has begun to broach the sensitive and important topic of Chicano/Latino homosexuality is the Chicano sociologist Tomás Almaguer. Noting the paucity of research on Mexican and Latino men, Almaguer observed that Chicano men must negotiate a modern American gay identity with Mexican-Latino configurations of homosexual identity and behavior (1995, 418). With no ethnographic research to draw from, Almaguer developed a theoretical perspective on Latino gay men by combining 'perceptive anthropological research on homosexuality in México and Latin America' (1995, 419) with the writings of Chicana lesbians, which provide excellent insights on sexual behavior and identity.

Almaguer's thesis is deceptively simple. In the contemporary United States sexual categories and personages are 'defined in terms of sexual preference or object choice: same sex (homosexual), opposite sex (heterosexual), or both sexes (bisexual)' (1995, 419). This definition historically has led to a categorical 'condemnation of all same-sex behavior' (1995, 419). In the Mexican/Latino sexual system, on the other hand, homosexuality is defined not by object choice but by the distribution of power. Mexican men, then, are able to engage in homosexual acts without impugning their masculinity or heterosexual persona as long as they assume the active inserter role. A person is considered a *maricón* (homosexual) or a *joto* (queer) only if he assumes the passive, insertee role. 'Although stigma accompanies homosexual practices in Latin culture, it does not equally adhere to both partners. It is primarily the anal-passive individual (the *cochón* or *pasivo*)[5] who is stigmatized for playing the subservient, feminine role' (1995, 420). Not only is the *activo* or *machista* partner not stigmatized, but there is no clear linguistic category or label to classify him and, according to Almaguer, he is considered to be a normal male (1995, 420). Based on this analysis Almaguer comes to the incredible conclusion that 'there is no cultural equivalent to the modern "gay man" in the Mexican/Latin-American sexual system' (1995, 418).

Reading Almaguer's piece brought back many memories of my childhood, my dear Uncle Pepe, and my father. My father was undoubtedly macho in the positive Mexican sense of the word, but he never ridiculed or denigrated *Quintos* or gays. In fact, everyone in the family treated him with warmth, respect, and affection. After reflecting on Almaguer's thesis, I started to wonder whether my family was weird or pathological or whether there was something missing in his analysis.

To this day I don't know whether Uncle *Quintos* was the inserter or the insertee or both, but I do know that whether dominant or passive, he was unquestionably gay and his identity as a gay man transcended his sexual encounters. Although there may be some truth to Almaguer's assertion that 'homosexuality in México is typically shrouded in silence' (1995, 421), it strikes me as a gross oversimplification to say that only passive participants in homosexual encounters assume a gay identity. I know that my uncle had gay friends and that he participated in the gay world, that there are gay bars and clubs in *La Zona Rosa* and in other parts of Mexico City, and that certain cities like Guadalajara are reputed to have a large concentration of homosexuals.

Several years ago my adult nephew and I were visiting the city of Morelia in the state of Michoacan. It was evening, and we were sitting at an out door restaurant in the *portales*, or main downtown plaza, when we began to notice an abundance of male couples strolling by, holding hands or walking arm-in-arm. We were shocked not only by the number of visibly gay couples but by their open display of affection. We later learned that an international gay conference was being held in the city.

I, therefore, respectfully disagree with Almaguer's conclusion that there is no Mexican equivalent of the modern gay man. Although homosexual activities may be somewhat more clandestine, there is growing acceptance of gays in large metropolitan areas. Almaguer is correct in asserting that by retaining an active, inserter position, Latino men can engage in homosexual activity without impugning their heterosexual, macho identity, but he is wrong in calling this a distinctive Mexican/Latino cultural pattern. As we have seen in films such as *Deliverance* and, more recently, *Pulp Fiction*, working-class white men also sodomize other men without defining themselves as homosexual. The same pattern is repeated daily in American prisons, where the strongest, most violent, and most 'macho' men attack weaker effeminate victims.

In an insightful article written more than thirty years ago, 'The Social Integration of Queers and Peers' (1961), sociologist Albert Reiss made the same observation about working-class delinquent boys that Almaguer has made about Mexican/Latino men. Reiss reported that working-class youths are able to engage in homosexual relations with adult gay men without defining themselves as homosexuals as long as they assume the dominant role in the sexual exchange and get paid for sex. But if a boy were to assume the insertee role and perform oral sex on the adult homosexual or grant sexual favours without charge, he would be ostracized and termed 'queer' by his peers. Thus what is essential in retaining heterosexual identity for these young men is that they assume a traditionally dominant sex role.

Though I disagree with Almageur's characterization of homosexuality among Mexican and Latino men, he is to be commended for addressing the Chicano male gay experience and for opening up a dialogue and discussion on an important and neglected subject. If we are to gain a full understanding of men and gender in the Latino community, it is essential that we begin to examine not only conventional manifestations of machismo and heterosexuality but also the full range and variety of masculinities.

The proposed new field of Chicano/Latino men's studies lies at the intersection of Chicano feminism, Chicano studies, and men's studies. However, because Chicanas and Chicanos share a common historical, sociopolitical, cultural, linguistic, and racial bond as members of an oppressed group, we cannot look to Anglo men – and their new men's studies – for direction. They are, after all, the source of our oppression. We must first come to grips with our own oppression as men and women of color before we can begin to generate and articulate paradigms that will have liberating, rather than oppressive, consequences. We must develop a flexible and transcendent view of our history and culture that enables us to gain a better understanding of racial, cultural, class, and gender oppression and to create an emancipatory vision of our past, present, and future. In the end, we must first look within ourselves and then to each other for liberation.

NOTES

1 A few works have focused on African-American men, but these works were written by African-Americans and emerged largely outside of the TNMS (Wilkinson and Taylor 1977; Staples 1978 and 1982; Wallace 1978).
2 Other works within men's studies have also failed to address Latino men. See Clatterbaugh (1990) and Easthope (1990).
3 See, for example, Richard Rodriguez's (1992) *Days of Obligation: An Argument with My Mexican Father*, and '"Sissy" Warriors Vs. "Real" Men: A Perspective on Gays in the Military' (1995). For a discussion of homosexuality in Chicano literature, see Juan Bruce-Novoa (1992).
4 Argentinean writer Manuel Puig (1994) provides an insightful analysis of the relationship between a gay male and a revolutionary who share a cell in prison in *El beso de la mujer araña* (The Kiss of the Spider Woman).
5 *Cochón* is a term used in Nicaragua to refer to passive homosexuals. It is derived from the word *colchon*, or mattress, and refers to the fact that the active party gets on top of the passive one, as on a mattress. There is obviously a contradiction here in that Almaguer is implying that there are active,

inserter homosexuals, whereas in the next breath he notes that only the passive one is defined as a *maricón*.

REFERENCES

Acosta-Belén, Edna, and Christine E. Bose. 1993. *Researching Women in Latin America and the Caribbean*. Boulder, Colo.: Westview Press.

Almaguer, Tomás. 1995. 'Chicano Men: A Cartography of Homosexual Identity and Behavior.' In *Men's Lives*, ed. Michael S. Kimmel and Michael A. Messner, 418–431. Boston: Allyn & Bacon.

Bose, Christine E., and Edna Acosta-Belén. 1995. *Women in the Latin American Development Process*. Philadelphia: Temple University Press.

Brod, Harry, ed. 1987. *The Making of Masculinities: The New Men's Studies*. Boston: Allen & Unwin.

Bruce Novoa, Juan. 1992. 'Homosexuality and the Chicano Novel.' In *Homosexuality in Literary Studies*, ed. Wayne R. Dynes and Stephen Donaldson. New York: Garland Press.

Canaan, Joyce E., and Christine Griffin. 1990. 'The New Men's Studies: Part of the Problem or Part of the Solution?' In *Men, Masculinities & Social Theory*, ed. Jeff Hearn and David Morgan. London: Unwin Hyman.

Carrigan, Tim, Bob Connell, and John Lee. 1985. 'Toward a New Sociology of Masculinity.' *Theory and Society* 14, no. 5: 551–604.

Clatterbaugh, Kenneth. 1990. *Contemporary Perspectives on Masculinity*. Boulder, Colo.: Westview Press.

Connell, R. W. 1995. *Masculinities*. Cambridge: Polity, and Berkeley: University of California Press.

Córdova, Teresa, Norma Cantú, Gilberto Cárdenas, and Juan Garcia, eds. 1984. *Chicana Voices: Intersections of Class, Race, and Gender*. Colorado Springs: National Association for Chicano Studies.

de la Torre, Adela, and Beatriz M. Pesquera. 1993. *Building with our Hands: New Directions in Chicana Studies*. Berkeley: University of California Press.

Easthope, Anthony. 1990. *What a Man's Gotta Do: The Masculine Myth in Popular Culture*. Boston: Unwin.

Franklin, Clyde W. II. 1988. *Men and Society*. Chicago: Nelson-Hall.

Garcia, Alma. 1989. 'The Development of Chicana Feminist Discourse, 1970–1980.' *Gender & Society* 3 (June): 217–238.

Hearn, Jeff, and David Morgan. 1990. *Men, Masculinities and Social Theory*. London: Unwin Hyman.

Kimmel, Michael. 1996. *Manhood in America*. New York: The Free Press.

Lopata, Helena Z., and Barrie Thorne. 1978. 'On the Term "Sex Roles."' *Signs: Journal of Women in Culture and Society* 3: 718–721.

Melville, Margarita B., ed. 1980. *Twice a Minority: Mexican American Women*. St. Louis: C. V. Mosby.

Mirandé, Alfredo, and Evangelina Enríquez. 1981. *La Chicana: The Mexican-American Woman*. Chicago: University of Chicago Press.

Mora, Magdalena, and Adelaide R. del Castillo, eds. 1980. *Mexican Women in the United States: Struggles Past and Present*. Los Angeles: Chicano Studies Research Center Publications, University of California, Los Angeles.

Moraga, Cherríe. 1993. *The Last Generation*. Boston: South End Press.

Puig, Manuel. 1994. *El beso de la mujer araña*. New York: Vintage.

Reiss, Albert J., Jr. 1961. 'The Social Integration of Queers and Peers.' *Social Problems* 9: 102–120.

Rodriguez, Richard. 1992. *Days of Obligation: An Argument with My Mexican Father*. New York: Penguin.

—— 1995. '"Sissy" Warriors Vs. "Real" Men: A Perspective on Gays in the Military.' In *Men's Lives*, ed. Michael S. Kimmel and Michael A. Messner. Boston: Allyn & Bacon.

Sánchez, Rosaura, and Rosa Martínez Cruz, eds. 1977. *Essays on la Mujer*. Los Angeles: Chicano Studies Research Center Publications, University of California, Los Angeles.

Staples, Robert. 1978. 'Masculinity and Race: The Dual Dilemma of Black Men.' *Journal of Social Issues* 34 (winter): 169–183.

—— 1982. *Black Masculinity: The Black Male's Role in American Society*. San Francisco: Black Scholar Press.

Wallace, Michele. 1978. *Black Macho and the Myth of the Superwoman*. New York: Warner Books.

Wilkinson, Doris Y., and Ronald I. Taylor, eds. 1977. *The Black Male in America: Perspectives on his Status in American Society*. Chicago: Nelson-Hall.

20

Man: The Invisible Gendered Subject?

Stephen M. Whitehead

Introduction

Many social and other commentators now concur that significant transformations have occurred in respect of women's opportunities and expectations during the past few decades. Indeed, some go so far as to
suggest that the end of grand (gendered) narratives, universal (gendered)
role models and shifts in (gendered) public and private power/space,
signal a new social 'disorder' (Fukuyama, 1997). Others have suggested
that the 'end of masculinity' is upon us (MacInnes, 1998) and with it the
end of patriarchy and the gender order. Elsewhere, questions have
emerged with regard to the future of feminism and the subsequent arrival
of a 'post-feminist' era, a time when women's opportunities and expectations are said to be multiplying at the expense of men's (Walter, 1997;
also Wilkinson, 1994). Heralding a new gender order, women are, then,
said by some to be standing poised to grasp the power-base vacated by
men/masculinity in crisis (Horrocks, 1994). In one respect these are
seductive notions, for they speak to a personal/political agenda long at
the forefront of feminism. Yet might this celebration be somewhat premature? Profound changes appear to have occurred in the way many
women perceive themselves and their opportunities, certainly; but more
to the point, to what extent have men changed?

In critically examining the above question this chapter's focus is not on
men's practices as such. Rather, following a feminist post-structuralist
understanding of self and identity, the chapter suggests that before positive, equitable change can take place in men's practices some movement
or transformation must first occur in men's subjective perception of their

own gendered identity: they must come to some appreciation of how 'being a man' might affect and influence their expectations and experiences, in a multitude of settings. For men, this act of self-reflexivity would be particularly profound for it would serve to position them away from the centre and, consequently, women and 'others' away from the margins.

Gendered epistemology, ontology and reflexivity

The question of self-reflexivity is, then, central to the notion of personal and political change, a point explored in depth by, amongst others, Giddens (1991), Beck et al. (1995), Bourdieu (1992), and Foucault (1983). However, unlike for example Giddens (1991), this chapter is not presupposing a conscious agency of the individual, a place where recourse to some authentic knowledge or ethical self is achievable.[1] Neither is it being suggested that the self exists merely as a monad; free-floating, unencumbered by language, culture or social codes.[2] On the contrary, the concept of self which is being utilised here draws on a post-structuralist understanding of identity, wherein the 'individual' ceases to exist as a concrete, self-knowing, grounded person, but is replaced by the discursive subject; framed in and formed by the various and contrasting subject positions which serve to provide both the *means* of social interaction and *sense* of self-hood (see Mouffe, 1995; Game, 1991; Weedon, 1991; Saco, 1992 for elaboration). The act of reflexivity is, then, understood as an act of (gender) identity signification (Butler, 1990), wherein a 'person' engages in reflexively interpreting the social phenomena in which they find themselves, in part to mitigate the ontological insecurities of everyday life (Giddens, 1991). However, this is not to suggest, as Giddens does, that the 'reflexive project of self' is a consciously mediated action and experience in which the individual seeks to sustain coherent, 'yet continuously revised, biographical narratives' through 'multiple choice' (1991: 5). Rather, following Foucault (1983, 1988), I suggest that the 'self-reflexive actor' is never outside the (discursive) script, while not disallowing the potential for some modifications on their part. As Foucault puts it: 'The subject constitutes himself [sic] in an active fashion, by the practices of self, these practices are nevertheless not something that the individual invents by himself. They are patterns that he finds in his culture and which are proposed, suggested and imposed on him by his culture, his society and his social group' (1988: 11). However, having located self-reflexivity thus, questions are now raised as to the notion of gendered epistemology: can a feminist critical project survive the fractured, contingent 'reality' of postmodernity and post-structuralism (Assiter, 1996; Holmwood, 1995)? This is a key question for it cuts to the notion of the personal/ political (feminist/womanist) actor, grounded in (but resisting) the epistemological configurations of a 'robust patriarchal hegemony' (Ledwith and Colgan, 1996). The personal/political position that arises from resistance to such malestream ideology has been well documented elsewhere (see, for example, Stanley and Wise, 1993; Harding, 1991; Assiter, 1996), but is exemplified in the notion of a feminist-standpoint epistemology. This perspective considers women (as a marginalised group) to have uniquely valid insights materially grounded in the localised practices of the everyday world. Framed within the ruling (male) apparatus, women's insights are thus understood to provide unique knowledge of both women's oppression and men's oppressiveness.

Although the notion of a feminist epistemology is seen to provide many feminists with a bedrock from which to challenge and circumvent malestream ideology (O'Brien, 1981), the question as to whether or not there is a single feminist standpoint, or indeed that such a concept has a reification, continues to be hotly debated both by feminists and other commentators (see, for example, Hartsock, 1983; Harding, 1991; Smith, 1988; Holmwood, 1995; McLennon, 1995; Hammersley, 1992; Lennon, 1995). Certainly the concept of a singular epistemology, determined through a pre-given order of experiences, inevitably confronts the 'postmodern turn' of contingent and fractured identities (Holmwood, 1995). One feminist supporting the notion of a singular feminist standpoint is Hartsock (1983), who draws on the Marxist concept of the proletariat in order to recognise the 'particular and privileged vantage point [that women occupy] in respect of understanding "male supremacy"' (1983: 284). By contrast, Harding (1991), in questioning any notion of a singular 'feminist standpoint' or indeed, of an identity 'woman', appears to be aligning more closely with the multiplicity of indentities highlighted in post-structuralist and postmodern perspectives (see Lennon, 1995 for discussion). In so doing, Harding avoids the accusation of being drawn into the gender dichotomising which underpins much of the enlightenment and (malestream) modernist philosophising. For can any group of individuals be said to have a unique and valid everyday knowledge? Does not this perspective repeat the essentialistic, Cartesian assumption of 'core truths'? Certainly Hekman (1990) makes this very point, as, in a similar way, does Butler (1990).[3] Both argue against those deterministic assumptions that seek to privilege any particular epistemology. The question remains then, can there be a privileging of women's knowledge – is 'woman' a universal category?

Following a post-structuralist position, I would argue that neither 'man' nor 'woman' are reducible to a priori, essential or grounded ontologies. Yet ontological security, informed by the localised knowledges (as discourses) available to subjects, would appear to be a core given of a person's immersion in and search for (self)-identity (Giddens, 1991). In this respect, one's location in the social field, albeit across multiple subject positions (Mouffe, 1995), is both an expression of power/resistance, and a statement of 'reality' for that subject as social actor (Foucault, 1988). Thus feminist-standpoint epistemology, in giving voice to a 'reality' which exists 'out there' for the political category 'woman', is providing a language for further developing a personal/ political position from which to promote and exercise previously silent or silenced discourses. What emerges from this understanding is still a (discursive) subject but, as Foucault acknowledges, not one which is completely passive and unknowing, nor indeed, without validity. Rather, this subject has revolutionary potential, can resist and, in part, re-position herself through the means of her subjectivity – through language and discourse (see also Kristeva, 1986).

This perspective would appear to be substantially reinforced empirically by the recognition that despite centuries of male dominance, a significant number of women in European, American and Australasian countries, and indeed beyond, are now exercising a degree of independence and self-reflexivity, vis-à-vis gender relationships, which would have been literally unthinkable for most women only a few generations earlier. In this respect, the gendered subjectivities of millions of women, across all social classes and ethnic groupings, appears to have undergone change (see Beck and Beck-Gernsheim, 1995; Giddens, 1992 for discussion). And feminism can be credited with being a major political and discursive factor here, for it has provided a public language and consequent political verification with which to enable the self-reflexivity required for such epistemological and ontological transformation. In this respect, the issue of equal opportunities for women is now partly resolved. For those previously marginalised now have access to languages, knowledges and ways of being which assist in both 'resolving' ontological insecurity while validating that 'individual' as a personal/political actor in an otherwise stridently dichotomised landscape. But by definition equal opportunities, as practice, can never be wholly achieved by ontological transformations in a singular political category. Thus the question remains: to what extent have men changed?

Changing men, changing masculinities

The critical interrogation of men and masculinities is a relatively recent phenomenon, emerging out of the second-wave feminism of the 1970s and 1980s.[4] Prior to this, history was very much his-story, throughout which intellectual 'developments' continued to assume men as the given centre, with malestream thinking being exemplified across psychology, sociology and most other academic disciplines (Hearn and Morgan, 1990). Now even those (men) writers not previously known for their engagement with critical gender enquiry feel able, or obliged, to make some contribution to 'understanding gender' (see, for example, Giddens, 1992; Fukuyama, 1997). In this respect at least, some change has occurred in the subjectivities of some men, a transformation for which feminism can take much or most of the credit. Thus, whether one concurs with, for example, Giddens in respect of instrumentally engaged 'pure relationships' or Fukuyama's 'social disorder' thesis, there remains a strong sense of movement and transformation in respect of contemporary gender positionings.

While the critical analysis of men is barely two decades old, the developments ensuing from such study have been rapid and profound. It is now commonplace, for example, to assume the multiplicity of masculinities, the significance of social and cultural influences on masculinities, and the importance of recognising historical shifts in dominant and subordinated ways of being a man. The relationships between men, masculinities and, for example, work, language, discourse, identity, psychoanalysis, power, criminality, violence, sexuality, and ethnicity have been explored in some depth (see Whitehead, forthcoming, for overview and discussion), while the hegemonic characteristic of some forms of masculinity has been interrogated almost to exhaustion (see Kerfoot and Whitehead, 1998b for discussion). However, as this critical enquiry has developed more subtle and sophisticated perspectives, so has a tension emerged between balancing this recognition of differences between men with the 'fact' of patriarchy, 'gender order', and other such blanket political categorisations of male oppression. This dilemma is, of course, one which feminist scholars are fully familiar with in respect of women, sisterhood, political assertion and resistance (see Nicholson, 1990 for discussion).

The question of 'men's sameness' is, then, directly linked to the debates surrounding a core feminist/womanist epistemology and ontology examined earlier. The fundamental question is, however, slightly different. For in examining or seeking to find a core masculine epistemological form, the issue is simply whether or not most men are even aware they have a gender, not, as in the case of women, whether their gender awareness constitutes an ontological and unitary standpoint. Michael Kimmel captures the dilemma quite succinctly: 'When I look in the mirror... I see a human being – a white middle-class male – gender is invisible to me because that is where *I* am privileged. I am the norm. I believe most men do not know they have a gender' (quote taken from Middleton, 1992: 11). As Middleton (p. 11) goes on to note, the notion of a male self-reflexive subject is problematic because 'men don't see what they are seeing when they see themselves'. Middleton suggests this 'blocked re-flexivity' to be a result of masculinity's 'denial of emotion', an aspect of men's ontological relationship to self and other. In this respect, Giddens' understanding of self-reflexivity is fundamentally compromised. For while on one hand he promotes the notion of late modernity as being characterised by individualism and the project of self (Giddens, 1991), in terms of gender and sexual relationships he notes that men are 'lagging behind [women] in the transitions now occurring... in Western culture' (Giddens, 1992: 59). While prepared to accept 'masculinity as problem-atic' (1992) in terms of men's transformations of self, Giddens, like many male sociologists, appears unable, or unwilling, to offer an explanation as to why this might be.

Not surprisingly it has been feminists who have alerted men to the transparent 'obliviousness' in their 'gendered attitudes, prejudices and motivations' (Roberts, 1984; also Segal, 1990). Thus a challenge is presented to men which some male academics have responded to in a positive and personal manner (see, for example, Hearn, 1987; Morgan, 1992; Rutherford, 1992; Tolson, 1977; Jackson, 1990). Yet, as within the academic community, the responses to feminism outside academe have been diverse if not confused. Where writers such as Hearn, Morgan, Tolson and Rutherford can be termed 'pro-feminist' – men working with feminists to transform the existing 'gender order' – others, for example Bly (1990) and McCartney (1992), have sought to reconfirm men's power and social positioning through recourse, and retreat to an essentialistic mythopoetic, sometimes Christian-based, masculinity. A similar anti-feminist response can be found in the various men's rights movements. Emerging out of 'consciousness-raising' groups of the early 1970s, men's rights advocates found a political platform, and ready support from many other men over issues of child maintenance, child custody, equal opportunities at work, and the rigidity of traditional (Western) male sex roles (see Messner, 1997 for elaboration). Thus the 'changing masculinities' which at first glance seem apparent, on closer examination are seen to be less about men's enlightenment and more about strategic responses to perceived loss of gendered power. Similarly, the 'new man', of which much was expected in the late 1980s, turned out in the main to be no more than yet another media invention; a catchy but simplistic outcome of the tabloidisation of complex social phenomena.

The responses by the mythopoetic and men's rights movements to feminism confirm the capacity of the masculine subject to shift in response to external imperatives, while maintaining location within the social and cultural parameters which would define and confirm its gendered status and identity (Kerfoot and Whitehead, 1998a). Thus, at a fundamental level, little is either changed or challenged for men. And this is an important point. For while it is possible to argue that masculinity is fundamentally illusory (see MacInnes, 1998), it is less easy to deny the political ramifications of masculinity as language and practice in most social arenas. Moreover, the automatic loss of status and material privilege for men which goes with equity and equality for women would appear, for many men, to be a bridge too far (see Morgan, 1990 for discussion). There is a material actuality to masculinity which serves to confirm and reinforce the politicised categories of man and woman. Thus those men able/prepared to perceive themselves as gendered subjects have, at some point, to address both material issues vis-à-vis women, and, on a highly personal level, those questions pertaining to masculine identity. For in engaging in alternative discursive realities, certainly those articulated within a (pro)-feminist frame, men are required to engage reflexively with their own ontological security as it has come to be 'achieved' in a maleist[5] paradigm. Clearly there are both opportunities and threats here. For in confronting and attempting to 'resolve' the existential question 'Who am I as man?', the occupier of this particular gendered configuration is increasingly denied refuge in traditional ways of being a man. The opportunity that ensues from such social and individual transformation should not, I suggest, be seen simply in terms of material advantage (there is unlikely to be any), but in the multiplicity of ontological positions which then become available to those men prepared to disengage from hegemonic, oppressive patterns of masculine behaviour. Simply put, those men who do positively respond to the questions laid down by feminists/feminisms are likely to have opened to them multiple and positive ways of being a man, outside of traditional gender stereotypes.

Women and men talking of gender

The research from which the following quotes are drawn was a larger project investigating the changing work cultures of UK postcompulsory education, and, specifically, men managers' experience and perception of this change.[6] The qualitative interviews were designed to elicit men managers' subjective interpretations of working in a rapidly changing, male-dominated, organisational setting. In addition, a small number of interviews were undertaken with women education managers. The quotes provide an interesting comparative analysis of women's and men's subjective understanding of their gender and its relationship to organisational experience and advancement.

The politicised epistemology of the woman manager

From very early in the research it became clear that whatever other imperatives might be influencing or driving a changing education work culture, e.g. government policy, post-industrialisation, and so on, other key influences were at work in the institutional setting. However, these influences were apparently being experienced and understood quite differently by women and men managers. This expression of gendered separateness was not only in respect of (un)equal opportunities and gendered cultural formations, but also related to gendered epistemology. For what emerged from talking to women managers was the politicised epistemology which they had constructed for themselves, and, importantly, had been constructed by, as a result of organisational (and other) experiences. The sense that these women had both of being women and of being positioned as 'outsiders' or 'intruders' (Ledwith and Colgan, 1996; Gherardi, 1995) as a consequence of their gender was quite acute. Typical of this was Interviewee 1, a woman principal of a large UK college. She recalled the physical and verbal intimidation she had suffered at the hands of men since assuming charge of her college:

> On one memorable occasion a man just stormed into my office and shouted at me in a really threatening manner. He just used his physical presence to try to intimidate me . . . I have had my car scratched and damaged in the car park on more than one occasion. It has been very difficult at times . . . I've suffered from violent nightmares on a number of occasions. But I'm still here.

Even outside her college, for example when attending large national education functions, this principal is constantly reminded of her 'uniqueness' in respect of the gendered constitution of education senior management: 'I've considered not going to any more big national functions for college principals and senior managers. It's just a men's club.'

This woman was, however, responding to the traditional gendered constitution of UK colleges in a practical, yet political fashion; she was slowly restructing her senior management teams, and in the process bringing more women into the higher echelons of the institution. She stated her intention quite clearly: to feminize the college by 'empowering a group of women at senior management level'.

A second woman principal, Interviewee 2, was responding to 'equal opportunities issues in education' in a similar way to the first. That is, she was active both in terms of her own college in trying to facilitate a college culture of 'co-operation rather than competition', while also being involved in the UK 'National Network for Women Managers in Further and Continuing Education'. Again, there is this strong sense of 'woman' as a political category, which simultaneously transcends and yet informs organisational, and individual, processes and experiences.

The gendered subjectivities of these two women principals are similarly reflected in accounts other women further education, senior managers give of their experiences climbing the 'greasy pole', an example being the research into women in education management undertaken by the Further Education Development Agency (1997):

> The current FE culture favours the macho-style principal who will be a 'hatchet man' in a downsizing. (1997: 54)
>
> The glass ceiling does exist, so don't assume your problems are necessarily your own fault. (1997: 59)
>
> The only way to beat the system that I have found, in what is still a male-dominated profession, is to consistently deliver what you promise. (1997: 28)

Of course, Interviewees 1 and 2 do have the advantage of being prominent and visible, not least because, as women, they still represent a minority of senior managers in postcompulsory education (FEDA, 1997). Consequently, their views on gender issues are often sought and both are quite prominent spokeswomen for education at a national level. So when I asked them questions about gender and management, their epistemological and ontological awareness was already 'switched on', and, moreover, finely tuned and readily articulated. By contrast, an interview I undertook with a woman middle manager employed in a large northern UK college gave a more 'real' feel for being unplanned and therefore more spontaneous. The unique circumstances of the interview probably contributed to the emotional outpourings which ensued. Thus it was this interview as much as any other which emphasised for me the epistemological gulf between men and women (managers).

This manager, together with her male colleague, had arranged to visit my college to discuss possible links and developments between our respective departments. The connection arose from a visit I had made to their college three weeks earlier. During that visit I had interviewed their head of department for the wider research project. At the conclusion of the interview the head of department and I had discussed areas of mutual interest in respect of new course developments. We agreed that I would meet two of his team to further this. I was duly contacted and, sensing an opportunity to undertake a further interview with a man manager, I asked the male colleague if he would partake in the research when he visited my college. This he agreed to do. Subsequently, the three of us met at my college, in a private room with little possibility of interruption. Knowing that only a few weeks earlier I had interviewed their line manager, both individuals were intrigued as to what the interview and the wider research project were about. I was unable to reveal too much, both because I had to maintain confidentiality and because I had arranged to interview the male colleague later that day – I felt that discussing the research focus in depth prior to the interview would only 'tarnish' the response I was likely to get from him. However, I did reveal that I was investigating issues around men college managers, in particular looking at gender in education organisations. Quite unprompted, the woman manager immediately went into a lengthy and revealing diatribe on her experiences as a manager in that particular college, and of how being a woman affected and influenced all aspects of her working, and non-working life. She spoke of the ways (gendered) expectations were created around her which were both powerful and, at times, very constraining. These expectations of, for example, language, dress, ambition, opportunity and skill confronted her in both the dominant culture of the college and in the everyday minutiae of intersubjective communication. It was a gendered condition which both repelled her and which she yet felt compelled to continuously 'manage'; an investment in emotional labour and (gendered) identity work which Gherardi (1995) describes as 'schizogenic' for women managers in organisational life. Her unscripted and unexpected response was very illuminating, not angry or bitter, but very matter of fact. It seemed that my comments to her about the research aims had triggered an 'alternative' epistemological form, one which seldom raised its head in her everyday presentation of self as a power-dressed, hard-headed manager.

What was equally revealing was her colleague's response to all this, for he was completely nonplussed. When I later interviewed him (alone) he admitted that although the two had worked closely together for over fourteen years, he had never heard her talk like that: about her gender, about being a woman in the organisation. As a result of hearing her engage in what was in effect for him a new language, it appeared his perception of her had shifted. It was as if a new person was revealed, one who no longer fitted the comfortable stereotypes which, as he saw it, had previously 'secured' both his and her (organisational) identities.

This experience, underlined in the responses I received from women senior managers, confirmed the sense of difference between men and women in these colleges. Not just in terms of equal opportunities, but at a much more fundamental level: in terms of knowledge, understanding and self-awareness. Like it or not, as women in these gendered organisations they had to be political. They were given little choice.

Man – the invisible gendered subject?

The responses from women managers were in stark contrast to those I received from men managers. The interviews with the men usually lasted for over 90 minutes and were quite extensive and revealing of their experiences and perceptions of new cultures and associated practices in UK education (see Whitehead, 1998, 1999). In the interviews with the men managers I always ended with the same question: 'Do you think your experiences in education, as a manager, have in any way been affected by you being a man?' The question was clearly designed to elicit a similar response to that which I had garnered so readily, and often unprompted, from women managers. That is, in what ways had gender been a factor in terms of career progression, experience of organisational life, and, ultimately, broader life experiences. However, unlike the women I spoke to, these men appeared to be floored by this question. On occasions it was as if I had spoken in an incomprehensible language. The majority had no sense of what the question meant or was referring to. They appeared never to have reflected on themselves as men, indeed, never felt the need to reflect on themselves as men. Their manhood, maleness, masculinity was a given, a universal 'fact'. It was as if all else revolved around this, with them as the centre. It was like questioning the existence of the sun, sky, or air we breathe:

Response 1: 'Mmm . . . interesting; can you expand on that to help me?'
Response 2: 'I don't know . . . I really don't know how I could answer that.'
Response 3: 'I don't know . . . I've just been lucky really.'
Response 4: 'That is difficult. Difficult to give you a realistic answer . . . I'm not a woman.'
Response 5: 'Mmm . . . [pause] . . . mmm . . . another question to ask my wife!'
Response 6: 'I don't know. I can't answer that.'
Response 7: 'Don't know; most of my appointments have been women.'
Response 8: 'No idea . . . I can't answer that question.'

Response 9: 'I've never thought about it; I don't treat women differently.'
Response 10: 'I'm not aware of it, not conscious of it ... a difficult question.'
Response 11: 'I don't think so ... you can't know.'
Response 12: 'Oh God! I don't know ... I've always tried to treat men and women similarly.'
Response 13: 'No, I'm lucky, I've always worked with men.'
Response 14: 'Difficult to answer that; I've never been a woman.'

Some made what appeared to be a brave attempt at responding to the question in a positive, reflective way, but tended to get lost as they talked, often bringing into their answer points related to 'not knowing women', 'treating them all equally', and so on. Many tended to tail off as they tried to engage with the 'intricacies' of the question:

Response 15: 'Yes, but I'm not sure where I go with that.'
Response 16: 'Yes, but ...'
Response 17: 'I'm not sure; it must have been ... yes, it's made a difference.'
Response 18: 'Yes, I tend to be more logical, a systems man.'
Response 19: 'Yes, because I work in a male-orientated environment.'

Respondent 19 was the only manager who equated the gendered environment in which he lived and worked with his own gender and sense of being. For all the other managers any connection escaped them. Certainly any critical understanding of themselves as 'men' was beyond them. For many, the question was pointless, some implying that I should ask women what it meant for them to be men.

Discussion and conclusion

In suggesting that women 'know us better than we know ourselves', maybe these men managers have made a valid point, albeit unintentionally. For while it does appear to be the case that many women are experiencing some significant transformation in their gendered subjectivities, particularly those women who daily confront masculinist cultures, the evidence for men changing is less pronounced. And in this respect the argument put forward by, amongst others, Stanley and Wise (1993) and Hartsock (1983) for recognising the particular knowledges of women as more valid, in comparison that is to many men's, seems verified. For women, despite the progress made in European, Australasian and American countries towards gender justice, remain positioned as the 'other', particularly in respect of organisationally specific, hegemonic forms of masculinity. Thus, while recognising the diversity of women's lives, and not wishing to assign essentialistic anchors to either 'man' or 'woman', I would suggest that women's marginalisation does provide an 'epistemic privilege' informed by 'strong reflexivity' (Lennon, 1995: 141; also Assiter, 1996; Benhabib and Cornell, 1987). This would go a significant way to explaining why womanist epistemological formations are outside the understanding of most, or at least many, men. A knowledge divide which is apparent from this, albeit specifically located, research.

While recognising that self-reflexivity is a tool by which a person comes to some 'understanding' of themselves vis-à-vis available discourses, it would appear inadequate to assume, as Giddens does, that the 'I' consequently disengages from its gendered self as a result of this process. It may well be, as Beck and Beck-Gernsheim (1995: 24) argue, that 'people are shaking off rigid gender roles', an 'individualisation process' which challenges the 'very foundations of industrial society'. More likely it is the case that the new knowledges now available to women, mainly as a result of feminism, provide a voice, resonance and political verification for their new 'trajectories of self' (Giddens, 1991). Thus the pluralisation of possibilities for women seems apparent, especially in respect of the increasing multiplicity of female ontologies.

The same cannot, however, be said of men. In examining the likelihood of men changing, Morgan (1990) concludes that, whether at home or at work, men are unlikely to actively seek a diminishment of 'personal status' (see also Heath, 1987). Yet even this pessimistic viewpoint assumes that men are able to see the 'nature' of the gendered worlds in which they live. For one would expect some degree of self-awareness in respect of gender before an individual embarks on what Giddens (1991) has described as the 'reflexive project of self', in this instance, men changing.

In addition, given that there is in post-structuralist terms no 'pre-discursive reality' (Mitchell and Rose, 1982), a further question emerges regarding the capacity of the self to 'know itself' outside of discourse. As Lacan (1977) implies, how can 'I' step outside that which constitutes 'me'; what knowledge exists prior to its language and practice? For contrary to some perspectives (see, for example, Connell, 1993; Middleton, 1992), I would argue that masculinity (as language, practice and symbol) is a *discursive construct*, providing a ready and privileged means of gender signification for men (Butler, 1990). Change can only come, then, through the subject's immersion in and inculcation of alternative discourses, not through recourse to some pre-discursive reality. The accomplishment of feminist thought has been to propagate alternative discourses; new knowledges and ways of being which have had resonance for countless women, far beyond the cells of academe. However, as discussed, for many men adoption of (pro)feminism is complex, fraught and potentially threatening to their ontological security given the decentring of men and masculinity inherent in feminist discourse.[7] Thus the question of men changing remains unresolved. Yet, at the very least, it is crucial that men come to some understanding and appreciation of the wider implications of what being a man means for their gendered subjectivity, that is, if there is to be what Connell (1995) describes as 'gender justice'. If real change is to occur across both genders, not just with women, then there has to be a deeper response by men, other than an instrumental one – typified in 'essentialist retreats' – to the challenges posited by women in respect of power, influence and material (dis)advantage.

From the comments I have recorded, together with my own understanding of the masculine subject and hegemonic masculine ways of being, I very much doubt that many men are able to readily grasp the 'gendered reality' which surrounds them, and indeed significantly forms them. But this act of gendered self-reflexivity would appear critical if change in men's practices is to come about. It is possible, of course, that women's re-positioning through multiple ontological locations provides the pressure for men to reflect on themselves as men. For in the act of re-positioning themselves, women are centring themselves, or at the very least making a political statement as 'non-Other'. And certainly there is some evidence for this in some areas of the social network. However, I would suggest that the higher echelons of professional and organisational life remain most resistant to this type of transformation. The reasons for this are twofold: firstly the continued numerical dominance of men across the public sphere and, secondly, the masculinist work cultures now entrenched across organisational life. Certainly there is little evidence that either gendered condition is abating (Ledwith and Colgan, 1996; Connell, 1998; Whitehead and Moodley, 1999). Thus, while on the surface at least, equal opportunities in organisations appears to have an unstoppable momentum, even to the extent of it now being labelled an 'obsession' by some (see, for example, Conway, 1998), to assume deeper cultural shifts would be premature. For the dominant epistemological form in professional and managerial life remains highly gendered, structured as it has been by the partial, incomplete but dominant understandings and perspectives of countless men. To talk, then, of fundamental social gender transformations is somewhat premature, given that only one half of society appears to be experiencing such a personal, and political, shift.

ACKNOWLEDGEMENT

I would like to thank Sheila Scraton and Jeff Hearn for their support in the larger research project informing this chapter.

NOTES

1   Much of the debate on self-reflexivity continues to be framed in an under-standing of the self as a dichotomised entity, wherein the expression of, and possibilities for, life narratives are seen to be determined by the structural conditions presupposing such agency. Moreover, the debate posits self-reflexivity in different ways. For example, as 'unintentional self-dissolution' (Beck, in Beck et al., 1995; as the uncovering of unthought categories (Bour-dieu, 1992); and as a tool in the conscious trajectories of self (Giddens, 1991).
2   The 'unencumbered monad' relates to Sartre's conception of the existential self. Such a concept has been critiqued by feminists for being a male vision, one which ignores the unique situatedness of, for example, female embodi-ment (see McNay, 1994; Benhabib and Cornell, 1987).
3   See also Benhabib and Cornell (1987) for discussion.
4   Earliest examples of critical gender enquiry by men into men and masculin-ities include those of Tolson, 1977; Pleck, 1976; Fein, 1978.
5   I use the term 'maleist' to describe a male-centred view of the world, one which, by definition, posits female, girl/woman, feminine as marginal, partial, and for ever relational to male.
6   There is an extensive and growing literature on the gendered constitution of organisations, and the particular masculinities (see Collinson and Hearn, 1996) and ways of being man (see Kerfoot and Knights, 1996) which serve to reinforce and validate managerial and professional identities (see also Dent and Whitehead, forthcoming, for examples).
7   See Morgan (1992) and Jardine and Smith (1987) for discussion as to the many tensions and ambiguities for men in feminism.

REFERENCES

Assiter, A. (1996) *Enlightened Women: Modernist Feminism in a Postmodern Age* (London, Routledge).
Beck, U. and Beck-Gernsheim, E. (1995) *The Normal Chaos of Love* (Cam-bridge, Polity).
Beck, U., Giddens, A. and Lash, S. (1995) *Reflexive Modernisation* (Cambridge, Polity).

Benhabib, S. and Cornell, D. (Eds) (1987) *Feminism as Critique* (Cambridge, Polity).

Bly, R. (1990) *Iron John: A Book about Men* (Reading, MA: Addison-Wesley).

Bourdieu, P. (1992) *An Invitation to Reflexive Sociology* (Cambridge, Polity).

Butler, J. (1990) *Gender Trouble* (New York, Routledge).

Collinson, D. L. and Hearn, J. (Eds) (1996) *Men as Managers, Managers as Men* (London, Sage).

Connell, R. W. (1993) The Big Picture: Masculinities in Recent World History, *Theory and Society*, 22, pp. 597–623.

Connell, R. W. (1995) *Masculinities* (Cambridge, Polity).

Connell, R. W. (1998) Masculinities and Globalization, *Men and Masculinities*, 1, 1, pp. 3–23.

Conway, D. (1998) Just the Job, or the Worst of all Worlds? *The Times*, 27 April, 1998, p. 22.

Dent, M. and Whitehead, S. (Eds) (forthcoming) *Managing Professional Identities: Knowledge Performativity and the 'New' Professional* (London, Routledge).

Fein, R. (1978) Research on Fathering: Social Policy and an Emergent Perspective, *Journal of Social Issues*, 34, 1, pp. 201–226.

Foucault, M. (1983) Structuralism and Poststructuralism: An Interview with Michel Foucault, *Telos*, 55, pp. 195–211.

Foucault, M. (1988) The Ethic of Care for the Self as a Practice of Freedom, in J. Bernauer and D. Rasmussen (Eds) *The Final Foucault* (Cambridge, Mass.: MIT Press).

Fukuyama, F. (1997) *The End of Order* (London, Social Market Foundation).

Further Education Development Agency (1997) *Women at the Top in Further Education* (London, FEDA).

Game, A. (1991) *Undoing the Social* (Milton Keynes, Open University Press).

Gherardi, S. (1995) *Gender, Symbolism and Organizational Cultures* (London, Sage).

Giddens, A. (1991) *Modernity and Self-Identity* (Cambridge, Polity).

Giddens, A. (1992) *The Transformation of Intimacy* (Cambridge, Polity).

Hammersley, M. (1992) On Feminist Methodology, *Sociology*, 26, 2, pp. 187–206.

Harding, S. (1991) *Whose Science, Whose Knowledge?* (Milton Keynes, Open University Press).

Hartsock, N. C. M. (1983) The Feminist Standpoint: Developing the Ground for a Specifically Feminist Historical Materialism, in S. Harding and M. B. Hintikka (Eds) *Discovering Reality* (Dordrecht, Reidel).

Hearn, J. (1987) *The Gender of Oppression* (Brighton, Wheatsheaf).

Hearn, J. and Morgan, D. (1990) *Men, Masculinities and Social Theory* (London, Unwin Hyman).

Heath, S. (1987) Male Feminism, in A. Jardine and P. Smith (Eds) *Men in Feminism* (London, Methuen).

Hekman, S. J. (1990) *Gender and Knowledge: Elements of a Postmodern Feminism* (Cambridge, Polity).

Holmwood, J. (1995) Feminism and Epistemology: What Kind of Successor Science? *Sociology*, 29, 3, pp. 411–428.

Horrocks, R. (1994) *Masculinity in Crisis: Myths, Fantasies and Realities* (London, Macmillan).

Jackson, C. (1990) *Unmasking Masculinity* (London, Unwin Hyman).

Jardine, A. and Smith, P. (Eds) (1987) *Men in Feminism* (London, Methuen).

Kerfoot, D. and Knights, D. (1996) The Best is Yet to Come? The Quest for Embodiment in Managerial Work, in D. L. Collinson and J. Hearn (Eds) *Men as Managers, Managers as Men* (London, Sage).

Kerfoot, D. and Whitehead, S. (1998a) 'Boys Own' Stuff: Masculinity and the Management of Further Education, *The Sociological Review*, 46, 3, pp. 436–457.

Kerfoot, D. and Whitehead, S. (1998b) W(h)ither Hegemonic Masculinity. Paper given to the Gendering the Millennium international conference, University of Dundee, 11–13 September, 1998.

Kristeva, J. (1986) A New Type of Intellectual: The Dissident, in T. Moi (Ed) *The Kristeva Reader* (New York, Columbia University Press).

Lacan, J. (1977) *Ecrits: A Selection* (tr. A. Sheridan) (London, Tavistock).

Ledwith, S. and Colgan, F. (Eds) (1996) *Women in Organizations: Challenging Gender Politics* (London, Macmillan).

Lennon, K. (1995) Gender and Knowledge, *Journal of Gender Studies*, 4, 2, pp. 133–143.

McCartney, B. (Ed) (1992) *What Makes a Man? The 12 Promises That Will Change Your Life* (Colorado Springs, CO: Nav Press).

MacInnes, J. (1998) *The End of Masculinity* (Buckingham, Open University Press).

McLennon, G. (1995) Feminism, Epistemology and Postmodernism: Reflections on Current Ambivalence, *Sociology*, 29, 3, pp. 391–410.

McNay, L. (1994) *Foucault: A Critical Introduction* (Cambridge, Polity).

Messner, M. A. (1997) *The Politics of Masculinities* (London, Sage).

Middleton, P. (1992) *The Inward Gaze: Masculinity and Subjectivity in Modern Culture* (London, Routledge).

Mitchell, J. and Rose, J. (Eds) (1982) *Feminine Sexuality: Jacques Lacan and 'Ecole Freudienne'* (London, Macmillan).

Morgan, D. H. J. (1990) Issues of Critical Sociological Theory: Men in Families, in J. Sprey (Ed) *Fashioning Family Theory* (London, Sage).

Morgan, D. H. J. (1992) *Discovering Men* (London, Routledge).

Mouffe, C. (1995) Feminism, Citizenship and Radical Democratic Politics, in L. Nicholson and S. Seidman (Eds) *Social Postmodernism: Beyond Identity Politics* (Cambridge, Cambridge University Press).

Nicholson, L. J. (Ed) (1990) *Feminism/Postmodernism* (New York, Routledge).

O'Brien, M. (1981) *The Politics of Reproduction* (London, Routledge and Kegan Paul).

Pleck, J. H. (1976) The Male Sex Role, *Journal of Social Issues*, 32, pp. 155–164.

Roberts, Y. (1984) *Man Enough: Men of Thirty-Five Speak Out* (London, Chatto).

Rutherford, J. (1992) *Men's Silences* (London, Routledge).

Saco, D. (1992) Masculinity as Signs: Poststructuralist Approaches to the Study of Gender, in S. Craig (Ed) *Men, Masculinity and the Media* (London, Sage).

Segal, L. (1990) *Slow Motion: Changing Masculinities, Changing Men* (London, Virago).

Smith, D. E. (1988) *The Everyday World as Problematic: A Feminist Sociology* (Milton Keynes, Open University Press).

Stanley, L. and Wise, S. (1993) *Breaking Out Again: Feminist Ontology and Epistemology* (London, Routledge).

Tolson, A. (1977) *The Limits of Masculinity* (London, Tavistock).

Walter, N. (1997) *The New Feminism* (London, Little, Brown and Company)

Weedon, C. (1991) *Feminist Practice and Poststructuralist Theory* (Oxford, Basil Blackwell).

Whitehead, S. (1998) Disrupted Selves: Resistance and Identity Work in the Managerial Arena, *Gender and Education*, 10, 2, pp. 199–215.

Whitehead, S. (1999) From Paternalism to Entrepreneurialism: The Experience of Men Managers in UK Postcompulsory Education, *Discourse: Studies in the Cultural Politics of Education*, 20, 1, pp. 57–72.

Whitehead, S. (forthcoming) *Men and Masculinities: Key Themes and New Directions in the Sociology of Masculinity* (Cambridge, Polity).

Whitehead, S. and Moodley, R. (Eds) (1999) *Transforming Managers: Gendering Change in the Public Sector* (London, UCL Press).

Wilkinson, H. (1994) *No Turning Back: Generations and the Genderquake* (London, Demos).

21

Masculinity Politics on a World Scale

R. W. Connell

Writings across the sociology of masculinity have made important changes in our understanding of masculinities and men's practices, emphasizing the plurality and hierarchy of masculinities, and their collective and dynamic character. These gains have been achieved mainly by close-focus research methods. But in a globalizing world, we must pay attention also to very large-scale structures. An understanding of the world gender order is a necessary basis for thinking about men and masculinities globally. Hegemony in the contemporary gender order is connected with patterns of trade, investment, and communication dominated by the North. A transnational business masculinity, institutionally based in multinational corporations and global finance markets, is arguably the emerging dominant form on a world scale.

We might propose, then, that the hegemonic form of masculinity in the current world order is the masculinity associated with those who control its dominant institutions: the business executives who operate in global markets, and the political executives who interact (and in many contexts, merge) with them. I will call this *transnational business masculinity*. This is not readily available for ethnographic study, but we can get some clues to its character from its reflections in management literature, business journalism, and corporate self-promotion, and from studies of local business elites (e.g. Donaldson 1977).

As a first approximation, I would suggest this is a masculinity marked by increasing egocentrism, very conditional loyalties (even to the corporation), and a declining sense of responsibility for others (except for purposes of image making). Gee, Hull, and Lankshear (1996), studying recent management textbooks, note the peculiar construction of the executive in 'fast capitalism' as a person with no permanent commitments, except (in effect) to the idea of accumulation itself. Transnational business masculinity is characterized by a limited technical rationality (management theory), which is increasingly separate from science.

Transnational business masculinity differs from traditional bourgeois masculinity by its increasingly libertarian sexuality, with a growing tendency to commodify relations with women. Hotels catering to businessmen in most parts of the world routinely offer pornographic videos, and in some parts of the world there is a well-developed prostitution industry catering for international businessmen. Transnational business masculinity does not require bodily force, since the patriarchal dividend on which it rests is accumulated by impersonal, institutional means. But corporations increasingly use the exemplary bodies of elite sportsmen as a marketing tool (note the phenomenal growth of corporate 'sponsorship' of sport in the last generation) and indirectly as a means of legitimation for the whole gender order.

Recognizing global society as an arena of masculinity formation allows us to pose new questions about masculinity politics. What social dynamics in the global arena give rise to masculinity politics, and what shape does global masculinity politics take?

The gradual creation of a world gender order has meant many local institutions of gender. Gender instability is a familiar theme of poststructuralist theory, but this school of thought takes as a universal condition a situation that is historically specific. Instabilities range from the disruption of men's local cultural dominance as women move into the public realm and higher education, through the disruption of sexual identities that produced 'queer' politics in the metropole, to the shifts in the urban intelligentsia that produced 'the new sensitive man' and other images of gender change.

One response to such instabilities, on the part of groups whose power is challenged but still dominant, is to reaffirm *local* gender orthodoxies and hierarchies. A masculine fundamentalism is, accordingly, a common response in gender politics at present. A soft version, searching for an essential masculinity amongst the myths and symbols, is offered by the mythopoetic men's movement in the United States and by the religious revivalists of the Promise Keepers (Messner 1997). A much harder version is found, in that country, in the right-wing militia movement brought to world attention by the Oklahoma City bombing (Gibson 1994), and in contemporary Afghanistan, if we can trust Western media reports, in the militant misogyny of the Taliban. It is no coincidence that in the two latter cases, hardline masculine fundamentalism goes together with a marked anti-internationalism. The world system – right enough – is seen as the source of pollution and disruption.

Not that the emerging global order is a hotbed of gender progressivism. Indeed, the neoliberal agenda for the reform of national and international economies involves closing down historic possibilities for gender reform. Not only has it subverted the gender compromise represented by the metropolitan welfare state, it also undermined the progressive-liberal agendas of sex-role reform represented by affirmative action programs, antidiscrimination provisions, child care services, and the like. Rightwing parties and governments have been persistently cutting such programs, in the name of either individual liberties or global competitiveness. Through these means, the patriarchal dividend to men is defended or restored, without an *explicit* masculinity politics in the form of a mobilization of men.

Within the arenas of international relations, the international state, multinational corporations, and global markets, there is nevertheless a deployment of masculinities and a reasonably clear hegemony. The transnational business masculinity described above has had only one major competitor for hegemony in recent decades, the rigid, control-orientated masculinity of the military, and the military-style bureaucratic dictatorships of Stalinism. With the collapse of Stalinism and the end of the cold war, Big Brother (Orwell's famous parody of this form of masculinity) is a fading threat, and the more flexible, calculative, egocentric masculinity of the fast capitalist entrepreneur holds world stage.

We must, however, recall two important conclusions of the ethnographic moment in masculinity research: that different forms of masculinity exist together and that hegemony is constantly subject to challenge. These are possibilities in the global arena too. Transnational business masculinity is not completely homogenous: variations of it are embedded in different parts of the world system, which may not be completely compatible. We may distinguish a Confucian variant, based in East Asia, with a stronger commitment to hierarchy and social consensus, from a secularized Christian variant, based in North America, with more hedonism and individualism and greater tolerance for social conflict. In certain arenas, there is already conflict between the business and political leaderships embodying these forms of masculinity: initially over human rights versus Asian values, and more recently over the extent of trade and investment liberalization.

If these are contenders for hegemony, there is also the possibility of opposition to hegemony. The global circulation of 'gay' identities (Altman 1996) is an important indication that nonhegemonic masculinities may operate in global arenas, and may even find a certain political articulation, in this case around human rights and AIDS prevention.

Critiques of dominant forms of masculinity have been circulating for some time among heterosexual men, or among groups that are

predominantly heterosexual. English-language readers will be most familiar with three Anglophone examples: the antisexist or profeminist men's
groups in the United States, with their umbrella group NOMAS (National
Organization for Men Against Sexism), which has been running since the
early 1980s (Cohen 1991); the British new left men's groups, which
produced the remarkable magazine *Achilles Heel* (Seidler 1991); and the
Canadian White Ribbon campaign, the most successful mass mobilization
of men opposing men's violences against women (Kaufman 1997).

There are parallel developments in other language communities. In
Germany, for instance, feminists launched a discussion of gender of men
in the 1980s (Metz-Goeckel and Mueller 1986; Hagemann-White and
Rerrich 1988), which has been followed by an educational (Kindler
1993), a popular-psychology (Hollstein 1992), and a critical (*Widersprueche* 1995; BauSteineMaenner 1996) debate among men about
masculinities and how to change them. In Scandinavia, gender reform
and debates about men (Oftung 1994) have led to the 'father's quota' of
parental leave in Norway (Gender Equality Ombudsman 1997) and to a
particularly active network of masculinity researchers. In Japan, a media
debate about men's liberation and some pioneering books about
changing masculinities (Ito 1993; Nakamura 1994) have been followed
by the foundation of a men's center and diversifying debates on change.

These developments at national or regional levels have very recently
begun to link internationally. An International Association for the Studies of Men has begun to link men involved in critical studies of masculinity. Certain international agencies, including the United Nations
Educational, Scientific and Cultural Organization (UNESCO) (1997),
have sponsored conferences to discuss the policy implications of new
perspectives on masculinity.

Compared with concentration of institutional power in multinational
businesses, these initiatives remain small-scale and dispersed. They are,
nevertheless, important in potential. I have argued that the global gender
order contains, necessarily, greater plurality of gender forms than any
local gender order. This must reinforce the consciousness that masculinity is not one fixed form. The plurality of masculinities at least symbolically prefigures the unconstrained creativity of a democratic gender order.

Concluding note on research

If the perspective set out in this chapter holds well, it suggests a significant refocusing of the research agenda on masculinities. There is already

a move beyond strictly local studies in the direction of comparative studies from different parts of the world (Cornwall and Lindisfarne 1994; UNESCO 1997). My argument suggests moving beyond this again, to study of the global arena itself, both as a venue for the social construction of masculinities and as a powerful force in local gender dynamics. Such a move will require a reconsideration of research methods, since the life-history and ethnographic methods that have been central to recent work on masculinities give limited grasp on the very large-scale institutions, markets, and mass communications that are in play on the world scale. Finally, the typical researcher of recent years – the individual scholar with a research project – will need to be supplemented by international teams, able to work together for significant periods, to investigate issues of the scale and complexity we must now address.

REFERENCES

Altman, Dennis. 1996. Rupture or continuity? The internationalisation of gay identities. *Social Text* 48(3): 77–94.

BauSteineMaenner, ed. 1996. *Kritische Maennerforschung* [Critical research on men]. Berlin: Argument.

Cohen, Jon. 1991. NOMAS: Challenging male supremacy. *Changing Men* (Winter/Spring): 45–46.

Cornwall, Andrea, and Nancy Lindisfarne, eds. 1994. *Dislocating masculinity: Comparative ethnographies*. London: Routledge.

Donaldson, Mike. 1997. Growing up very rich: The masculinity of the hegemonic. Paper presented at the conference Masculinities: Renegotiating Genders, June, University of Wollongong, Australia.

Gee, James Paul, Glynda Hull, and Colin Lankshear. 1996. *The new world order: Behind the language of the new capitalism*. Sydney: Allen & Unwin.

Gender Equality Ombudsman. 1997. *The father's quota*. Information sheet on parental leave entitlements, Oslo.

Gibson, J. William. 1994. *Warrior dreams: Paramilitary culture in post-Vietnam America*. New York: Hill and Wang.

Hagemann-White, Carol, and Maria S. Rerrich, eds. 1988. *FrauenMaennerBilder* [Women, imagining, men]. Bielefeld: AJZ-Verlag.

Hollstein, Walter. 1992. *Machen Sie Platz, mein Herr! Teilen statt Herrschen* [Sharing instead of dominating]. Hamburg: Rowohlt.

Ito, Kimio. 1993. *Otokorashisa-no-yukue* [Directions for masculinities]. Tokyo: Shinyo-sha.

Kaufman, Michael. 1997. Working with men and boys to challenge sexism and end men's violence. Paper presented at UNESCO expert group meeting on Male Roles and Masculinities in the Perspective of a Culture of Peace, September, Oslo.

Kindler, Heinz. 1993. *Maske(r)ade: Jungen- und Maennerarbeit fuer die Praxis* [Work with youth and men]. Neuling: Schwaebisch Gmuend und Tuebingen.

Messner, Michael. 1997. *The politics of masculinities: Men in movements*. Thousand Oaks, CA: Sage.

Metz-Goeckel, Sigrid, and Ursula Mueller. 1986. *Der Mann: Die Brigitte-Studie* [The male]. Beltz: Weinheim & Basel.

Nakamura, Akira. 1994. *Watashi-no Danseigaku* [My men's studies]. Tokyo: Kindaibugei-sha.

Oftung, Knug, ed. 1994. *Menns bilder og bilder av menn* [Images of men]. Oslo: Likestillingsradet.

Seidler, Victor J. 1991. *Achilles Heel Reader. Men, sexual politics and socialism*. London: Routledge.

United Nations Educational, Scientific and Cultural Organization (UNESCO). 1997. *Male roles and masculinities in the perspective of a culture of peace: Report of expert group meeting. Oslo, 24–28 September 1997*. Paris: Women and a Culture of Peace Programme, Culture of Peace Unit, UNESCO.

Widersprueche, 1995. Special Issue. Maennlichkeiten. Vol. 56/57.

Index

Index compiled by Zeb Korycinska